Getting Started with Nano Server

Transform your Datacenter into headless servers with
Microsoft® Nano Server

Charbel Nemnom

BIRMINGHAM - MUMBAI

Getting Started with Nano Server

Copyright © 2017 Packt Publishing

First published: June 2017

Production reference: 1280617

Published by Packt Publishing Ltd.
Livery Place
35 Livery Street
Birmingham
B3 2PB, UK.

ISBN 978-1-78217-522-3

www.packtpub.com

Credits

Author
Charbel Nemnom

Copy Editor
Safis Editing

Reviewers
Patrick Lownds
Aleksandar Nikolic

Project Coordinator
Shweta H Birwatkar

Commissioning Editor
Kunal Parikh

Proofreader
Safis Editing

Acquisition Editor
Rahul Nair

Indexer
Mariammal Chettiyar

Content Development Editor
Mamata Walkar

Graphics
Kirk D'Penha

Technical Editor
Varsha Shivhare

Production Coordinator
Nilesh Mohite

About the Author

Charbel Nemnom is a **Microsoft Most Valuable Professional** (**MVP**) for Cloud and datacenter management and technical evangelist with 5nine Software and Unidesk Corporation. Charbel has extensive infrastructure expertise and a vast knowledge of a variety of Microsoft technologies. He has over 15 years of professional experience in the IT field and guides technical teams to optimize the performance of mission-critical enterprise systems. He has worked as a system and network engineer, senior consultant, and regional technical manager and has a history of successful enterprise projects in the IT, banks, education, and publishing sectors. He works as a virtualization consultant and cloud architect in the MENA region. He authored *Getting Started with Nano Server*, co-authored *Windows Server 2016 Hyper-V Cookbook Second Edition*, and reviewed *Hyper-V Best Practices* books (all by Packt Publishing).

Charbel also runs his blog at charbelnemnom.com where he blogs often about software - defined Datacenter and Cloud computing.

Charbel is Microsoft, Cisco, and VMware certified and holds the following credentials:

VCA-DCV, MCP, MCSA, MCTS, MCITP, MCS, MCSE, CCNP, ITIL® and PMP®. You can also follow him on Twitter @CharbelNemnom and like his Facebook page @CharbelNemnomMVP.

Books don't write, edit, and publish themselves. I would like to say a big thank you to my family and friends for their support and patience while I was busier than usual the last one year and a half, and for always supporting the crazy things I want to do. They are the reason that I can fulfill my dream and follow my passion.

Of course, the book wouldn't be possible at all without the Packt Publishing team for supporting all the authors and reviewers during this project. I want to say a big thank you to the Acquisition Editor Rahul Nair, Content Development Editor Mamata Walkar and Mehvash Fatima, the Project Coordinator Shweta Birwatkar, and the Technical Editor Varsha Shivhare.

A big thank you to the Technical Reviewers and fellow MVPs Patrick Lownds from United Kingdom and Aleksandar Nikolic from Serbia, who offered great feedback, comments, and support through the course of this project. I would also like to thank a dear friend, Marco Brodkorb, from Germany. Thank you, guys!

Finally, I want to thank the Microsoft product group individually and give them the credit they deserve for helping me make this book as good as possible (if I've missed anyone, I'm truly sorry): Ben Armstrong, Sarah Cooley, Steven Ekren, Claus Joergensen, Cosmos Darwin, Elden Christensen, Subhasish Bhattacharya, Andrew Mason, Anders Ravnholt, Dan Harman, Refaat Issa, Venkat Yalla, Chris Van Wesep, Sarah Blodgett, Sue Hartford, Samuel Li, Rajani Janaki Ram, Rochak Mittal, Aditi Gangwar, Neela Syam Kolli, Shon Shah, Sneha Agrawal, Swapnil Sumbe, Manish Jha, Gautam Deora, Mahesh Narayanan, Krati Jain, Ravi Chivukula, Nirbhay Singh, Ashish Mehndi, Nipun Arora, and Schumann Ge.

About the Reviewers

Patrick Lownds is a master-level solution architect at **Hewlett Packard Enterprise's (HPE)** Pointnext, COE, in the Hybrid IT practice and is based in London, UK.

Patrick is also a current Microsoft **Most Valuable Professional (MVP)** for **Cloud and Datacenter Management (CDM)** and has worked in the IT industry since 1988 on various technologies, including Windows Server Hyper-V, System Center, Windows Azure Pack, and Microsoft Azure. In his current role, he works mainly with the most recent versions of Windows Server, System Center, Azure, and Azure Stack, and has participated in the Windows Server 2016, System Center 2016, and Microsoft Azure stack's early adoption program.

Patrick has previously contributed to *Mastering Hyper-V Deployment*, *Microsoft Private Cloud Computing*, and *Windows Server 2012 Hyper-V Installation and Configuration Guide*, all of which were published by Wiley and Sybex and *Windows Server 2016 Hyper-V Cookbook* by Packt.

He is a community blogger for HPE and tweets in his spare time--his Twitter handle is `@patricklownds`.

When not consulting, speaking, or writing, he can be most often found on a rugby pitch teaching contact rugby to children of various ages.

Aleksandar Nikolic is a **Microsoft Most Valuable Professional (MVP)** for Cloud and Datacenter Management and Microsoft Azure, a co-founder of PowerShellMagazine.com, and the community manager of PowerShell.com. Aleksandar has more than 17 years of experience as a system administrator. He also delivers PowerShell and Azure training courses around the world and is a frequent speaker at IT conferences.

www.PacktPub.com

For support files and downloads related to your book, please visit `www.PacktPub.com`.

Did you know that Packt offers eBook versions of every book published, with PDF and ePub files available? You can upgrade to the eBook version at `www.PacktPub.com` and as a print book customer, you are entitled to a discount on the eBook copy. Get in touch with us at `service@packtpub.com` for more details.

At `www.PacktPub.com`, you can also read a collection of free technical articles, sign up for a range of free newsletters and receive exclusive discounts and offers on Packt books and eBooks.

`https://www.packtpub.com/mapt`

Get the most in-demand software skills with Mapt. Mapt gives you full access to all Packt books and video courses, as well as industry-leading tools to help you plan your personal development and advance your career.

Why subscribe?

- Fully searchable across every book published by Packt
- Copy and paste, print, and bookmark content
- On demand and accessible via a web browser

Customer Feedback

Thanks for purchasing this Packt book. At Packt, quality is at the heart of our editorial process. To help us improve, please leave us an honest review on this book's Amazon page at https://www.amazon.com/dp/1782175229.

If you'd like to join our team of regular reviewers, you can e-mail us at customerreviews@packtpub.com. We award our regular reviewers with free eBooks and videos in exchange for their valuable feedback. Help us be relentless in improving our products!

Table of Contents

Preface

Thank you for purchasing *Getting Started with Nano Server*. The book you are holding is the result of 15 years of experience in the IT world and over 17 years of Windows Server experience that started with Windows Server 2000, moved on to Windows Server 2012 R2 and now, includes Windows Server 2016 and Nano Server. Modern data centers need a highly optimized server platform to run infrastructure services, distributed cloud-based applications, and containers apps based on the microservice architecture.

Nano Server is the first operating system released by Microsoft that was designed to deploy less on your servers, have less that you have to patch and reboot, and have fewer components that you actually need on your servers. Nano Server is a much scale down version of Windows Server that was built for higher density and more efficient OS resource utilization. Now moving to the cloud journey with Microsoft Azure, large server installations that have a lot of things installed require patching and rebooting, which interrupts service delivery. Nano Server is a deep refactoring initially focused on the CloudOS infrastructure and born-in-the-cloud applications; these applications were written with cloud patterns that allow you to run on top of Nano Server, and most importantly, highly optimized base OS images for Nano containers, so you can create containerized applications that are much smaller, more manageable, and easily shareable across different environments.

Our aim in this book is to provide you with the information you need to be immediately effective in deploying, managing, and administering Nano Server environments.

We hope that you get as much from reading this book as we did from writing it. Please be sure to post any questions, comments, or suggestions you may have about the book on the online author forum. Your feedback is important to us, in order to develop the best books possible in the future.

What this book covers

Chapter 1, *Introduction to Nano Server*, covers why Microsoft developed Nano Server and why we need a server that is optimized for the cloud for running the fabric for born-in-the-cloud applications and for running Windows Server and Hyper-V containers. Nano Server is a different approach for Microsoft and for everyone; it comes from a historical position that started with Server Core in Windows Server 2008. It's completely a new headless operating system.

Chapter 2, *Getting Started with Nano Server*, focuses on how to get started with Nano Server. It covers how to add roles and features and how to create and customize a Nano image using a single line of PowerShell. This chapter also covers how to build and customize a Nano image using Nano Server Image Builder, the new graphical user interface-based wizard; and finally, we show you how to customize a Nano image using DISM.

Chapter 3, *Deploying Nano Server in a Virtual Machine and on Physical Hardware*, Covers how to create Nano Server images using Hyper-V Manager and Windows PowerShell. We also discuss the four deployment options for Nano Server on a bare-metal physical machine using WinPE and WDS; and lastly, we cover how to deploy a Nano Server VM in Microsoft Azure.

Chapter 4, *Deploying Hyper-V Cluster on Nano Server*, covers the steps needed to deploy Nano Server as compute, storage, and a hyper-converged cluster using **Storage Spaces Direct (S2D)** technology. There is also an introductory overview of running Nano Server as a compute and storage cluster in this chapter.

Chapter 5, *Deploying, Managing, and Monitoring Nano Server with System Center 2016*, focuses on how to manage and monitor Nano Server using System Center Virtual Machine Manager and System Center Operations Manager 2016. We show you how to deploy Nano Server using VMM as a Hyper-V host using bare-metal deployment, and as a virtual machine using VM templates. Lastly, we show you how you can push the Operations Manager agent to Nano Server using the operations console with Windows PowerShell.

Chapter 6, *Managing Nano Server with Windows PowerShell and Windows PowerShell DSC*, covers how to effectively manage a Nano Server installation using remote server graphic tools, Windows PowerShell remoting, and PowerShell **Desired State Configuration (DSC)**.

Chapter 7, *Managing Nano Server with Third-Party Tools*, focuses on how to administer Nano Server using 5nine Manager from 5nine Software, and we show you how to create and manage a Nano Server Failover cluster.

Chapter 8, *Running Windows Server Containers and Hyper-V Containers on Nano Server*, focuses on Windows containers and how they can change the way we deploy applications. We also cover the benefits of using containers and how they can integrate with Dev and Ops team to accelerate application delivery. Finally, we show you how to deploy and run Windows Server and a Hyper-V container on top of Nano Server using a Nano base OS image running IIS.

Chapter 9, *Troubleshooting Nano Server*, demonstrates how to troubleshoot a Nano Server installation using the Nano recovery console, **Emergency Management Services (EMS)**, kernel debugging, and **Setup and Boot Event Collection (SBEC)**, which is a new feature of Windows Server 2016. Lastly, we show you how to retrieve and read Nano Server Windows event logs and display them in a nicely formatted HTML report.

Chapter 10, *Running Other Workloads on the Nano Server*, covers how to run DNS and IIS on Nano Server. We also cover additional updates and tools that will help you streamline your experience using Nano Server. Finally, we discuss the future of Nano Server and Windows Server.

What you need for this book

To follow along on with this book, you need Windows Server 2016 ISO media, including System Center 2016 Virtual Machine Manager and System Center 2016 Operations Manager. We strongly believe in learning by doing; therefore, we encourage you to try out all of the technologies and principles covered in this book. You don't need a huge server. For most topics, you could use a single machine with Windows Server 2016 installed, 16 GB of memory, and by enabling Hyper-V nested virtualization, you could enable a few virtual machines to run concurrently. Ideally, having at least two physical workstations or servers will help you with the high availability clustering concepts. With Windows 10, the Hyper-V client is included in the box, so even without any kind of real server, it is possible to explore all the features introduced in Nano Server.

Who this book is for

This book is intended for anyone who wants to learn and master Nano Server and take advantage of all exciting new features that Windows Server 2016 has to offer. If you have basic knowledge of Windows Server and virtualization, it will be helpful, but it's not a requirement. If you are an architect, a consultant, a system administrator, or really anyone who just wants more knowledge about Nano Server, this book is for you as well.

Please note that in some chapters we go into advanced topics that may seem over your head. In those cases, don't worry. Focus on the preceding elements that you understand better and implement and practice them to nurture your understanding. Then, when you feel ready, come back to the more advanced topics and read them multiple times. Repetition is the key. The more you repeat, the more you understand.

Conventions

In this book, you will find a number of text styles that distinguish between different kinds of information. Here are some examples of these styles and an explanation of their meaning.

Code words in text, database table names, folder names, filenames, file extensions, pathnames, dummy URLs, user input, and Twitter handles are shown as follows: "We are copying `NanoServer` folder from the mounted ISO image into `C:\NanoServer` locally."

A block of code is set as follows:

```
Import-Module "C:\NanoServer\
NanoServerImageGenerator\NanoServerImageGenerator.psd1" -Verbose
```

Any command-line input or output is written as follows:

```
bcdedit.exe /set "{default}" description "Windows Nano Server 2016"
```

New terms and **important words** are shown in bold. Words that you see on the screen, for example, in menus or dialog boxes, appear in the text like this: "Right Click your WDS server in the **Windows Deployment Services** console and select **Configure Server**."

Warnings or important notes appear in a box like this.

Tips and tricks appear like this.

Reader feedback

Feedback from our readers is always welcome. Let us know what you think about this book-what you liked or disliked. Reader feedback is important for us as it helps us develop titles that you will really get the most out of.

To send us general feedback, simply e-mail `feedback@packtpub.com`, and mention the book's title in the subject of your message.

If there is a topic that you have expertise in and you are interested in either writing or contributing to a book, see our author guide at `www.packtpub.com/authors`.

Customer support

Now that you are the proud owner of a Packt book, we have a number of things to help you to get the most from your purchase.

Downloading the example code

You can download the example code files for this book from your account at `http://www.p acktpub.com`. If you purchased this book elsewhere, you can visit `http://www.packtpub.c om/support` and register to have the files e-mailed directly to you.

You can download the code files by following these steps:

1. Log in or register to our website using your e-mail address and password.
2. Hover the mouse pointer on the **SUPPORT** tab at the top.
3. Click on **Code Downloads & Errata**.
4. Enter the name of the book in the **Search** box.
5. Select the book for which you're looking to download the code files.
6. Choose from the drop-down menu where you purchased this book from.
7. Click on **Code Download**.

Once the file is downloaded, please make sure that you unzip or extract the folder using the latest version of:

- WinRAR / 7-Zip for Windows
- Zipeg / iZip / UnRarX for Mac
- 7-Zip / PeaZip for Linux

The code bundle for the book is also hosted on GitHub at `https://github.com/PacktPubl ishing/Getting-Started-with-Nano-Server`. We also have other code bundles from our rich catalog of books and videos available at `https://github.com/PacktPublishing/`. Check them out!

Downloading the color images of this book

We also provide you with a PDF file that has color images of the screenshots/diagrams used in this book. The color images will help you better understand the changes in the output. You can download this file from `https://www.packtpub.com/sites/default/files/downloads/GettingStartedwithNanoSe rver_ColorImages.pdf`.

Errata

Although we have taken every care to ensure the accuracy of our content, mistakes do happen. If you find a mistake in one of our books-maybe a mistake in the text or the code-we would be grateful if you could report this to us. By doing so, you can save other readers from frustration and help us improve subsequent versions of this book. If you find any errata, please report them by visiting http://www.packtpub.com/submit-errata, selecting your book, clicking on the **Errata Submission Form** link, and entering the details of your errata. Once your errata are verified, your submission will be accepted and the errata will be uploaded to our website or added to any list of existing errata under the Errata section of that title.

To view the previously submitted errata, go to https://www.packtpub.com/books/content/support and enter the name of the book in the search field. The required information will appear under the **Errata** section.

Piracy

Piracy of copyrighted material on the Internet is an ongoing problem across all media. At Packt, we take the protection of our copyright and licenses very seriously. If you come across any illegal copies of our works in any form on the Internet, please provide us with the location address or website name immediately so that we can pursue a remedy.

Please contact us at copyright@packtpub.com with a link to the suspected pirated material.

We appreciate your help in protecting our authors and our ability to bring you valuable content.

Questions

If you have a problem with any aspect of this book, you can contact us at questions@packtpub.com, and we will do our best to address the problem.

1
Introduction to Nano Server

Nano Server is a new headless, 64-bit only, deployment option in Windows Server 2016 that has been optimized for data centers and for next-generation, distributed applications. Nano Server is the future of Windows Server; it is similar to Windows Server in Server Core mode, but significantly smaller, has no local logon capability, and only supports 64-bit applications, tools, and agents. It takes up far less disk space, sets up significantly faster, and requires far fewer updates and restarts much faster than Server with Desktop Experience.

In this chapter, we will cover the following topics:

- The story behind Nano Server
- The journey to Nano Server
- What makes Nano Server unique?
- Nano Server improvements

The story behind Nano Server

Microsoft has done a great job with Nano Server. Nano Sever was announced in April 2015 and shipped with the release of Windows Server 2016 in October 2016. But before we start to dive deeply into Nano Server, we would like to share with you a little background behind why Microsoft developed Nano Server:

http://blogs.technet.com/b/windowsserver/archive/2015/04/08/microsoft-announc es-nano-server-for-modern-apps-and-cloud.aspx.

Business impact

Microsoft is always listening to customer's feedback, and one constant feedback was server reboots are impacting my business, because, when you reboot a server, you need to plan ahead of time and schedule a maintenance window in order to avoid downtime. The next piece of feedback was, why do I have to reboot a server because of a patch to a certain component that I never use on my server? And if a reboot is required, the systems need to be back in service as soon as possible. The constant feedback was, we just want the components needed to accomplish our goals and nothing more.

Infrastructure impact

The size of server images have increased over time; large server images take a long time to deploy and configure, especially when you work with virtual machines.

Storing and maintaining virtual machine templates requires too much disk space, when it comes to mobility by moving virtual machines around using live migration. Thus, it will require a lot of network bandwidth as well.

With full blown server images, the infrastructure requires too many resources; if the operating system consumes fewer resources, you can increase virtual machines' density, and with higher VM density, you can lower the cost and increase efficiency in your environment.

Security impact

IT security is no longer just about protecting your computers and minimizing potential downtime and lost productivity. It's about protecting your valuable business data, your customers' personal details, and your company's reputation. We saw the headlines in the last couple of years about online attacks and credit card numbers being stolen. There was a 40% increase in the number of large companies targeted by cyber-attacks in 2014, as criminals hijack infrastructures and attack from within, according to the largest cybersecurity companies research; a cyberattack has even caused confirmed physical damage for the second time ever. As an example, a hacker was able to remotely control a vehicle and shut it down. Security has become a number one priority in every firm today.

We can no longer afford the security risks of the install everything, everywhere approach.

Basically, having a large server installation that has a lot of things installed, that you don't necessarily really need, opens you up to more of these attacks. The less you have installed on your server, the less ports you have to open. This in turn reduces the ways a hacker can try to attack your systems. So that's really sort of the area that Microsoft took the lead on and created the genesis of Nano Server.

The journey to Nano Server

Now going back, let's tell the story from the beginning. Starting with the Windows NT and 3.1 days, after Windows Server came Windows NT and really, what Microsoft did at that time was they took the client and installed everything on it. All the roles and features were in the box. You could just deploy what you wanted and you were up and running. In fact, Mark Russinovich (CTO of Microsoft Azure), claimed that he discovered the registry key that will allow you to convert your client OS into a Server. That approach continues through Windows Server 2003 when they started to separate some of the roles and features.

Server Core

The big change occurred in Windows Server 2008 and Microsoft introduced Windows Server Core as an installation option. This was really the first step toward having to deploy less on your servers, have less that you have to patch and reboot, and have fewer components that you don't necessary need on your servers. What I mean by the installation option is, when you first start installing the operating system, you have the option to choose between Server Core or Server with Desktop Experience installation.

Once you deploy Server Core or Server with Desktop Experience, then you can start adding roles and features that you want to run on top as shown in *Figure 1*, small boxes on top.

For Windows Server 2008 and Windows Server 2008 R2, the choice between Server Core and a full installation had to be made at installation time and couldn't be changed without reinstalling the OS:

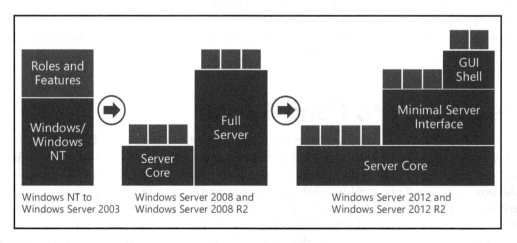

Figure 1: Windows NT - Windows Server 2012 R2 journey (image source: Microsoft)

However, with Windows Server 2012 and 2012 R2, Microsoft has offered the installation options in a way that you can start by deploying Server Core. Then there is a package that you can add to move up to **Full Server** or you can install a Full Server and then remove the server graphic shell and **Graphical Management Tools and Infrastructure** and convert back down to Server Core is as showing in *Figure 2*. In other words, the graphical shell and the management infrastructure are features that can be added and removed at any time, requiring only a reboot, making it easy to switch between the Server Core and Full Server with GUI. Microsoft also introduced the minimal Server interface so you can actually uninstall Internet Explorer and `Explore.exe` and have just **Microsoft Management Console (MMC)** and Server Manager, which results in less patching. The **Minimal Server Interface** has fewer benefits than Server Core but it does provide a nice middle-ground versus Server with Desktop Experience:

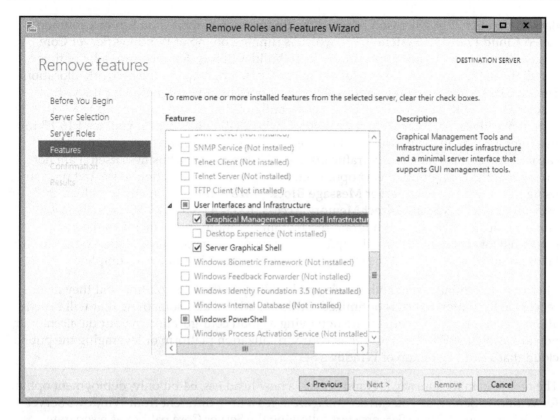

Figure 2: Removing the graphical management tools in Windows Server 2012 R2

Cloud journey

Now moving to the cloud journey with Microsoft Azure, a large server installation that has a lot of things installed, requires patching, and reboots which interrupt service delivery. Azure doesn't use live migration and doesn't use failover clustering. When they have to take down a host in an Azure data center, it does require the virtual machine to be taken down and restarted as well. So, with a large number of servers and large OS resource consumption, it generates a lot of **Cost of goods sold (COGS)** for them. COGS are the direct costs attributable to the production of the services sold by Microsoft Azure. Thus, by provisioning, large host images compete for the network resources. As mentioned in the **Business impact** section earlier in this chapter, deploying all those hosts and then re-imaging all of them when a new patch comes out, requires a lot of network bandwidth. Many service providers (not only Microsoft Azure) are over provisioning their network so that they can have enough capacity for live migration or for re-provisioning servers.

Back in October 2014, Microsoft released the first version of their Cloud-in-box solution called **Cloud Platform System** (**CPS**) which is running on top of Windows Server Core, System Center, and Windows Azure Pack. To build a CPS system, requires a lot of time; installing all that software takes a lot of time and patching impacts the network allocation. Since a CPS system is an on-premises solution, it does use live migration for the virtual machines. So, with fully loaded CPS 4 racks, configuration would support up to 8,000 virtual machines. So, if each VM is configured with 2 GB of RAM, then you need 16 TB to live migrate over all the networks. Thus, we conclude that you need to have enough capacity to handle that network traffic instead of using it for the business itself. I am not saying that the configuration isn't optimized in CPS in a live migration sense, but they are using live migration over **Server Message Block** (**SMB**) protocol directly to offload the network traffic to **Remote Direct Memory Access** (**RDMA**) NICs, which is really fast. However, it still takes time to migrate 16 TB of information, and as mentioned earlier, server reboots result in service disruption. The reboot for the compute Hyper-V host in CPS takes around 2 minutes, and the storage host takes around 5 minutes to complete.

Microsoft determined from both Azure and building up the CPS solution that they need a server configuration which is optimized for the cloud and also something that will benefit all their customers, whether you are deploying a cloud configuration in your data center or you are using just Windows Server as your virtualization platform or leveraging the public cloud that's running on top of Windows Server.

The next step in the journey is Nano Server, a new headless, 64-bit only, deployment option for Windows Server, as you can see in *Figure 3*. It's a little different from Windows Server 2012 R2 in *Figure 1*. Nano Servers start following the Server Core pattern as a separate installation option. Therefore you can install Nano Server and then there is sub-set of roles and features that you can add on top. The installation options that we have in Windows Server 2016 are **Nano Server**, **Server Core**, and **Server with a Desktop Experience**. Microsoft made a significant change in Windows Server 2016 where you cannot move between different installation options anymore as in Windows Server 2012 R2, just because of some of the changes they had to make in order to implement Nano Server and Server with a Desktop Experience:

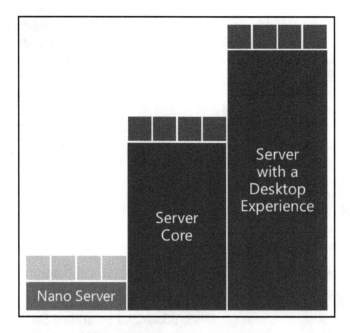

Figure 3: Nano Server journey (image source: Microsoft)

Nano Server is deep refactoring initially focused on the CloudOS infrastructure. With Nano Server, you can deploy Hyper-V hosts as a compute platform. You can deploy a scale-out file server as storage nodes and clusters, so that you can do clustered storage servers or clustered Hyper-V hosts and do live migration across nodes. The Nano Server team is continuously working on supporting born-in-the cloud applications; those applications were written with cloud patterns which allow you to run on top of Nano Server. Nano Server can be installed on your physical machines, or it can be installed as a guest virtual machine, and it will also serve as the base OS for Hyper-V containers. Please refer to Chapter 8, *Running Windows Server Containers and Hyper-V Containers on Nano Server*, for more details about Windows Server containers and Hyper-V containers running on top of Nano Server.

Nano Server is a separate installation option. It's a self-contained operating system that has everything you need. The major difference between Nano Server and Server Core is that none of the roles or features are available in the image same as we get in Server Core and Full Server. The side by side store is when you go to add or install additional roles and features with Windows Server; it never prompts you for the media, as the binary data that is required already exists on your hard disk within the OS. However, in Nano Server, all the infrastructure roles (Hyper-V, storage, clustering, DNS, IIS, and so on) live in a series of separate packages, so you have to add them to the image. In this case, your base Nano Server image will always stay very small. As you start adding roles and features to Nano Server, each role becomes an additional package, as the Hyper-V role for example which only requires the Nano Server base OS, so it will always be small and tight. If you are adding another role that requires a 500 MB file, that will be another 500 MB file to be added to the Nano Server image as a separate package. Nano Server has full driver support, so any driver that works for Windows Server 2016, will work with Nano Server as well.

As of the first release of Nano Server 2016, these are the key roles and features supported to run on Nano Server:

- Hyper-V, clustering, storage, DNS, IIS, DCB, PowerShell DSC, shielded VMs, Windows defender, and software inventory logging
- Core CLR, ASP.NET 5, and PaaSv2
- Windows Server containers and Hyper-V containers
- System Center Virtual Machine Manager (SCVMM) and System Center Operations Manager (SCOM)

Nano Server - management

Without a GUI, it's not easy to carry out the daily management and maintenance of Nano Server. In fact, all the existing graphical tools, such as Hyper-V Manager, failover cluster manager, Server Manager, registry editor, file explorer, disk and device manager, server configuration, computer management, users and groups are compatible to manage Nano Server remotely.

The Nano Server deployment option of Windows comes with full PowerShell remoting support. The purpose of the core PowerShell engine is to manage Nano Server instances at scale. PowerShell remoting includes WMI, Windows Server cmdlets (network, storage, Hyper-V, and so on.), PowerShell **Desired State Configuration (DSC)**, remote file transfer, remote script authoring, and debugging. PowerShell relies on the .NET Framework; as you may have noticed Nano Server is a small and tiny OS and only has the Core **Common Language Runtime (CLR)**. The Core CLR is a tiny subset of the .NET Framework; the PowerShell team went ahead and refactored PowerShell to run on Core CLR, which was a huge effort. The good news is that PowerShell users probably will not miss the most important features. It has full language compatibility and supports PowerShell remoting, so you can use the most popular remote commands, such as `Invoke-Command`, `New-PSSession`, `Enter-PSSession`, and so on.

The PowerShell Core is available in every image of Nano Server; it's not an optional package. Each Nano Server image contains, by default, Core CLR that takes up 45 MB of space; PowerShell itself takes about 8 MB of space, and there is 2 MB available for two built-in modules. Remoting is turned on by default, so a Nano Server installation will be always ready to be remoted into and be managed remotely.

What makes Nano Server unique?

One of the unique capabilities of Nano Server is the ability to be deployed as a massively scaled down version of the server OS. Microsoft dabbled with this idea in Windows Server 2008 when they introduced Server Core, but Nano Servers are substantially smaller than Server Core deployments.

How is this possible?

- No GUI, no notepad, and no `cmd.exe` window.

- The OS has been stripped of everything that is not needed in a cloud environment; in particular the UI stack, the x86 subsystem (WOW64), and unnecessary APIs.

- Nano Server does not include MSI as an installation technology due to dependencies and the open-ended nature of MSI custom actions. Microsoft introduced the Windows Server App (WSA) instead, which is an installer framework designed to install and service applications safely and reliably, using a declarative manifest. WSA does not support custom actions, so will not have the reliability and uninstall issues of MSI.

- Minimal packages and features in the base image. The Nano Server team have stripped down this OS to a minimal set of APIs and features. You will probably find some of your utilities missing here, but that's ok because it similarly has another and probably better API that accomplishes the same functionality.

Basically, Microsoft is producing an OS that does not try to support legacy systems. However, the DevOps mindset is far more effective at managing server cattle versus pets, which is an analogy made by Jeffery Snover (Microsoft technical fellow, lead architect for Cloud and Enterprise Group and PowerShell architect).

At this scale, we don't have the time or resources to be accessing our instances via a remote desktop and clicking buttons or dragging windows. If one server becomes sick, we put it out of its misery quickly and replace it and be up and running in a couple of seconds. The idea behind Nano Server is to eliminate the need to sit in front of a server forever. UIs do not belong on servers.

Nano is a lightweight server OS and made to be accessed and managed remotely.

Nano Server improvements

Microsoft has published several numbers and preliminary results for Nano Server around servicing, security, resource utilization and deployment improvements, compared to Server Core and Server with Desktop Experience deployment. In this section, we will highlight the improvements based on those results for you to understand the benefits on what Nano Server brings to your environment.

Servicing improvements

The numbers shown in *Figure 4* are based on analysis done by Microsoft for all Windows patches that were released in 2014. These numbers fall under three categories as the following:

- Important bulletins
- Critical bulletins
- Reboots required

If you had Nano Server installation options available in 2014, Nano Server had nine important bulletins versus Server Core which had 23 and Server with Desktop Experience that had 26. The interesting one is critical bulletins; Nano Server had two versus Server Core that had eight and Server with Desktop Experience 23. The critical bulletin is a security fix for something that Microsoft has found that people are trying to exploit. This is rated as critical and must be deployed as quickly as possible. So, for the entire year, Nano Server had only two of those critical updates. However, the important bulletins help in overall quality of the system. For Nano Server, there were three reboots required for the entire year, Microsoft is working hard to bring the reboot number from three to only two; Server Core had six and Server with Desktop Experience had 11. Thus for 11 months, you had to reboot your servers because of patches that were applicable to them, whereas for Nano Server, you had to reboot only thrice. Here you can see the uptime benefits of deploying Nano Server:

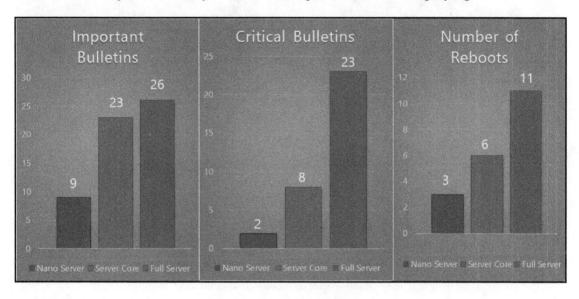

Figure 4: Nano Server servicing improvements (image source: Microsoft)

Security improvements

Now moving to the security improvements, we are comparing Nano Server with Server Core. As shown in *Figure 5* for drivers loaded, we have 73 for Nano and Server Core has 98, Microsoft did not change a lot in the driver's space. However, for services running, they made some significant improvements. In this area, Nano Server had 28 services running versus Server Core which had 47, little less than half. As for ports open, Nano Server was almost a third less compared to Server Core; Nano Server had 12 versus Server Core which had 30. This is the exposure on your network in ways that things can be attacked; vulnerability might be exposed in your systems. The drivers loaded are the hardware drivers and the drivers loaded by the system:

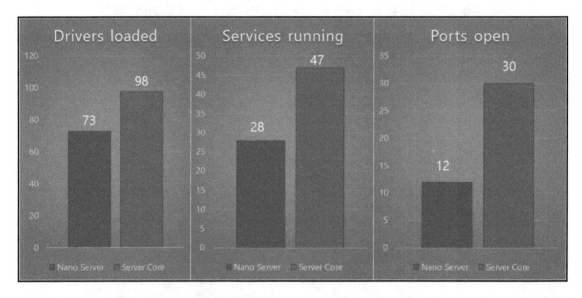

Figure 5: Nano Server security improvements (image source: Microsoft)

Resource utilization improvements

As for the resource utilization side, the process count, as shown in *Figure 6*, Nano Server had 21 versus Server Core that had 26; there has not been too much work done in this area. The boot I/O is a good change here where Nano Server has 108 MB versus Server Core's 306 MB, so 198 MB less of things loading during the boot process and I/O on the disk, that helps speed-up the boot time. Considering the kernel memory in use, Nano Server had 61 MB versus Server Core that had 139 MB, so more resources are available for other things running on your servers:

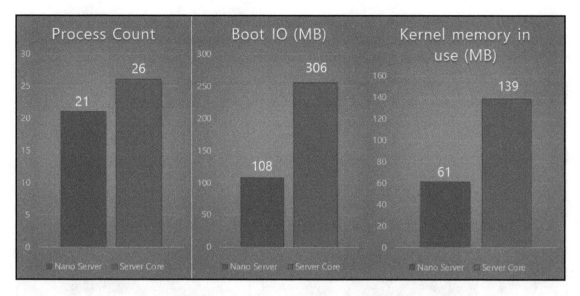

Figure 6: Nano Server resource utilization improvements (image source: Microsoft)

Deployment improvements

Finally, the deployment improvements are shown in *Figure 7*. For setup time, Nano Server takes just 35 seconds compared with almost 5 minutes for Server Core. This is a huge improvement here. You will see where these 35 seconds came from in Chapter 3, *Deploying Nano Server in a Virtual Machine and on Physical Hardware*. You don't have to actually use Windows setup. Basically, you copy an image that you already created an unattended file for; that 35 seconds setup includes the time to create the unattended file. As for physical deployment using commodity hardware 100 MB switch with **Windows Deployment Server (WDS)** and PXE boot, Nano Server was fully provisioned in 3 minutes, whereas Server Core using the exact same configuration just switching to a Server Core image was 19 minutes. This is quite an improvement. The setup time is a one-time operation typically; the reboot time took only 15 seconds using the same hardware with spindle disks. The reboot times might vary based on your hardware especially with SSDs. This is quite impressive.

For the disk footprint, Nano Server is 460 MB; that's why it can boot and deploy so quickly, whereas Server Core is almost 5.42 GB. This is assuming you did not add any extra packages; as an example, with the Hyper-V (compute) package, the image will be under 460 MB, because Hyper-V is such a small footprint of hypervisor.

As for VHD size, there is a little bit of overhead here. When you are running in a virtual machine, as you can see, Windows Server Core went up from almost 5.42 GB to a little over 6 GB, and Nano Server goes from 460 MB to 480 MB:

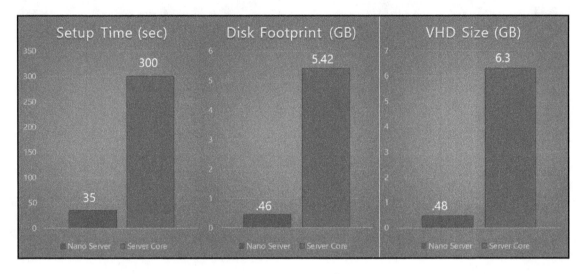

Figure 7: Nano Server deployment improvements (image source: Microsoft)

Summary

In this chapter, we covered why Microsoft developed Nano Server, and why we need a server that is optimized for the cloud for running the fabric. For born-in-the-cloud applications, for running Hyper-V containers and Windows Server containers, it's a different approach for Microsoft and for everyone actually; it's one that's coming from a position historically starting with Server Core in Windows Server 2008 and going forward. It's a completely new, headless operating system.

Continue now to `Chapter 2`, *Getting Started with Nano Server*, to learn more about how to get started with Nano Server.

2
Getting Started with Nano Server

As we discussed in `Chapter 1`, *Introduction to Nano Server*, Nano Server has absolutely no local GUI and it takes up far less disk space. Server roles and optional features exist outside of Nano Server, and we refer to them as packages. Those packages can be added to Nano Server image on demand. Microsoft developed Nano Server with just enough OS. In other words, it's only the OS and the components of the OS that we need for the function which is required, and nothing more. With Nano Server, the 400 MB base image basically holds **Windows Management Instrumentation** (**WMI**), reverse forwarders for application compatibility, and a PowerShell core. Nano Server installation will always be ready to be remoted into and can be managed remotely using remote PowerShell, or with any standard **Remote Server Administration Tools** (**RSAT**) GUIs such as Hyper-V Manager, failover cluster manager, and Server Manager. If any additional roles and features are needed, we can have them actually installed online with a package management (`a.k.a OneGet`) provider, we can inject them at image creation as well, or we can copy them over a running Nano Server and install them using the DISM tool or Nano Server PowerShell module.

Nano Server is fully supported using the same drivers that exist in the Server Core installation of Windows Server 2016.

The main key roles and features for Nano Server are:

- Hyper-V compute role, storage (Scale-out File Serve, Storage Spaces Direct, Storage Replica), and failover clustering
- Born-in-the-cloud application is the modern-day web server for Core CLR, ASP.NET 5, Node.js, and PaaS v2
- Base operating system for Windows Server containers and Hyper-V containers

In this chapter, we will cover the following topics:

- Getting started with Nano Server
- Building and customizing a Nano Server image using Windows PowerShell
- Building and customizing a Nano Server image using Nano Server image builder
- Customizing a Nano Server image using DISM

Getting started with Nano Server

Unlike the other installation options, whether in Server with Desktop Experience or Server Core, as shown in *Figure 1*, Nano Server basically exists in the folder of the ISO image on the media, and we need to add the package for the role and feature that we need. For example, if we need to make Nano Server a compute host (Hyper-V), we need to add a compute package using DISM or PowerShell. We will cover the syntax in a bit:

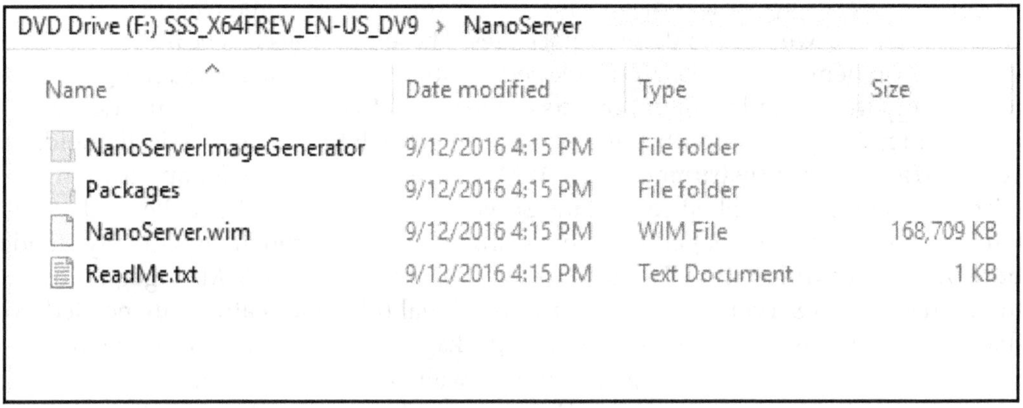

DVD Drive (F:) SSS_X64FREV_EN-US_DV9 › NanoServer			
Name	Date modified	Type	Size
NanoServerImageGenerator	9/12/2016 4:15 PM	File folder	
Packages	9/12/2016 4:15 PM	File folder	
NanoServer.wim	9/12/2016 4:15 PM	WIM File	168,709 KB
ReadMe.txt	9/12/2016 4:15 PM	Text Document	1 KB

Figure 1: Nano Server. Windows Server 2016 media

Nano Server quick start

Microsoft provided two of the main scripts on the Nano Server image itself. When you go to the `NanoServer` folder on the ISO media, you will find `NanoServer.wim` which is a file-based disk image format that will help you to deploy the Nano Server operating system. In addition, you will find a very small text file called `ReadMe` which actually tells you this: For detailed information on deploying and managing Nano Server, please go to this link: `http://www.aka.ms/nanoserver`.

Under the `NanoServerImageGenerator` folder, you will find one script and one PowerShell module, as shown in *Figure 2*:

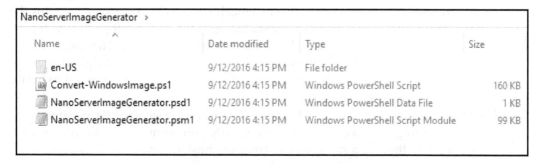

Figure 2: Nano Server. Image generator and PowerShell module

You can use these scripts to generate, build, and customize a Nano Server image for:

- A physical machine
- A virtual machine

The good news is that Microsoft made it easy to build your Nano Server image in such a way that you can write a single PowerShell command. That's all you need to build your Nano Server image from scratch. You can specify the package(s) that you need to be included as part of the image. You can add the computer name, administrator password, and IP address.

This single PowerShell command will take care of the customization to build the image that fits your environment.

Nano Server customizations

You can customize Nano Server using the `NanoServerImageGenerator` PowerShell module or using the DISM tool. Microsoft divides the customizations into required and optional packages, as shown here:

With the `required` parameters, you can set the following:

- Adding the right set of drivers. Microsoft has the OEM drivers package. If you want to host Nano Server on a physical machine, the OEM package contains the inbox drivers that are used to ship with Server Core. Microsoft packaged these for convenience purposes, so you can test Nano Server without having to bump into situations where you have to download a driver or find the right driver for your machine. Alternatively, you can use the guest drivers if you want to host Nano Server in a virtual machine.

- Adding the required roles and features. You can create a Nano Server image without adding any role or feature, but ideally you want to run Nano Server for a purpose, whether it's a storage host, compute host, or you want to run, for example, ASP.NET applications on top of Nano Server.

- Set the Administrator password which is required. If you don't specify a computer name, the Operating System will generate a random computer name during setup for you.

- The last one is converting WIM to VHD(X), which is required if you want to use Nano Server in a VM. However, there is a way to apply the WIM image as it is, without conversion to the physical hardware. We will cover that in Chapter 3, *Deploying Nano Server in a Virtual Machine and on Physical Hardware.*

With the `optional` parameters, you can set the following:

- Add computer name
- Add the IP address, DNS, and gateway
- Join Nano Server to the domain
- Set dual boot with `bcdboot` more on that in Chapter 3, *Deploying Nano Server in a Virtual Machine and on Physical Hardware*
- Enable **Emergency Management Services** (**EMS**): more on that at the end of this chapter
- Add packages: see further for more information

Nano Server roles and features

The `NanoServer` folder in the ISO image has a packages sub-folder, as shown in the following *Figure 3*:

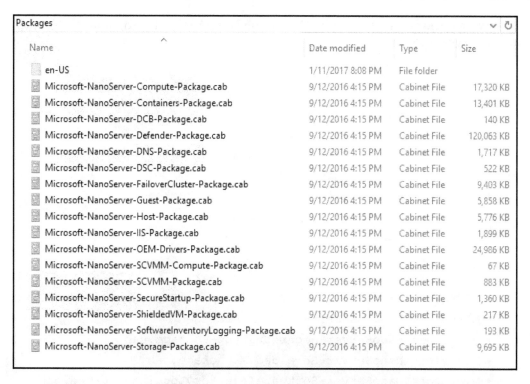

Figure 3: Nano Server, Roles, and Features

Role or feature:

- Hyper-V role
- Failover clustering
- File Server role and other storage components
- Container host
- DNS server
- IIS Server
- Windows defender antimalware, including a default signature file

The following packages are supported to work on Nano Server, based on the GA version of Windows Server 2016:

- `Microsoft-NanoServer-Compute-Package`
- `Microsoft-NanoServer-Containers-Package`
- `Microsoft-NanoServer-DCB-Package`
- `Microsoft-NanoServer-Defender-Package`
- `Microsoft-NanoServer-DNS-Package`
- `Microsoft-NanoServer-DSC-Package`
- `Microsoft-NanoServer-FailoverCluster-Package`
- `Microsoft-NanoServer-Guest-Package`
- `Microsoft-NanoServer-Host-Package.cab`
- `Microsoft-NanoServer-IIS-Package`
- `Microsoft-NanoServer-OEM-Drivers-Package`
- `Microsoft-Windows-Server-SCVMM-Compute-Package`
- `Microsoft-Windows-Server-SCVMM-Package`
- `Microsoft-NanoServer-SecureStartup-Package.cab`
- `Microsoft-NanoServer-ShieldedVM-Package.cab`
- `Microsoft-NanoServer-SoftwareInventoryLogging-Package.cab`
- `Microsoft-NanoServer-Storage-Package`

Building and customizing a Nano Server image using Windows PowerShell

First, you need to mount Windows Server 2016 ISO media on any Windows 10 or Windows Server 2016 machine.

Assuming the drive letter for the mounted image is **E:**

Run the following PowerShell cmdlet:

```
Copy "E:\NanoServer""C:\NanoServer" -Recurse
```

We are copying the `NanoServer` folder from the mounted ISO image into `C:\NanoServer` locally.

Import the `NanoServerImageGenerator.psd1` PowerShell module by running the following command:

```
Import-Module "C:\NanoServer\
NanoServerImageGenerator\NanoServerImageGenerator.psd1" -Verbose
```

```
PS C:\NanoServer> # Import NanoServerImageGenerator.psd1 PowerShell module
Import-Module "C:\NanoServer\NanoServerImageGenerator\NanoServerImageGenerator.psd1" -Verbose
VERBOSE: Loading module from path 'C:\NanoServer\NanoServerImageGenerator\NanoServerImageGenerator.psd1'.
VERBOSE: Loading module from path 'C:\NanoServer\NanoServerImageGenerator\NanoServerImageGenerator.psm1'.
VERBOSE: Importing function 'Edit-NanoServerImage'.
VERBOSE: Importing function 'Get-NanoServerPackage'.
VERBOSE: Importing function 'New-NanoServerImage'.

PS C:\NanoServer>
```

Figure 4: Nano Server. Import PowerShell Module

After importing the new PowerShell module using the `-Verbose` parameter, you will notice we have in fact imported three commands: `New-NanoServerImage`, `Get-NanoServerPackages`, and `Edit-NanoServerImage`:

- The `New-NanoServerImage` creates a new Nano Server image.
- The `Edit-NanoServerImage` makes changes to an existing image that you already built. For example, you have created an image that has the Hyper-V compute package and you have been using it for a while. Now, if you decide that you want to add the clustering role, then you can edit the image to add the clustering package instead of creating a new one.
- The `Get-NanoServerPackages` lists all supported packages on the media.

To generate a VHD(X) from `NanoServer.WIM` by using the `New-NanoServerImage` function, open Windows PowerShell as Administrator and run the following:

```
Cd C:\NanoServer

$Password = Read-Host -Prompt "Please specify local Administrator
password" -AsSecureString

New-NanoServerImage -MediaPathE: `
-BasePathC:\NanoServer\ `
-TargetPathC:\NanoServer\NanoServer01.vhdx `
-DeploymentTypeGuest `
-EditionDatacenter `
-ComputerName"NANO-01" `
-AdministratorPassword$Password `
-InterfaceNameOrIndexEthernet `
```

```
-Ipv4Address192.168.1.10 `
-Ipv4SubnetMask255.255.255.0 `
-Ipv4Dns192.168.1.9 `
-Ipv4Gateway192.168.1.1 `
-EnableRemoteManagementPort `
-Verbose
```

Let's dive into the parameters that we used in this example:

- `-MediaPath` : This is the root of the DVD drive or the ISO image (`E:` in my case), where your media is.
- `-BasePath`: This is the `local` folder on your machine that you specify where the command is going to keep a copy of the Nano Server binaries. In other words, next time you use the command to create a Nano Server image, you don't have to use `-MediaPath` anymore. You can just use `-BasePath`, because it already has a copy of the binaries, so you will save the copy time.
- `-TargetPath`: This is the location path where you want to generate your final image. You can specify any folder you want, but make sure you specify the extension you want. In this example, we specified VHDX, because that was what I wanted. You can specify VHD, VHDX, or WIM as well.
- `-DeploymentType`: This is a very important parameter when you are generating a Nano image. This will be guest or host, depending on whether you want to deploy a virtual machine or a physical Nano Server. In this example, we specified guest; you can consider the guest the same as integration services in Hyper-V. Integration Services (also called integration services) are the set of synthetic drivers which allow a virtual machine to communicate with the host operating system.
- `-Edition`: This parameter helps you to choose a `Standard` or `Datacenter` edition. For more information about pricing and licensing for Windows Server 2016, please check the following link: `https://www.microsoft.com/en-us/clou d-platform/windows-server-pricing`.
- `-ComputerName`: This is the name of the Nano Server computer.

- `-AdministratorPassword`: This is the local Admin password (the one we specified at the beginning of the script).
- `-InterfaceNameOrIndex`: This parameter helps you to change the IP settings of a network adapter; you'll need to use this parameter in conjunction with the following IP parameters. The first NIC adapter will always be named Ethernet.
- `-Ipv4Address`, `-Ipv4SubnetMask`, `-Ipv4Dns`, `-Ipv4Gateway-`: are self-explanatory and enable the setting of static addresses; if you don't specify these parameters, Nano Server will look for the DHCP server on the network.
- `-EnableRemoteManagementPort`: This parameter opens port 5985 for inbound TCP connections for **Windows Remote Management** (**WinRM**) to manage Nano Server across different subnets.

After running the previous script, you will get a Nano Server VHDX image with just enough OS, without any role or feature added.

If you created a VHDX Nano image and you want to use this image in Hyper-V, please make sure to choose generation 2 virtual machine (this is very important). VHDX means generation 2, in this case, for Nano Server and VHD means generation 1. More on this in `Chapter 3`, *Deploying Nano Server in a Virtual Machine and on Physical Hardware*.

 You can download the previous script `New-NanoServerImage`, which is a companion for this book.

Advanced settings

The `New-NanoServerImage` supports an extended set of advanced parameters as well:

- `-MaxSize`: If you need larger images, you can supply `-MaxSize` to create a larger, dynamically expanding VHD(X) (that is, `MaxSize` 100 GB). If you don't use this parameter, the default disk size is 4 GB.
- `-LogPath`: This parameter sets the location where you want to save the logs created while building the Nano image.
- `-EnableRemoteManagementPort`: If you need to open port 5985 for inbound TCP traffic to connect using WinRM from a different subnet.
- `-MergePath`: If you need to embed your own script or binaries into the Nano Server image, you can supply `-MergePath` to copy a file or a directory into the root of the image (that is, `-MergePath .\tools`).

- `-EnableEMS`: This enables EMS and boot EMS on the image. See `Chapter 10`, *Running Other Workloads on the Nano Server,* for more information.
- `-EMSPort`: This is the port on which to enable the EMS. The default is `1`.
- `-EMSBaudRate`: This is the baud rate to use for EMS. The default is `115200` bps.
- `-DomainName`: This joins the image to the specified domain performing an offline join. For more information, see the domain join in `Chapter 3`, *Deploying Nano Server in a Virtual Machine and on Physical Hardware.*
- `-ReuseDomainNode`: When joining a domain, reuse a node with the same name if it exists already in the domain.
- `-ServicingPackagePath`: With this parameter, you can add servicing packages that you download from the Microsoft update catalog (multiple packages are possible at once, added as a comma separated list; these packages should be extracted from `.msu` to `.cab` format).
- `-SetupComplete-Command`: With this parameter, you can add custom commands as part of `setupcomplete.cmd`. See *Customizing a Nano Server Image Using DISM* in this chapter for more information.
- `-UnattendPath`: With this parameter, you can add the location of your own custom `unattend.xml` file. See *Customizing a Nano Server Image Using DISM* in this chapter for more information.
- `-Package`: This is the specific parameter that adds the packages that don't have a specific parameter. See the *Adding Packages* section in this chapter for more information.
- `-OEMDrivers`: This is the specific parameter that adds the OEM drivers package. These drivers are the same set of drivers that exist in Server Core, which includes a variety of network and storage controller drivers.
- `-SetupUI`: This parameter is brought about the same way as with the packages choice. This is used internally by the Nano Server image builder, and the recommended method is still to use the `-Package` parameter (see *Building and customizing a Nano Server image using Nano Server image builder* section for more information).

Adding packages

For adding packages, you can use the following package switches which are supported with the `New-NanoServerImage` command:

- `-Storage`: This allows you to add the File Server role and other storage components
- `-Compute`: This allows you to add the compute (Hyper-V) role
- `-Defender`: This allows you to add the Windows defender feature
- `-Clustering`: This allows you to add the clustering role
- `-Containers`: This allows you to add the containers role (see `Chapter 8`, *Running Windows Server Containers and Hyper-V Containers on Nano Server*)

The list of packages supported on Nano Server will keep growing over time. Therefore, instead of adding a new switch for each package, the Nano Server team has added a new parameter `-Package` that supports a comma separated list of all the packages that you want to include.

If you want to add the Hyper-V server role, failover clustering, and the storage role, you can use the `-Package` parameter as shown in the example covered earlier, followed by the name of each package, as shown in the following example:

```
-PackageMicrosoft-NanoServer-Compute-Package,Microsoft-
NanoServer-FailoverCluster-Package,Microsoft-NanoServer-
Storage-Package
```

Building and customizing a Nano Server image using Nano Server image builder

The Nano Server image builder is a new GUI-based wizard which helps you create a custom Nano Server image and bootable USB media. The Nano Server image builder is based on the inputs you provide; it generates images for deployment and it also creates reusable PowerShell scripts that allow you to automate the image creation process.

To create a Nano Server image using the Nano Server image builder, there are three resources you must have ready. These resources include:

- **Windows Assessment and Deployment Kit (ADK)** (https://developer.micro soft.com/en-us/windows/hardware/windows-assessment-deployment-kit)

- Nano Server image builder (https://www.microsoft.com/en-us/download/details.aspx?id=54065)
- Windows Server 2016 ISO file (https://www.microsoft.com/en-us/evalcenter/evaluate-windows-server-2016)

From the machine that you will use to create the Nano Server image using the Nano Server image builder, you need to install the Windows ADK.

Launch Nano Server image builder and select the preferred method of creating the image, as shown in *Figure 5*:

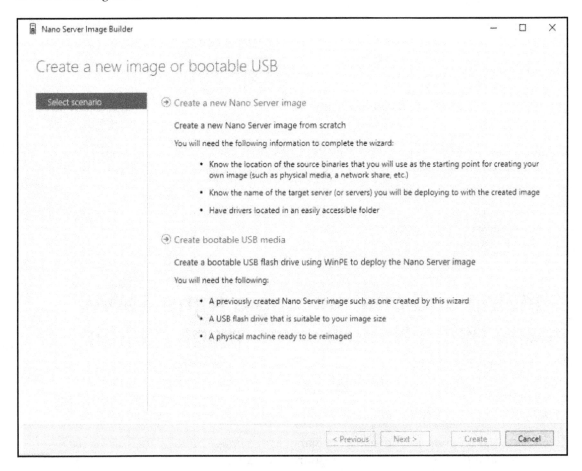

Figure 5: Nano Server image builder

Make sure you have already downloaded Windows Server 2016 ISO; you can extract the media to a folder on your local machine or mount the ISO, click on **Create a new Nano Server image**, specify the location of the Windows Server media as shown in *Figure 6*, and then click **Next**:

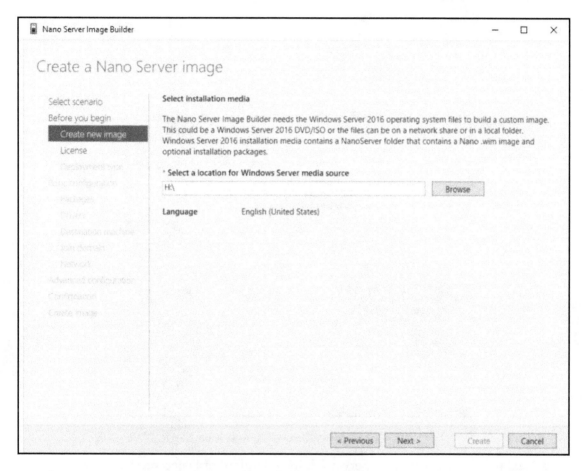

Figure 6: Nano Server image builder. Create a Nano Server image

Accept the License Agreement, click **Next**, and then choose your deployment type:

- Virtual machine images can be .vhd or .vhdx
- Physical machine images can be .vhd, .vhdx, or .wim

In this example, we will select a virtual machine image, as shown in *Figure 7*:

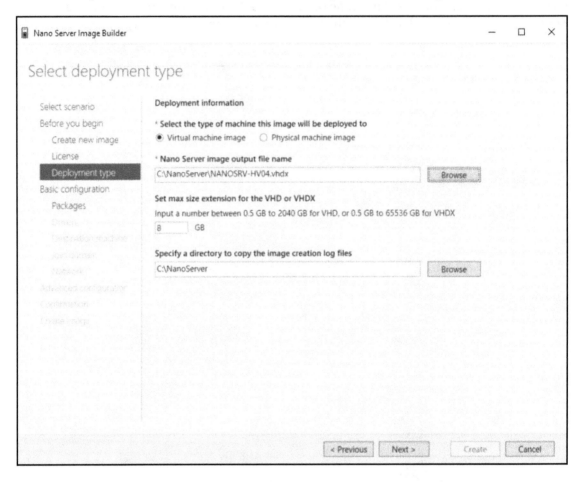

Figure 7: Nano Server image builder. Select deployment type

Click **Next** twice. Select the Nano Server Edition (Standard or Datacenter) and the components that you want to include, as shown in *Figure 8*. In my case, I'll use it as a Hyper-V, file server, and failover clustering service, so I've selected those roles. Including Windows PowerShell **Desired State Configuration** (**DSC**) is useful too (as you do need some way to configure the OS after it is installed), and having some sort of anti-malware is recommended too, so include **Windows Server Antimalware** for defender. Beyond that, it depends on what you want the Nano Server to do:

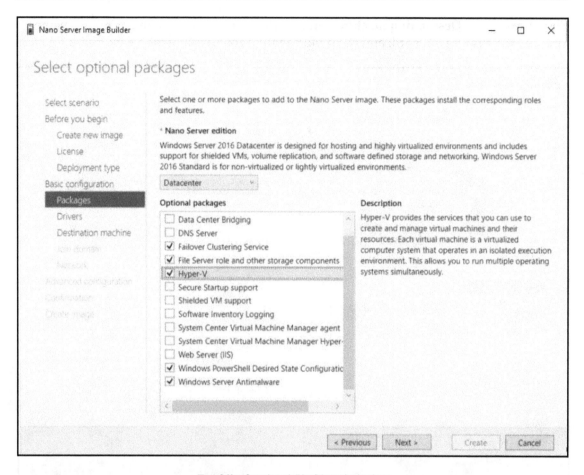

Figure 8: Nano Server image builder. Select optional packages

Click **Next**; here you can add additional drivers provided by the OEM vendor if you are creating a Nano image for a physical machine. In my case, the virtual machine integration components for Hyper-V have been selected automatically, which enables VMs to have a more consistent state and enables the guest to use synthetic devices.

Click **Next**; in the **Destination machine** information you need to give the computer name, local Administrator password, and the preferred time zone, as shown in *Figure 9*:

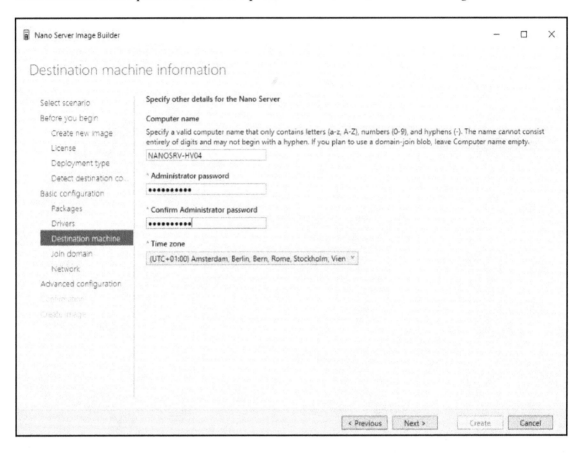

Figure 9: Nano Server image builder. Destination machine information

Click **Next**; you can enter a domain name to use as an existing active directory account, or you can provision a computer account metadata `blob` file.

Click **Next**; in the **Set network** you can enable remote PowerShell management from all subnets, enable VLAN ID, and configure network settings (DHCP or static), as shown in *Figure 10*:

Figure 10: Nano Server image builder. Set network

Click **Next**. You can proceed and select **Create basic Nano Server image** or **Continue to configure advanced settings**. Advanced settings options are: add servicing update packages, embed files and commands to run when setup completes, enable **Emergency Management Services**, enable support for development scenarios, and debugging methods.

In this example, we will create a basic Nano Server image. When ready, click **Create** and the image creation will start. In my case, the image creation completed in 2 minutes and 25 seconds, as shown in *Figure 11*, but this depends on your machine speed. As mentioned earlier, you can also copy the PowerShell command and use it later to automate the image creation process:

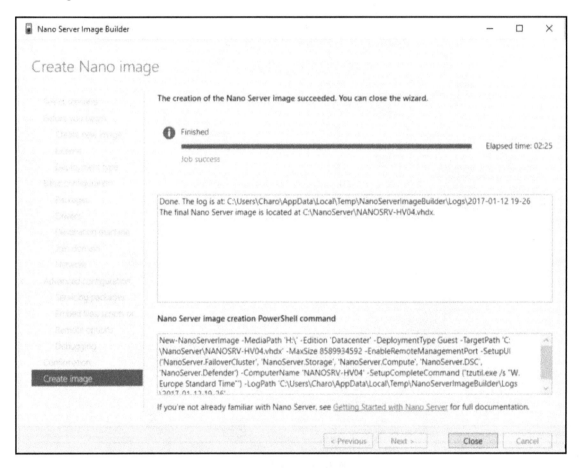

Figure 11: Nano Server image builder. Creating Nano Server image file

Customizing a Nano Server image using DISM

DISM is the tool of choice for adding packages in online and offline modes. The following example uses the offline version of DISM to add a package:

- `Dism /Add-Package /PackagePath:.\packages\<package>`
- `Dism /Add-Package /PackagePath:.\packages\en-us\<package>`

 For each package you want to add, you must run two DISM commands, one for the package path in the `Packages` folder, as shown in *Figure 3* earlier. But underneath that, you will find another folder called `en-US` or whatever localization you have bought from Microsoft. In my example here, we are using `en-US` for English-United States; `fr-BE` is for French-Belgium, and so on.

Customizing a Nano image using unattend.xml file

To customize Nano Server using DISM so you can manage it remotely, you need to set an administrator password.

The simplest way is using an `unattend.xml` file, as shown in the following example:

```
<?xml version='1.0' encoding='utf-8'?>
<unattend xmlns="urn:schemas-microsoft-com:unattend"
xmlns:wcm="http://schemas.microsoft.com/WMIConfig/2002/State"
xmlns:xsi="http://www.w3.org/2001/XMLSchema-instance">

<settings pass="offlineServicing">
<component name="Microsoft-Windows-Shell-Setup"
processorArchitecture="amd64" publicKeyToken="31bf3856ad364e35"
language="neutral" versionScope="nonSxS">
<ComputerName>NanoServer01</ComputerName>
</component>
</settings>

<settings pass="oobeSystem">
<component name="Microsoft-Windows-Shell-Setup"
processorArchitecture="amd64" publicKeyToken="31bf3856ad364e35"
language="neutral" versionScope="nonSxS">
```

```
<UserAccounts>
<AdministratorPassword>
<Value>Passw0rd!</Value>
<PlainText>true</PlainText>
</AdministratorPassword>
</UserAccounts>
<TimeZone>Romance Standard Time</TimeZone>
</component>
</settings>

<settings pass="specialize">
<component name="Microsoft-Windows-Shell-Setup"
processorArchitecture="amd64" publicKeyToken="31bf3856ad364e35"
language="neutral" versionScope="nonSxS">
<RegisteredOwner>My Team</RegisteredOwner>
<RegisteredOrganization>My Corporation</RegisteredOrganization>
</component>
</settings>
</unattend>
```

In this sample, the `unattend.xml` file does not add the Nano Server to a domain. Therefore, you should use it if you want to run the Nano Server as a standalone machine or if you want to wait and join it later to a domain. The values for `ComputerName` and `AdministratorPassword` are merely examples.

Please note that by using `unattend.xml` you can also include domain join information. We will get into that in a bit.

The `unattend.xml` file must be placed under the `C:\Windows\panther` folder in the Nano Server image.

You can download a sample of `unattend.xml` file for standalone and domain joined as a companion to this book.

Injecting unattend.xml into VHD(X)

After creating the `unattend.xml` file which includes your customized settings, we need to inject it into the image.

To create a VHD(X) image, please refer to the *Building and customizing a Nano Server image Using Windows PowerShell* and *Building and customizing a Nano Server image using Nano Server Image Builder* sections covered earlier.

Injecting the `unattend.xml` into a VHD(X) basically involves mounting the image first.

There are four steps involved to inject the `unattend.xml` file, as follow:

1. Before we inject the `unattend.xml` file, we should create a `mount` directory.

    From an elevated command prompt, run the following command:

    ```
    dism /Mount-Image /ImageFile:.\NanoServer.vhdx /Index:1
    /MountDir:.\mountdir
    ```

    Please update the extension of the image VHD(X) according to the image created earlier.

2. Apply the `unattend.xml` file that you already created and customized by running the following command:

    ```
    dism /image:.\mountdir /Apply-Unattend:.\unattend.xml
    ```

3. Create a `Panther` folder under `C:\Windows\` (this folder is used by Windows systems for storing files during setup). Copy the `unattend.xml` file to it using the following two commands:

    ```
    md .\mountdir\windows\panther
     copy .\unattend.xml .\mountdir\windows\panther
    ```

What this does is basically, when the image is booting, the offline servicing section of the `unattend.xml` file will execute without any reboot. However, with `oobeSystem` and `specialize`, the content of those two sections of the `unattend.xml` will execute on boot, so as the Nano Server boots, they will execute.

4. Unmount the VHD with `/commit` which is very important to keep these changes by running the following command:

```
dism /Unmount-Image /MountDir:.\mountdir /Commit
```

We would prefer to use Windows PowerShell that we covered earlier to create and customize a Nano image using the Nano PowerShell module.

Optional customizations

There are other optional customizations that can be used with DISM to further customize Nano Server for your environment, which include:

- Set computer name
- Run commands on first boot, for example, set a static IP address
- Domain join
- Enabling Emergency Management Services (EMS)
- Installing agents and tools

We will get into each of the previous optional settings in more detail.

Set computer name

To set the computer name, the simplest way is with an `unattend.xml` file, as shown in *Figure 12*:

```
<?xml version="1.0" encoding="UTF-8"?>
<unattend xmlns:xsi="http://www.w3.org/2001/XMLSchema-instance"
xmlns:wcm="http://schemas.microsoft.com/WMIConfig/2002/State" xmlns="urn:schemas-microsoft-
com:unattend">
  <settings pass="offlineServicing">
    <component language="neutral" versionScope="nonSxS" publicKeyToken="31bf3856ad364e35"
    processorArchitecture="amd64" name="Microsoft-Windows-Shell-Setup">
      <ComputerName>INSERT_NAME_HERE</ComputerName>
    </component>
  </settings>
  <settings pass="oobeSystem">
    <component language="neutral" versionScope="nonSxS" publicKeyToken="31bf3856ad364e35"
    processorArchitecture="amd64" name="Microsoft-Windows-Shell-Setup">
      <UserAccounts>
        <AdministratorPassword>
          <Value>INSERT_PWD_HERE</Value>
          <PlainText>true</PlainText>
        </AdministratorPassword>
      </UserAccounts>
      <TimeZone>Pacific Standard Time</TimeZone>
    </component>
  </settings>
  <settings pass="specialize">
    <component language="neutral" versionScope="nonSxS" publicKeyToken="31bf3856ad364e35"
    processorArchitecture="amd64" name="Microsoft-Windows-Shell-Setup">
      <RegisteredOwner>INSERT_OWNER_HERE</RegisteredOwner>
      <RegisteredOrganization>INSERT_COMPANY_HERE</RegisteredOrganization>
    </component>
  </settings>
</unattend>
```

Figure 12: Nano Server computer name, unattend.xml

You need to place `unattend.xml` inside the `C:\Windows\Panther` folder as discussed earlier.

Run commands on first boot

`SetupComplete.cmd` is a command file that, if found on boot by Windows under this location (`C:\Windows\Setup\Scripts\`), will be executed once and then never again, even if it's still in the same location afterward.

In the following example, we are setting a static IP address using command prompt. The trick here is that we are executing a PowerShell command by adding `PowerShell.exe` in the `.cmd` file. Because there is no PowerShell environment here, we follow this by adding `–command` and everything after that is a single command placed between quotation marks. It's very important for the command to be a single line, because every `PowerShell.exe` has its own environment. Therefore, we put everything related to setting the static IP address into one PowerShell command.

Create a `SetupComplete.cmd` file and copy the following command:

```
powershell.exe –command "Import-Module
C:\windows\system32\windowspowershell\v1.0\Modules\Microsoft.PowerShell.Uti
lity\Microsoft.PowerShell.Utility.psd1; Import-Module
C:\windows\system32\WindowsPowerShell\v1.0\Modules\NetAdapter\NetAdapter.ps
d1; $ifa = (Get-NetAdapter –Name Ethernet).ifalias; netsh interface ip set
address $ifa static 192.168.100.11"
```

In the previous example, we imported the module that is responsible for the utility module called (`Microsoft.PowerShell.Utility.psd1`), and then we imported another module called `NetAdapter.psd1`, because we are using `Get-NetAdapter` including the `ifalias` parameter. Then we specified `netsh interface ip` and finally, we set the static IP address `192.168.100.11`.

This is a very nice trick for setting once at Windows boot only.

Another command could be running a scheduling task, for example where you can create a scheduling task and add it to the `SetupComplete.cmd` file as well, so it would be an excellent idea to use any one-time operation that you want to setup on first boot with `SetupComplete.cmd`.

To copy `SetupComplete.cmd` into the Server VHD(X) image, you need to use the following DISM commands:

From an elevated command prompt, run the following command:

```
dism /Mount-Image /ImageFile:.\NanoServer.vhdx /Index:1
/MountDir:.\mountdir
```

Create the `Setup` and `Scripts` folders and then copy in the `Setupcomplete.cmd` file:

```
md .\mountdir\Windows\Setup
md .\mountdir\Windows\Setup\Scripts
copy .\SetupComplete.cmd .\mountdir\Windows\Setup\Scripts
```

Finally, unmount the VHD(X) image by running the following command:

```
dism /Unmount-Image /MountDir:.\mountdir /Commit
```

Domain join

You can also join Nano Server to a domain using the `djoin.exe` command line.

We have two ways of doing that:

- The first option is a blob-based domain join. It means that you should generate a blob from a domain joined machine located in the same domain, and then copy that blob over to Nano Server. Then, apply that blob to the image in offline or online mode.
    - To harvest a data blob from a domain machine that is already running Windows Server 2016, from an elevated command prompt, run the following command:

        ```
        djoin.exe /provision /domain <domain-name> /machine
        <machine-name> /savefile .\odjblob
        ```

- Next, we need to copy that harvest data blob <odjblob> into the Nano Server machine using PowerShell remoting, and then join it to the domain by running the following command:

    ```
    $Session = New-PSSession -ComputerName <NanoServer> -Credential
    ~\Administrator

    Copy-Item -ToSession $Session -Path 'C:\odjblob' -Destination
    C:\ -Recurse -Verbose

    $Session | Enter-PSSession
    djoin /requestodj /loadfile C:\odjblob /windowspath c:\windows
    /localos
     shutdown /r /t 5
    Exit-PSSession
    ```

- The second option is to generate a blob on a machine that is joined to the same domain as well, and then open that `blob` file `<odjblob>` that you generated and copy its content inside the `unattend.xml` file under the `<AccountData>` section, as shown in *Figure 13*. Then, use that `unattend.xml` file to apply the domain join on boot in the Nano Server image.
  - To harvest a data blob from a domain machine that is already running Windows Server 2016, we need to use the same step as described previously with `djoin.exe` command:

```xml
<?xml version="1.0" encoding="UTF-8"?>
<unattend xmlns:xsi="http://www.w3.org/2001/XMLSchema-instance"
xmlns:wcm="http://schemas.microsoft.com/WMIConfig/2002/State" xmlns="urn:schemas-microsoft-
com:unattend">
    <settings pass="offlineServicing">
        <component language="neutral" versionScope="nonSxS" publicKeyToken="31bf3856ad364e35"
        processorArchitecture="amd64" name="Microsoft-Windows-UnattendedJoin">
            <OfflineIdentification>
                <Provisioning>
                    <AccountData>
                        AAAAAAARUABLEABLEABAoAAAAAAAMABSUABLEABLEABAwAAAAAAAABbMAAdYABc8AB
                    </AccountData>
                </Provisioning>
            </OfflineIdentification>
        </component>
    </settings>
</unattend>
```

Figure 13: Nano Server domain join, unattend.xml

- Add the contents of the `odjblob` file to the `unattend.xml` file
- Inject the `unattend.xml` file into the Nano Server image as discussed earlier

If you have multiple Nano Servers that you want to join to the domain, you should generate one blob for each Nano machine, because the blob has computer name information. If you specify a blob using the `unattend.xml` file as shown in *Figure 13*, you cannot specify a computer name in the `unattend.xml` file as well. This will contradict, as the blob already holds the computer name when you are generating it from the `djoin.exe`.

Emergency management services

Since things don't always go as we planned, Microsoft added Emergency Management Services (EMS) to Nano Server.

Emergency Management Services (EMS) is a feature that offers remote management and system recovery options when other server administrative options are not possible. It is also needed for headless systems in which there is no GUI available, as in the case of Nano Server.

The communication works through the **System Administration Channel** (**SAC**) feature of Windows Server. The SAC channel offers several administrative features, such as enabling a Windows cmd.exe channel for Windows CLI access, listing processes running on the system, obtaining IP address information, retrieving server hardware information, and rebooting the server, to name just a few. Another important feature of the SAC channel is the ability to watch the boot and install progress of the server. See the TechNet article on EMS and SAC at technet.microsoft.com/en-us/library/cc778042(v=ws.10).aspx for more information.

PuTTY is one of the tools that can be used in this case. The good news is that network and server vendors such as HPE and Dell EMC sometimes use redirect. So, they use EMS over TCP/IP to redirect serial ports to the network card called **Virtual Serial Port** (**VSP**). Thus, if you have a baseboard management port in your server, such as ILO or iDRAC, you can access a Nano Server machine over EMS in this way.

See Chapter 9, *Troubleshooting Nano Server,* for a walkthrough example that uses Windows EMS to manage HPE ProLiant servers.

If you want to use EMS, you can enable it in your boot configuration using bcedit. You can set EMS to on and then specify the port that you will communicate on, followed by the EMSBAUDRATE as well, which typically is 115200.

From an elevated command prompt, run the following:

```
bcdedit /ems {GUID for Nano Server boot option} ON
bcdedit /emssettings EMSPORT:<port> EMSBAUDRATE:115200
```

Installing agents and tools

Microsoft does not support MSI in Nano Server. There is a reason for this. Firstly, MSI is built primarily for local installation, so remote installation can be problematic. Secondly, when you uninstall software that was installed using MSI, there is never a guarantee that everything will be cleaned up after the process is completed. A complete uninstall means all the registry entries they have and all the files that we ever put on disk should have been cleaned up. This has never been a guarantee with MSI in the past. Thirdly, MSI is being used to create custom scripts. In other words, people who use the feature to merely write scripts and deploy them to their system make things even worse when they come back and uninstall things afterward. All of this jeopardizes the reliability and stability of the system. With these drawbacks and the fact that MSI relies on a large chunk of .NET Framework which is not supported on Nano Server, Microsoft made the conscious decision to not include MSI support in Nano Server. Instead, they created a new installer based on xFormat. It is the format used by the Windows Store for all Windows Store apps, whether modern or legacy, and the **Windows Server App** (**WSA**) installer, which is not just for Nano Server but for all Windows Server 2016. WSA is important as it is the officially supported Server Installer going forward and is the only installer available on Nano Server. WSA promises a complete and clean uninstall and never leaves the system in an unreliable or unstable state.

With WSA, you can package apps so that you have a declarative, intent-based installer.

Examples of the tools and agents that can be installed using the new xFormat installer include System Center Virtual Machine Manager, System Center Operations Manager, and System Center Configuration Manager. These agents, whether they're Microsoft or non-Microsoft, and all the ISV vendors who are writing antivirus software, database software and so on, will use the new installer to install their tools and apps on it. Since it's a headless environment, the tool could be fully remoteable, in which case you can use everything you want either through PowerShell remoting or through a GUI outside, but it will run against the Nano Server as a server.

Summary

In this chapter, we discussed how to get started with Nano Server, covering how to add roles and features, and how you can create and customize a Nano image using a single line of PowerShell. We also discussed how to build and customize a Nano image using Nano Server image builder, the new GUI-based wizard, and finally we showed you how to customize a Nano image using the DISM tool.

Continue now to `Chapter 3`, *Deploying Nano Server in a Virtual Machine and on Physical Hardware*, to learn more about how to deploy Nano Server in your environment.

3
Deploying Nano Server in a Virtual Machine and on Physical Hardware

In `Chapter 2`, *Getting Started with Nano Server*, we talked about how to get started with Nano Server and explored all the requirements to create and customize a Nano Server image using Windows PowerShell, Nano Server image builder, and the DISM tool.

In this chapter, we will deploy Nano Server and cover the following topics:

- Nano Server roles and features
- Deploying Nano Server in a virtual machine
- Deploying Nano Server on a physical machine
- Deploying Nano Server in Microsoft Azure

Nano Server roles and features

In this section, we will dive deeply into covering all the roles and features that are part of Nano Server in Windows Server 2016. In the table, you can see the various roles and features, and the deployment type (physical or virtual machine), including a short description that will help you to choose the right role for your environment:

Role / Feature	Physical / Virtual Machine	Description
Compute-Package	Both	Hyper-V role
Storage-Package	Both	Storage role Note: This package is only available for the Datacenter edition of Nano Server
FailoverCluster-Package	Both	Failover Clustering role
Containers-Package	Both	Running Windows Server Containers and Hyper-V Containers
DNS-Package	Both	Running DNS Server
IIS-Package	Both	Running IIS Server
Defender-Package	Both	Anti-malware Defender package
OEM-Drivers-Package	Physical	The OEM package for Nano Server contains the same drivers that ship in-box with Server Core for physical machine deployment.
SCVMM-Package	Both	Helps in managing, deploying, and monitoring Nano Server with VMM
DSC-Package	Both	PowerShell DSC helps to simultaneously configure large numbers of Nano servers in push mode
DCB-Package	Both	DCB package is needed when configuring Network Datacenter Bridging
ShieldedVM-Package	Both	Deploying shielded virtual machines on top of Nano Server with Hyper-V role. Note: This package is only available for the Datacenter edition of Nano Server
SecureStartup-Package	Both	Provides support for secure startup
SoftwareInventoryLogging-Package	Both	SIL is a feature which helps server administrators retrieve a list of the Microsoft software that is installed on their servers. Note that SIL package in Nano server is agent only, not the aggregator.

Following is the description for each role:

- `Compute-Package`: It is the Hyper-V role which is applicable primarily for physical machines, however starting with Windows Server 2016 and Windows 10 build 10565 and later, Microsoft introduced Nested Virtualization where you can leverage this feature and host Nano Server with the compute role in a virtual machine.
- `FailoverCluster-Package`: It is a straightforward role. It can be used with Hyper-V or with file servers. The cluster role works either if Nano Server is hosted in a VM or on a physical machine.
- `Storage-Package`: It will add the necessary file server services and other storage components, such as scale-out File Servers, storage spaces direct, and storage replica.

 This package is only available for the datacenter edition of Nano Server. However, the Storage and failover clustering packages contain all the storage features in this first release. If you install failover clustering you'll have Storage Spaces Direct, but you won't be able to use it in the Standard edition as it calls licensing APIs and will not run, you'll only be able to use traditional clustering.

- **Containers-Package**: It will add the container role to turn Nano Server into a container host. Thus, you can start deploying Windows Server containers and Hyper-V Containers on top of Nano Server. For more information about Windows Server and Hyper-V containers, see `Chapter 8`, *Running Windows Server Containers and Hyper-V Containers on Nano Server*.
- **DNS-Package**: It will add the DNS server on top of Nano Server. The DNS can run both on a physical and a virtual machine. However, there are some catches, which we will cover in `Chapter 10`, *Running Other Workloads on the Nano Server*.
- **IIS-Package**: It will add the necessary binaries to run IIS and certain features of that service. The IIS role can also run on a physical and a virtual machine. However, not all features are supported. See `Chapter 10`, *Running Other Workloads on the Nano Server*, for more information.
- **Defender-Package**: It is the Antivirus and the optional threat protection package that works in a VM or on a physical machine. See `Chapter 10`, *Running Other Workloads on the Nano Server*, for more information.

- **OEM-Drivers-Package**: It is a collection of all the inbox drivers that Microsoft shipped with Server Core 2016, it makes testing Nano Server a lot easier, of course for optimization you would absolutely want to just pick the drivers that you need for Nano Server and nothing more, but this is a convenience feature more than anything else, which contains most of the common hardware drivers that used to ship with Server Core for use on physical machines with Nano installations.

- **SCVMM-Package**: **System Center Virtual Machine Manager** (**SCVMM**) works on both physical and virtual machines, the VMM agent can be added into the Nano Server image to help manage, monitor, and deploy VM templates. Please note that **System Center Operations Manager** (**SCOM**) is also supported on Nano Server. However, the SCOM agent is deployed in a different way. See Chapter 5, *Deploying, Managing, and Monitoring Nano Server with System Center 2016* for more information.

- **DSC-Package**: It works on both physical and virtual machines, the PowerShell **Desired State Configuration** (**DSC**) tool makes it possible to apply a configuration to a Nano Server, for example by using a single script you can adapt to simultaneously configure large numbers of Nano Servers.

- **DCB-Package**: **Datacenter Bridging** (**DCB**) provides hardware-based bandwidth allocation to a specific type of network traffic and enhances Ethernet transport reliability with the use of priority-based flow control. Hardware-based bandwidth allocation is essential if traffic bypasses the operating system and is offloaded to a converged network adapter. DCB is supported over **Internet Small Computer System Interface** (**ISCSI**), **Remote Direct Memory Access** (**RDMA**), over converged Ethernet (RoCE), or **Fiber Channel over Ethernet** (**FCoE**). Priority-based flow control is essential if the upper layer protocol, such as Fiber Channel, assumes a lossless underlying transport. It is very important to enable DCB with RDMA over Converged Ethernet. In this way, if you are using Nano Server as a storage fabric, the storage traffic will have the right priority, preventing packet loss.

- **The shielded VM-Package**: It is the host guardian that provides everything necessary to provision shielded virtual machines. Note that this package is only available in the datacenter edition of Nano Server.

- **Secure startup-Package**: It includes support for BitLocker, **Trusted Platform Module** (**TPM**), volume encryption, platform identification, cryptography providers, and other functionality related to secure startup which is a prerequisite for Shielded VMs.

- **Software inventory logging-Package**: It is a feature that helps server administrators to retrieve a list of the Microsoft software installed on their servers. Note that the **Software Inventory Logging (SIL)** package in Nano Server is agent only, not the aggregator. More information can be found here: `https://t echnet.microsoft.com/en-us/library/dn268301(v=ws.11).aspx`.

There are some additional roles and features that don't come in a package, but are certainly important, such as MPIO, NIC teaming, and using an SSH provider.

Deploying Nano Server in a VM

Before we deploy Nano Server in a virtual machine, we need to create a Nano Server image. You can do this using PowerShell or using Nano Server image builder. In this chapter, we will use Windows PowerShell. For a more thorough explanation of deployment and configuration options for Nano Server, see `Chapter 2`, *Getting Started with Nano Server*.

First, you need to have a Windows Server 2016 or Windows 10 machine. Upon doing so, you'll have to create a folder on the machine that you can use to store the items to be used for the Nano Server creation process. For instance, you might create a folder named `C:\NanoServer`. After creating this folder, there are four resources you must have saved to that folder. These resources are:

- `NanoServerImageGeneratorPowerShell` module
- `Convert-WindowsImage.ps1` script
- `NanoServer.wim` file
- Windows Server 2016 ISO file

In fact, all these resources are included in Windows Server 2016 ISO media in the `NanoServer` folder, you can mount the ISO image and copy the required components, then verify all are in the correct folder.

Next, open Windows PowerShell and import the `NanoServerImageGenerator.psd1` module using the following command (see *Figure 1*):

```
Import-Module "C:\NanoServer\
NanoServerImageGenerator\NanoServerImageGenerator.psd1" -Verbose
```

```
PS C:\NanoServer> # Import NanoServerImageGenerator.psd1 PowerShell module
Import-Module "C:\NanoServer\NanoServerImageGenerator\NanoServerImageGenerator.psd1" -Verbose
VERBOSE: Loading module from path 'C:\NanoServer\NanoServerImageGenerator\NanoServerImageGenerator.psd1'.
VERBOSE: Loading module from path 'C:\NanoServer\NanoServerImageGenerator\NanoServerImageGenerator.psm1'.
VERBOSE: Importing function 'Edit-NanoServerImage'.
VERBOSE: Importing function 'Get-NanoServerPackage'.
VERBOSE: Importing function 'New-NanoServerImage'.

PS C:\NanoServer>
```

Figure 1. Import Nano Server PowerShell module

When doing so, you can start creating the image using the `New-NanoServerImage` cmdlet, but you must specify a few parameters to use within the Nano Server that you are creating. These parameters are divided into required and optional.

Required parameters

- `MediaPath`: The root of the DVD drive contains the mounted ISO file that you are using.
- `BasePath`: The base path is a local folder on your machine that you specify where the command will keep a copy of the required Nano Server files and packages. This is very helpful, so next time you run `New-NanoServerImage`, you no longer have to specify the `MediaPath`, and instead you can just specify the `BasePath` and avoid the time of the copy operation.
- `TargetPath`: The target path is the path where you want to save your specialized Nano Server image, so that could be a folder where you actually keep, for example, your `VHD(X)`/`WIM` files, you can name them anything that is descriptive. If you are creating a `VHD(X)` image, you need to make sure that you specify the extension you want to use, `.VHDX` or `.VHD`, more on this later.
- `AdministratorPassword`: The password to be used for the built-in local Administrator account.
- `DeploymentType`: This will be `Guest` or `Host`, depending on whether you want to deploy a virtual machine or physical Nano Server.
- `Edition`: This parameter helps you to choose between standard or datacenter edition.

Optional parameters

- `ComputerName`: The Nano Server computer name, this is going to be the machine name of either the VM or physical machine.
- `Package`: The packages parameter supports a comma separated list of all packages that you wish to install into the Nano Server. You can find a list of available packages on the mounted ISO image in the `NanoServer\Packages` folder.
- `InterfaceNameOrIndex`: The alias name of the Ethernet adapter inside Nano Server. The first NIC adapter will always be named Ethernet.
- `IPv4Address`: This sets the given IPv4 static address that you want to assign on the interface specified by the `InterfaceNameOrIndex` parameter.
- `IPv4SubnetMask`: This sets the given IPv4 subnet mask that you want to assign on the interface specified by the `InterfaceNameOrIndex` parameter.
- `IPv4Dns`: This sets the given IPv4 DNS Server (can be multiple DNS servers) on the interface specified by the `InterfaceNameOrIndex` parameter.
- `IPv4Gateway`: This sets the given IPv4 default gateway that you want to assign on the interface specified by the `InterfaceNameOrIndex` parameter.
- `IPv6Address`: This sets the given IPv6 static address that you want to assign on the interface specified by the `InterfaceNameOrIndex` parameter.
- `IPv6Dns`: This sets the given IPv6 DNS Server on the interface specified by the `InterfaceNameOrIndex` parameter.
- `DomainName`: The domain name that Nano Server will be a member of.
- `ReuseDomainNode`: When joining a domain, reuse a node with the same name if it exists already in the domain.
- `DomainBlobPath`: This parameter lets you join the image to the domain as specified in the given domain blob. For more information, see the domain join in this chapter.
- `Storage`: This parameter will add the storage package.
- `Compute`: This parameter will add the Hyper-V role.
- `Defender`: This parameter will add the anti-malware package.
- `Clustering`: This parameter will add the failover clustering role.

- `Containers`: This allows you to add the containers role. See Chapter 8, *Running Windows Server Containers and Hyper-V Containers on Nano Server* for more information.
- `OEMDrivers`: This is used to add the OEM Drivers package useful for physical machine deployment. Those drivers are the same set of drivers that exist in Server Core.
- `DriverPath`: If you need additional drivers or a specific set of drivers, you can add them with this parameter. This is useful when you are deploying Nano Server to a bare-metal machine. The drivers can be obtained from your favorite OEM vendor. The path should contain the drivers in `.inf` format.

 The drivers need to be signed otherwise the command will fail.

- `CopyPat`: This parameter specifies the additional `directory` path on the computer where you create the image. This directory including the files in it will be added to the `root` of the Nano Server image.
- `LogPath`: This sets the location where you want to save the logs created while building the image. The default path is the current folder from where you are creating the image (that is, `C:\NanoServer\Logs`).
- `MaxSize`: If you need larger images, you can supply `- MaxSize` to create a larger, dynamically expanding VHD(X). If you don't use this parameter, the default disk size is 4 GB.
- `OfflineScriptArgument`: This accepts a hash table of arguments when you want to add a customer script.
- `OfflineScriptPath`: This accepts an array of paths to PowerShell scripts, with the possibility to pass arguments through the `OfflineScriptArgument` parameter.
- `EnableRemoteManagementPort`: This parameter will open port 5985 for inbound TCP traffic to connect and manage Nano Server using WinRM from a different subnet.

- `EnableEMS`: This enables **Emergency Management Services (EMS)** and BootEMS on the image. See `Chapter 10`, *Running Other Workloads on the Nano Server,* for more information.
- `EMSPort`: This is the port on which to enable the EMS. The default is `1`.
- `EMSBaudRate`: This is the baud rate to use for EMS. The default is `115200` bps.
- `DebugMethod`: With this parameter, you will enable kernel debugging on the target Nano image with the specified method. You can use a Serial Port, TCP/IP network, Firewire or USB. See `Chapter 10`, *Running Other Workloads on the Nano Server,* for more information.
- `Development`: This is used to perform tests on Nano Server, which allows unsigned drivers, copy debugger binaries, and more. Not used in production.
- `ServicingPackagePath`: This parameter helps you to add servicing stack and cumulative updates that you download from the Microsoft Update catalog (multiple packages are possible).
- `SetupComplete` command : With this parameter, you can add custom commands as part of `setupcomplete.cmd`. See `Chapter 2`, *Getting Started with Nano Server, Customizing a Nano Server Image Using* section *DISM* for more information.
- `UnattendPath`: With this parameter, you can add the location of your own, custom, `unattend.xml` file. See `Chapter 2`, *Getting Started with Nano Server, Customizing a Nano Server Image Using DISM* section for more information.
- `Internal`: This is something specific for Microsoft, and not to be used in production.
- `SetupUI`: This parameter is about same way as with the `Package` parameter. This is used internally by the Nano Server image builder, and the recommended method is still to use the `Package` parameter covered earlier. See `Chapter 2`, *Getting Started with Nano Server, Building and customizing a Nano Server image using Nano Server image builder* section for more information.

Upon completing these procedures, you've created the Nano Server image VHDX ready to be deployed on Hyper-V (see *Figure 2*):

```
PS C:\> New-NanoServerImage -MediaPath "$($DVDDriveLetter):"
               -BasePath C:\NanoServer\
               -TargetPath C:\NanoServer\NanoServerVM01.vhdx
               -MaxSize 8GB
               -DeploymentType Guest
               -Edition Datacenter
               -ComputerName "NANO-VM01"
               -AdministratorPassword $Password
               -InterfaceNameOrIndex Ethernet
               -Ipv4Address 192.168.1.10
               -Ipv4SubnetMask 255.255.255.0
               -Ipv4Dns 192.168.1.9
               -Ipv4Gateway 192.168.1.1
               -EnableRemoteManagementPort
               -ServicingPackagePath $ServicingPackage
               -SetupCompleteCommand ('tzutil.exe /s "W. Europe Standard Time"')

Done. The log is at: C:\NanoServer\Logs\2017-01-16_13-08-18-58
```

Figure 2. The Nano Server VHD created with the script

Once the VHDX file is created, you can simply copy the VHDX file to Hyper-V server and create a new virtual machine. Please note that the VM must be a generation 2 VM .VHDX image means generation 2 in this case for Nano Server and VHD means generation 1. However, this rule does not apply for Server with Desktop Experience and Server Core, VHDX can be generation 1 or generation 2.

Deploying Nano Server VM in Hyper-V

In this section, we will deploy Nano Server in a virtual machine. In order to do so, you have two options, either you can use Hyper-V Manager or PowerShell, we will cover both options.

Hyper-V Manager

1. Launch Hyper-V Manager and navigate to **New | Virtual Machine**.

2. In the **New Virtual Machine Wizard**, choose a name, for example
   NanoServerVM01 (see *Figure 3*):

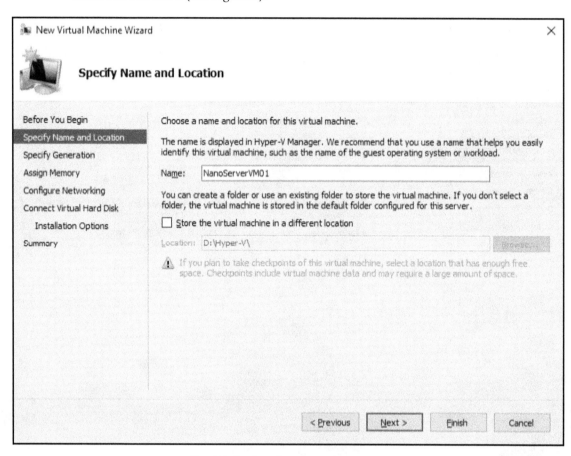

Figure 3. The Nano Server VM creation with Hyper-V Manager

3. Make sure you choose **Generation 2** virtual machine; this is very important (see *Figure 4*):

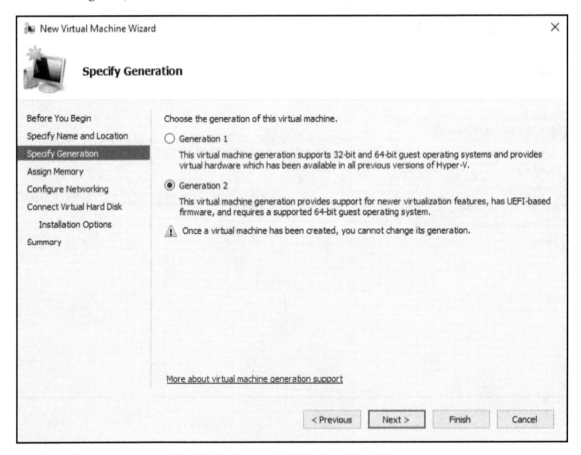

Figure 4. The Nano Server generation 2 VM creation with Hyper-V Manager

4. Next, assign the amount of startup memory for this VM (see *Figure 5*):

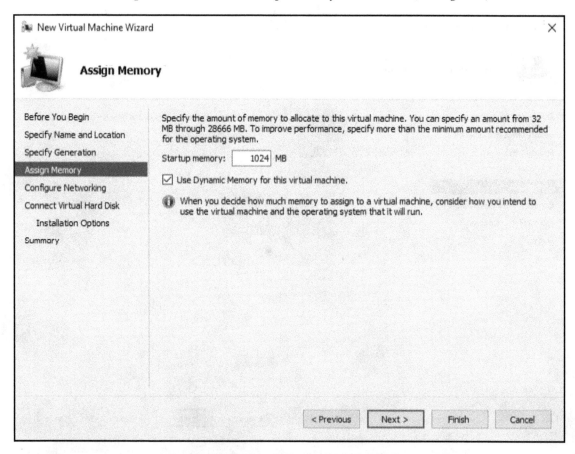

Figure 5. Assign Startup memory for Nano Server VM with Hyper-V Manager

5. Next, connect Nano Server VM to the appropriate virtual switch (see *Figure 6*):

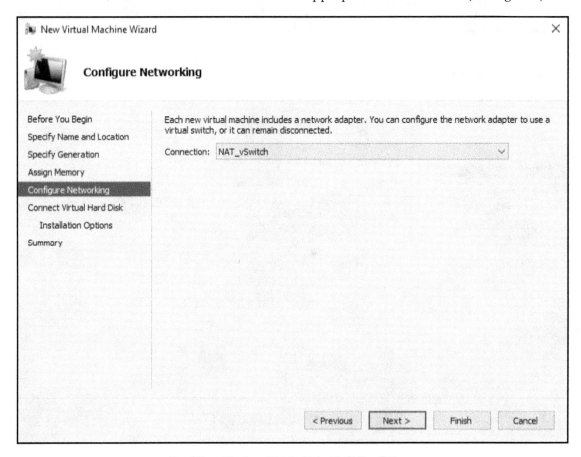

Figure 6. Connect Nano Server VM to the virtual switch with Hyper-V Manager

6. Next, attach the Nano Server VHD(X) image file which we created earlier (see *Figure 7*):

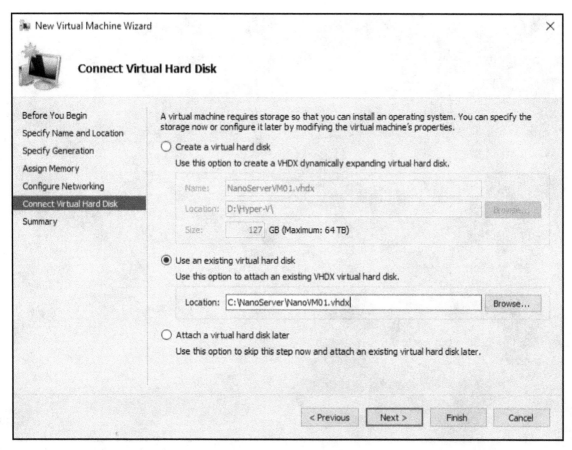

Figure 7. Attach Nano Server VHD(X) with Hyper-V Manager

7. Click **Next|Finish**.
8. Connect to the virtual machine using Hyper-V Manager and click **Start**.

9. Wait a couple of seconds and you will see the Nano recovery console (see *Figure 8*):

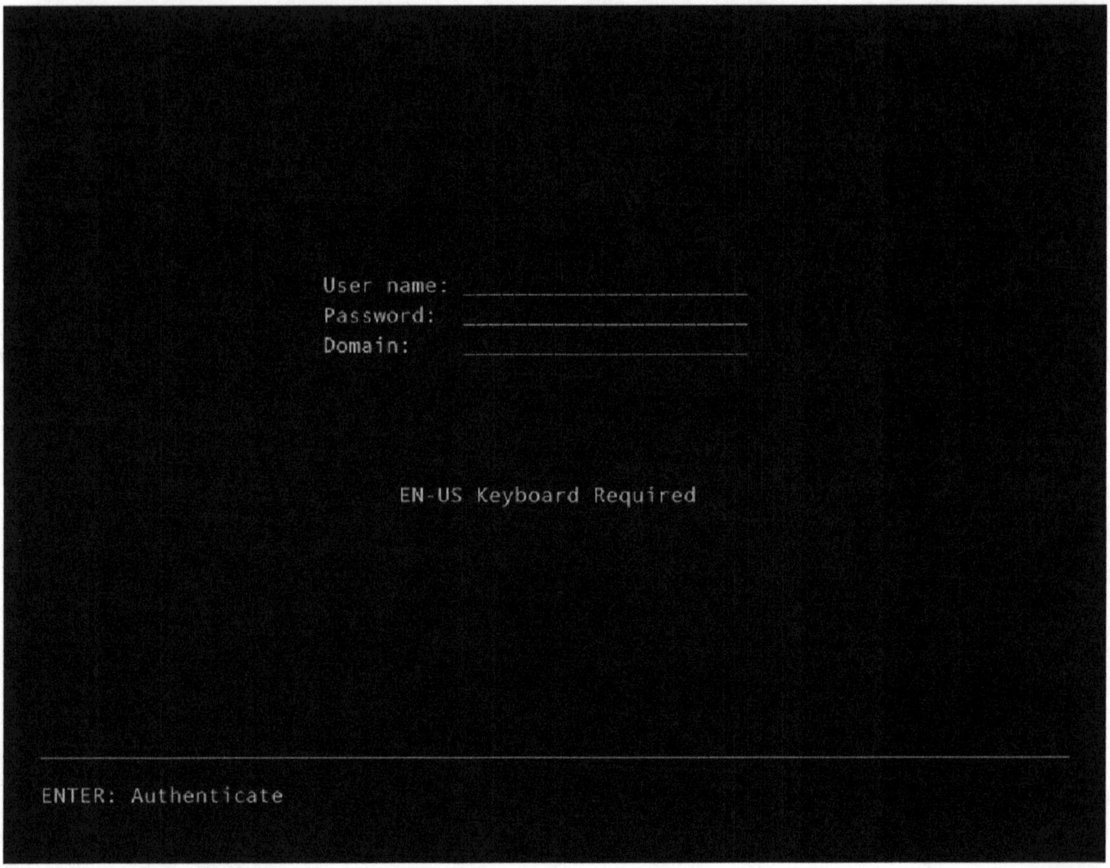

```
                    User name:  _____
                    Password:   _____
                    Domain:     _____




                    EN-US Keyboard Required








  _____
  ENTER: Authenticate
```

Figure 8. Nano Server login screen in Hyper-V Manager

10. Enter the administrator password you specified when creating the image, and press *Enter* to log onto Nano Server (see *Figure 9*):

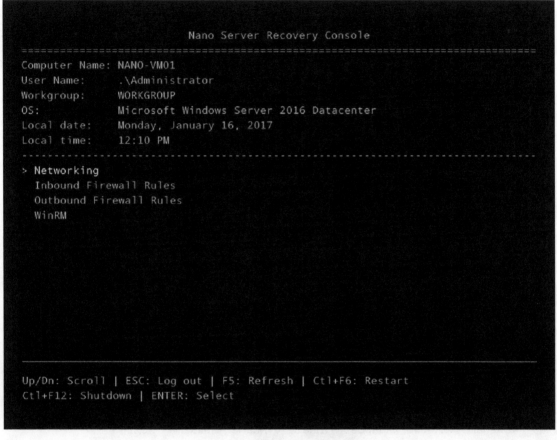

```
                        Nano Server Recovery Console
==============================================================================
Computer Name: NANO-VM01
User Name:     .\Administrator
Workgroup:     WORKGROUP
OS:            Microsoft Windows Server 2016 Datacenter
Local date:    Monday, January 16, 2017
Local time:    12:10 PM
- - - - - - - - - - - - - - - - - - - - - - - - - - - - - - - - - - - - - - -

> Networking
  Inbound Firewall Rules
  Outbound Firewall Rules
  WinRM



------------------------------------------------------------------------------
Up/Dn: Scroll | ESC: Log out | F5: Refresh | Ctl+F6: Restart
Ctl+F12: Shutdown | ENTER: Select
```

Figure 9. Nano Server recovery console

11. The recovery console will open showing you basic information, you can use the IP address assigned to start managing Nano Server remotely using Windows PowerShell, more on this in Chapter 6, *Managing Nano Server with Windows PowerShell and Windows PowerShell DSC* .

See also Chapter 9, *Troubleshooting Nano Server*, for more information about the recovery console.

PowerShell

We strongly encourage you to use PowerShell if you are not doing so already, please remember Nano Server has been optimized for large deployment whether on-premises or in the public cloud, you will soon find out it's more convenient to use PowerShell instead of clicking next, or finish.

In this step, we will create a Nano Server VM using Windows PowerShell. First, we need to define some variables:

```
# Variables
$vSwitchName01 = "NAT_vSwitch"
$InstallRoot = "C:\NanoServer"
$VMName = "NanoServerVM01"
$NanoServerImage = "C:\NanoServer\NanoServerVM01.vhdx"

# Create a new VHD(X) file
New-VHD -Path ($InstallRoot + "\$VMName\NanoServerVM01_D.vhdx") -
SizeBytes 50GB -Dynamic | Out-Null

# Create Nano Server VM
New-VM -VHDPath $NanoServerImage -Generation 2 -MemoryStartupBytes 2GB
-Name $VMName -Path $InstallRoot -SwitchName $vSwitchName01 | Out-Null

# Set vCPU count to 4
Set-VMProcessor -VMName $VMName -Count 4

# Set AutomaticStopAction and AutomaticStartAction
Set-VM -VMName $VMName -AutomaticStopAction ShutDown -
AutomaticStartAction StartIfRunning

# Rename vNIC Adapter name to MGMT
Rename-VMNetworkAdapter -VMName $VMName -NewName "MGMT"

# Set vNIC Device Naming to On
Set-VMNetworkAdapter -VMName $VMName -Name "MGMT" -DeviceNaming On

# Add additional SCSI Controller and attach the new VHD(X)
Add-VMScsiController -VMName $VMName
Add-VMHardDiskDrive -VMName $VMName -ControllerType SCSI -
ControllerNumber 1 -ControllerLocation 0 -Path ($InstallRoot +
"\$VMName\NanoServerVM01_D.vhdx")

# Start Nano Server VM
Start-VM -Name $VMName | Out-Null
Get-VM -Name $VMName
```

Upon running this script, you've created and hosted a new Nano Server VM on Hyper-V in just a couple of seconds (see *Figure 10*):

```
CharbelNemnom.com #> $vSwitchName01 = "NAT_vSwitch"
CharbelNemnom.com #> $InstallRoot = "C:\NanoServer"
CharbelNemnom.com #> $VMName = "NanoServerVM01"
CharbelNemnom.com #> $NanoServerImage = "C:\NanoServer\NanoServerVM01.vhdx"
CharbelNemnom.com #>
CharbelNemnom.com #> # Create a new VHD(X) file
CharbelNemnom.com #> New-VHD -Path ($InstallRoot + "\$VMName\NanoServerVM01_D.vhdx") -SizeBytes 50GB -Dynamic | Out-Null

CharbelNemnom.com #>
CharbelNemnom.com #> # Create Nano Server VM
CharbelNemnom.com #> New-VM -VHDPath $NanoServerImage -Generation 2 -MemoryStartupBytes 2GB -Name $VMName -Path $Install
Root -SwitchName $vSwitchName01 | Out-Null
CharbelNemnom.com #>
CharbelNemnom.com #> # Set vCPU count to 4
CharbelNemnom.com #> Set-VMProcessor -VMName $VMName -Count 4
CharbelNemnom.com #>
CharbelNemnom.com #> # Set AutomaticStopAction and AutomaticStartAction
CharbelNemnom.com #> Set-VM -VMName $VMName -AutomaticStopAction ShutDown -AutomaticStartAction StartIfRunning
CharbelNemnom.com #>
CharbelNemnom.com #> # Rename vNIC Adapter name to MGMT
CharbelNemnom.com #> Rename-VMNetworkAdapter -VMName $VMName -NewName "MGMT"
CharbelNemnom.com #>
CharbelNemnom.com #> # Set vNIC Device Naming to On
CharbelNemnom.com #> Set-VMNetworkAdapter -VMName $VMName -Name "MGMT" -DeviceNaming On
CharbelNemnom.com #>
CharbelNemnom.com #> # Add additional SCSI Controller and attach the new VHD(X)
CharbelNemnom.com #> Add-VMSscsiController -VMName $VMName
CharbelNemnom.com #> Add-VMHardDiskDrive  -VMName $VMName -ControllerType SCSI -ControllerNumber 1 -ControllerLocation 0
 -Path ($InstallRoot + "\$VMName\NanoServerVM01_D.vhdx")
CharbelNemnom.com #>
CharbelNemnom.com #> # Start Nano Server VM
CharbelNemnom.com #> Start-VM -Name $VMName | Out-Null
CharbelNemnom.com #> Get-VM -Name $VMName

Name            State   CPUUsage(%) MemoryAssigned(M) Uptime          Status              Version
----            -----   ----------- ----------------- ------          ------              -------
NanoServerVM01 Running 0               2048           00:00:04.7410000 Operating normally 8.0
```

Figure 10. Create Nano Server VM using PowerShell

 All scripts provided in this chapter are accompanied with this book.

Deploying Nano Server on a physical machine

There are actually a few ways to deploy Nano Server to a physical bare-metal machine, you can use one of the following options. Deploying Nano Server on a physical machine:

- Dual-boot a Nano Server VHD or VHD(X).
- PxE-boot a bare-metal machine and install Nano Server from WDS using a VHD or VHD(X).
- PxE-boot a bare-metal machine and install Nano Server from WDS using a WIM file.
- Booting a bare-metal machine into WinPE and deploying Nano Server using a WIM file.

Regardless of the deployment method used, the default Nano Server image that ships with Windows Server 2016 requires customization. Customizations include adding Nano Server packages based on the role the server will play in the environment, the addition of boot critical drivers, and an `Unattend.xml` file to complete the setup. This chapter covers the most common deployment scenarios.

Dual-boot a Nano Server VHD or VHD(X)

The easiest way to have multiple Windows versions available on the same machine is to place some of them into VHD(X)s, and then you can boot an OS directly from a VHD(X).

This way of deployment is assuming that you already have a physical machine with existing Windows OS installed, it's not a bare-metal deployment, we will get into that in a bit.

To quickly deploy Nano Server on a physical computer, you need to have a generalized Nano Server VHD or VHDX image ready.

We will create a new VHDX image using PowerShell; The computer name will be `NANO-HV01`. The deployment type is `Host` for physical machine, we will have the OEM drivers installed for most common hardware including the drivers provided by the hardware vendor by using the `-DriverPath` parameter. We will add `Microsoft-NanoServer-SecureStartup-Package` for UEFI boot. We will add the compute package for Hyper-V, as well as clustering, storage features, and enabling Remote Management across subnets.

Open Windows PowerShell as administrator and run the following command:

```
# Import NanoServerImageGenerator.psd1 PowerShell module
Import-Module
"C:\NanoServer\NanoServerImageGenerator\NanoServerImageGenerator.psd1"
-Verbose

# Enter Administrator Password
$Password = Read-Host -Prompt "Please specify local Administrator
password" -AsSecureString


# Servicing Update Packages
$ServicingPackage = @(
 "C:\NanoServer\Updates\Windows10.0-KB3199986-x64.cab"
 "C:\NanoServer\Updates\Windows10.0-KB3213986-x64.cab"
 )

# Create New Nano Server Image
New-NanoServerImage -BasePath C:\NanoServer\ `
 -TargetPath C:\NanoServer\NanoServer01.vhdx `
 -ComputerName "NANO-HV01" `
 -AdministratorPassword $Password `
 -DeploymentType Host `
 -Edition Datacenter `
 -OEMDrivers `
 -DriverPath C:\NanoServer\HPE-Drivers `
 -Compute `
 -Clustering `
 -Storage `
 -Package Microsoft-NanoServer-SecureStartup-Package `
 -EnableRemoteManagementPort `
 -ServicingPackagePath $ServicingPackage `
 -SetupCompleteCommand ('tzutil.exe /s "W. Europe Standard Time"')
```

> If the physical server uses BIOS instead of UEFI, then make sure to change
> `NanoServer01.vhdx` to `NanoServer.vhd` and remove `Microsoft-NanoServer-SecureStartup-Package`.

If you noticed in the script above, we eliminated the `-MediaPath` parameter and just used the `-BasePath`, this will save us two steps. The first one is copying from the ISO image to the local folder, and the second one is converting the WIM image to VHD because we did that in the previous section, and since the physical computer in this example does support UEFI, we created the image as VHDX.

1. Copy the VHDX that this script creates to the physical computer, either manually or with PowerShell. In this example, we will use the new feature which was introduced in PowerShell V5.0 (copying files from one machine to another through `-ToSession` and `-FromSession` parameters). Please note that Windows **Management Framework** (**WMF**) version 5.0 is required to be installed on the target machine if it's running an OS earlier than Windows Server 2016 or Windows 10 for the following command to work (see *Figure 11*):

2. Log in as an administrator on the physical server where you want to run the Nano Server:

```
$ip = "172.16.19.21"
$s = New-PSSession -ComputerName $ip -Credential
~\Administrator
Copy-Item -ToSession $s -Path .\NanoServer01.vhdx -Destination
c:\
```

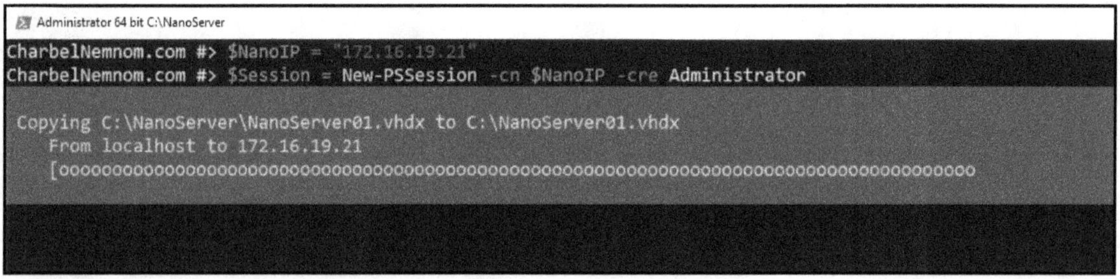

Figure 11. Copying Nano Server image using PowerShell

3. Configure the physical machine to boot from this new VHDX. To do that, follow these steps:

   1. We need to add an entry to the boot database using `bcdboot`, but before we add this entry, let's look at the current boot database by running bcdedit (see *Figure 12*):

```
Windows Boot Manager
--------------------
identifier              {bootmgr}
device                  partition=\Device\HarddiskVolume1
path                    \EFI\Microsoft\Boot\bootmgfw.efi
description             Windows Boot Manager
locale                  en-US
inherit                 {globalsettings}
bootshutdowndisabled    Yes
default                 {current}
resumeobject            {b080498f-dc02-11e6-93a7-1c98ec115207}
displayorder            {current}
                        {778882db-d778-11e1-ba01-d89d671a537c}
toolsdisplayorder       {memdiag}
timeout                 10

Windows Boot Loader
--------------------
identifier              {current}
device                  partition=C:
path                    \Windows\system32\winload.efi
description             Windows Server 2016
locale                  en-US
inherit                 {bootloadersettings}
recoverysequence        {b0804991-dc02-11e6-93a7-1c98ec115207}
recoveryenabled         Yes
isolatedcontext         Yes
allowedinmemorysettings 0x15000075
osdevice                partition=C:
systemroot              \Windows
resumeobject            {b080498f-dc02-11e6-93a7-1c98ec115207}
nx                      OptOut
```

Figure 12. Bcdedit output on physical machine

As you can see, we have a single entry as identifier called `{current}`.

2. Next, we need to add a new entry to the BCD store, so in addition to the current operating system, which in this example is listed as Windows Server 2016, we would like to add another boot entry. In order to do that we need to use the `bcdboot` command.

3. On the target server, mount the VHDX that we copied in an earlier step, and configure it to boot from this new VHDX. To do that, follow these steps:

```
# Nano Server 2016 VHD Image
$NanoImage = "C:\NanoServer01.vhdx"

# Mount the VHD Image
Mount-DiskImage $NanoImage -Verbose

# Get the Drive Letter of the VHD image
(Get-DiskImage -ImagePath $NanoImage | Get-Disk |
 Get-Partition | Get-Volume).DriveLetter
```

In this example, the VHDX is mounded on the E:\drive as shown in *Figure 13*:

```
PS C:\> # Nano Server 2016 VHD Image
PS C:\> $NanoImage = "C:\NanoServer01.vhdx"
PS C:\>
PS C:\> # Mount the VHD Image
PS C:\> Mount-DiskImage $NanoImage -Verbose
PS C:\>
PS C:\> # Get the Drive Letter of the VHD image
PS C:\> (Get-DiskImage -ImagePath $NanoImage | Get-Disk | Get-Partition | Get-Volume).DriveLetter
E
PS C:\>
```

Figure 13. Mount Nano Server VHDX image on physical machine

4. Run `bcdboot e:\windows /v.`

If `bcdboot.exe` worked correctly, you should see the following message:

```
"Boot files successfully created."
```

5. **Dismount the VHDX by running**: `Dismount-DiskImage $NanoImage` verify the new boot entry in the BCD store by running `bcdedit.exe`. You should see a new Windows boot loader entry with the device setting pointing to Nano Server VHD(X) file. In our example, `vhd=[C:]\NanoServer01.vhdx`.

6. As you can see in *Figure 14*, `bcdboot` has updated all boot files (such as `bootmgr`), and took the bcd template from the Nano image you want to boot from, stamped it into the BCD store, and updated the device paths. Now, you will know for sure that the path is correct, the entry is correct, and the binaries have supported versions:

```
Windows Boot Manager
--------------------
identifier              {bootmgr}
device                  partition=\Device\HarddiskVolume1
path                    \EFI\Microsoft\Boot\bootmgfw.efi
description             Windows Boot Manager
locale                  en-us
inherit                 {globalsettings}
bootshutdowndisabled    Yes
default                 {default}
displayorder            {default}
                        {current}
                        {778882db-d778-11e1-ba01-d89d671a537c}
toolsdisplayorder       {memdiag}
timeout                 30

Windows Boot Loader
-------------------
identifier              {default}
device                  vhd=[C:]\NanoServer01.vhdx
path                    \windows\system32\boot\winload.efi
description             Windows Server 2016
locale                  en-us
inherit                 {bootloadersettings}
isolatedcontext         Yes
allowedinmemorysettings 0x15000075
osdevice                vhd=[C:]\NanoServer01.vhdx
systemroot              \windows
nx                      OptIn
hypervisorlaunchtype    Auto
```

Figure 14. Nano Server VHDX - Boot loader BCD Store

You could possibly accomplish something similar with the `bcdedit` command, but with `bcdedit` you would need to manually set the VHD path, which is easy to get wrong. If you are not careful while copying different entries, you will end up booting the OS with an incorrect boot configuration. On top of that, `bcdedit` will not update the binaries, which could result in an unsupported configuration. As best practice, please use `bcdboot`.

7. Since we already have Windows Server 2016 installed on the same physical machine, we now have two entries with the same name in Windows boot manager (Windows Server 2016). However, `bcdboot` set Nano Server as default boot. You can easily change the description by running the following command:

```
bcdedit.exe /set "{default}" description "Windows Nano Server
2016"
```

8. You could also enable the EMS in the new boot entry. See `Chapter 9, Troubleshooting Nano Server`, for more information. Assuming the identifier string of the newly added boot loader is `{default}`, run the following commands:

```
bcdedit.exe /set "{default}" bootems on
bcdedit.exe /set "{default}" ems on
```

9. You can verify the boot entry in the BCD store again by running, `bcdedit.exe` (see *Figure 15*):

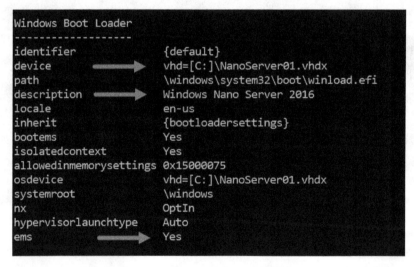

Figure 15. Nano Server VHDX - Boot loader BCD Store

10. Reboot the physical machine now. You should see two boot entries. The Nano Server image should appear first in the Windows Boot Manager as `Windows Nano Server 2016 [EMS Enabled]` (see *Figure 16*):

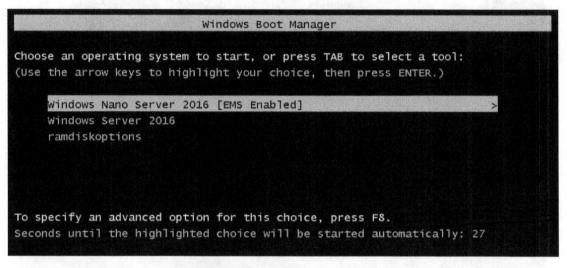

Figure 16. Nano Server boot process on physical machine

11. Wait for a couple of seconds until Nano Server boots and then log onto the recovery console, as shown in *Figure 17* using the user name (in this case: `Administrator`) and the password you supplied while creating the Nano Server image.

```
User name: Administrator_____
Password:  ********  _____
Domain:             _____




ENTER Authenticate
```

Figure 17. Nano Server recovery console login screen

12. In our example here, we have DHCP server deployed on the network. You can get the IP address and use PowerShell remoting to connect to and start managing the physical Nano machine (see *Figure 18*), more on this in Chapter 6, *Managing Nano Server with Windows PowerShell and Windows PowerShell DSC*.

You can also manage Nano Server from different network subnets, as a requirement, the remote management port switch was enabled as part of creating the image.

```
                    Network Adapter Settings
=============================================================================
Embedded LOM 1 Port 4
HP Ethernet 1Gb 4-port 331i Adapter #4
- - - - - - - - - - - - - - - - - - - - - - - - - - - - - - - - - - - - - - -
State             Started
MAC Address       1C-98-EC-11-52-07

Interface
DHCP              Enabled
IPv4 Address      172.16.19.21
Subnet mask       255.255.0.0
Prefix Origin     DHCP
Suffix Origin     DHCP

Interface
DHCP              Enabled
IPv6 Address      fe80::50f1:4017:f9fd:236d
Prefix Length     64
Prefix Origin     Well Known
Suffix Origin     Link
_____

Up/Dn: Scroll | ESC: Back | F4: Toggle | F10: Routing Table
F11: IPv4 Settings | F12: IPv6 Settings
```

Figure 18. Nano Server recovery console - Network adapter settings

PxE-boot a bare-metal machine and install Nano Server from WDS using a VHD, VHD(X), or WIM file

Deploying Nano Server using WDS can be accomplished using a Nano Server image in VHD, VHD(X), or WIM format that contains customizations including Nano Server packages and drivers, prior to adding the image to the WDS server.

This section describes using Microsoft WDS to perform a bare-metal deployment of Nano Server. For instructions on how to create and modify a VHD image, please refer to the section titled *Creating a custom Nano Server VHD(X) image* and for instructions on how to create and modify WIM files, please refer to the section titled *Creating a custom Nano Server WIM image*. The Nano Server WIM, VHD, or VHDX file can be added to the WDS server using the same steps described here.

In this section, we will configure the WDS environment for automated deployments using two `unattend.xml` files. The first one is for automating the WinPE phase of setup using a client `unattend.xml` file. The second one is automating the remainder of the deployment using an image `unattend.xml` file. This section covers both files.

Preparing the environment

But before we get to building the actual deployment, we need to install all the pre-requisites:

1. Active Directory Domain Services (ADDS, DNS, DHCP)
2. Prepare the Nano Server VHD Image
3. Install and configure the WDS Role

In addition to the components listed above, the following components are also required for a successful deployment and management of Nano Server:

*   Microsoft Windows Server 2016 ISO Media
*   Windows 10 assessment and deployment kit
*   Required hardware drivers from the OEM vendor

The ADK contains deployment tools such as the **Deployment Imaging Servicing and Management** (**DISM**) command-line tool, DISM PowerShell cmdlets, Windows **System Image Manager** (**SIM**), and so on. Windows SIM is a GUI-based utility used to create and modify `unattend.xml` files. The ADK is as a free download from the Microsoft download site. Windows PowerShell or DISM is required to perform offline image customization such as adding Windows features and for platform driver injection.

ADK 10 provides support for Windows 10 and Windows Server 2016 image and is available for download at `http://go.microsoft.com/fwlink/p/?LinkId=526740`.

 Previous versions of the ADK are not compatible with Nano Server.

Active Directory Domain Services (ADDS, DNS, DHCP)

This chapter assumes the reader is familiar with Active Directory, DNS and DHCP. we don't have to cover how to install AD, DHCP and DNS. For more information, consult the Active Directory Domain Services guide at `https://technet.microsoft.com/en-us/libr ary/dd448614.aspx`, the DNS at `https://technet.microsoft.com/en-us/library/cc 730921(v=ws.11).aspx` and the dynamic host configuration protocol at `https://technet.m icrosoft.com/en-us/library/dd145320(v=ws.10).aspx`.

Creating a custom Nano Server VHD(X) image

We will create a new VHD image using PowerShell; The computer name will be `NANO-HV01`, we will have the OEM drivers and custom drivers added to the image using (`-DriverPath`) parameter for physical machines deployment, we will add the compute role for Hyper-V, as well as clustering, storage feature, and enable remote management port, and finally we will add it to the domain.

You need to run this script from a computer running Windows Server 2016 or Windows 10 that is already a domain joined to the same domain, thus the computer account for Nano Server will be created in Active Directory. This process is known as offline domain join:

```
# Import NanoServerImageGenerator.psd1 PowerShell module Import-
Module"C:\NanoServer\NanoServerImageGenerator\NanoServerImageGenerator.
psd1"-Verbose# Enter Administrator Password$Password=Read-Host-
Prompt"Please specify local Administrator password"-AsSecureString#
Servicing Update Packages$ServicingPackage=@(
        "C:\NanoServer\Updates\Windows10.0-KB3199986-x64.cab"
    "C:\NanoServer\Updates\Windows10.0-KB3213986-x64.cab" ) # Create New
Nano Server ImageNew-NanoServerImage-BasePathC:\NanoServer\`
                    -TargetPathC:\NanoServer\NANO-HV01.vhd`
                        -ComputerName"NANO-HV01"`
                        -AdministratorPassword$Password`
                        -DeploymentTypeHost`
                        -EditionDatacenter`
                        -DomainNameVIRT.LAB`
```

```
                        -OEMDrivers`
                                -DriverPathC:\NanoServer\HPE-Drivers`
                                -Compute`
                                -Clustering`
                                -Storage`
                        -EnableRemoteManagementPort`
                                -ServicingPackagePath$ServicingPackage`
                                -SetupCompleteCommand('tzutil.exe /s "W.
    Europe Standard Time"')
```

If your system supports EFI, please make sure to change the image file format to VHD(X).

Look in active directory, and see the computer account for Nano Server is auto-created.

Creating a custom Nano Server WIM image

This section describes the process of customizing a Nano Server WIM image. The deployment scenarios which support the use of WIM images are:

- Deploying from a WDS server (covered in this section).
- WinPE boot environment (covered in subsequent section).

Please refer to the specific deployment section for any special configuration steps related to that particular scenario.

Before starting, please be sure to perform the steps described in the *Prerequisites* section covered earlier.

The WIM image contains two separate editions:

- Windows Server 2016 SERVERSTANDARDNANO
- Windows Server 2016 SERVERDATACENTERNANO

You have to decide which edition of Nano Server to use prior to creating a customized image. The edition is specified during image creation using the parameter, -Edition, followed by standard or datacenter:

1. Open an administrative PowerShell session on your management machine, and change the directory to the location of the Nano Server image. In our example, it is C:\NanoServer.

2. Import the `NanoServerImageGenerator.psd1` file into the PowerShell session using the following command:

```
Import-
Module"C:\NanoServer\NanoServerImageGenerator\NanoServerImageGenera
tor.psd1"-Verbose
```

3. The next step is to determine which Nano Server packages to add to the image. For a complete list of packages, please refer to the section titled *Nano Server Roles and Features* covered at the beginning of this Chapter. In this example, Nano Server will be installed on a bare-metal server targeted to run Hyper-V, we will specify a hostname of `NANO-HV01`, enable the remote management port, and enable EMS functionality. Finally, we will add the following packages and drivers to the image:
   - Compute
   - Failover clustering
   - OEM driver package
   - Hardware vendor drivers (that is HPE, Dell EMC, Cisco and so on)

4. The following is the command that will be used to create our custom WIM image:

```
# Servicing Update Packages$ServicingPackage=@(
        "C:\NanoServer\Updates\Windows10.0-KB3199986-x64.cab"
"C:\NanoServer\Updates\Windows10.0-KB3213986-x64.cab" ) # Create
New Nano Server ImageNew-NanoServerImage-BasePathC:\NanoServer\`
                -TargetPathC:\NanoServer\NANO-HV01.wim`
                        -ComputerName"NANO-HV01"`
                        -AdministratorPassword$Password`
                        -DeploymentTypeHost`
                        -EditionDatacenter`
                        -OEMDrivers`
                        -DriverPathC:\NanoServer\HPE-
Drivers`

                        -Compute`
                        -Clustering`
                        -EnableRemoteManagementPort`
                        -EnableEMS`
                        -
ServicingPackagePath$ServicingPackage`
                        -SetupCompleteCommand('tzutil.exe
/s "W. Europe Standard Time"')
```

For UEFI secure boot support add `-package Microsoft-NanoServer-SecureStartup-Package`.

5. The next step is to create an `unattend.xml` file to complete the deployment. It is recommended that you use **Windows System Image Manager (WSIM)** to customize the XML for your environment. For more information on WSIM, please refer to the Microsoft article at, `http://technet.microsoft.com/en-us/library/cc722301(v=ws.10).aspx`.

In the companion of this book, we've included unattend XML sample files for BIOS based servers as well as UEFI based servers and for Nano Server image customization. Use the appropriate version in the following step.

6. After creating or modifying the example unattend file, apply the `unattend.xml` file by editing the offline image as follows:

```
Edit-NanoServerImage-BasePathc:\NanoServer\-
TargetPathc:\NanoServer\NANO-HV01.wim-
UnattendPathC:\NanoServer\Unattend.xml
```

If the target image has been already booted, the requested changes will not be applied using the `-UnattendPath` parameter.

7. The image now is ready for deployment using WDS.

Installing and Configuring the WDS Role

The process described in this section configures the WDS environment for automated deployments using the client unattend file. The `unattend.xml` file is associated with a pre-staged device for customizing the WinPE phase of setup.

However, the previous unattend file that we add it using `Edit-NanoServerImage`, is associated with the image for automating post-WinPE stages of setup and is usually referred to as the image unattend file.

You might need to update the unattend XML files provided with this book to match your environment.

This section also describes the process for injecting out-of-the-box drivers into the `boot.wim` file used for WDS deployments:

1. Install Windows Deployment Service from Server Manager or using PowerShell:

   ```
   Install-WindowsFeature-NameWDS-IncludeAllSubFeature-
   IncludeManagementTools-verbose
   ```

2. Configure Windows Deployment Service from the Tools menu in Server Manager.
3. Right-click your WDS server in the Windows Deployment Services console and select Configure Server (see *Figure 19*):

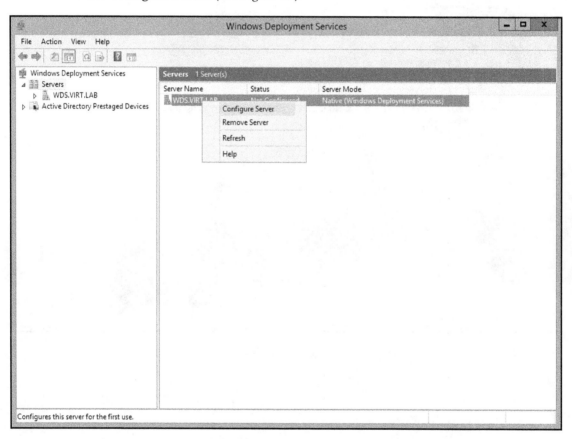

Figure 19. Configure Windows Deployment Service

4. In the **Windows Deployment Services Configuration Wizard**, click **Next**, and then select **Integrated with Active Directory** in the Install Options page (see *Figure 20*):

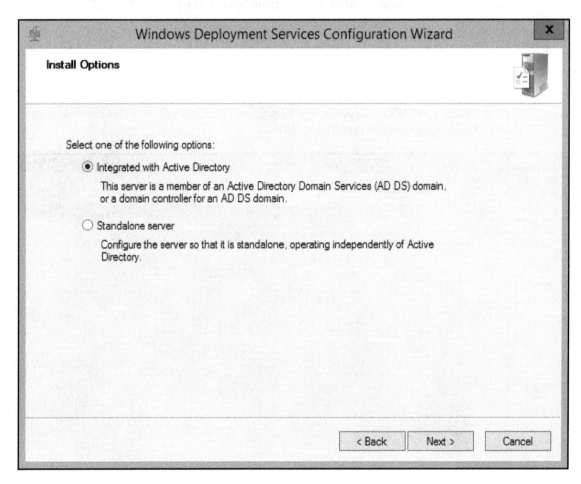

Figure 20. Configure Windows deployment Service integrated with AD

5. Select the default in the Remote Installation Folder Location and the Proxy DHCP Server pages. In the **PxE Server initial Settings**, select **Respond to all client computers (known and unknown)** (see *Figure 21*):

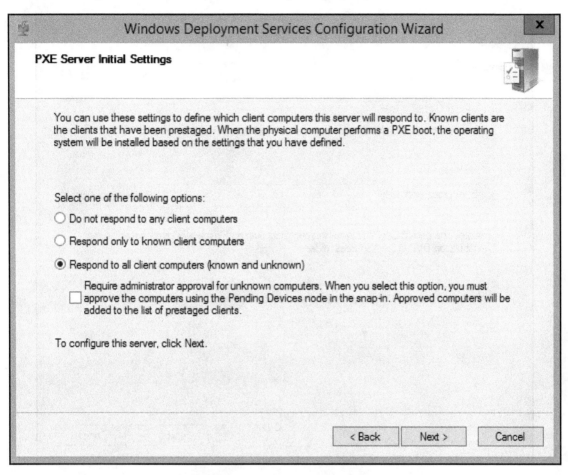

Figure 21. Configure Windows Deployment Service Respond to all clients

6. Once the server is configured, Right-click on **Boot Images** and select **Add Boot Image**. Select `boot.wim` from the "Sources" folder on your media disk or ISO file, and select the defaults for the rest of the wizard (see *Figure 22*):

Figure 22. Add boot image "boot.wim" in WDS

7. Right-click on **Install Images** and select **Add Install Image**. In the image group page, create an image group named **Nano Server Image** (see *Figure 23*):

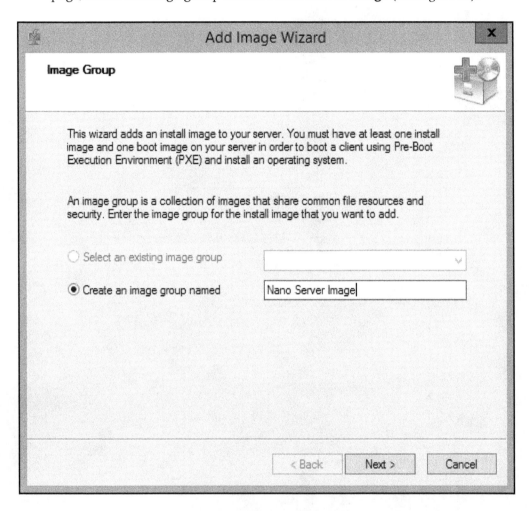

Figure 23. Add Nano Server image "boot.wim" in WDS

8. In the **Image File** page, select Nano Server VHD(X) or the Nano Server WIM file that you've prepared at the beginning of this section (see *Figure 24*):

Figure 24. Adding Nano Server WIM image in WDS

9. Click **Open** and **Next** to continue (see *Figure 25*). Select the image(s) you wish to add to the WDS server:

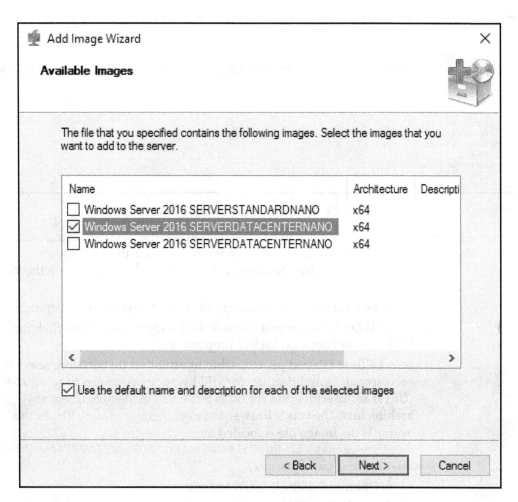

Figure 25. Adding Nano Server WIM image in WDS

10. Click **Next** to continue.
11. Click **Next** and then **Finish** to complete the operation.

12. The image should be added to the Nano Server Image folder on the WDS server (see *Figure 26*):

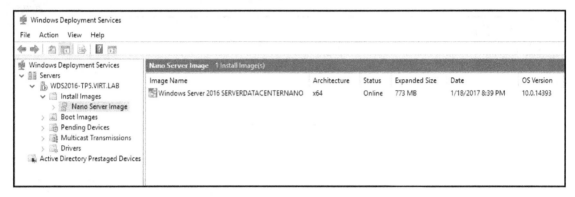

Figure 26. Nano Server successfully added to the WDS server

13. After adding Nano Server image to the WDS server, the next step is to associate the unattend.xml file to the image in order to automate the installation:

    1. First, be sure a Nano Server WIM or VHD(X) image exists on the WDS server.

    2. Next, be sure the unattend.xml file already exists on the server.

    3. In the WDS Management Console, in the right pane, right-click the WDS Server Name and select **Properties**.

    4. Select **Client** tab and select **Enable unattended installation**, select the corresponding architecture, for UEFI systems you need to select **x64 (UEFI) architecture** and for BIOS Systems you need to select **x64 architecture**, then click **Browse** to select unattend.xml file. In this example the image file is located at, d:\RemoteInstall\WdsClientUnattend\NanoBIOSClientUnatte nd-WDS.xml (see *Figure 27*).

    5. Click Open and then click **OK** to continue.

    6. Click **Apply** and **OK** to complete the operation.

    7. This completes the process for configuring a Nano Server image for automated deployments.

If a change has been made to the unattend file in the future, you need to repeat the steps above to reapply the unattend file to the install image. This is necessary because WDS imports the `unattend.xml` file into the folder structure of the associated image on the WDS server. For instance, in our example above, the `NanoServerUnattend.xml` file is copied to the following location: `D:\RemoteInstall\Images\Nano Server\NanoServerCompute\Unattend\`:

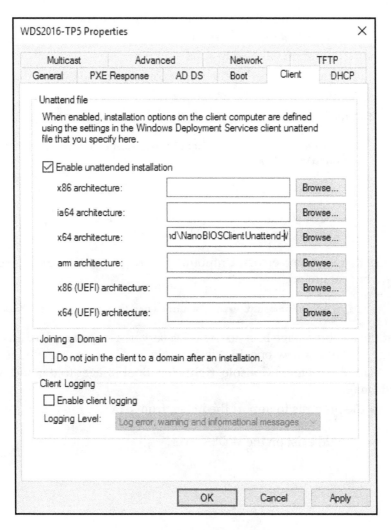

Figure 27. WDS Server Client image properties

14. In some situations, it may be necessary to add out-of-the-box drivers for boot-critical devices because they are not included as part of Windows Server 2016 media. In our example, it's HPE dynamic smart array B120i controller.
15. Logon to the WDS server and open the WDS Management Console.
16. Copy the B120i driver to a folder located on the WDS server.
17. Locate the desired `boot.wim` file from the list of boot images.
18. Right-click the image and select the **Export Image** option.
19. Export the image to a folder on the WDS server and give it a name such as `d:\images\CustomBoot.wim`.
20. Open a ADK or CMD shell to the folder containing the exported image.
21. Create a mount folder for the image, `mkdir d:\images\mount`.
22. Mount index 2 of the image by using the following command:

```
Dism.exe /mount-wim /wimfile:d:\images\CustomBoot.wim /index:2
/mountdir:d:\images\mount
```

23. Add the B120i driver to the image using the following command:

```
Dism.exe /image:d:\images\mount /add-driver
/driver:d:\Images\B120i\hpsa2.inf
```

24. Ensure there were no errors. Unmount the image and save the changes using the following command:

```
Dism.exe /unmount-wim /mountdir:d:\images\mount /commit
```

25. Add the custom image back to the WDS server. You can replace an existing image, or create a new one. In this example, we'll create a new `boot.wim` file. In the WDS Management Console, right-click Boot Images folder and select **Add Boot Image**.
26. Follow the prompts to import the image from `d:\images\CustomBoot.wim`.

A new boot image should exist on the WDS server.

You can now PXE boot your physical machine and install that customized image of Nano Server with Hyper-V and failover clustering enabled (see *Figure 28*):

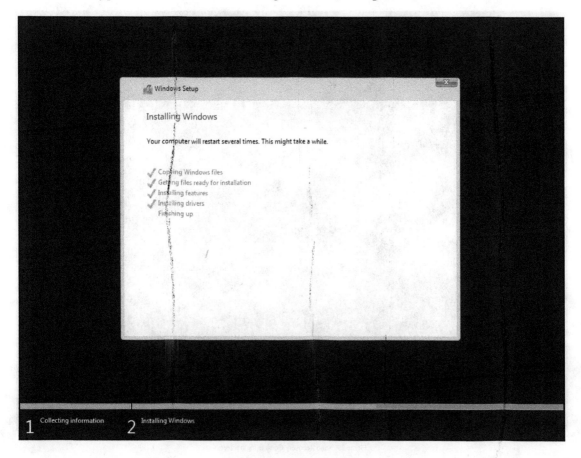

Figure 28. Installing Nano Server using WDS

The rest of the deployment should be automated. At the end of setup, the Nano Recovery Console login screen should appear, similar to *Figure 29*:

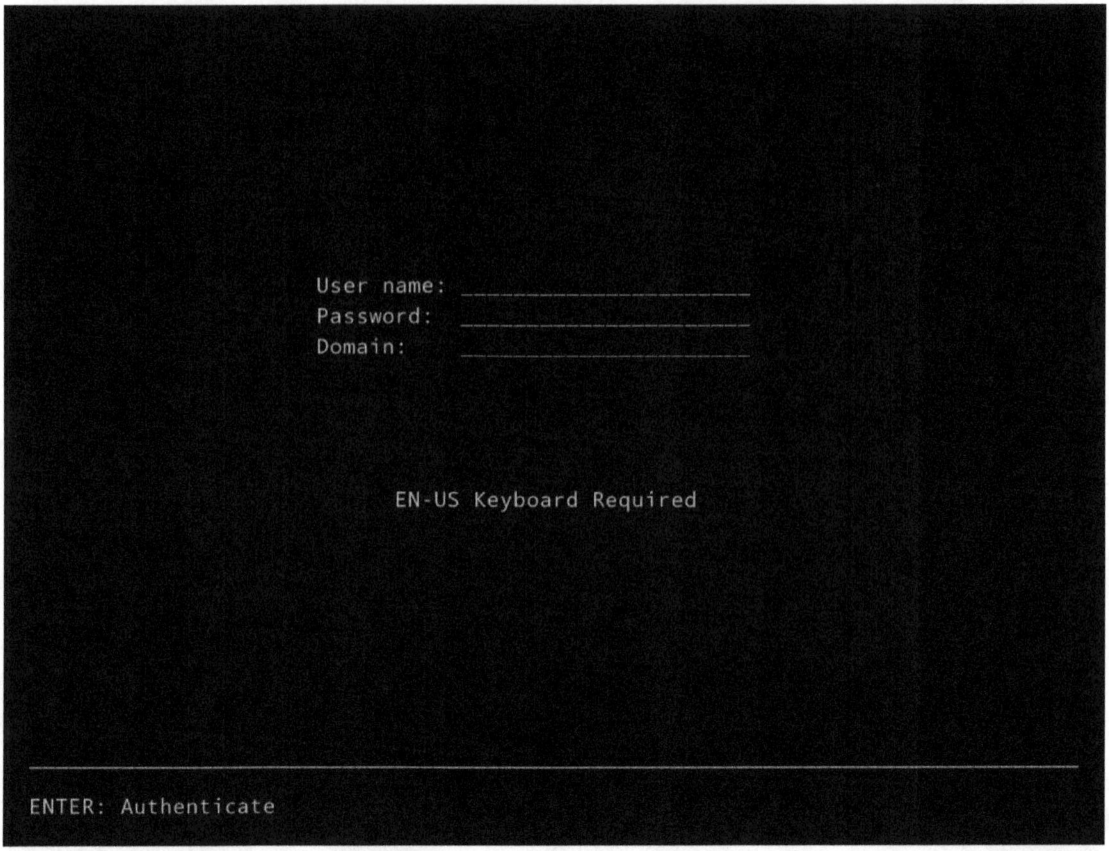

```
                        User name:    _____
                        Password:     _____
                        Domain:       _____




                              EN-US Keyboard Required








    _____

    ENTER: Authenticate
```

Figure 29. Nano Recovery Console login screen

Booting a bare-metal machine into WinPE and deploying Nano Server using a .wim file

One of the deployment methods for Nano Server is deploying a WIM image to disk from a WinPE boot environment. There are multiple options available for booting into WinPE such as:

- Deployment from WinPE ISO image using **Baseboard Management Controller (BMC)**
- Deployment from WinPE USB thumb drive

- Deployment from WinPE PXE boot
- Deployment from WinPE with network and without WDS

This chapter covers the last scenario, deployment from WinPE with network and without WDS. You can choose the method best for your environment. But before doing so, we need to create a WinPE bootable image.

The following points will be covered in this section:

- Prerequisites
- Setting up WinPE environment
- Deployment from WinPE with network and without WDS
- Creating custom WinPE boot image that has PowerShell enabled
- Creating a WinPE ISO image
- Creating a WinPE bootable USB thumb drive

Prerequisites

Before starting, be sure to perform the steps described in the previous section titled *Preparing the environment*. In addition, be sure to complete all desired customizations to Nano Server VHD(X) image as described in the section titled, *Creating a Custom Nano Server VHD(X) Image*.

Setting up the WinPE environment

The Windows Assessment and Deployment Kit (Windows ADK) includes a batch file that creates an environment for working with WinPE images. This batch file requires two arguments. The first one is the architecture type of the target image, and since Nano Server is 64-bit, we will use amd64. The second argument is, the working folder. In our example, the location for the WinPE folder is d:\TempPE\.

1. In the Deployment and Tools CMD session, change directories to C:\Program Files (x86)\Windows Kits\10\Assessment and Deployment Kit\Windows Preinstallation Environment\.
2. Run the copype.cmd file with the appropriate arguments as the following:

```
copype.cmd amd64 d:\TempPE\
```

3. This command creates the specified directory for you. Ensure there were no errors during this operation.

4. Included in the files copied is a `boot.wim` file that we will be modifying. The `boot.wim` image is located at `D:\TempPE\media\sources\boot.wim`.

5. The `boot.wim` file will be used in the subsequent section *Deployment from WinPE with network and without WDS*.

If it is necessary to inject specific boot-critical drivers in your custom WinPE `boot.wim` image, please check with your preferred hardware vendor to get those drivers before you continue with the remaining steps.

Please refer to the previous section where we showed you how to inject HPE dynamic smart array B120i controller to Windows `boot.wim` image.

At this time, you could create a bootable copy of WinPE that would be able to boot the physical hardware and present you with access to both the network and storage devices. But the goal here is to automate the deployment of Nano Server without WDS, so we will perform a few more steps.

Deployment from WinPE with network and without WDS

The process of installing Nano Server using WinPE can be automated through scripting instead of manual installation.

In this example, we will show you how to deploy Nano Server from WinPE which involves PXE booting and automating Nano Server deployment.

This example is fully automated through PowerShell, so you can PXE boot your servers without WDS and have WinPE complete the installation with no human interaction. This process requires to have a DHCP server deployed in your environment to PXE boot.

Creating a custom WinPE boot image that has PowerShell enabled

The Windows Assessment and Deployment Kit (Windows ADK) includes a `winpe.wim` image that creates an environment for working with WinPE images. The WIM file is really a specialized archive that holds all of the files for the Windows operating system. The first is the architecture type of the target image. Thus, we will use `amd64` for Nano Server:

1. First we'll store the location of the PowerShell packages to be installed and the location for the temporary Windows PE media in two PowerShell variables named `$WinADK` and `$WinPETemp`. Open Windows PowerShell and run the following:

```
$WinADK="C:\Program Files (x86)\Windows Kits\10\Assessment and
Deployment Kit\Windows Preinstallation
Environment\amd64\WinPE_OCs"
$WinPETemp="D:\TempPE"
```

2. In order to modify `boot.wim` image, we need to mount it to make it available to the system. The following DISM command mounts the file. This will open the WIM file for editing. It will extract the structure to a target folder where we can add files and content:

```
Mount-WindowsImage -ImagePath
"$WinPETemp\Media\Sources\boot.wim" -Index 1 -Path
"$WinPETemp\Mount"
```

3. At this point, we need to add a PowerShell package to the WIM file to enhance its capabilities, because it is so much easier to script in PowerShell. The list of all packages (OCS files) can be found in the `WinPE_OCS` folder.

    To do this, we use the `Add-WindowsPackage` cmdlet. The following commands demonstrate how to install the six optional PowerShell components to extend WMI capability in a Windows PE environment that are required for this example. You will notice that there are two CAB files per component--the component and its associated language pack. Both are required to be installed. Additionally, the added components often need to be added in a specific sequence. The following list follows the prescribed sequence:

```
$CABfiles=@("$WinADK\WinPE-WMI.cab","$WinADK\en-us\WinPE-
WMI_en-us.cab","$WinADK\WinPE-NetFX.cab","$WinADK\en-us\WinPE-
NetFX_en-us.cab","$WinADK\WinPE-Scripting.cab","$WinADK\en-
us\WinPE-Scripting_en-us.cab","$WinADK\WinPE-
PowerShell.cab","$WinADK\en-us\WinPE-PowerShell_en-
us.cab","$WinADK\WinPE-StorageWMI.cab","$WinADK\en-us\WinPE-
StorageWMI_en-us.cab","$WinADK\WinPE-
DismCmdlets.cab","$WinADK\en-us\WinPE-DismCmdlets_en-
us.cab")Foreach($CABfilein$CABfiles) {Add-WindowsPackage-
PackagePath"$CABFile"-Path"$WinPeTemp\Mount"-IgnoreCheck}
```

4. Next, we need to modify `Startnet.cmd` in WinPE to connect to a network share that contains the fully automated scripts including the VHD(X) created in the section titled, *Creating a Custom Nano Server VHD(X) Image.*

5. Open `Startnet.cmd` with your favorite editor (`Notepad` in this example):

```
Notepad "$WinPETemp\Mount\Windows\System32\Startnet.cmd"
```

6. And then add the following commands (see *Figure 30*):

```
Net use S: \\<IP>\TempPE /User:<username><pwd>
PowerShell "Set-ExecutionPolicy Bypass -Force"
PowerShell ".S:\NanoServerBIOSDeployment-WithoutWDS.ps1"
exit
```

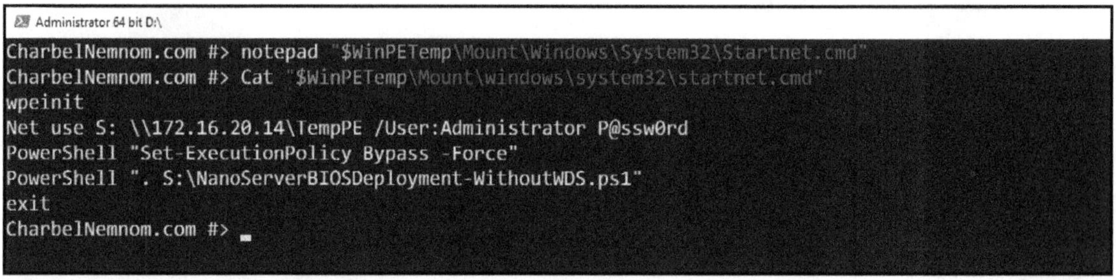

Figure 30. Startnet.cmd customized

During your initial testing and debugging of your scripts, you may want to remove the exit command at the end of `Startnet.cmd`. This allows you to manipulate your scripts within WinPE. Please note that the exit command will cause WinPE to automatically reboot the system when it's completed.

7. Exit notepad and save `Startnet.cmd`.

8. Dismount the Windows image by running the following command:

```
Dismount-WindowsImage -path "$WinPETemp\Mount" -save
```

9. Copy `NanoServerBIOSDeployment-WithoutWDS.ps1` and Nano Server VHD(X) image to the `TempPE` shared folder on your network.

> We provided the scripts for both BIOS and UEFI mode deployment accompanied with this chapter.

10. The **TempPE** shared folder will look similar to *Figure 31*:

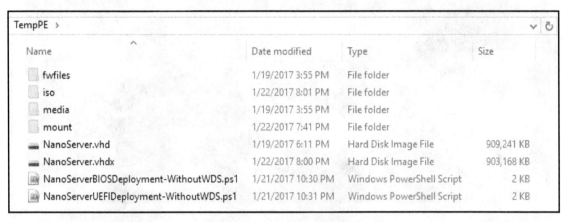

Figure 31. TempPE Shared Folder content

11. The final step is to decide which WinPE boot method to use. You can boot from WinPE ISO image or WinPE USB thumb drive, please refer to the section titled *Creating WinPE ISO image* or *Creating WinPE bootable USB thumb drive*. You need to use the customized WinPE boot image which we edited in this section. In our example, it's located at `D:\TempPE\Media\boot.wim`.

12. PXE boot your physical machine and observe hands-off Nano Server deployment (see *Figure 32*):

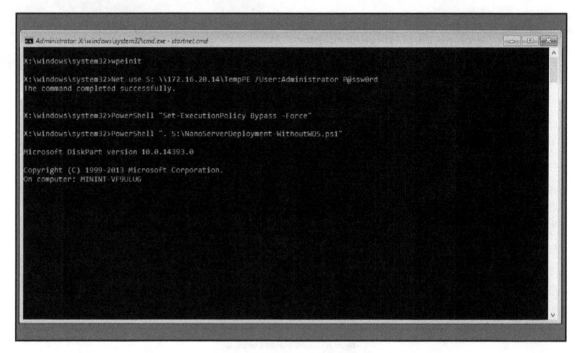

Figure 32. PXE Boot Physical Machine

13. The rest of the deployment is automated. At the end of setup, the system will reboot and Nano recovery console login screen should appear similar to *Figure 33*:

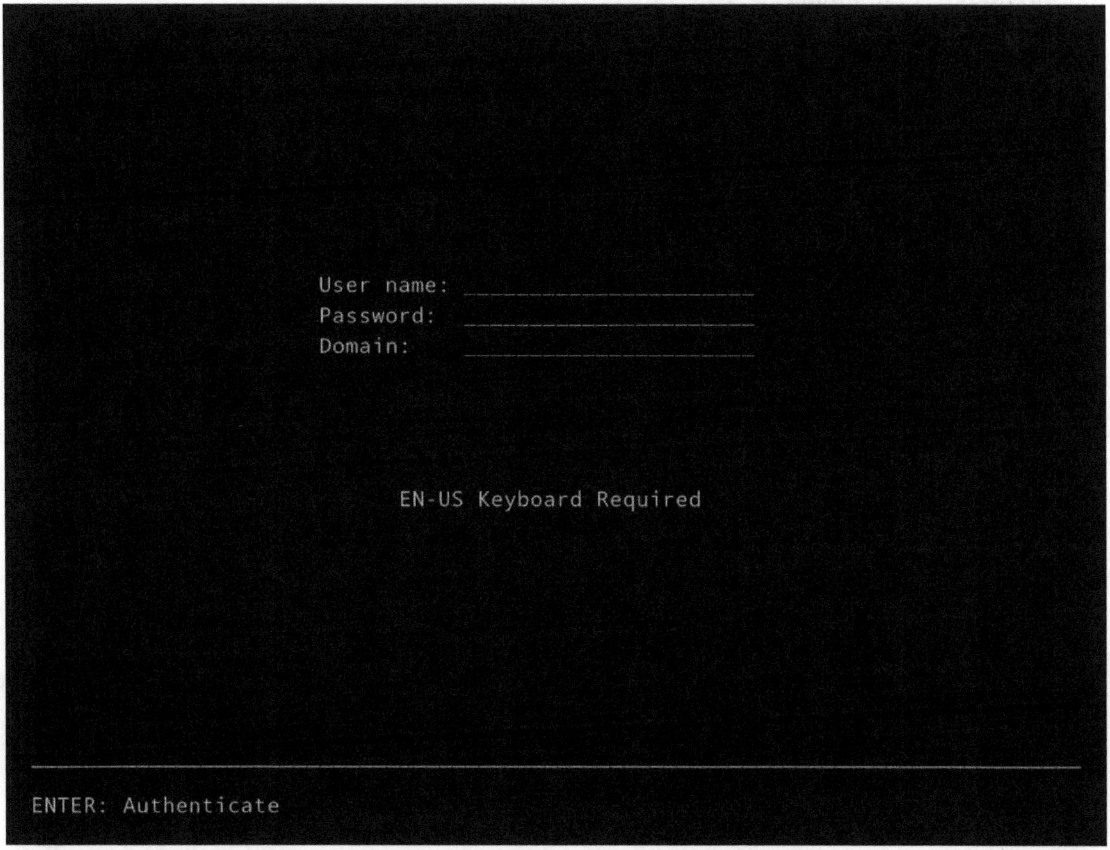

```
                              User name: _____
                              Password:  _____
                              Domain:    _____



                          EN-US Keyboard Required




ENTER: Authenticate
```

Figure 33. WinPE completed - Nano Server recovery console

Creating a WinPE ISO image

This step is only required if you will be booting WinPE from an ISO image, such as booting from the BMC port such as HPE iLO IRC or **integrated Dell Remote Access Controller (iDRAC)**. Otherwise, skip to *Creating WinPE bootable USB thumb drive* section.

The ADK ships with a batch file that creates an ISO image from the contents of the `d:\winpe_amd64\media` folder. The script name is `MakeWinPEMedia.cmd` and is located at, `C:\Program Files (x86)\Windows Kits\10\Assessment and Deployment Kit\Windows Preinstallation Environment`.

1. First, make sure your running a ADK CMD session with elevated privileges.
2. Change directories to the folder containing `MakeWinPEMedia.cmd` `"C:\Program Files (x86)\Windows Kits\10\Assessment and Deployment Kit\Windows Preinstallation Environment\"`.
3. Make sure the destination folder exists before running the script. For example, `mkdir d:\TempPE\iso`.
4. Run the command, `MakeWinPEMedia.cmd /iso d:\TempPE d:\TempPE\iso\nanoserver_winpe.iso`.
5. If the operation was successful, you can go back to the previous section titled, *Deployment from the network using WinPE without WDS*, and PXE boot your physical machine from that ISO file.

Creating a WinPE bootable USB thumb drive

This step is only required if you will be deploying Nano Server from a USB thumb drive. The process for creating a USB bootable WinPE image is nearly identical to creating a bootable ISO image described in the previous section.

The ADK ships with a batch file that creates a bootable USB WinPE environment using the contents of the `d:\TempPE\media` folder which the case in our example.

The script name is `MakeWinPEMedia.cmd` and is located at, `C:\ProgramFiles (x86)\Windows Kits\10\Assessment and Deployment Kit\Windows Preinstallation Environment`:

1. First, make sure your deployment and imaging tool shell is running with elevated privileges.
2. Change folders to the folder containing `MakeWinPEMedia.cmd`.
3. Insert the USB thumb drive in your computer and be sure Windows assigns it a drive letter and the drive partition style is MBR. If there is no drive letter assigned, format the USB drive as FAT32 and assign it one. Make a note of the drive letter. For this example, we will assume the USB drive letter is F.

4. Run the command, `MakeWinPEMedia.cmd /ufd d:\TempPE F:`
5. If the operation was successful, the USB drive is ready.
6. Safely eject the USB drive from your computer and boot your physical machine.

Deploying Nano Server in Microsoft Azure

The last deployment option for Nano Server is Microsoft Azure. As of today, there are two methods to do so, you can create Nano Server VM using the Nano Server image from the Azure gallery, or bring your own Nano Server to Azure.

When bringing your Nano Server VHD image to Azure simply use the parameters `-DeploymentType Guest` and `-EnableRemoteManagement` when building the image on-premises before you send the VHD to Microsoft Azure.

For more information on how to upload your own VHD, please check here: `https://azure.microsoft.com/en-us/documentation/articles/virtual-machines-create-upload-vhd-windows-server/`.

In this example, we will show you how to deploy Nano Server using Azure helper PowerShell module which is developed by the Nano Server team, however, you can deploy the same through Azure marketplace at `https://portal.azure.com` as shown in *Figure 34*:

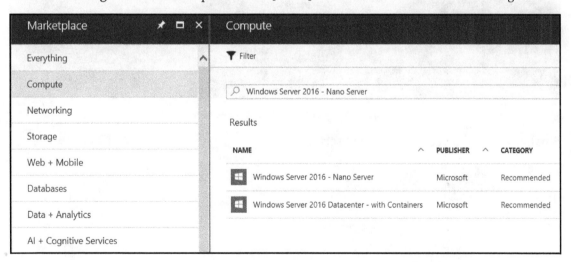

Figure 34. Azure Marketplace: Windows Server 2016 Nano Server

Requirements

We have three requirements to deploy Nano Server in Azure:

Download and extract the zip file for Nano Server Azure Helper PowerShell module at

```
https://msdnshared.blob.core.windows.net/media/2016/10/NanoServerAzureHelper_
20160927.zip.
```

The Azure Helper module requires **Azure Resource Manager** (**AzureRM**) cmdlets to be installed on your management computer.

In order to do so, please open an elevated Windows PowerShell or Windows PowerShell ISE, and run the following command to install Azure resource manager PowerShell module (see *Figure 35*):

```
Install-Module AzureRM -Verbose
```

```
CharbelNemnom.com #> Install-Module AzureRM -Verbose
VERBOSE: Using the provider 'PowerShellGet' for searching packages.
VERBOSE: The -Repository parameter was not specified.  PowerShellGet will use all of the registered repositories.
VERBOSE: Getting the provider object for the PackageManagement Provider 'NuGet'.
VERBOSE: The specified Location is 'https://www.powershellgallery.com/api/v2/' and PackageManagementProvider is 'NuGet'.
VERBOSE: Searching repository 'https://www.powershellgallery.com/api/v2/FindPackagesById()?id='AzureRM'' for ''.
VERBOSE: Total package yield:'1' for the specified package 'AzureRM'.
VERBOSE: Performing the operation "Install-Module" on target "Version '3.3.0' of module 'AzureRM'".

Untrusted repository
You are installing the modules from an untrusted repository. If you trust this repository, change its InstallationPolicy
cmdlet. Are you sure you want to install the modules from 'PSGallery'?
[Y] Yes  [A] Yes to All  [N] No  [L] No to All  [S] Suspend  [?] Help (default is "N"): Y
VERBOSE: The installation scope is specified to be 'AllUsers'.
VERBOSE: The specified module will be installed in 'C:\Program Files\WindowsPowerShell\Modules'.
VERBOSE: The specified Location is 'NuGet' and PackageManagementProvider is 'NuGet'.
VERBOSE: Downloading module 'AzureRM' with version '3.3.0' from the repository 'https://www.powershellgallery.com/api/v2
VERBOSE: Searching repository 'https://www.powershellgallery.com/api/v2/FindPackagesById()?id='AzureRM' for ''.
VERBOSE: Searching repository 'https://www.powershellgallery.com/api/v2/FindPackagesById()?id='AzureRM.Profile'' for ''.
VERBOSE: Searching repository 'https://www.powershellgallery.com/api/v2/FindPackagesById()?id='Azure.Storage'' for ''.
VERBOSE: Searching repository 'https://www.powershellgallery.com/api/v2/FindPackagesById()?id='AzureRM.Profile'' for ''.
VERBOSE: Searching repository 'https://www.powershellgallery.com/api/v2/FindPackagesById()?id='AzureRM.AnalysisServices'
```

Figure 35.Install Azure Resource Manager PowerShell Module

Finally, we need an active Azure subscription.

Creating Nano Server in Azure

1. Browse to the local folder where you extracted the Azure Helper module and import it (see *Figure 36*):

```
CharbelNemnom.com #> cd .\NanoServerAzureHelper_20160927\
CharbelNemnom.com #> Import-Module .\NanoServerAzureHelper.psm1 -Verbose
VERBOSE: Loading module from path 'C:\NanoServer\NanoServerAzureHelper_20160927\NanoServerAzureHelper.psm1'.
VERBOSE: Exporting function 'Copy-Cert'.
VERBOSE: Exporting function 'New-AzureVMCert'.
VERBOSE: Exporting function 'Protect-CustomString'.
VERBOSE: Exporting function 'Unprotect-CustomString'.
VERBOSE: Exporting function 'Protect-CustomFiles'.
VERBOSE: Exporting function 'Unprotect-CustomFiles'.
VERBOSE: Exporting function 'Unprotect-DockerCerts'.
VERBOSE: Exporting function 'Initialize-DockerCerts'.
VERBOSE: Exporting function 'New-NanoServerAzureVM'.
VERBOSE: Exporting function 'Set-HelperAzureRmCustomScript'.
VERBOSE: Importing function 'Copy-Cert'.
VERBOSE: Importing function 'Initialize-DockerCerts'.
VERBOSE: Importing function 'New-AzureVMCert'.
VERBOSE: Importing function 'New-NanoServerAzureVM'.
VERBOSE: Importing function 'Protect-CustomFiles'.
VERBOSE: Importing function 'Protect-CustomString'.
VERBOSE: Importing function 'Set-HelperAzureRmCustomScript'.
VERBOSE: Importing function 'Unprotect-CustomFiles'.
VERBOSE: Importing function 'Unprotect-CustomString'.
VERBOSE: Importing function 'Unprotect-DockerCerts'.
CharbelNemnom.com #>
```

Figure 36.Import Nano Server Azure helper

2. Make sure `AzureRM` module is imported and then log in to your Azure account by running the following command (see *Figure 37*):

```
CharbelNemnom.com #> Login-AzureRmAccount

Environment          : AzureCloud
Account              :
TenantId             :
SubscriptionId       :
SubscriptionName     : Visual Studio Premium with MSDN
CurrentStorageAccount :
```

Figure 37. Login to AzureRM

3. Run the following commands to create a resource group and a key vault, if you haven't already (see *Figure 38*). In our example, we chose `West Europe` because this is the closest Azure datacenter to us:

```
New-AzureRmResourceGroup-Name"NanoResourceGroup"-Location'West
Europe'
```

```
New-AzureRmKeyVault-VaultName"NanoServerVault"-
ResourceGroupName"NanoResourceGroup"-Location'West Europe'-
EnabledForDeployment
```

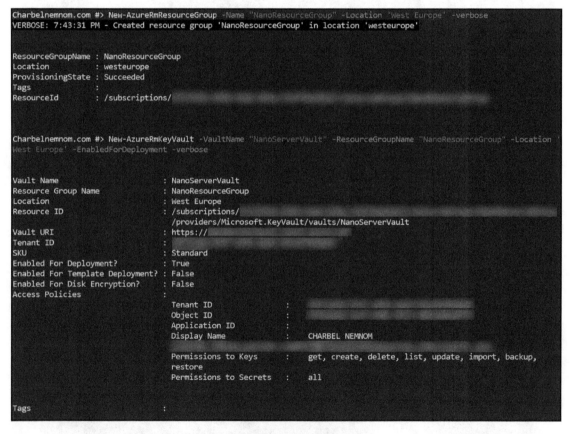

Figure 38.New Azure Resource Manager Group

4. We are ready now to create a Nano Server VM. In the same PowerShell window run the following commands, you will be prompted for an administrator password:

```
# Set Azure location$location='WestEurope'# Get Nano image SKU
for an offer$NanoImageSku=Get-AzureRmVMImageSku-
Location$location-PublisherName"MicrosoftWindowsServer"-
Offer"WindowsServer"|Where-Object{$_.Skus -like"*Nano*"} #
Create New Nano Azure VMNew-NanoServerAzureVM-Location'West
Europe'-VMName"NanoAzureVM"-AdminUsername"NanoAdmin"-
VaultName"NanoServerVault"-
ResourceGroupName"NanoResourceGroup"-
StorageAccountName"nanoazurestorageacc"-
ImageSku$NanoImageSku.Skus -Verbose
```

5. If you switch to Azure portal at `https://portal.azure.com`, you can see the VM Status is **Creating** (see *Figure 39*):

Figure 39.New Azure Nano VM - Azure Portal

6. Wait until the VM is completely provisioned.

7. To establish a secure PowerShell remote session to Nano Server VM in Azure, you need to note the FQDN string from DNS settings by running the following command:

```
Get-AzureRmPublicIpAddress -ResourceGroupName
"NanoResourceGroup"
```

8. Observe the output of this cmdlet and copy the FQDN string, under DNS settings. It will look something like: `nanoazurevm.westeurope.cloudapp.azure.com`, it might be different in your environment.

9. Use the FQDN noted in the previous step and establish a secure session connection by running the following command (see *Figure 40*):

10. You will be prompted for the administrator password.

```
Enter-PSSession -ConnectionUri
"https://nanoazurevm.westeurope.cloudapp.azure.com:5986" -
Credential NanoAdmin
```

```
Administrator 64 bit C:\NanoServer\NanoServerAzureHelper                                          —  □  ×
CharbelNemnom.com #> Enter-PSSession -ConnectionUri "https://nanoazurevm.westeurope.cloudapp.azure.com:5986/WSMAN" -Cred
ential NanoAdmin
[nanoazurevm.westeurope.cloudapp.azure.com]: PS C:\Users\NanoAdmin\Documents> cd /
[nanoazurevm.westeurope.cloudapp.azure.com]: PS C:\> Get-ComputerInfo oss*1

OsServerLevel
-------------
   NanoServer  ◄──────

[nanoazurevm.westeurope.cloudapp.azure.com]: PS C:\> _
```

Figure 40. Connect to Nano Server VM in Azure

As you can see, we were able to deploy and access a Nano Server VM in Microsoft Azure from a local machine.

If you want to access the same Nano VM in Azure from another management machine, you need to export the certificate from the original machine and import it to another one, the steps are documented at the following link: `http://blogs.technet.com/b/nanoserver/archive /2015/11/19/nano-server-iaas-image-in-the-azure-gallery.aspx`.

Summary

In this chapter, we discussed the current roles and features which are available for Nano Server in Windows Server 2016, we covered how to create a Nano Server VHD(X) image, then we showed you how to deploy that image in a virtual machine using Hyper-V Manager and Windows PowerShell, and lastly, we discussed the four deployment options for Nano Server on a physical machine using WinPE and WDS.

Nano Server can also be deployed in Microsoft Azure. You can use the Azure helper PowerShell module to automate the deployment, or you can deploy the same through Azure marketplace.

Continue now to `Chapter 4`, *Deploying Hyper-V Cluster on Nano Server*, to learn more about how to deploy Nano Server with compute and storage roles for a clustered environment.

4
Deploying Hyper-V Cluster on Nano Server

In Chapter 3, *Deploying Nano Server in a Virtual Machine and on Physical Hardware*, we covered how to create Nano Server images, then we showed you how to deploy the image in a virtual machine using Hyper-V Manager and in Windows PowerShell. We also discussed the deployment options for Nano Server on a bare-metal machine using WinPE and WDS, and lastly we covered how to deploy Nano Server in Microsoft Azure.

As discussed earlier in this book, Nano Server was created to serve as cloud fabric and infrastructure for Hyper-V storage, clustering and networking, which is our focus in this chapter, and it was also designed to be a deployment option for cloud application (platform-as-a-service v2 and ASPT.NET v5 applications).

This chapter will give you both a specific standalone example of how to deploy Nano Server as a compute cluster and storage using a hyperconverged solution with **Storage Spaces Direct** (**S2D**), and an introductory overview of the following topics:

- Nano Server as a compute cluster
- Nano Server as a storage cluster

In this chapter, we will also be focusing heavily on Windows PowerShell to build and deploy Nano Server as a compute and storage cluster.

Nano Server as a compute cluster

Hyper-V roles are one of the common workloads we expect most people will run on Nano Server. The compute role is the Hyper-V role which is applicable primarily for physical machines however, starting with Windows Server 2016, Microsoft introduced nested virtualization where we can leverage this feature and host Nano Server with compute role in a virtual machine. Nested virtualization was primarily enabled for Hyper-V containers. For more information about Windows containers and Hyper-V containers, please refer to `Chapter 8`, *Running Windows Server Containers and Hyper-V Containers on Nano Server*.

The storage and the cluster role work both whether Nano Server is hosted in a VM or on a physical machine.

As discussed in `Chapter 6`, *Managing Nano Server with Windows PowerShell and Windows PowerShell DSC*, Nano Server management must be done remotely; in other words, you should be using management tools such as **System Center Virtual Machine Manager** (**SCVMM**), Windows PowerShell, and **Remote Server Administration Toolkit** (**RSAT**) from your management PC, because you cannot log in into Nano Server directly and do the configuration locally. Moreover, the management PC must run the same build as Nano Server; you cannot manage Nano Server with an older version of Hyper-V Manager or FCM, or an older version of PowerShell.

Deploying a Nano Server as a Hyper-V cluster

As we expect Hyper-V to become an important role for Nano Server, it's very important to deploy Hyper-V as a highly available role. The good news is that failover clustering works the same as on any Windows Server (Server with Desktop Experience, Server Core, and free Hyper-V Server).

Concisely, failover cluster is a group of independent servers that work together to increase the availability, and scalability of clustered roles (formerly called clustered applications such as virtual machines, SQL databases, and services). You need to make sure you have redundant hardware deployed everywhere to avoid a single point of failure, including storage, network adapters, switches, servers, and applications.

The clustered servers (called nodes) are connected by physical (Ethernet) cables and by software. Shared storage must be accessible by all nodes at the same time. If one or more of the cluster nodes fail, other nodes begin to provide the service (a process known as failover), as shown in *Figure 1*:

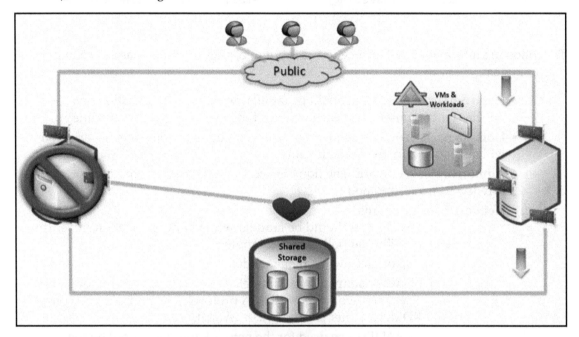

Figure 1. Failover clustering: Failover process

In addition, the clustered roles are proactively monitored to verify that they are working properly (a process known as heartbeat). If they are not working, they are restarted or moved to another node. Failover clusters also offer **Cluster Shared Volume (CSV)** functionality that gives a consistent, distributed namespace that clustered roles such as applications, SQL databases, and virtual machines can use to access shared storage from all nodes. When an unplanned failover happens, the users experience a minimum disruption in service; however, with certain applications, such as virtual machines, if we have planned maintenance, we can move those VMs between hosts with no downtime (a process called live migration).

Failover clusters can be managed by using the FCM console and the failover clustering PowerShell cmdlets. You can also use the tools in file and storage services to manage file shares on file server clusters.

For more information about what's new in failover clustering in Windows Server 2016, please check the following article:

```
https://technet.microsoft.com/en-us/windows-server-docs/comput
e/failover-clustering/whats-new-failover-clustering-windows-se
rver.
```

The following information will be needed as input to configure and manage the Nano cluster system:

- **Nano Server names**: You should be familiar with your organization's naming policies for computers, and each will need to have a unique server name
- **Domain name**: You will be joining Nano computers to your domain, and you will need to specify the domain name
- **Administrator password**: The domain account must have Administrator privileges on all Nano nodes
- **Network configurations**:
    - DHCP: You should be familiar with your organization's IP address distribution policies for computers.
    - Top of rack switch make/model.
    - Network adapter make/model. Are you using RDMA adapters? There are two types of RDMA protocols; note which type your RDMA adapter is (RoCEv2 or iWarp).
    - VLAN ID to be used for the network interfaces used by the Management OS including live migration, backup, cluster, and storage networks.

This section includes instructions to install and configure the components of a Hyper-V cluster using Windows Server 2016 and Nano Server.

The act of deploying a Hyper-V cluster system can be divided into three high-level phases:

- Deploying a Nano Server as compute host
- Configuring the network
- Creating and configuring a Hyper-V cluster

Deploying a Nano Server as compute host

Nano Server as a compute is used to host virtual machines on top of Hyper-V, either in clusters or not.

This process includes the following tasks:

1. Acquiring the ISO image of Windows Server 2016 Datacenter edition.
2. Creating the new Nano Server images.
3. Copying the new Nano Server images to the host machines.
4. Rebooting into the new Nano Server image.
5. Connecting and managing Nano Servers from the management machine.

Acquiring the ISO image of Windows Server 2016 Datacenter edition

You can download a copy of the Windows Server 2016 Datacenter ISO from TechNet evaluation center (`https://www.microsoft.com/en-us/evalcenter/evaluate-windows-server-2016`) for your image creation and note the path.

Creating the new Nano Server images

This section describes how to create the Nano Server VHD(X) file to be used on physical machines using the pre-installed device drivers. We need to create a VHD(X) that includes the OEM drivers, and failover clustering features including SCVMM packages, and enables remote management and emergency management services. If you have drivers that are recommended by your hardware vendor, it is simplest to inject the network drivers into the image; you can do this by using the `-DriversPath` parameter and adding the drivers to the image. If your deployment is using an RDMA adapter and datacenter bridging, then make sure to include `Microsoft-NanoServer-DCB-Package` in the PowerShell command string below, so the DCB package is included in the example.

If you are going to manage the servers with System Center and you add `Microsoft-NanoServer-SCVMM-Compute-Package`, then do not use the `-Compute` option for the Hyper-V role, because this server will be managed by VMM and already has the compute option.

 It's very important also to add the SCVMM packages in the right order or the deployment will fail.

The following steps will illustrate this process:

1. On the management machine, mount the Windows Server 2016 `.ISO`. To mount the ISO, in **File Explorer**, select and right click on **ISO**, then choose **Mount**. Once the mounted drive is opened, navigate to the `\NanoServer\NanoServerImageGenerator` directory and copy the contents to a `local` directory to your desired working folder on your management machine where you want to create and store your new Nano Server images. The drive mounted in this example is `E:\`.

2. Start an elevated Windows PowerShell console, then change the directory to the folder in which you've copied the contents in *step 1* and then import the Nano Server PowerShell module by using the following command:

```
Import-Module NanoServerImageGenerator.psd1 -Verbose
```

You will see the following screen (see *Figure 2*):

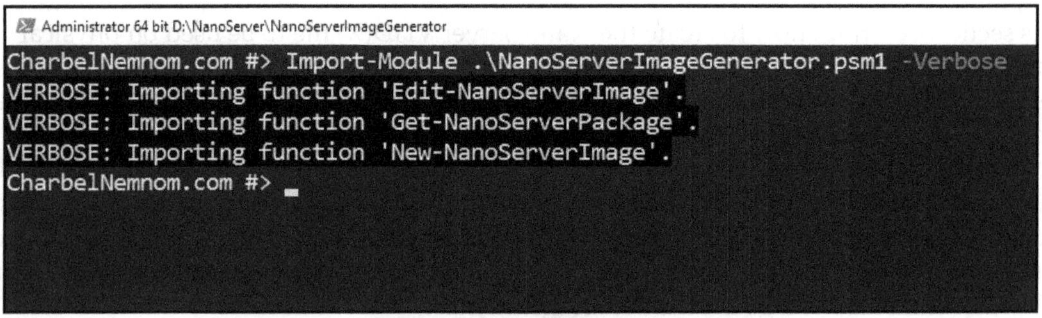

Figure 2. Importing Nano PowerShell module

3. Copy the network drivers that are recommended by your favorite hardware vendor to a directory and note the path. The example in the next step will use the following:

```
D:\NanoServer\HP-Nano
```

4. In this step, you will create a unique image for each Nano host machine. We need four images, one for each physical host for the Hyper-V cluster setup, so we will create a VHDX for a physical machine that includes the SCVMM and DCB packages by running the following script on the management machine which is a member of the same domain where Nano Server will be deployed. The script will prompt you for an administrator password for the new VHDX.

Type carefully and note your password for later use. You will use this password later to log in to the Nano Server Recovery Console.

It is strongly recommended to download and install the latest updates. Windows updates can be added to the Nano Server image in pre-deployment fashion or post-deployment. See `Chapter 10`, *Running Other Workloads on Nano Server*, for more information.

In the following example, we downloaded Windows updates manually from the Microsoft update catalog and added them to the image:

```
# Windows Server 2016 ISO Image
Media$ServerISO="C:\NanoServer\WindowsServer2016.ISO"# Mount the ISO
ImageMount-DiskImage$ServerISO# Get the Drive Letter of the disk ISO
image$DVDDriveLetter=(Get-DiskImage$ServerISO|Get-Volume).DriveLetter#
Import NanoServerImageGenerator.psd1 PowerShell moduleImport-
Module"C:\NanoServer\NanoServerImageGenerator\NanoServerImageGenerator.psd1
"-Verbose# Enter Administrator Password$Password=Read-Host-Prompt"Please
specify local Administrator password"-AsSecureString# Domain
Name$myDomainFQDN="VIRT.LAB"# Servicing Update Packages$ServicingPackage=@(
                "C:\NanoServer\Updates\Servicing Stack
Update\Windows10.0-KB4013418-x64.msu" "C:\NanoServer\Updates\Cumulative
Update\Windows10.0-KB4023680-x64.msu" )# Nano Packages$NanoPackage=@(
            "Microsoft-NanoServer-DCB-Package" "Microsoft-NanoServer-
SCVMM-Package" "Microsoft-NanoServer-SCVMM-Compute-Package" )1..4|ForEach-
Object{New-NanoServerImage -MediaPath"$($DVDDriveLetter):\"`
                -BasePathC:\NanoServer\`
                -TargetPathC:\NanoServer\NANOSRV-HV0$_.vhdx`
                        -MaxSize20GB`
                        -DeploymentTypeHost`
                        -EditionDatacenter`
                        -ComputerNameNANOSRV-HV0$_`
                        -AdministratorPassword$Password`
                        -DomainName$myDomainFQDN`
                        -ReuseDomainNode`
                        -Clustering`
                        -Package$NanoPackage`
                        -DriversPathD:\NanoServer\HP-Nano`
```

```
                                        -OEMDrivers`
                                        -EnableRemoteManagementPort`
                                        -EnableEMS`
                                        -ServicingPackagePath$ServicingPackage`
                                        -SetupCompleteCommand('tzutil.exe /s "W.
    Europe Standard Time"')
    }# Dismount Windows Server 2016 ISO ImageDismount-DiskImage$ServerISO
```

Once you've completed this task, you should have four VHDXes, as shown in *Figure 3*, for each of the four Hyper-V cluster systems that you are provisioning. If the server uses BIOS to boot instead of UEFI, then you need to change the previous script from `NANOSRV-HV0$_.VHDX` to `NANOSRV-HV0$_.VHD`:

Name	Date modified	Type
NANOSRV-HV01.vhdx	6/8/2017 6:38 PM	Hard Disk Image File
NANOSRV-HV02.vhdx	6/8/2017 6:58 PM	Hard Disk Image File
NANOSRV-HV03.vhdx	6/8/2017 7:17 PM	Hard Disk Image File
NANOSRV-HV04.vhdx	6/8/2017 7:37 PM	Hard Disk Image File

Figure 3. Nano Server Hyper-V images

Copying the new Nano Server images to the host machines

Copy the VHDX files that you created earlier to each respective host machine and configure each machine to boot from the new VHDX by performing the following steps.

The tasks described in this example assume that the servers will be used for Hyper-V cluster, the nodes are booted into an existing Windows Server operating system, and they are accessible to the network. We are using dual-boot from VHDX:

1. Log in as administrator on the Host machines that will be part of the Hyper-V cluster system.
2. Mount the VHDX. If you are using Windows Explorer, the mount is carried out by right-clicking on the VHDX file and **mount**. In this example, it is mounted under `E:\`

3. Open Windows PowerShell as administrator and change the prompt to the `Windows` directory of the mounted VHDX. In this example, the command would be as follows:

```
cd e:\Windows
```

4. Enable booting to the VHDX by running the following command:

```
Bcdboot.exe e:\Windows
```

5. Unmount the VHDX. If you are using Windows Explorer, the unmount is carried out by right-clicking on the drive letter, and selecting **eject**. This step is very important. The system may have issues booting if you don't unmount the VHDX.
6. Repeat the steps described in steps 1-5 on each physical machine.

Rebooting into the new Nano Server image

Perform the following steps:

1. Reboot the host machines. They will automatically boot into the new Nano Server.
2. After the host machines are booted, log into the Nano recovery console. You will need to enter `Administrator` for the username and the password you specified earlier when creating the image. You can also specify the domain name and login with a user who is a member of the administrators group.
3. Note the IP address of each Nano Server. You will use these IP addresses in the networking section (more on that in a bit).

4. You can get the IP address from the DHCP server if you have DHCP deployed in your environment, or you can select **Networking** in the Nano recovery console and press *Enter*. Select the network adapter that is being used to connect to the system to manage it and then press *Enter*. Note your IPv4 address, as shown in *Figure 4*, for later use:

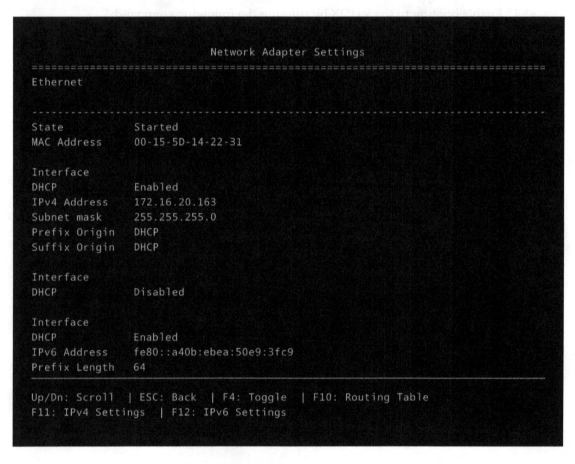

Figure 4. Nano Server recovery console: network adapter settings

Connecting and managing Nano Servers from a management machine

Perform the following steps:

1. Connect to and manage Nano Servers from a management machine that has the same build of Windows Server 2016 and RSAT installed.

2. Launch Hyper-V Manager on the management machine and add the four Nano Servers, as shown in *Figure 5*, and make sure you can connect to each Nano host:

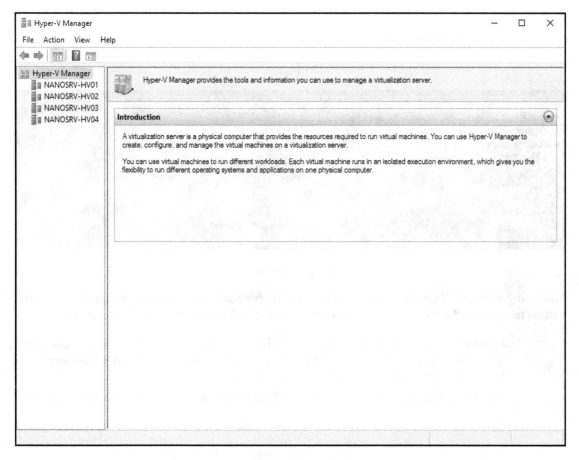

Figure 5. Hyper-V Manager console: Nano Servers

3. You can also use PowerShell remoting by using either the Nano Server name or the IP address that you acquired from the recovery console in the earlier step.

4. Open Windows PowerShell on the management machine and run the following commands. You will be prompted for a password; enter the local administrator password you specified when creating the Nano Server images:

```
Set-itemwsman:localhost\client\trustedhosts -Value"NANOSRV-*"-
Force$NanoServer01="NANOSRV-HV01"$Cred=Get-
Credential"~\Administrator"Enter-PSSession-ComputerName
$NanoServer01-Credential $CredSet-Location C:\Get-ComputerInfo
w*x,oss*l
```

5. After you enter the credentials, (see *Figure 6*):

```
CharbelNemnom.com #> Set-item wsman:localhost\client\trustedhosts -Value "NANOSRV-*" -Force
CharbelNemnom.com #> $NanoServer01 = "NANOSRV-HV01"
CharbelNemnom.com #> $Cred = Get-Credential "~\Administrator"
CharbelNemnom.com #> Enter-PSSession -ComputerName $NanoServer01 -Credential $Cred
[NANOSRV-HV01]: PS C:\Users\Administrator\Documents> Set-Location C:\
[NANOSRV-HV01]: PS C:\> Get-ComputerInfo w*x, oss*l

WindowsBuildLabEx                                 OsServerLevel
-----------------                                 -------------
14393.1198.amd64fre.rs1_release_sec.170427-1353   NanoServer
```

Figure 6. Nano Server PowerShell Remote Session

Managing a Hyper-V cluster system including cluster and virtualization components often means using a domain account that is a member of the Administrators group on each node:

1. From the management machine, open the Windows PowerShell console and run the following commands to add your domain account(s) in the administrators local security group simultaneously on all four nodes.
2. Please update the domain account and password according to your environment:

```
$Cred=New-object-typenameSystem.Management.Automation.PSCredential
-argumentlist ".\Administrator", (ConvertTo-SecureString"PWS"-
AsPlainText-Force) $Nodes="NANOSRV-HV01","NANOSRV-HV02","NANOSRV-
HV03","NANOSRV-HV04"Invoke-Command-ComputerName $Nodes-Credential
$Cred-ScriptBlock {Netlocalgroup Administrators VIRT\ClusterMgmt
/add
}
```

Configuring the network

The following example assumes that you already have dual RDMA NIC ports in each node. The Hyper-V virtual switch must be deployed with RDMA-enabled host virtual NICs. In Windows Server 2016, separate NICs are no longer needed for RDMA. The Converged NIC feature is a feature that allows the virtual NICs on the host (vNICs) to expose RDMA to the host management OS and share the bandwidth of the NICs between the RDMA traffic and the VM and other TCP/UDP traffic in a fair and manageable manner.

The diagram in *Figure 7* illustrates the software architecture changes in Windows Server 2016:

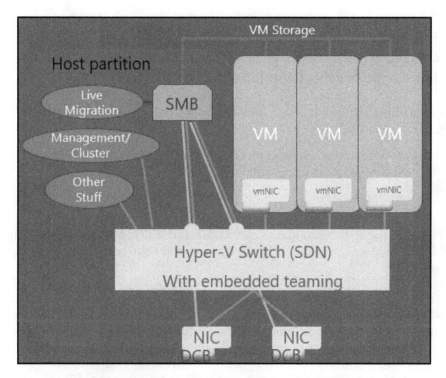

Figure 7. Converged NIC with RDMA-enabled host vNICs (image source: Microsoft)

The configuration for this example is based on a network adapter that implements RDMA using RoCEv2 from Mellanox. Network QoS for this type of RDMA requires that the Top of Rack (TOR) switches have specific capabilities set called **Data Center Bridging** (**DCB**) for the network ports that the physical NICs are connected to.

While DCB is not needed for Internet Wide Area RDMA Protocol (iWARP) networks, testing has found that all Ethernet-based RDMA technologies work better with DCB. Because of this, you should consider using DCB even for iWARP RDMA deployments as well.

DCB is used to mean all four of the following technologies:

- **Priority-based Flow Control** (**PFC**), standardized in IEEE 802.1 Qbb
- **Enhanced Transmission Selection** (**ETS**), standardized in IEEE 802.1 Qaz
- Congestion notification, standardized in IEEE 802.1 Qau
- **Data Center Bridging Capabilities Exchange Protocol** (**DCBX**)

In summary, Windows Server is only interested in the first two technologies of DCB, PFC, and ETS.

 For more information about **Quality of Service** (**QoS**) and DCB, please refer to the following article: `https://technet.microsoft.com/en-us/network/bb530836.aspx`.

Perform the following steps from a management machine using a PowerShell remote session and the `Invoke-Command` cmdlet to connect and configure the network adapter for each Nano Server:

1. Set a network QoS policy for SMB, which is the protocol that the software-defined storage system uses, including live migration and other SMB types of traffic. This example assumes that the virtual machine storage will be live on storage spaces direct in a separate cluster (disaggregated or converged model):

```
Invoke-Command-ComputerName$Nodes-Credential$Cred-
ScriptBlock{New-NetQosPolicy"SMB"-
NetDirectPortMatchCondition445-PriorityValue8021Action3}
```

2. The output should look something like this (see *Figure 8*):

```
[NANOSRV-HV01]: PS C:\> New-NetQosPolicy "SMB" -NetDirectPortMatchCondition 445 -PriorityValue8021Action 3

Name            : SMB
Owner           : Group Policy (Machine)
NetworkProfile  : All
Precedence      : 127
JobObject       :
NetDirectPort   : 445
PriorityValue   : 3
```

Figure 8. New NetQoS Policy

3. Turn on flow control for SMB using the following command:

```
Invoke-Command-ComputerName$Nodes-Credential$Cred-
ScriptBlock{Enable-NetQosFlowControl-Priority3}
```

4. Make sure flow control is off for other type of traffic using the following command:

```
Invoke-Command-ComputerName $Nodes-Credential $Cred-ScriptBlock {
Disable-NetQosFlowControl -Priority0,1,2,4,5,6,7}
```

5. Apply the network QoS policy to all NICRDMA adapters. In this example, we have only two RDMA NICs on each Nano host; you can use the wildcard character * for the Name, as shown in the following example:

```
Invoke-Command-ComputerName $Nodes-Credential $Cred-ScriptBlock {
Get-NetAdapterQos -Name"*"|Enable-NetAdapterQos
}
```

6. Create a Traffic class and give the SMB 50% of the bandwidth minimum. The name of the class will be SMB as shown in the following example:

```
Invoke-Command-ComputerName$Nodes-Credential$Cred-ScriptBlock{New-
NetQosTrafficClass"SMB"-Priority3-BandwidthPercentage50-
AlgorithmETS}
```

In this example, the SMB traffic has 50% of the bandwidth at least and the other traffic will share the remaining 50%.

Priority Flow Control (PFC) must also be configured on Top of Rack switches; more on that in a bit.

The following is a sample of configuring DCB and PFC on the Cisco Nexus 3172 switch series. In this example, we will use the following VLANs:

VLAN	VLAN name	VLAN description
10	MGMT_OS	Management OS
11	SMB	SMB dedicated network
12	Live migration	Hyper-V live migration
13	Backup	Backup and replication
14	CSV	Cluster communication

```
#Global Cisco Switch settings:
 switch#configure terminal
 switch(config)#class-map type qos match-all RDMA
 switch(config-cmap-qos)#match cos 3
 switch(config-cmap-qos)#exit
 switch(config)#class-map type queuing RDMA
 switch(config-cmap-que)#match qos-group 3
 switch(config-cmap-que)#exit
 switch(config)#policy-map type qos QOS_MARKING
 switch(config-pmap-qos)#class RDMA
 switch(config-pmap-c-qos)#set qos-group 3
 switch(config-pmap-c-qos)#class class-default
 switch(config-pmap-c-qos)#exit
 switch(config-pmap-qos)#exit
 switch(config)#policy-map type queuing
 QOS_QUEUEING
 switch(config-pmap-qeue)#class type queuing RDMA
 switch(config-pmap-c-qeue)#bandwidth percent 100
 switch(config-pmap-c-qeue)#class type queuing
 class-default
 switch(config-pmap-c-qeue)#exit
 switch(config-pmap-qeue)#exit
 switch(config)#policy-map type queuing
 INPUT_QUEUING
 switch(config-pmap-qeue)#class type queuing RDMA
 switch(config-pmap-c-qeue)#pause buffer-size
 101920 pause-threshold 46800 resume-threshold
 34320
 switch(config-pmap-c-qeue)#class type queuing
 class-default
 switch(config-pmap-c-qeue)#exit
 switch(config)#class-map type network-qos RDMA
 switch(config-cmap-nqos)#match qos-group 3
```

```
switch(config-cmap-nqos)#exit
switch(config)#policy-map type network-qos
QOS_NETWORK
switch(config-pmap-nqos)#class type network-qos
RDMA
switch(config-pmap-nqos-c)#mtu 2240
switch(config-pmap-nqos-c)#pause no-drop
switch(config-pmap-nqos-c)#class type network-qos
class-default
switch(config-pmap-nqos-c)#mtu 9216
switch(config-pmap-nqos-c)#exit
switch(config-pmap-nqos)#policy-map type network-
qos jumbo-queuing
switch(config-pmap-nqos)#class type network-qos
class-default
switch(config-pmap-nqos-c)#mtu 9216
switch(config-pmap-nqos-c)#exit
switch(config-pmap-nqos)#exit
switch(config)#copy running-config startup-con
```

The buffer sizes differ from the Nexus switch in the canonical configuration.

The canonical buffer sizes are: pause buffer-size `101920`, pause-threshold `46800`, resume-threshold `34320`:

```
#Individual Cisco switch interface configuration:switch#configure
terminalswitch(config)#interface Ethernet1/1switch(config-if)#priority-
flow-control mode onswitch(config-if)#switchport mode
trunkswitch(config-if)#switchport trunk native vlan 10switch(config-
if)#switchport trunk allowed vlan 11-14switch(config-if)#spanning-tree
port type edge trunk
```

7. Create the Hyper-V virtual **Switch Embedded Teaming (SET)** which is connected to both physical NIC adapters, and enable RDMA vNIC.

8. SET is an alternative NIC Teaming solution in Windows Server 2016 that can be used for Hyper-V deployments with or without a **Software-Defined Networking (SDN)** stack. SET is only supported in Nano Server; however, LBFO teaming solution is not supported in Nano.

For more information about SET, please refer to the following articles:

- https://technet.microsoft.com/en-us/library/mt403349.a spx
- https://charbelnemnom.com/2015/12/deploying-switch-emb edded-teaming-set-on-hyper-v-using-powershell-dsc-pow ershell-dsc-hyperv/

9. Before creating the virtual switch, you need to find the physical network adapter's names on the host by running the following command:

```
Get-NetAdapter|FTName, InterfaceDescription, Status, LinkSpeed
```

10. Once you have figured out the names of the NICs, you can then create the Hyper-V virtual switch by running the following command from the management machine. You may notice a message that your PowerShell session lost connection. This is expected and your session will reconnect:

```
Invoke-Command-ComputerName $Nodes-Credential $Cred-ScriptBlock
{New-VMSwitch-Name SETvSwitch-NetAdapterName
"Ethernet","Ethernet 2"-EnableEmbeddedTeaming $true}
```

11. Add host vNICs to the virtual switch. This configures a vNIC from the virtual switch that we just created in *step 12*. As shown in the following example, we will add five host vNICs for SMB multichannel, live migration, cluster, and backup. The host management vNIC is automatically created in Step 12 when we create the `SET` virtual switch:

```
Invoke-Command-ComputerName $Nodes-Credential $Cred-ScriptBlock
{Add-VMNetworkAdapter-SwitchName SETvSwitch-Name SMB_1-
managementOS Add-VMNetworkAdapter-SwitchName SETvSwitch-Name
SMB_2-managementOSAdd-VMNetworkAdapter-SwitchName SETvSwitch-
Name LiveMigration-managementOS Add-VMNetworkAdapter-SwitchName
SETvSwitch-Name Cluster-managementOSAdd-VMNetworkAdapter-
SwitchName SETvSwitch-Name Backup-managementOS
}
```

12. Next, we need to set the IP address for each host vNIC accordingly. The following script will automate the IP address assignment on all nodes:

```
# Number of Node in the Hyper-V Cluster$ServerCount =4# SMB_1
and SMB_2 Network ID for nodes$SMB_ID="10.11.0."# Backup
Network ID for nodes$Backup_ID="10.13.0."# Start IP address for
nodes$Backup_Network=11$SMB_Network=11For($i=1; $i-
le$ServerCount; $i++)
{$SMB_IP=$SMB_ID+$SMB_Network$Backup_IP=$Backup_ID+$Backup_Netw
orkInvoke-Command-ComputerName"NANOSRV-HV0$i"-Credential$Cred-
ScriptBlock{
 Param($SMB_Network,$SMB_ID,$SMB_IP,$Backup_IP)
   New-NetIPAddress-InterfaceAlias"vEthernet (SMB_1)"-
IPAddress$SMB_IP-PrefixLength"24"-
TypeUnicast$SMB_Network++$SMB_IP=""$SMB_IP=$SMB_ID+$SMB_Network
New-NetIPAddress-InterfaceAlias"vEthernet (SMB_2)"-
IPAddress$SMB_IP-PrefixLength"24"-TypeUnicastNew-NetIPAddress-
```

```
InterfaceAlias"vEthernet (Backup)"-IPAddress$Backup_IP-
PrefixLength"24"-TypeUnicast
} -
ArgumentList$SMB_Network,$SMB_ID,$SMB_IP,$Backup_IP$Backup_Netw
ork++$SMB_Network++$SMB_Network++}
```

13. If you noticed in the script above, we did not set the IP address for live migration and cluster networks; in fact, they'll work out of the box due to IPv6 APIPA. Additionally, it's even a little faster as there is no NetBIOS involved for IPv6; however, NetBIOS is recommended to be disabled when using IPv4 for live migration, CSV, and cluster networks. As for SMB multichannel, both vNICs can be on the same subnet (VLAN ID 11) as well; this is a new enhancement in Windows Server 2016 failover clustering.

14. Next, we need to disable DNS registration for storage, cluster, backup, and live migration network adapters, except for host management vNIC, by running the following commands:

```
Invoke-Command-ComputerName$Nodes-Credential$Cred-
ScriptBlock{Get-DnsClient|Where-Object{$_.InterfaceAlias -
ne"vEthernet (SETvSwitch)"} |Set-DNSClient-
RegisterThisConnectionsAddress$False }
```

15. Next, we need to configure the host vNICs to use a different VLAN. Please make sure the VLANs are also defined on your Top of Rack switches:

```
Invoke-Command-ComputerName $Nodes-Credential $Cred-ScriptBlock
{Set-VMNetworkAdapterVlan-VMNetworkAdapterName "SMB_1"-VlanId
11-Access -ManagementOSSet-VMNetworkAdapterVlan-
VMNetworkAdapterName "SMB_2"-VlanId 11-Access -ManagementOSSet-
VMNetworkAdapterVlan-VMNetworkAdapterName "LiveMigration"-
VlanId 12-Access -ManagementOSSet-VMNetworkAdapterVlan-
VMNetworkAdapterName "Backup"-VlanId 13-Access -
ManagementOSSet-VMNetworkAdapterVlan-VMNetworkAdapterName
"Cluster"-VlanId 14-Access -ManagementOS }
```

16. You can also verify the VLANID is set by running the following command:

```
Invoke-Command-ComputerName $Nodes-Credential $Cred-ScriptBlock
{
Get-VMNetworkAdapter -SwitchNameSETvSwitch-ManagementOS|Get-
VMNetworkAdapterVlan
}
```

17. Please make sure to also disable and enable each host vNIC adapter by running the following commands so that the VLANs are active:

```
Invoke-Command-ComputerName $Nodes-Credential $Cred-ScriptBlock
{Disable-NetAdapter"vEthernet (SMB_1)","vEthernet
(SMB_2)","vEthernet (LiveMigration)","vEthernet
(Backup)","vEthernet (Cluster)"-Confirm:$falseEnable-
NetAdapter"vEthernet (SMB_1)","vEthernet (SMB_2)","vEthernet
(LiveMigration)","vEthernet (Backup)","vEthernet (Cluster)" }
```

18. In the final step, we need to enable RDMA on the host vNIC adapters by running the following command from the management machine:

```
Invoke-Command-ComputerName $Nodes-Credential $Cred-ScriptBlock
{Enable-NetAdapterRDMA"vEthernet (SMB_1)","vEthernet
(SMB_2)","vEthernet (LiveMigration)","vEthernet (Backup)"
}
```

Creating and configuring a Hyper-V cluster

Configuring a Hyper-V cluster in Windows Server 2016 includes the following steps:

1. First, we will run the cluster validation tool to ensure that the Nano nodes are configured correctly to create a Hyper-V cluster. The cluster validation runs to test and verify that the configuration appears suitable to successfully function as a failover cluster.

   Use the following PowerShell command to confirm a set of servers for use as a Hyper-V cluster:

   ```
   $Nodes="NANOSRV-HV01","NANOSRV-HV02","NANOSRV-HV03","NANOSRV-
   HV04"Test-Cluster-Node$Nodes-IncludeInventory,Network,"System
   Configuration"-Verbose
   ```

The output report should look something like this (see *Figure 9*):

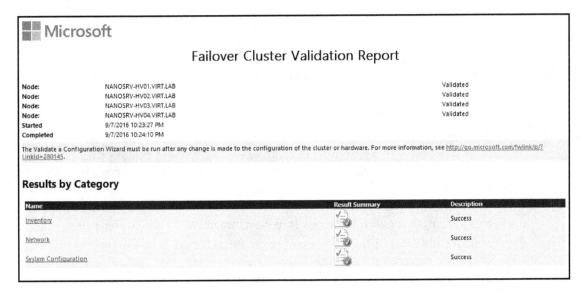

Figure 9. Failover cluster validation report

In the PowerShell example above, we removed the storage option from the cluster validation test, because we will store the VM on a S2D cluster over SMB (more on that in the next section).

2. In the second step, we will create a Hyper-V cluster with four nodes that you have confirmed for cluster creation in Step 1 by using the following PowerShell command:

The `-NoStorage` parameter is important to be added to the cmdlet, because will use Storage Spaces Direct for shared storage.

3. In the following command, the `ClusterName` placeholder should be replaced with a NetBIOS name that is unique and 15 characters or less. If you don't have a DHCP server in your environment, then add the `-StaticAddress` parameter with the appropriate IP address:

```
New-Cluster-NameNANOHV-CLU-Node$Nodes-NoStorage-
StaticAddress172.16.20.159/24-
IgnoreNetwork10.11.0.0/24,10.13.0.0/24-Verbose
```

4. After running the previous command, you will receive a warning message which states that `There were issues while creating the clustered role that may prevent it from starting.`

   You can safely ignore this warning. This warning is due to no disks being available for the cluster quorum. It's recommended that a file share witness or cloud witness is configured after creating the cluster. We will configure a cloud witness in the next step.

5. In this step, we will configure the cloud witness. In Windows Server 2016, Microsoft introduced a new type of failover cluster witness besides disk witness and file share witness called cloud witness. Cloud witness leverages Microsoft Azure's blob storage to read and write to a blob file. Cloud witness will be used as an arbitration point in case of split-brain resolution.

6. The requirement for cloud witness is to have an active Azure subscription.

7. In your Azure subscription, you need to create a storage account; for this purpose, we've created a storage account named `nanohvcloudwitness`, and the resource group named `NANOHV-RG`, as shown in *Figure 10*:

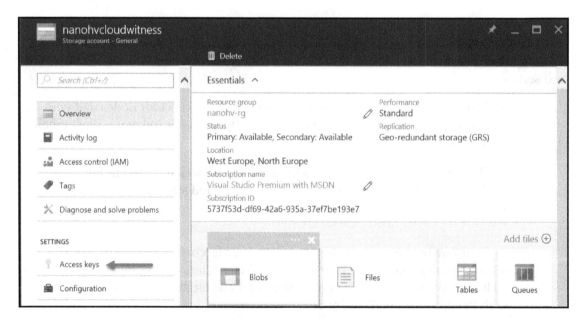

Figure 10. Cloud witness

A storage account gets two access keys and two connection strings. The reason for this is that you can regenerate the keys, and have your workloads use the other key without having any downtime for your workload.

The storage account can be used for multiple clusters as well. In fact, we will use the same storage account to configure the Storage Spaces Direct cluster in the next section.

8. In Azure, the work is done. The rest will happen on-premises. We'll configure the cluster with the cloud witness by running the following PowerShell one-liner. Please update the `-AccessKey` parameter with your key accordingly:

```
Set-ClusterQuorum-ClusterNANOHV-
CLU-CloudWitness-AccountNamenanohvcloudwitness-AccessKey<Access
Key>
```

9. You can also set the cluster quorum using failover Cluster Manager from the management machine, as shown in *Figure 11*:

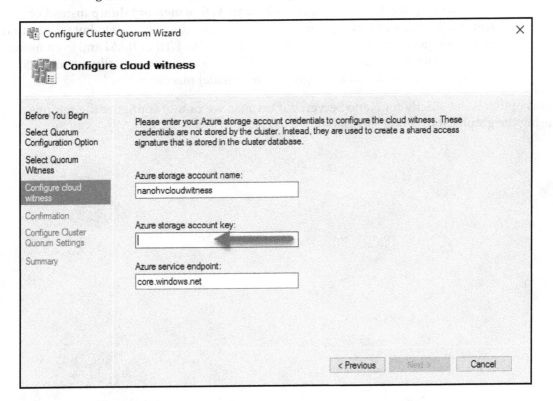

Figure 11. Configure cloud witness in failover cluster manager

10. Once you're done, you can check the cluster quorum by running the following `Get-ClusterQuorum` command:

```
Get-ClusterQuorum-ClusterNANOHV-CLU
```

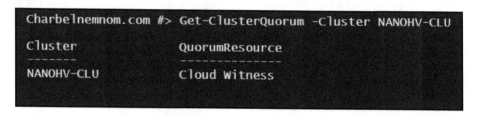

Figure 12. Get-ClusterQuorum Output

11. In this step, we will set the cluster memory dump to active. In Windows Server 2016, Microsoft added a new option for creating memory dumps when a system failure occurs. The new option is called **Active memory dump**.

It's recommended to set the Hyper-V host to **Active memory dump** instead of **Automatic memory dump,** which is the default setting, because today we can find on the market large memory servers with 256 GB to 1 TB of RAM and even more. And for troubleshooting issues with the Hyper-V hosts, we usually do not need the part of the RAM that is assigned to the virtual machines.

This option is not strictly for Nano Server, but because we cannot configure the settings using the graphical user interface, as shown in *Figure 13*:

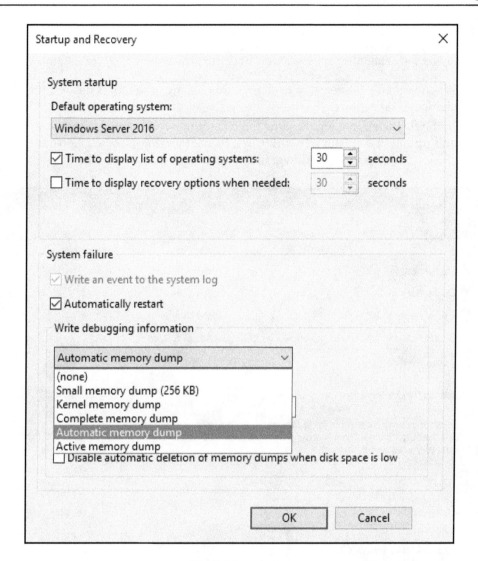

Figure 13. Active memory dump

Therefore, we need to set it in the registry on each Nano node by running the following PowerShell command:

```
Invoke-Command-ComputerName$Nodes-Credential$Cred-ScriptBlock{
    # Configure Active memory dumpSet-
ItemProperty-PathHKLM:\System\CurrentControlSet\Control\CrashControl-NameCr
ashDumpEnabled-value1New-
ItemProperty-PathHKLM:\System\CurrentControlSet\Control\CrashControl-
NameFilterPages-Value1# CrashDumpEnabled = 7 = Automatic memory dump
```

```
(default).# CrashDumpEnabled = 1 = Complete memory dump.# CrashDumpEnabled
= 1 and FilterPages = 1 = Active memory dump.Get-
ItemProperty-PathHKLM:\System\CurrentControlSet\Control\CrashControl}
```

12. When you edit the registry to change this setting, a reboot is needed for the change to take effect.
13. In the final step, we will rename the cluster network names to match the function and update the cluster network roles. But before doing so, let's look at the current cluster networks using failover cluster manager (see *Figure 14*):

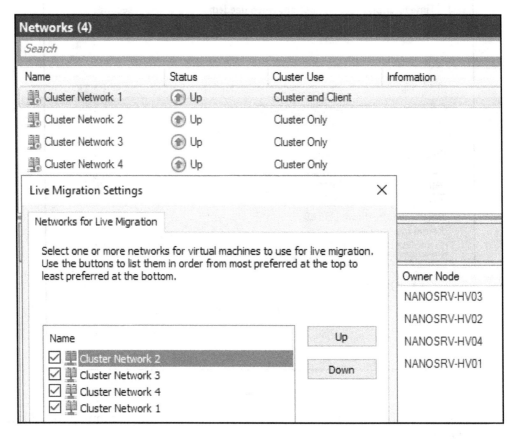

Figure 14. Cluster Networks: Failover cluster manager

14. From the management machine, run the following script to update the cluster networks. Please update the IP addresses and names according to your environment:

```
# Update Cluster Network Names to Match Function and Update Cluster
Network Roles$Cluster ="NANOHV-CLU"Get-ClusterNetwork-
Cluster$Cluster|Format-List*# Rename Management OS Network and
Enable for client and cluster communication(Get-ClusterNetwork-
Cluster$Cluster|Where-Object{$_.Address -eq"172.16.20.0"}).name
="ManagementOS"(Get-ClusterNetwork-Cluster$Cluster-
Name"ManagementOS").Role =3# Rename Live Migration Network and
Enable for Cluster Communication only(Get-ClusterNetwork-
Cluster$Cluster|Where-Object{$_.Address -eq""}).name
="LiveMigration"(Get-ClusterNetwork-Cluster$Cluster-
Name"LiveMigration").Role =1# Rename SMB Network and Disable for
Cluster Communication(Get-ClusterNetwork-Cluster$Cluster|Where-
Object{$_.Address -eq"10.11.0.0"}).name ="SMB_A_B"(Get-
ClusterNetwork-Cluster$Cluster-Name"SMB_A_B").Role =0# Rename
Backup Network and Disable for Cluster Communication(Get-
ClusterNetwork-Cluster$Cluster|Where-Object{$_.Address -
eq"10.13.0.0"}).name ="Backup"(Get-ClusterNetwork-Cluster$Cluster-
Name"Backup").Role =0# Configure Live Migration NetworksGet-
ClusterResourceType-Cluster$Cluster-Name"Virtual Machine"|Set-
ClusterParameter-NameMigrationExcludeNetworks-
Value([String]::Join(";",(Get-ClusterNetwork-Cluster$Cluster|Where-
Object{$_.Name -ne"LiveMigration"}).ID))
```

15. Once you run this script, you can check **Networks** in failover cluster manager, as shown in *Figure 15*:

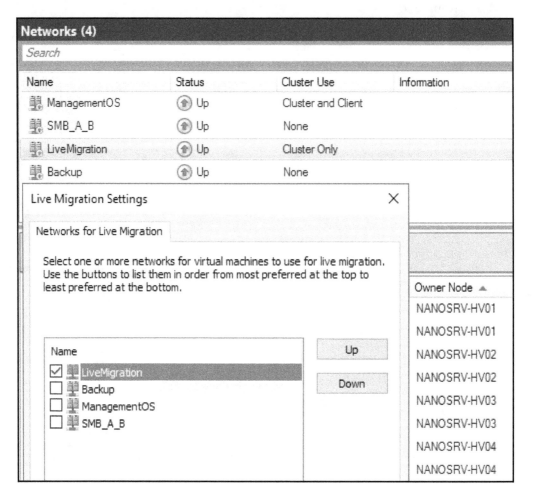

Figure 15. Cluster Networks Renamed: Failover Cluster Manager

Once Nano Server as compute cluster has been created, you can start deploying clustered virtual machines; please refer to the next section for a sample deployment.

Nano Server as a storage cluster

As mentioned at the beginning of this chapter, Nano Server can also be used as a storage system. In Windows Server 2016, Microsoft added a new type of storage called S2D. S2D enables the building of highly available storage systems with local attached disks, and without the need for any external SAS fabric (that is, shared JBODs or enclosures).This is a significant step forward for Microsoft in Windows Server 2016 SDS which reduces hardware and operation costs.

In Windows Server 2016, S2D delivers us two deployment models: private cloud hyper-converged, where S2D and the hypervisor (Hyper-V) run on the same set of hardware, or private cloud storage, where Storage Spaces Direct is disaggregated called converged (separate storage cluster) from the hypervisor. The hyper-converged deployment groups compute and storage together. This simplifies the deployment model, while compute and storage are scaled at the same time. A private cloud storage deployment separates the compute and storage resources. This deployment model (see *Figure 16*) enables us to scale compute and storage independently for larger scale-out deployments and avoids overprovisioning:

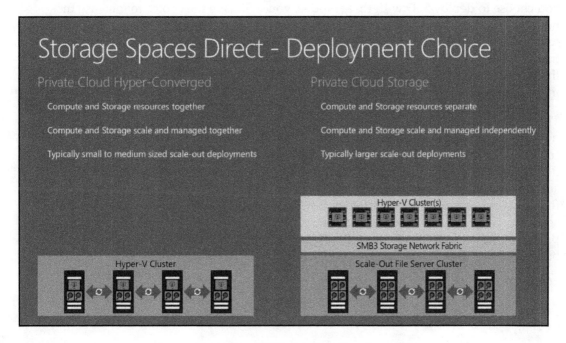

Figure 16. Storage S2D choice (image source: Microsoft)

This section gives the instructions to create a hyper-converged solution using S2D on top of Nano Server in Windows Server 2016. Please note that the disaggregated, (separate storage cluster) deployment is identically the same as the hyperconverged modell; the only difference is the way you present the VM storage to the hypervisor. In the hyperconverged deployment, the virtual machine's files are stored on clustered shared volume ReFS File System (CSVFS_REFS), however, in a disaggregated model, the VM storage is presented through scale-out File Server (file share) on top of the Clustered Shared Volume ReFS File System (CSVFS_REFS); over SMB3 network fabric. Once S2D is configured and the storage is available, configuring and provisioning Hyper-V is the same process and uses the same tools that you would use with any other Hyper-V deployment on a failover cluster.

In Windows Server 2016, S2D can be deployed by using from two nodes up to sixteen nodes. This is the minimum and maximum limit based on your fault tolerance requirements, and what Microsoft supports. If you choose to deploy S2D with two Nodes only, you will be limited to one failure, either drive or server, but not both, and the volume will be limited to mirror volume (two-way mirroring) resiliency. Mirroring is like distributed, software-defined RAID-1. It offers the fastest possible reads/writes, but isn't very capacity efficient, because you're effectively keeping full extra copies of everything. If you choose to deploy S2D with three Nodes, you will have the choice to increase the number of failures from one to two; in other words, you will ensure that all data remains safe and continuously accessible in the unlikely event that two drives fail simultaneously, or that two nodes go down simultaneously, or one drive fails and one node goes down. With the three nodes deployment choice, you will also be limited to mirror volume (three-way mirroring) resiliency.

The ideal deployment is to start with four nodes; this deployment gives you the choice to use mirroring and parity encoding at the same time, which can be referred to as mixed resiliency, or multi-resiliency, or is sometimes called hybrid volume resiliency. This deployment also gives you the choice to increase the number of failures from one to two simultaneously (two drives, or two nodes, or one drive and one node). S2D needs at least four servers to enable parity resiliency. Unlike mirroring, parity is like distributed, software-defined RAID-5 or RAID-6. And since the same volume can be part mirror and part parity, **Resilient File System (ReFS)** will automatically move data back and forth between these **tiers** in real time, depending on what's hot and what's cold.

ReFS is a new filesystem which was introduced in Windows Server 2012 and was designed to overcome issues that had become significant over the years since NTFS was conceived. In Windows Server 2016, Microsoft enhanced ReFS and it is now the preferred file system deployment for Storage Spaces Direct. This updated version offers many new capabilities for private cloud workloads, such as data integrity, resiliency to corruption and availability, and speed and efficiency.

Mirroring volume offers faster access to data, but is not very space-efficient. On the other hand, parity volume encoding incurs some computation time and cost to encode/decode data, but is far more space-efficient. This multi-resiliency volume gives the best of both worlds - fast, cheap writes of hot data, and better efficiency for cooler data.

S2D offers three volumes of resiliency type: Mirroring (two-way mirroring and three-way mirroring), dual parity (often called erasure coding), or a mix of the two (often called multi-resilient volume or MRV).

Please note that mirror volumes is faster than any other type of resiliency.

Microsoft coupled ReFS in Windows Server 2016 with the S2D scenario. They recommend running ReFS on S2D and Storage Spaces, and NTFS elsewhere; therefore, the story behind ReFS is the following technologies used together: ReFS, S2D, Storage Spaces, Multi-Resiliency Volume, and the S2D cache.

Finally, you can refer to the S2D calculator at `http://aka.ms/s2dcalc`, which will help you to efficiently size your storage deployment.

Deploying storage spaces direct on top of Nano Server

As we expect Hyper-V to become an important role for Nano Server, we would also expect that Nano Server will play a vital role as a software-defined storage host as well. The good news is that S2D works the same as on any Windows Server (Server with Desktop Experience, Server Core and Nano Server).

For more information about Storage Spaces Direct in Windows Server 2016, please check the following article:

`https://docs.microsoft.com/en-us/windows-server/storage/storage-spaces/storage-spaces-direct-overview`.

This section includes instructions on how to install and configure the components of Storage Spaces Direct in a hyper-converged model using Windows Server 2016 on top of four Nano Servers. The hardware we are using in this example is the following:

- 4 HP DL380 Gen 9, 2 X E5-2690v3, 256 GB Memory, 2 X 120 GB SATA SSD RAID-1 for the OS, 4X2 TB SATA HDD 7.2K RPM, 4X960 GB SATA SSD. HPE H240 12 GB 2-ports smart HBA, and two dual-port 10/25 GBE network interface controllers (NICs): HPE 10/25 GB/s 2-port 640 SFP28 Ethernet adapter and the HPE 10/25 GB/s 2-port 640 FLR-SFP28 Ethernet adapter. Both adapters are based on the Mellanox connect-X®-4 Lx 10/25 GBE controller (top of rack switch Cisco Nexus 3172 PQ-XLBIOS: version 3.4.0).

As you can see from this list, we have two Mellanox connect-X®-4 NICs (dual port, 10/25 GB). Both dual NICs support RDMA. However, in this example, the first Mellanox NIC will be used for normal management and VM traffic (management traffic includes live migration, backup, cluster, and OS management). We will use the second Mellanox NIC for the storage traffic.

Since we have four physical NICs, it's better to keep two standalone NICs for RDMA and use the other two for SET virtual switch. There are other reasons to do so, for example, if you plan to use SDN on top of S2D in the future. With this setup, storage NICs will be transparent and not managed by network controller, making it much easier to integrate both features. However, if you have only two physical NICs, then virtual RDMA (vRDMA), with management, cluster, SMB1, and SMB2 vNICs is the way to go, as we did in the *Deploying Nano Server as a Hyper-V cluster* section.

A question that you may ask is, how can we limit S2D SMB traffic on a specific NIC, since all traffic is considered as SMB? By default, SMB-multichannel (S2D) will automatically select only the RDMA adapters for SMB traffic, therefore if you need to force S2D traffic over dedicated NICs, then do not enable RDMA on the vNICs which are created on top of SET virtual switch. You need to enable RDMA only on the other two physical NICs. In Windows Server 2016, we don't have a network constraint feature for S2D as we have with storage replica. Storage replica is out of the scope of this book.

The act of deploying a hyper-converged system can be divided into three high-level phases:

- Creating and deploying Nano Server images
- Configuring the network
- Creating and configuring S2D

Since most of the steps are covered in the *Deploying Nano Server as a Hyper-V cluster* section at the beginning of this chapter, we will refer to them while deploying the hyper-converged system to minimize repetitive tasks - at the same time, we will highlight the new steps about configuring S2D. Please refer also to the information section at the beginning that we need as input as well.

Creating and deploying Nano Server images

This section describes how to create the Nano Server VHD(X) file to be used on physical machines using the pre-installed device drivers. We need to create a VHD(X) that includes the OEM drivers, storage, and failover clustering features including SCVMM packages, and that enables remote management and emergency management services.

Nano Server on a bare-metal (physical machine) can be deployed using multiple options; please refer to Chapter 3, *Deploying Nano Server in a Virtual Machine and on Physical Hardware,* for the complete details. In this guide, we will use the boot from VHDX option.

Please refer to the *Deploying Nano Server as compute host section* at the beginning of this chapter for more information.

The following steps will illustrate the OS deployment process:

1. In the first step, you will create a unique image for each Nano storage host. We need four images one for each physical machine in the hyper-converged system, so we will create a VHDX for a physical machine that includes the SCVMM and DCB packages by running the following script on the management machine which is a member of the same domain where the Nano Server will be deployed. The script will prompt you for an administrator password for the new VHDX (type carefully and note your password for later use; you will use this password later to log in to the new Nano Servers):

```
# Example definition of variable and values for hyper-converged
S2D# Import NanoServerImageGenerator.psd1 PowerShell moduleImport-
Module"C:\NanoServer\NanoServerImageGenerator\NanoServerImageGenera
tor.psd1"-Verbose# Enter Administrator Password$Password=Read-Host-
Prompt"Please specify local Administrator password"-AsSecureString#
Domain Name$myDomainFQDN="VIRT.LAB"# Servicing Update
Packages$ServicingPackage=@(
                "C:\NanoServer\Updates\Servicing Stack
Update\Windows10.0-KB4013418-x64.msu"
"C:\NanoServer\Updates\Cumulative Update\Windows10.0-KB4023680-
x64.msu" )# Nano Packages$NanoPackage=@(
            "Microsoft-NanoServer-DCB-Package" "Microsoft-
NanoServer-SCVMM-Package" "Microsoft-NanoServer-SCVMM-Compute-
```

```
Package" )1..4|ForEach-Object{New-NanoServerImage-
BasePathC:\NanoServer\`
                        -TargetPathC:\NanoServer\NANOSRV-S2D0$_.vhdx`
                              -MaxSize20GB`
                              -DeploymentTypeHost`
                              -EditionDatacenter`
                              -ComputerNameNANOSRV-S2D0$_`
                              -AdministratorPassword$Password`
                              -DomainName$myDomainFQDN`
                              -ReuseDomainNode`
                              -Storage`
                              -Clustering`
                              -Package$NanoPackage`
                              -OEMDrivers`
                              -DriversPathD:\NanoServer\HP-Nano`
                              -EnableRemoteManagementPort`
                              -EnableEMS`
                              -
ServicingPackagePath$ServicingPackage`
                              -SetupCompleteCommand('tzutil.exe /s
"W. Europe Standard Time"')
}
```

 We have included a -Storage parameter in the image.

2. Copy the VHDX files that you created in *Step 1* to each respective machine and configure each host machine to boot from the new VHDX. Please refer to the *Creating the new Nano Server images* section in this chapter for the complete details.
3. Reboot the host machines. They will automatically boot into the new Nano Server. After the host machines are booted, log into the Nano Recovery Console, and note the IP address of each Nano Server. You will use these IP addresses to connect to Nano Server and configure the network in the next section.

Configuring the network

The following example assumes that you already have two dual RDMA NIC ports in each node. As mentioned earlier, the Hyper-V virtual switch must be deployed in SET with RDMA-enabled host virtual NICs.

The configuration for this example is based on a network adapter that implements RDMA using RoCEv2 from Mellanox. Network QoS for this type of RDMA requires that the Top of Rack switches have a specific capabilities set called **Data Center Bridging** (**DCB**) and PFC enabled.

Open Windows PowerShell on the management machine and run the following commands using `Invoke-Command` to connect and configure the network on each Nano Server:

1. Set a network QoS policy for SMB, which is the protocol that the software-defined storage system uses:

```
$Cred=New-object-typenameSystem.Management.Automation.PSCredential-
argumentlist".\Administrator", (ConvertTo-SecureString"PWS"-
AsPlainText-Force) $Nodes="NANOSRV-S2D01","NANOSRV-S2D02","NANOSRV-
S2D03","NANOSRV-S2D04" Invoke-Command-ComputerName$Nodes-
Credential$Cred-ScriptBlock{New-NetQosPolicy"SMB"-
NetDirectPortMatchCondition445-PriorityValue8021Action3}
```

2. Turn on flow control for SMB:

```
Invoke-Command-ComputerName $Nodes-Credential $Cred-ScriptBlock {
Enable-NetQosFlowControl -Priority3}
```

3. Make sure the flow control is off for other traffic:

```
Invoke-Command-ComputerName$Nodes-Credential$Cred-
ScriptBlock{Disable-NetQosFlowControl-Priority0,1,2,4,5,6,7}
```

4. In this step, we will apply the network QoS policy to the target RDMA adapters. Use the name of the target adapters as shown in the following example. And since we will use one port from each Mellanox card for fault tolerance, we will apply the Network QoS respectively on each NIC interface on a different card. Please make sure to update the NIC names based on your environment:

```
Invoke-Command-ComputerName $Nodes-Credential $Cred-ScriptBlock
{
Enable-NetAdapterQoS -Name"HPE-640SFP01"Enable-NetAdapterQoS -
Name"HPE-640FLR-SFP01"}
```

5. In this step, we will create a Traffic class and give SMB 50% of the bandwidth minimum. In this example, the SMB traffic (live migration, backup, and so on) has 50% of the bandwidth at least and the VM traffic will share the remaining 50%:

```
Invoke-Command-ComputerName $Nodes-Credential $Cred-ScriptBlock
{New-NetQosTrafficClass"SMB"-Priority 3-BandwidthPercentage 50-
Algorithm ETS}
```

6. Please make sure to configure **Priority Flow Control** (**PFC**) and **Datacenter Bridging** (**DCB**) on the physical TOR switches; please refer to the example covered in *Step 9* on deploying Nano as a compute cluster, *Configure the Network* section.

7. In this step, we will create the Hyper-V virtual SET which is connected to both physical NIC adapters, and enable RDMA vNIC. We will select one NIC from each of the dual Mellanox adapters for fault tolerance:

```
Invoke-Command-ComputerName $Nodes-Credential $Cred-ScriptBlock
{New-VMSwitch-Name SETvSwitch-NetAdapterName
"HPE-640SFP01","HPE-640FLR-SFP01"-EnableEmbeddedTeaming $true}
```

While creating the vSwitch, you may notice a message that your PowerShell session lost connection. This is expected and your session will reconnect.

8. In this step, we will add host vNICs to the SET switch. This configures a virtual NIC (vNIC) from the virtual switch that you just configured in *Step 6* for the management OS to use. As shown in the following example, we will add three host vNICs for live migration, cluster, and backup. The host management vNIC is automatically added when we create the SET virtual switch. As for SMB traffic, we will use the two remaining physical NIC ports:

```
Invoke-Command-ComputerName $Nodes-Credential $Cred-ScriptBlock
{Add-VMNetworkAdapter-SwitchName SETvSwitch-Name LiveMigration-
managementOS Add-VMNetworkAdapter-SwitchName SETvSwitch-Name
Cluster-managementOSAdd-VMNetworkAdapter-SwitchName SETvSwitch-Name
Backup-managementOS
}
```

9. Next, we need to set the IP address for each host vNIC accordingly. The following script will automate the IP address assignment on all nodes including the SMB NICs:

```
# Number of Nodes in S2D hyper-converged Cluster$ServerCount=4#
SMB_1 and SMB_2 Network ID for nodes$SMB_ID="10.11.0."# Backup
Network ID for nodes$Backup_ID="10.13.0."# Start IP address for
nodes$Backup_Network=21$SMB_Network=21For($i=1; $i-le$ServerCount;
$i++){$SMB_IP=$SMB_ID+$SMB_Network$Backup_IP=$Backup_ID+$Backup_Net
workInvoke-Command-ComputerName"NANOSRV-S2D0$i"-Credential$Cred-
ScriptBlock{ Param($SMB_Network,$SMB_ID,$SMB_IP,$Backup_IP)
   New-NetIPAddress-InterfaceAlias"HPE-640SFP02"-IPAddress$SMB_IP-
PrefixLength"24"-
TypeUnicast$SMB_Network++$SMB_IP=""$SMB_IP=$SMB_ID+$SMB_NetworkNew-
NetIPAddress-InterfaceAlias"HPE-640FLR-SFP02"-IPAddress$SMB_IP-
PrefixLength"24"-TypeUnicastNew-NetIPAddress-
InterfaceAlias"vEthernet (Backup)"-IPAddress$Backup_IP-
PrefixLength"24"-TypeUnicast
} -
ArgumentList$SMB_Network,$SMB_ID,$SMB_IP,$Backup_IP$Backup_Network+
+$SMB_Network++$SMB_Network++}
```

10. Please update the interface alias names and IP addresses based on your environment.

11. In the final step, we need to disable DNS registration for storage, cluster, backup, and live migration network adapters; we need also to configure the host vNICs and pNICs to use a different VLAN and enable RDMA on each one. Please make sure the VLANs are also defined on top of rack switches. Please refer to the example in *step 15* through *step 19* on deploying Nano Server as Hyper-V cluster *Configure the Network* section.

Creating and configuring Storage Spaces Direct

Configuring S2D in Windows Server 2016 includes the following steps:

1. In this step, we will run the cluster validation tool to ensure that the Nano nodes are configured correctly to create the hyper-converged cluster using S2D:

```
# Test S2D hyper-converged cluster$Nodes= "NANOSRV-
S2D01","NANOSRV-S2D02","NANOSRV-S2D03","NANOSRV-S2D04"Test-
Cluster-Node$Nodes-IncludeInventory,Network,"System
Configuration","Storage Spaces Direct"-Verbose
```

The output report should look something like this (see *Figure 17*):

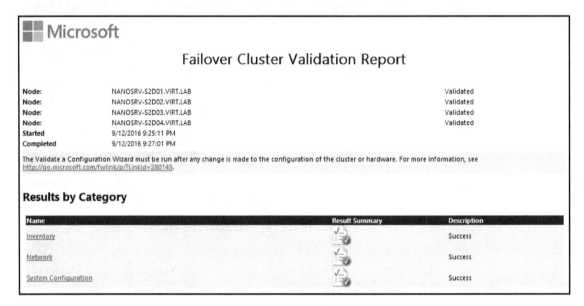

Figure 17. Failover cluster validation report

2. In this step, we will create the S2D cluster with four nodes using the following PowerShell command.

It is important to add the -NoStorage parameter to the cmdlet, otherwise the disks may be automatically added to the cluster and they will not be included in the S2D storage pool:

```
New-Cluster-NameNANOS2D-CLU-Node$Nodes-NoStorage-
StaticAddress172.16.20.155/24-IgnoreNetwork10.11.0.0/24,10.13.0.0/24-
Verbose
```

3. In this step, we will configure the cloud witness. We will use the same Azure storage account nanohvcloudwitness that we created in *step 3* of the, *Creating and configuring a Hyper-V cluster* section. Please update the -AccessKey parameter with your key accordingly:

```
Set-ClusterQuorum-Cluster NANOS2D-CLU-CloudWitness -AccountName
nanohvcloudwitness-AccessKey <AccessKey>
```

4. Please refer to s*tep 11* of the *Creating and configuring a Hyper-V cluster* section to set the cluster memory dump to **Active memory dump**.

5. Please refer to *step 14* of the *Creating and configuring a Hyper-V Cluster* section to rename the cluster network names to match the function, and update the cluster network roles.

6. After we create the cluster, we will enable the cluster storage Spaces Direct, which will put the storage system into the S2D mode and do the following automatically:

   - **Create a pool**: Creates a single large pool.
   - **Configure S2D cache**: If you are using multiple device types (NVMe, SSD, or HDD), the fastest are automatically used as a cache. Each faster device binds dynamically to several slower devices, to accelerate I/O for consistent low latency. These devices do not contribute to the overall capacity, since everything stored in cache is also stored elsewhere. It's strongly recommend to have a minimum of two cache drives to preserve performance if one cache drive fails.
     - If you are using one medium type only (that is, SSD, HDD, or NVMe), you can disable the autoconfiguration of the S2D cache by adding the `AutoConfig:0` parameter to the `Enable-ClusterS2D` cmdlet; in this case, the Software Storage Bus cache will not be active and you need to configure it manually. Please note that S2D uses a combination of bus type and media type to find cache devices. You cannot use devices partially for cache and the rest for capacity. The fastest devices will be either cache or capacity.
   - **Tiers**: S2D automatically created two storage tiers (known as resiliency) a mirror tier and a parity tier. The parity tier is called capacity and the mirror tier is called performance. The `Enable-ClusterS2D` command analyzes the devices and configures each tier with the mix of device types and resiliency, in other words, the storage tier details depend on the storage devices in the system, and thus vary from system to system.

Based on the storage that we have in each node, this results in 8.0 TB of HDDs and 3.8 TB of SSDs per node without fault tolerance. If you used the auto-configuration mode when enabling S2D cluster, all the SSDs will be consumed as cache and they will not contribute to storage in the traditional sense. The storage pool will only have four disks x 4 nodes x 2 TB HDD (32 TB) of total, physical RAW capacity you can use.

In this example, the usable capacity based on four nodes, two simultaneous hardware failures, and all SSDs will be used for cache only this results in 16 TB of usable capacity across the entire storage system.

If we use all the pool's space, we could create four volumes, each with 4 TB (4 TB x 8 TB = 32 TB). The consequence, which you should be aware of, is that if you experience a drive failure, Storage Spaces will not be able to do an immediate and in-place repair, meaning it will successfully repair only after you have replaced the physical failed device. If, instead, we reserve at least 2 TB of free space in the pool, then S2D will be able to restore resiliency immediately after drives fail, even before they are replaced.

However, and based on this example, Microsoft recommend setting aside 4 TB for in-place recovery (leaving two drives' worth, but it's just a recommendation). This value is based on your chosen fault tolerance; in this example, it's two and the largest drive is 2 TB.

At certain scales, they may recommend more, because repairs are constrained to happen on the local node. The 4 TB value above includes this consideration. Please note that this is a recommended reserve and is not enforced; if you don't have enough, repairs should simply wait for the replacement drive to complete.

In this example, if we create four volumes, each with 3.5 TB instead of 4 TB, they'll occupy 7 TB of footprint on the disk each (4 TB x 7 TB = 28 TB) RAW after reserve. This will leave 4 TB for in-place repair. This results in 14 TB of usable capacity across the entire storage system.

From the management machine, open Windows PowerShell and enable S2D by running the following command:

```
# Enable Storage Spaces Direct$Cluster="NANOS2D-CLU"Enable-
ClusterStorageSpacesDirect-CimSession$Cluster
```

 You can also use the node name instead of the cluster name when enabling S2D using the previous command.

With the two storage tiers automatically created by S2D, you can now create the following volumes:

- Mirror `volumes` (performance)
- Parity volumes (capacity)
- Multi-resilient volumes (Performance, and capacity)

But before creating the volumes, let's check the supported storage size for each tier (performance, capacity) by running the following commands:

```
Get-StorageTierSupportedSize-FriendlyNamePerformance-CimSession$Cluster
|Select@{l="TierSizeMin(GB)";e={$_.TierSizeMin/1GB}},@{l="PerformanceTierSi
zeMax(TB)";e={$_.TierSizeMax/1TB}},@{l="TierSizeDivisor(GB)";e={$_.TierSize
Divisor/1GB}}Get-StorageTierSupportedSize-FriendlyNameCapacity-
CimSession$Cluster
|Select@{l="TierSizeMin(GB)";e={$_.TierSizeMin/1GB}},@{l="CapacityTierSizeM
ax(TB)";e={$_.TierSizeMax/1TB}},@{l="TierSizeDivisor(GB)";e={$_.TierSizeDiv
isor/1GB}}
```

The output will look something like this (see *Figure 18*):

```
Charbelnemnom.com #> $ClusterName = "NANOS2D-CLU"
Charbelnemnom.com #> Get-StorageTierSupportedSize -FriendlyName Performance -CimSession $ClusterName
izeMin(GB)";e={$_.TierSizeMin/1GB}}, @{l="PerformanceTierSizeMax(TB)";e={$_.TierSizeMax/1TB}}, @{l="
;e={$_.TierSizeDivisor/1GB}}

TierSizeMin(GB) PerformanceTierSizeMax(TB) TierSizeDivisor(GB)
--------------- -------------------------- -------------------
              0                          0                   0


Charbelnemnom.com #> Get-StorageTierSupportedSize -FriendlyName Capacity -CimSession $ClusterName
izeMin(GB)";e={$_.TierSizeMin/1GB}}, @{l="CapacityTierSizeMax(TB)";e={$_.TierSizeMax/1TB}}, @{l="Tie
{$_.TierSizeDivisor/1GB}}

TierSizeMin(GB) CapacityTierSizeMax(TB) TierSizeDivisor(GB)
--------------- ----------------------- -------------------
              1            18.2392578125                   1
```

Figure 18. Storage Tier Supported Size

In this example, we have 0 TB of size on the performance (mirror) tier and around 18 TB of size on the capacity (parity) tier. We will keep 4 TB as reserve for immediate and in-place repair.

 If you have four servers, you will experience more consistent performance with eight total volumes than with seven or nine. This allows the cluster to distribute volume ownership (one server handles metadata orchestration for each volume) evenly among servers.

In this example, since we have four nodes, we will create four capacity (parity) volumes, one volume per node.

From the management machine, open Windows PowerShell and run the following script:

```
# Create four Capacity Volumes 3.5 TB each$Nodes="NANOSRV-S2D01","NANOSRV-
S2D02","NANOSRV-S2D03","NANOSRV-S2D04"Foreach($Nodein$Nodes) {New-Volume-
CimSession$Node-StoragePoolFriendlyNameS2D*-FriendlyName$Node-
FileSystemCSVFS_REFS-StorageTierFriendlyNameCapacity-StorageTierSizes3.5TB}
```

You can inspect the four volumes created above by the running the following command:

```
# Inspect the volumesGet-VirtualDisk-CimSession$Cluster |Get-
StorageTier|FTFriendlyName,ResiliencySettingName,MediaType,@{l="Size(TB)";e
={$_.Size/1TB}} -autosize
```

1. In this step, we will rename the volumes to their friendly names and distribute the volumes across all nodes.
2. Open Windows PowerShell from the management machine and run the following commands:

```
# Rename Volume friendly names and mount points
accordingly$CSVFS=Get-ClusterSharedVolume-
Cluster$ClusterForeach($Volin$CSVFS)
{If($Vol.SharedVolumeInfo.FriendlyVolumeName -match'Volume\d+$') {
 If($Vol.Name -match'\((.*)\)') {
$MatchStr1=$matches[1]$mountpoint=($vol.SharedVolumeInfo.FriendlyVo
lumeName) -replace'C:','C$' $vol.Name =$MatchStr1
$OwnerNode=($vol.OwnerNode).NameRename-Item-
Path\\$OwnerNode\$mountpoint -NewName$MatchStr1 }
 }
}# Distribute the Volumes across the four
nodesForeach($Nodein$Nodes) {Get-ClusterSharedVolume-
Cluster$Cluster-Cluster $Node |Move-ClusterSharedVolume-Node$Node}
```

The result in failover cluster manager and in the file system will look something like this (see *Figure 19*):

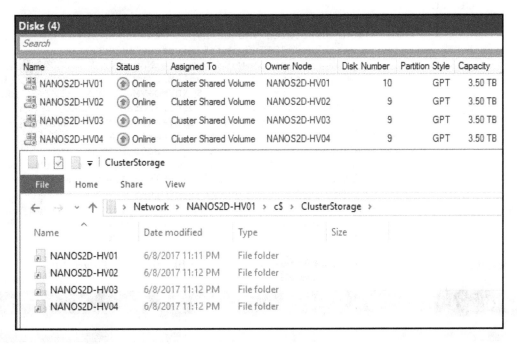

Figure 19. Failover Cluster Manager: Virtual Disks

3. In the final step, we will deploy a virtual machine on the nodes of the hyper-converged S2D cluster.

4. In this example, the virtual machine's VHDX files are stored on the clustered Shared Volume ReFS File System namespace just like clustered VMs on failover clusters. The storage cluster path is `C:\ClusterStorage\`.

5. You may use Windows PowerShell, Hyper-V Manager, or failover cluster manager tools to manage the storage and virtual machines, including System Center VMM.

6. Open Windows PowerShell from the management machine and run the following script to create a clustered VM on top of the hyperconverged S2D cluster:

```
# Create four Clustered VMs on hyper-converged S2D
cluster$vSwitchName="SETvSwitch"$Cluster="NANOS2D-
CLU"1..4|ForEach-Object{New-VM-ComputerNameNANOSRV-S2D0$_-
NameDEMO-VM0$_-MemoryStartupBytes512MB-
VHDPath"C:\ClusterStorage\vDisk0$_\DEMO-VM0$_\DEMO-VM0$_.vhdx"-
SwitchName$vSwitchName-Path"C:\ClusterStorage\vDisk0$_\"-
Generation2Set-VM-ComputerNameNANOSRV-S2D0$_-NameDEMO-VM0$_-
ProcessorCount2# Rename VM network interfaceGet-
VMNetworkAdapter-ComputerNameNANOSRV-S2D0$_-VMNameDEMO-
VM0$_|Rename-VMNetworkAdapter-NewName"vmNIC01" # Make the VM
highly availableAdd-ClusterVirtualMachineRole-Cluster$Cluster-
VMNameDEMO-VM0$_# Start Clustered VM$ClusteredVM=Get-
ClusterResource-Cluster$ClusterName|Where{$_.ResourceType -
eq"Virtual Machine"-and$_.State -eq"Offline"}Start-
ClusterResource-Cluster$Cluster -Name$ClusteredVM}
```

The result in failover cluster manager will look something like this (see *Figure 20*):

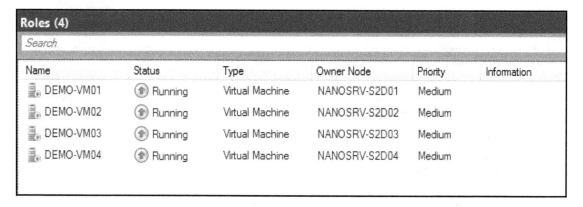

Figure 20. Failover cluster manager: virtual machines

Summary

In this chapter, we covered the required steps needed to deploy Nano Server as a compute, storage, and hyperconverged cluster using S2D technology, and an introductory overview of the following topics:

- Nano Server as a compute cluster
- Nano Server as a storage cluster

As discussed earlier in this chapter, Nano Server was created to serve as cloud fabric and infrastructure for a software-defined datacenter (Hyper-V, storage, clustering, and networking).

Continue now to `Chapter 5`, *Deploying, Managing, and Monitoring Nano Server with System Center 2016,* to learn more about how to manage and monitor Nano Server with System Center 2016 Virtual Machine Manager and System Center 2016 Operations Manager.

5
Deploying, Managing, and Monitoring Nano Server with System Center 2016

In Chapter 4, *Deploying Hyper-V Cluster on Nano Server*, we covered how to create a Hyper-V cluster on top of a Nano Server installation and we also covered Hyper-converged deployment with Nano Server and Storage Spaces Direct.

As discussed in this book, there are a variety of ways you can deploy and manage a Nano Server installation. However, System Center 2016 plays a vital role in deploying, managing, and monitoring a large Nano Server deployment at scale.

In this chapter, we will cover the following topics:

- Deploying Nano Server with System Center Virtual Machine Manager 2016
- Managing Nano Server with System Center Virtual Machine Manager 2016
- Monitoring Nano Server with System Center Virtual Machine Manager 2016

Deploying Nano Server with system center virtual machine manager 2016

If you are familiar with **System Center Virtual Machine Manager** (**SCVMM**) deployment methods, Nano Server deployment is mainly the same compared to Server with Desktop Experience and Server Core. The user experience with Nano Server using the SCVMM console is completely the same, except for bare-metal (physical machine) and server-based VM domain join deployment. The virtual hard disk VHD(X) you want to use for the physical computer profiles will be a Nano Server VHD(X) including SCVMM packages.

In this section, we will cover how to deploy Nano Server as a Hyper-V host in VMM using bare-metal deployment, and we will also cover how to deploy domain-join Nano Server as a virtual machine using VM templates.

VMM bare-metal deployment

The procedures in this section describe how to use VMM to discover physical computers on the network, automatically install Nano Server, and provision the computers into managed Hyper-V hosts or host clusters.

This section will also describe how to create a Nano Server VHD(X) image for bare-metal deployment using the pre-installed device drivers. We need to create a VHD(X) that includes the OEM drivers, storage, and failover clustering features, including SCVMM packages, and enable remote management and emergency management services. If your hardware needs a specific set of drivers that are not included in the OEM drivers (for example to boot or connect to a network), then you need to use the `-DriversPath` parameter and add the needed drivers to the image.

Preparing a Nano Server VHD(X) for a physical machine

Before you start deploying Nano Server to a bare-metal machine, you need to make sure the following packages are added to the Nano Server image that we will use in the steps that follow.

The packages are listed in the following order:

1. Adding the SCVMM package, `Microsoft-NanoServer-SCVMM-Package`, will ensure that the VMM agent is part of the image.
2. Adding the SCVMM compute package, `Microsoft-NanoServer-SCVMM-Compute-Package`, will ensure that the image has the Hyper-V role enabled and you can manage the physical host using SCVMM.
3. For the File Server role, use `-Storage` along with `Microsoft-NanoServer-SCVMM-Package`.
4. For the clustering feature, use `-Clustering` along with `Microsoft-NanoServer-SCVMM-Package`.
5. For the Hyper-Converged model, use `-Storage` and `-Clustering` along with `Microsoft-NanoServer-SCVMM-Package` and `Microsoft-NanoServer-SCVMM-Compute-Package`.

 `Microsoft-NanoServer-SCVMM-Compute-Package`: Includes services for monitoring a Hyper-V host using SCVMM `Microsoft-NanoServer-SCVMM-Package`: Includes services for monitoring a physical or virtual machine using SCVMM

If you install `Microsoft-NanoServer-SCVMM-Compute-Package`, then do not use the `-Compute` parameter for the Hyper-V role, because this server will be managed by VMM and already has the compute option added by the SCVMM compute package.

It's very important to add the packages in the right order as shown in the example below or the deployment will fail.

The following steps will illustrate this process:

1. Mount the Windows Server 2016 ISO medium on your machine. In this example, it's mounted under the H drive.
2. Start Windows PowerShell as an administrator, and run the following script to create a VHD for physical machine deployment that includes the SCVMM packages. You will be prompted for an administrator password:

```
#region variables$ComputerName='NANOSRV-HV01'# Staging path
for new Nano image$StagingPath='C:\'# Path to Windows Server
2016 ISO file $MediaPath='H:\'$DriverPath='C:\NanoServer\HPE-
Drivers'$Path=Join-Path-Path$StagingPath-
ChildPathNanoServer$Password=Read-Host-Prompt"Please specify
local Administrator password"-AsSecureString#endregion #region
Copy source filesif(-not(Test-Path$StagingPath)) {
```

```
   mkdir$StagingPath
}if(-not(Test-Path$Path)) {

  $NanoServerSourcePath=Join-Path-Path$MediaPath-
ChildPathNanoServer-Resolve Copy-Item-
Path$NanoServerSourcePath-Destination$StagingPath-Recurse}
#endregion #region Generate Nano ImageImport-Module-Name(Join-
Path-Path$Path-ChildPathNanoServerImageGenerator) -Verbose
$ServicingPackagePath=@(
  'C:\NanoServer\Updates\Servicing stack update\Windows10.0-
kb3211320-x64.msu' 'C:\NanoServer\Updates\Cumulative
Update\Windows10.0-kb3213986-x64.msu')
  $NanoServerImageParameters=@{

  ComputerName =$ComputerName MediaPath =$MediaPath BasePath
=(Join-Path-Path$Path-ChildPath$ComputerName)
  # .vhd for BIOS and .vhdx for UEFI system TargetPath =Join-
Path-Path$Path-ChildPath($ComputerName+'.vhd')
  AdministratorPassword =$Password Clustering =$true Package
='Microsoft-NanoServer-Storage-Package','Microsoft-NanoServer-
SCVMM-Package','Microsoft-NanoServer-SCVMM-Compute-Package'
OEMDrivers =$true DriverPath =$DriverPath
EnableRemoteManagementPort =$true EnableEMS =$true
DeploymentType ='Host' Edition ='Datacenter'
ServicingPackagePath =$ServicingPackagePath}
  New-NanoServerImage@NanoServerImageParameters-
Verbose#endregion
```

The previous script will create a VHD image file using the Windows Server 2016 ISO
mounted as H:\ drive. When creating the VHD, it uses a folder called NanoServer located
on the root C drive. The VHD file is placed under the same folder and called NANOSRV-HV01.
In this example, the computer name is set to NANOSRV-HV01 including the OEM drivers and
external drivers for HPE ProLiant servers. If the server uses UEFI to boot instead of BIOS,
then you need to change NANOSRV-HV01.vhd to NANOSRV-HV01.vhdx. We enabled the
remote management port and EMS. Finally, we added the latest Windows Server updates.

 If you forgot to add the SCVMM packages while creating the Nano Server
image, you can add them later using online or offline methods. More on
that in the next section.

Copy the VHD image to the VMM library.

Add a **Preboot Execution Environment** (PXE) Server to the VMM fabric by carrying out the following steps:

1. Click **Fabric|Servers|Add|Add Resources|PXE Server.**
2. In **Computer name** specify the PXE server name as shown in *Figure 1.*
3. Add the credentials for an account that has local administrator permissions on the WDS server.
4. In the **Jobs** view verify that the job status is **Completed** successfully. Verify that the PXE server is added in **Fabric| Servers|PXE Servers|Home|Show|Fabric Resources|PXE Servers**. The agent status should be **Responding**.

PXE is a specification that defines how a client-server environment boots from network software on a client. It needs standard network protocols, such as DHCP and TFTP. In this example, we will use **Windows Deployment Services (WDS)**: a server technology made by Microsoft for the network-based installation of Windows operating systems.

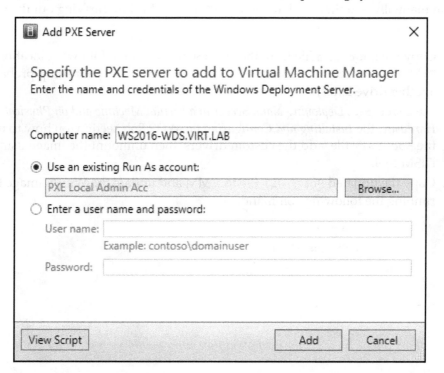

Figure 1. Adding PXE Server in virtual machine manager

When you install Windows deployment services you should install both the deployment server and transport server options. You don't need to add any images to WDS. During host deployment, VMM uses the virtual hard disk that we've created earlier and is stored in the VMM library. In addition, you don't need to configure any settings on the PXE Response tab. VMM offers its own PXE provider.

The PXE (WDS) server must be in the same subnet as the physical Nano Servers that you want to provision.

When you add a PXE server into VMM, you must specify an account that has local administrator permissions on the PXE (WDS) server. You can enter a user name and password or specify a run as account predefined in VMM.

If your new physical server needs special drivers, your Windows Server image may not include those drivers, the bare-metal deployment will fail due to not being able to connect to the network since the WinPE image does not include those drivers; therefore you need to inject them manually and then update the `WinPE` file in VMM by carrying out the following steps:

1. Copy the `Boot.wim` file from the WDS server from the following location: `E:\RemoteInstall\DCMgr\Boot\WIndows\Images` (your setup probably has another drive letter).
2. See `Chapter 3`, *Deploying Nano Server in a Virtual Machine and on Physical Hardware*, the *Installing and Configuring the WDS Role* section, on how to mount the `Boot.wim` file, add the custom drivers, then unmount the image using the DISM tool.
3. Copy the updated `Boot.wim` file to VMM and update the WinPE image by running the following command:

```
Publish-SCWindowsPE -Path D:\Boot.wim
```

Create a physical computer profile using the VHD generated earlier by carrying out the following steps:

1. Click **Library | Home | Create | Physical Computer Profile**.
2. In the **New Physical Computer Profiles Wizard | Profile Description**, type in a name and description and select **VM host**.
3. In OS **Image | Virtual hard disk file | Browse**, click the generalized Nano Server VHD that you added to the VMM library share as shown in *Figure 2*:

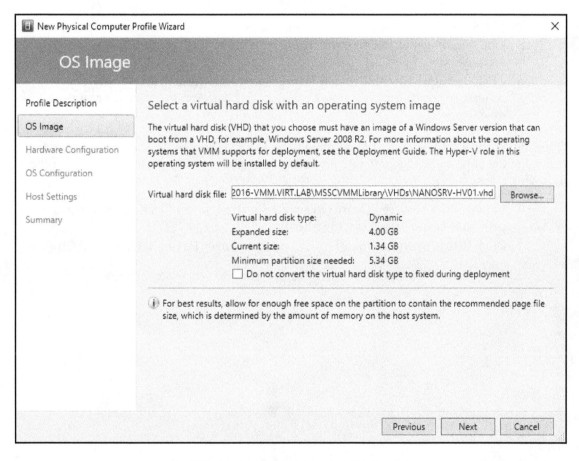

Figure 2. The wizard for creating a physical computer profile for Nano Server

4. If you are using VHDX for UEFI systems, and you are wondering why the image is not shown when you browse to choose a VHD, then you need to make sure that you specify and label the OS image in VMM library as Windows Server 2016 (standard or datacenter).

5. In **Hardware Configuration | Management NIC** select the network adapter you'll use to communicate with VMM and whether to use DHCP or a static address.

6. In **Disk and Partitions**, specify the partitioning scheme for the first disk. In this example, we are using MBR because the physical computer profile is BIOS. You can use GPT for UEFI systems.

7. In **OS Configuration** specify the domain that the Nano physical computer should join including **Run As account**. Specify the credentials for the local administrator account.

8. Click through to complete the wizard. You've now constructed a physical computer profile that you can use to deploy Nano Server on a bare-metal machine.

Once the physical computer profile is created and the PXE Server is added, you can now provision the bare-metal machine into a managed Nano Hyper-V host by carrying out the following steps:

1. In the **Add Resource Wizard | Resource location**, select **Physical computers to be provisioned as virtual machine hosts**.

2. Click **Fabric Servers | Home | Add | Add Resources | Hyper-V Hosts and Clusters**.

3. In **Credentials and Protocol** select **Run As account** with permissions to access the **Baseboard Management Controller** (**BMC**) of your server (please refer to your hardware vendor). In the **Protocol** list, click the out-of-band management protocol that your BMCs use as shown in *Figure 3*:

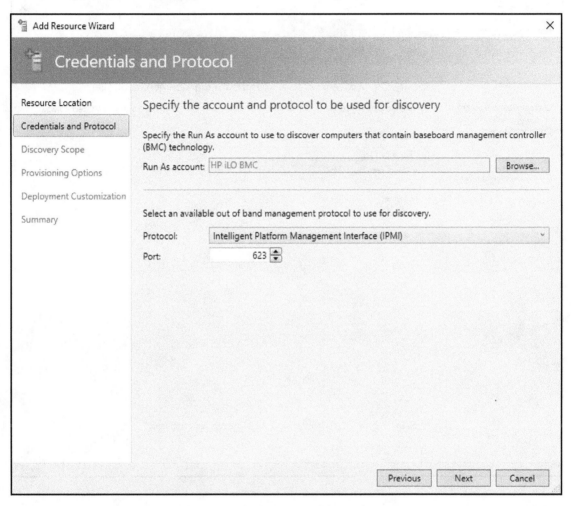

Figure 3. The wizard for adding resource: Credentials and Protocol

4. In **Discovery Scope**, specify the IP address scope that includes the IP addresses of the BMCs as shown in *Figure 4*. You can enter a single IP address, an IP subnet, or an IP address range. Select **Skip deep discovery**:

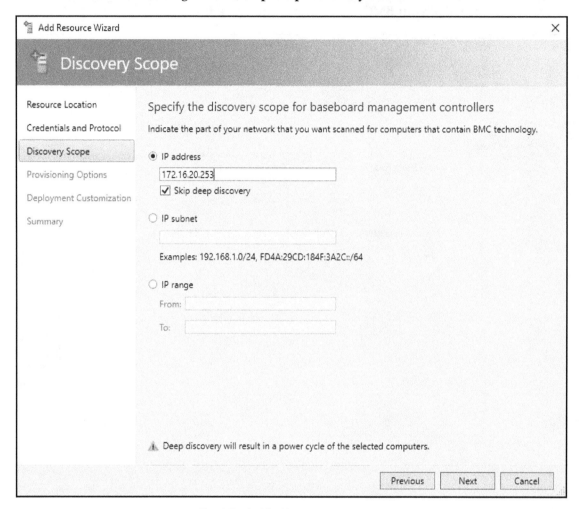

Figure 4. The wizard for adding resource: Discovery Scope

5. In **Provisioning Options**, click a host group for new Nano host(s) in this example the host group is named **Nano**. Select the physical computer profile that we created earlier as shown in *Figure 5*:

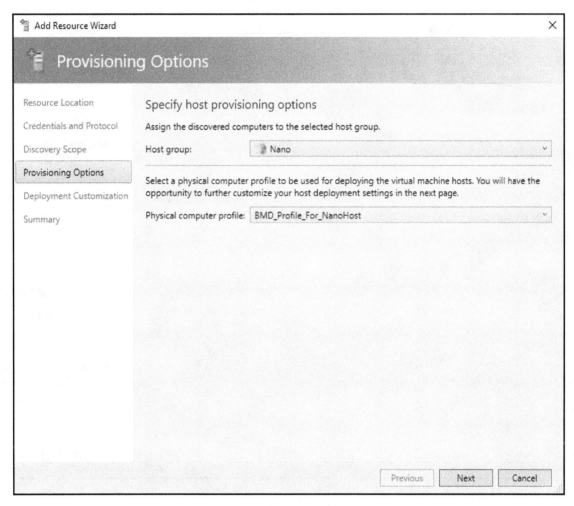

Figure 5. The wizard for adding resource: Provisioning Options

6. In **Deployment Customization**, enter the **Computer Name** and **Network Adapters** details as shown in *Figure 6*:

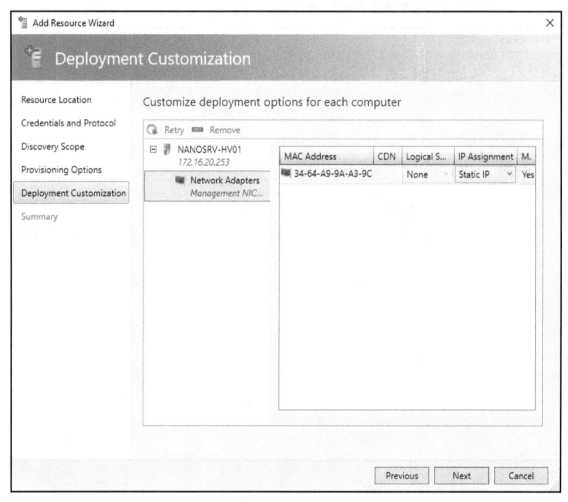

Figure 6. The wizard for adding resource: Deployment Customization

7. Click **Next** to complete the wizard. In **Summary**, confirm the settings as shown in *Figure 7*, and then click **Finish** to deploy the new Nano Server on a physical machine and bring it under VMM management:

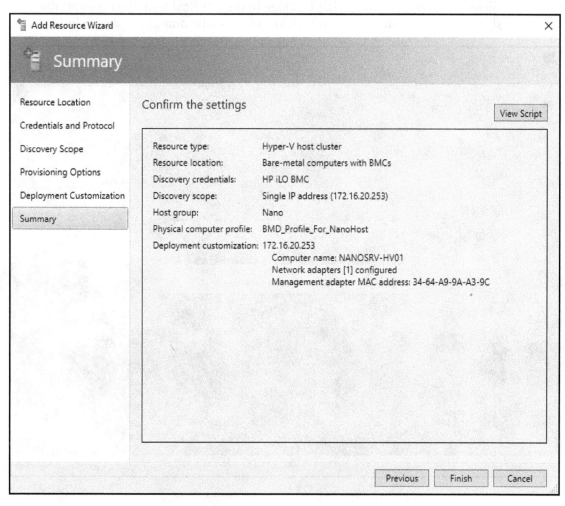

Figure 7. The wizard for adding resource: Summary

8. Deploying Nano Server on a bare-metal machine can take a while, as long as 15-25 minutes on some hardware. Behind the scenes, VMM will power/reboot the physical machine and wait to PXE boot, then it will format and create partition disks, transfer the Nano VHD(X) image to the physical host, then convert the dynamic VHD(X) to fixed VHD(X) and join it to the domain as shown in *Figure 8*:

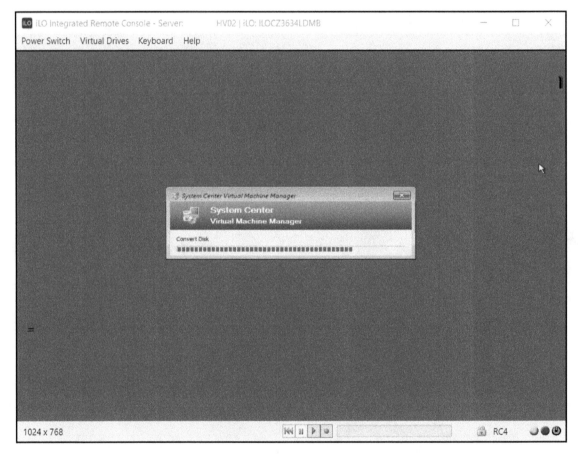

Figure 8. The wizard for adding resource: Summary

9. You can also view the job named `Create a new host from physical machine` in **VMM Jobs** view to inspect the complete deployment details (see *Figure 9*):

Step		Name	Status	Start Time	End Time
▶	⊟ 1	Create a new host from physical machine: NANOSRV-HV01 (BMC address: 172.16.19.22)	▮▮ 32 %	02-Feb-2017 4:27:14 AM	
✓	1.1	Create undeployed host	Completed	02-Feb-2017 4:27:14 AM	02-Feb-2017 4:27:14 AM
▶	⊟ 1.2	Provision physical computer: NANOSRV-HV01 (BMC address: 172.16.19.22)	▮▮▮▮▮▮▮ 96 %	02-Feb-2017 4:27:14 AM	
✓	1.2.1	Retrieving physical machine information	Completed	02-Feb-2017 4:27:14 AM	02-Feb-2017 4:27:14 AM
✓	1.2.2	Preparing the physical machine to boot/reboot	Completed	02-Feb-2017 4:27:14 AM	02-Feb-2017 4:27:14 AM
✓	1.2.3	Power on the physical machine using BMC	Completed	02-Feb-2017 4:27:14 AM	02-Feb-2017 4:27:32 AM
✓	1.2.4	Waiting for physical machine to PXE boot	Completed	02-Feb-2017 4:27:32 AM	02-Feb-2017 4:38:24 AM
✓	1.2.5	Process physical machine information	Completed	02-Feb-2017 4:38:24 AM	02-Feb-2017 4:38:24 AM
✓	1.2.6	Determine which custom code to run at this point	Completed	02-Feb-2017 4:38:24 AM	02-Feb-2017 4:38:24 AM
✓	1.2.7	Determine the boot disk location	Completed	02-Feb-2017 4:38:24 AM	02-Feb-2017 4:38:24 AM
✓	1.2.8	Format and partition disks	Completed	02-Feb-2017 4:38:24 AM	02-Feb-2017 4:38:39 AM
✓	1.2.9	Transfer VHD	Completed	02-Feb-2017 4:38:39 AM	02-Feb-2017 4:38:59 AM
✓	1.2.10	Convert Dynamic VHD to Fixed VHD	Completed	02-Feb-2017 4:39:00 AM	02-Feb-2017 4:39:40 AM
✓	1.2.11	Retrieve information about the OS being deployed	Completed	02-Feb-2017 4:39:40 AM	02-Feb-2017 4:39:40 AM
✓	1.2.12	Setup boot from native VHD	Completed	02-Feb-2017 4:39:40 AM	02-Feb-2017 4:39:45 AM
✓	1.2.13	Install matching drivers	Completed	02-Feb-2017 4:39:45 AM	02-Feb-2017 4:39:45 AM
✓	1.2.14	Deploy OS customization scripts	Completed	02-Feb-2017 4:39:45 AM	02-Feb-2017 4:39:48 AM
✓	1.2.15	Enable Multipath I/O feature	Completed	02-Feb-2017 4:39:48 AM	02-Feb-2017 4:39:51 AM
✓	1.2.16	Setup OS customization scripts	Completed	02-Feb-2017 4:39:51 AM	02-Feb-2017 4:39:52 AM
▶	1.2.17	Wait for physical machine to reboot and customization to be finished	▮▮▮ 44 %	02-Feb-2017 4:39:52 AM	
	1.3	Install Virtual Machine Manager agent	Not started		
	1.4	Run post-unattend script commands on 'NANOSRV-HV01'	Not started		
	1.5	Refresh host	Not started		
	1.6	Configure host created from physical machine	Not started		

Figure 9. This is how your bare metal Nano Server deployment job should look

10. To confirm that the host was added in VMM, click **Fabric | Servers | All Hosts |** host group, and verify that the new Nano host appears in the group.

VMM VM template deployment

The procedures in this section describe how to use SCVMM to deploy a Nano Server-based VM domain joined using VMM VM templates on top of a Windows Server 2016 Hyper-V host managed by SCVMM 2016 with update rollup 2.

This section will also describe how to create the Nano Server VHD(X) file to be used with VM templates using the pre-installed guest drivers. First, we need to create a VHD(X) image with the deployment type as **Guest**, including the container package and SCVMM packages, and enable the remote management port.

Preparing a Nano Server VHD for a virtual machine

When you start planning to deploy Nano Server-based virtual machines, you need to make sure the following packages are added into the Nano Server image that we will use in the steps that follow.

Follow the steps mentioned below to create a VHD(X) image for a virtual machine:

1. Mount the Windows Server 2016 ISO medium on your machine. In this example, it's mounted in the H drive.

2. Start Windows PowerShell as an administrator, and run the following script to create a VHD(X) for virtual machine deployment that includes the SCVMM packages. You will be prompted for an administrator password:

```
#region variables$ComputerName='NANOVM-01'# Staging path for
new Nano image$StagingPath='C:\'# Path to Windows Server 2016
ISO file $MediaPath='H:\'$Path=Join-Path-Path$StagingPath-
ChildPathNanoServer$Password=Read-Host-Prompt"Please specify
local Administrator password"-AsSecureString#endregion #region
Copy source filesif(-not(Test-Path$StagingPath)) {

 mkdir$StagingPath
}if(-not(Test-Path$Path)) {

 $NanoServerSourcePath=Join-Path-Path$MediaPath-
ChildPathNanoServer-Resolve Copy-Item-
Path$NanoServerSourcePath-Destination$StagingPath-Recurse}
#endregion #region Generate Nano ImageImport-Module-Name(Join-
Path-Path$Path-ChildPathNanoServerImageGenerator) -Verbose
$ServicingPackagePath=@(
 'C:\NanoServer\Updates\Servicing stack update\Windows10.0-
kb3211320-x64.msu' 'C:\NanoServer\Updates\Cumulative
Update\Windows10.0-kb3216755-x64.msu')
 $NanoServerImageParameters=@{

 ComputerName =$ComputerName MediaPath =$MediaPath BasePath
=(Join-Path-Path$Path-ChildPath$ComputerName)
 # .vhd for Gen1 VM and .vhdx for Gen2 VM TargetPath =Join-
Path-Path$Path-ChildPath($ComputerName+'.vhdx')
 AdministratorPassword =$Password Containers =$true Package
='Microsoft-NanoServer-SCVMM-Package','Microsoft-NanoServer-
SCVMM-Compute-Package' EnableRemoteManagementPort =$true
DeploymentType ='Guest' Edition ='Standard'
ServicingPackagePath =$ServicingPackagePath}
 New-NanoServerImage@NanoServerImageParameters#endregion
```

The previous script will create a VHDX image file using the Windows Server 2016 ISO mounted as `H:\` drive. When creating the image, it uses a folder called `NanoServer` located on the `root C` drive. The file is placed in the same folder called `NANOVM-01`. In this example, the computer name is set to `NANOVM-01` and includes guest drivers. We will deploy a generation 2 virtual machine; for this reason we created the image as VHDX. We enabled the remote management port, and finally we added the latest Windows Server updates.

We also added the SCVMM package, `Microsoft-NanoServer-SCVMM-Package`, to ensure that the VMM agent is available as part of an image, so you can manage the VM using VMM.

The SCVMM compute package, `Microsoft-NanoServer-SCVMM-Compute-Package`, will ensure that the image has the Hyper-V role enabled, so you can use Hyper-V nested virtualization.

The container package, `Microsoft-NanoServer-Containers-Package` will ensure that the image has the container role so you can deploy Windows Server containers and Hyper-V Containers; more on that in `Chapter 8`, *Running Windows Server Containers and Hyper-V Containers on Nano Server*.

Once the image is created, you need to copy it to VMM and refresh the library.

In virtual machine manager console, you need to create a new virtual machine template and use the VHD(X) created earlier. Click through the wizard; in the **Configure Operating System** page, please give the other information as needed and make sure you select the checkbox next to **Nano Server-based VM deployment** as shown in *Figure 10*. This will make sure Nano VM will join the domain during the deployment:

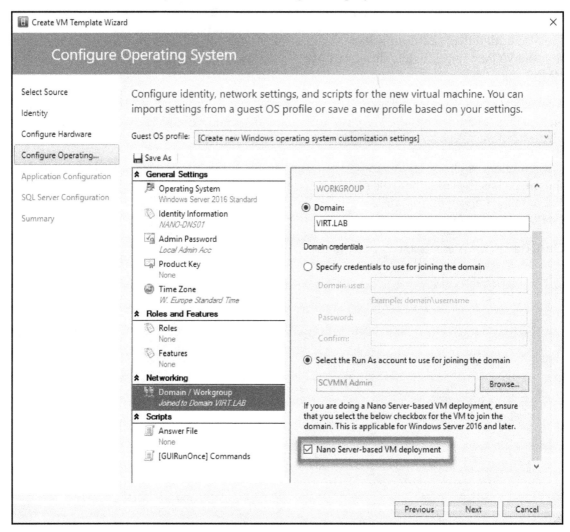

Figure 10. The wizard for Creating VM Template: Configure operating system

With the VM template ready, you can start deploying Nano VMs in same way as if you were deploying Server with desktop experience or Server Core. The deployment will take a couple of minutes since the VHD(X) image is very small. Behind the scenes, VMM will create an offline domain join object (`Blob`) for Nano VM and then apply that object to the Nano image in offline mode. When the virtual machine boots up for the first time, it picks the offline setting and joins the domain automatically as shown in *Figure 11*:

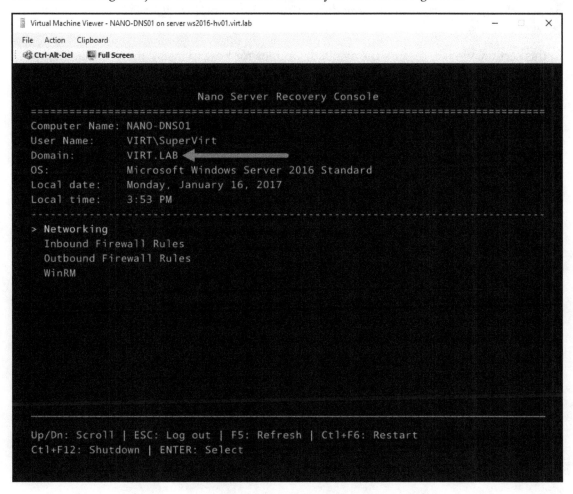

Figure 11. Nano Server-based VM deployment and domain joined

Managing Nano Server with system center virtual machine manager 2016

Managing Nano Server using virtual machine manager is like managing any other installation of Hyper-V Server with Desktop Experience, Server Core, and free Hyper-V Server. However, there are some key differences in how you install VMM agent on Nano Server.

In this section, we will discuss the available options for how to install the VMM agent; we will also discuss how to manage network teaming on Nano Server.

Installing the virtual machine manager agent on Nano Server

There are three methods available for installing the VMM agent on Nano Servers:

Nano Server Image Builder is a UI tool that will help you to build an installation image that you can use to deploy Nano Server for either Windows Server 2016 datacenter or Standard editions. The wizard creates an installation image starting with a standard source image without any role, and then you can customize it for your deployment; in this case you will add the VMM package as part of your image creation (pre-deployment option).

As shown in *Figure 12*, the wizard will also help you to create a USB bootable medium to install Nano Server on a machine ready for reimaging. This wizard will package your Nano Server information with the drivers and packages you have selected and create a single partition so you can easily install it on your server.

See `Chapter 2`, *Getting Started with Nano Server*, for more information about Nano Server image builder:

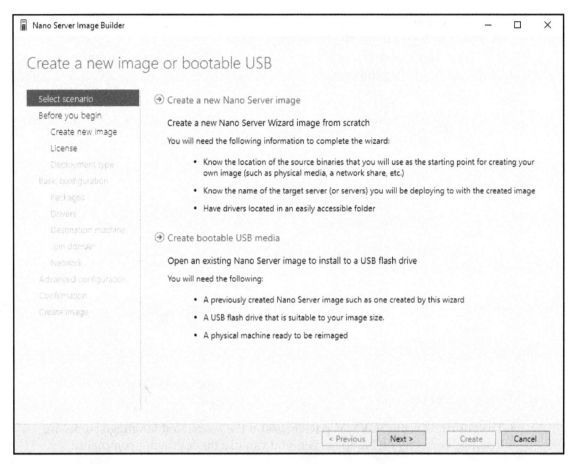

Figure 12. Nano Server image builder

The second method is manual agent installation, so users can run the PowerShell script as described at the beginning of this chapter to include the SCVMM package while creating the VHD(X) image, which is the recommended way. However, you might also need to install the VMM agent online (while Nano Server is running). To do so, follow these steps:

1. Copy the SCVMM Packages folder from the installation medium locally to the running Nano Server (for example, to C:\vmmpackages) using the following commands:

```
$NanoIP="172.16.19.21"$Cred=Get-
Credential"Domain\SuperNano"$Session=New-PSSession-
ComputerName$NanoIP-Credential$CredCopy-Item-
PathE:\vmmpackages-DestinationC:\vmmpackages-ToSession$Session
```

2. Use remote PowerShell to connect to a Nano Server-based host, and add the SCVMM packages using the following commands:

- To install `Microsoft-NanoServer-SCVMM-Package` use the following command:

```
dism /online /Add-package
/PackagePath:C:\vmmpackages\en-US\Microsoft-NanoServer-
SCVMM-Package_en-us.cab
```

```
dism /online /Add-package
/PackagePath:C:\vmmpackages\Microsoft-NanoServer-SCVMM-
Package.cab
```

- To install `Microsoft-NanoServer-SCVMM-Compute-Package` use the following command:

```
dism /online /Add-package /PackagePath:C:\vmmpackages\en-
US\Microsoft-NanoServer-SCVMM-Compute-Package_en-us.cab
```

```
dism /online /Add-package
/PackagePath:C:\vmmpackages\Microsoft-NanoServer-SCVMM-Compute-
Package.cab
```

- To confirm that the SCVMM packages and the associated language packs are installed correctly on Nano Server, you can use the following command:

```
dism /online /get-packages
```

Once the SCVMM packages are installed on a running Nano Server, you need to restart the server.

In this example, we are using system center virtual machine manager 2016 update rollup 2. If you are familiar with system center updates, Microsoft regularly releases update rollups every quarter or so. As of this writing, it's not possible to update the Nano Host agents directly from VMM console; in other words, there is currently no push-based installation of VMM agents. The update for the VMM agent will be pushed as part of the Nano ongoing cadence updates.

The third method is using Nano Server PowerShell package management. The Nano Server package provider is part of the package management (aka OneGet) PowerShell module. More information on OneGet can be found at `http://www.oneget.org/`.

A package management provider is an online repository supported by Microsoft. It requires that Nano Server has access to the Internet.

To install Nano Server packages from the online package repository by using the Nano Server package provider, please carry out the following. In this example, we are interested in installing the SCVMM packages only (you can install any package you want):

```
# Variables$NanoIP="172.16.19.21"$Session=New-PSSession-
ComputerName$NanoIP-credential"Domain\SuperNano"#region Install
NanoServer Roles and Features$Session|Enter-PSSessionSet-Location/#
Download Nano Server Package moduleSet-PSRepository-Name'PSGallery'-
InstallationPolicyTrustedInstall-Module-NameNanoServerPackage-
MinimumVersion1.0.1.0Import-PackageProviderNanoServerPackage-Verbose#
Find all available online Nano packages (en-us Language)Find-Package-
ProviderNameNanoServerPackage-cultureen-us# Filter SCVMM PackagesFind-
Package-ProviderNameNanoServerPackage-cultureen-us|Where-Object{$_.Name
-like"*SCVMM*"}# Install SCVMM package that depends on other packages
with a single command.# In this case, the dependency packages will be
installed as well.# Microsoft-NanoServer-SCVMM-Package, Microsoft-
NanoServer-Compute-Package, Microsoft-NanoServer-SCVMM-Compute-
PackageFind-NanoServerPackage*scvmm-compute*|install-package-
Force|Format-Table-AutoSize# Search for all Windows Packages installed
on the local machine.Get-Package-ProviderNameNanoServerPackage-
DisplayCulture|Format-Table-AutoSizeRestart-Computer#endregion
```

Once the SCVMM packages are added to the image using one of the methods described previously. You can then add Nano Server to VMM using Add resource wizard in the same way that you add a regular Windows server. For more information, please check the Add Windows servers as Hyper-V hosts or clusters in the VMM compute fabric topic on TechNet:

`https://technet.microsoft.com/en-us/system-center-docs/vmm/manage/manage-compute-add-existing-servers`.

Managing network teaming on Nano Server

In Windows Server 2016, Microsoft introduced a new type of networking teaming solution called **Switch Embedded Teaming** (**SET**) that is virtualization aware.

If you have deployed LBFO teaming solutions in Windows Server 2012/R2, SET is different from LBFO:

- SET needs to have the Hyper-V role enabled, because it's embedded into the Hyper-V virtual switch, which leads to a couple of results. Firstly, you don't have any team interfaces on the host anymore, you won't be able to build anything extra on top of it, you can't set a property on the team because it's part of the virtual switch, and thus all the properties are set directly on the Hyper-V virtual switch.
- SET is targeted to support **Software-Defined Networking** (**SDN**) switch capabilities.
- SET is specifically integrated with converged RDMA vNIC and SDN-QoS, and it's only supported in Nano Server; however, the LBFO teaming solution is not supported in Nano Server.

For more information about SET, you can read the NIC teaming Deployment guide for Windows Server 2016 which can be downloaded from the TechNet gallery:

`https://gallery.technet.microsoft.com/Windows-Server-2016-839cb607.`

This guide has authoritative content on SET and is updated regularly.

In the following procedures, we will show you how to create SET in SCVMM and deploy it on Nano Server, assuming you have a good understanding about the network fabric in VMM (logical network, VM networks, uplink port profile, logical switch, and IP address pool).

For more information about managing VMM network resources, please check the following article:

`https://technet.microsoft.com/en-us/system-center-docs/vmm/manage/managing-n`
`etwork-resources-with-vmm.`

Open VMM console and follow these steps:

1. Navigate to the **Fabric** workspace, right click on **Logical Switches**, and select **Create Logical Switch**.
2. At the **General** page, as shown in *Figure 13*, you can select **Embedded Team** in **Uplink mode**. Click **Next**:

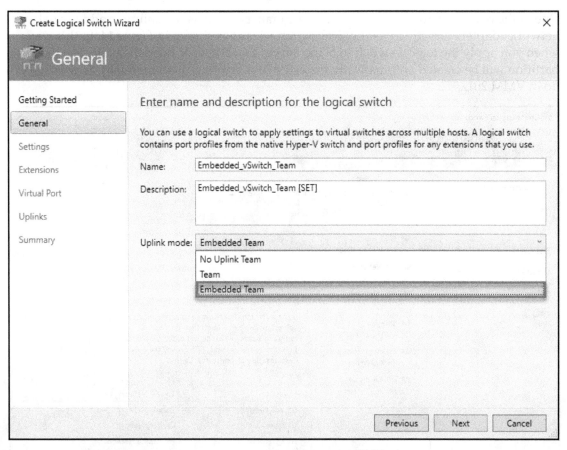

Figure 13. The wizard for creating logical switch in VMM: Uplink mode

3. At the **Settings** page, leave **Minimum bandwidth** mode at the default: **Weight**. Click **Next**.

4. On the **Extensions** page, click **Next**.

5. On the **Virtual Port** page, click **Add** and specify the port classifications for virtual ports that will be part of this logical switch.

6. At the **Uplinks** page, add an existing uplink port profile or create a new one.

One of the newest features in virtual machine manager 2016 is the ability to add virtual network adapters directly in the Logical switch wizard as shown in *Figure 14*. In this way, when you apply the logical switch to Nano Server as a Hyper-V host, the vNICs on the host partition will be created automatically instead of our creating them manually as we used to do in VMM 2012/R2:

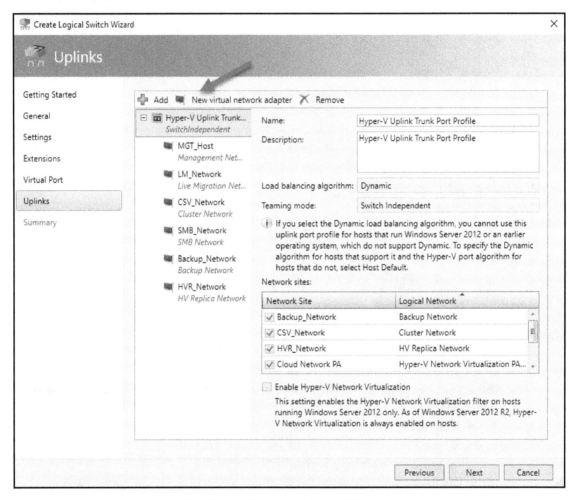

Figure 14. The wizard for creating logical switch in VMM: Uplinks

Once the logical switch is created, you can start deploying it by going to the properties of the Nano Hyper-V host: **Virtual Switches|New Virtual Switch|New Logical Switch**. Choose the embedded team logical switch that you just created as shown in *Figure 15*, and then click **OK**:

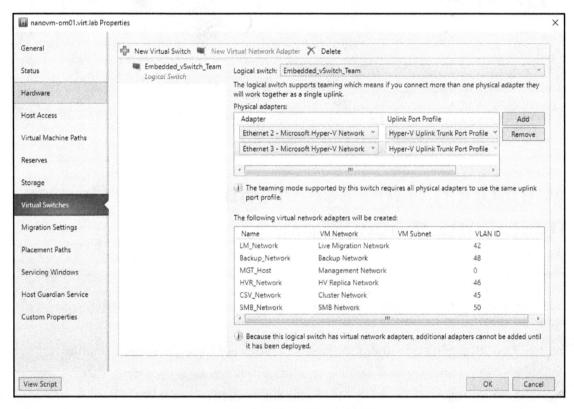

Figure 15. Deploy switch embedded teaming in VMM

Once the logical switch is created successfully, you can use PowerShell remoting and verify that SET is created successfully on Nano Server by running the following command:

```
Get-
VMSwitch|FLName,Extensions,BandwidthReservationMode,PacketDirctEnabled,Embe
ddedTeamingEnabled,IovEnabled,SwitchType,AllowManagementOS,NetAdapterInterf
aceDescription
```

The `EmbeddedTeamingEnabled` property is set to `True` as shown in Figure 16:

```
Charbelnemnom.com #> Get-VMSwitch -Name Embedded_vSwitch_Team | FL Name, Extensions, BandwidthReservationMode, PacketDir
ectEnabled, EmbeddedTeamingEnabled, IovEnabled, SwitchType, AllowManagementOS, NetAdapterInterfaceDescription


Name                         : Embedded_vSwitch_Team
Extensions                   : {Microsoft Windows Filtering Platform, Microsoft VMM DHCPv4 Server Switch Extension,
                               Windows Azure VFP Switch Extension, Microsoft NDIS Capture}
BandwidthReservationMode     : Weight
PacketDirectEnabled          : False
EmbeddedTeamingEnabled       : True  <------
IovEnabled                   : False
SwitchType                   : External
AllowManagementOS            : True
NetAdapterInterfaceDescription : Teamed-Interface
```

Figure 16. Embedded teaming is enabled

Monitoring Nano Server with System Center operations manager 2016

With system center 2016 operations manager you can now monitor Nano Server installations in a similar way to monitoring any other installation of Windows Server 2016 (Server with Desktop Experience, Server Core and Nano Server) by installing the operations manager agent. However, there are some key differences in how you install the agent on a Nano Server that we will cover in this section.

With SCOM 2016, you can monitor the basic operations of Nano Server by using the Windows Server 2016 operating system management pack.

Please note that Nano Server monitoring is supported only by SCOM 2016.

You can also monitor a Nano Server running the following workloads:

- Nano Server base OS
- Failover clusters including Nano Server cluster disk health, Nano Server cluster shared volume health, Nano Server cluster disk capacity, Nano Server cluster shared volume disk capacity, and Nano Server duplicated cluster disk
- **Domain Name System (DNS)** server
- **Internet Information Services (IIS)** server

You can download management packs for Windows Server 2016 including Nano support, from the following links:

- **Windows Server 2016 OS**: `https://www.microsoft.com/en-us/download/details.aspx?id=54303`
- **Windows Failover cluster**: `https://www.microsoft.com/en-us/download/details.aspx?id=54701`
- **DNS server**: `https://www.microsoft.com/en-us/download/details.aspx?id=54524`
- **IIS server**: `https://www.microsoft.com/en-us/download/details.aspx?id=54445`

The audit agent for sending and collecting security event logs is also supported on the monitored Nano Server. In Windows Server 2016, Microsoft added support for **Audit Collection Services**; the Audit Agent can send and collect security event logs, so allACS features will work fine as they used to work with full servers.

For more information about collecting security events using audit collection services in operations manager, please check the following article:

`https://technet.microsoft.com/en-us/system-center-docs/om/deploy/how-to-install-an-audit-collection-services-acs-collector-and-database.`

Installing the operations manager agent on Nano Server

Patching and life cycle management for Nano agents is supported from SCOM 2016 RTM onwards. You will not need additional management packs for this. The user can update the Nano agent from a patched management server, or you can download Nano updates and install them locally by running the update PowerShell script (more on that in a bit).

 Active directory integration is not supported for Nano agents. In other words, you cannot enable SCOM agents to query for secondary management servers/groups in the event a primary management server failed. Active directory integration is only supported for Server with desktop experience and Server Core.

The operations manager agent depends on the reverse forwarders package, which is now included by default in every Nano image.

Reverse Forwarders is a new technology that enables a subset of desktop Win32 binaries to run on Nano Server without recompilation.

Follow the instructions described at the beginning of this chapter on creating and installing Nano Server on either a physical or virtual machine.

Before you start deploying the SCOM agent, you need to make sure you join Nano Server to the same domain as the operations manager management Server.

There are two methods available for installing the operations manager agent on Nano Servers:

- Push-based installation of SCOM agents. The discovery wizard from the operations console can be used to find Nano Servers and install the agent. SCOM 2016 can now automatically discover Nano Server, Server with Desktop Experience, or Server Core of Windows Server 2016. Right now, we have two versions of the agent, one is for the Server with Desktop Experience, Server Core, and the second one is specifically tailored for Nano Server, the pushed-based agent installation option is going to identify the right agent to be installed seamlessly.

The process of installing the agent using the discovery wizard is straight forward by using **Device Management | Computer and Device Management Wizard** from the operations manager console as shown in *Figure 17*:

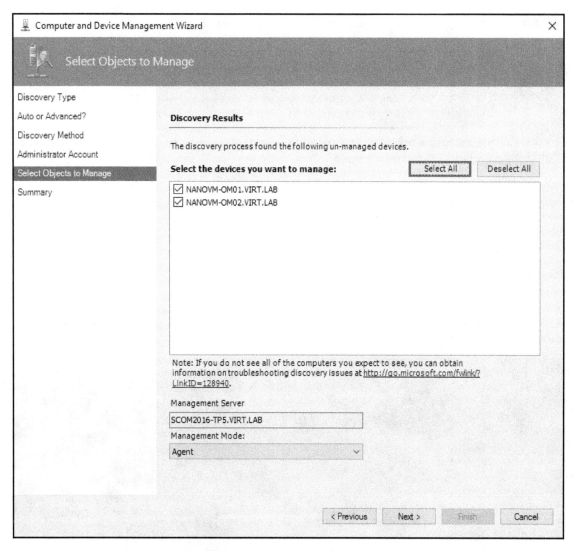

Figure 17. The discovery wizard: Computer and device management

After a couple of minutes deploying the SCOM agent, Nano Server(s) will report their health state in the agent-managed console.

Microsoft is also offering a manual agent installation method for Nano, so the users can run a PowerShell script to remotely install the SCOM agent on Nano Server.

The following procedure is for PowerShell-based agent installation only.

1. Log in to the operations manager management server, open the Windows PowerShell console, and navigate to the following path:

```
Cd "C:\Program Files\Microsoft System Center 2016\Operations
Manager\Server\AgentManagement\Nano\NanoServer"
```

2. Run the following script to install the agent manually on Nano Server, which is a member of the same domain.

```
# Install Nano Server SCOM
Agent.\InstallNanoServerScomAgentOnline.ps1-
ManagementServerFQDNSCOM2016.VIRT.LAB-
ManagementGroupNameSCOM2016-NanoServerFQDNNANOVM-OM03.VIRT.LAB-
BinaryFolder..\
```

Please adjust the management server FQDN, management group, and the Nano Server name to match your environment.

If the installation succeeded, you will see the `Installation successful!` message as shown in *Figure 18*:

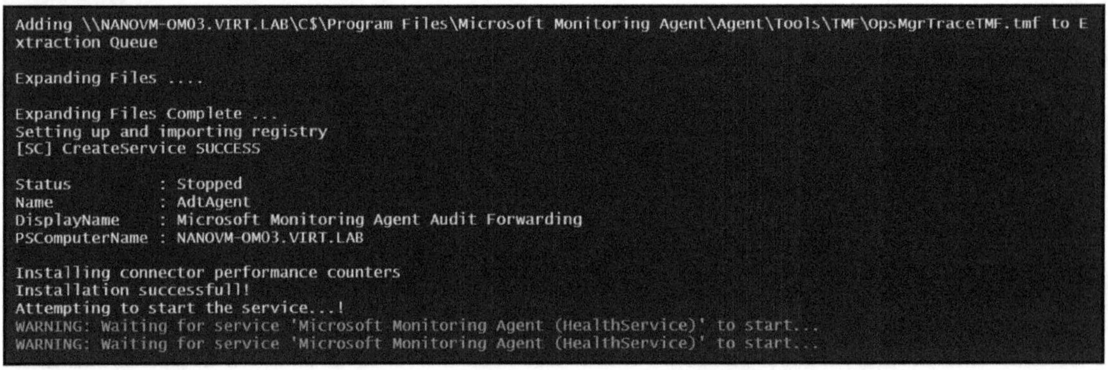

Figure 18. Installing the SCOM agent manually on Nano Server

3. Switch back to the operations manager console, open the **Pending Management** section of the administration pane, and then approve the Nano Server for management as shown in *Figure 19*:

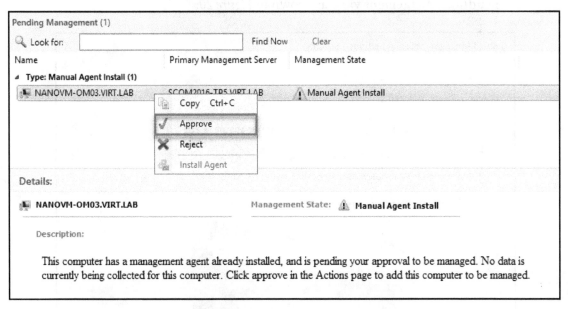

Figure 19. Approve Nano Server: Manual agent install

4. If Nano Server did not show up under **Pending Management** after installing the agent manually, then check the SCOM **Settings** section in the Administration pane and make sure you select **Review new manual agent installations in pending management view** as shown in *Figure 20*:

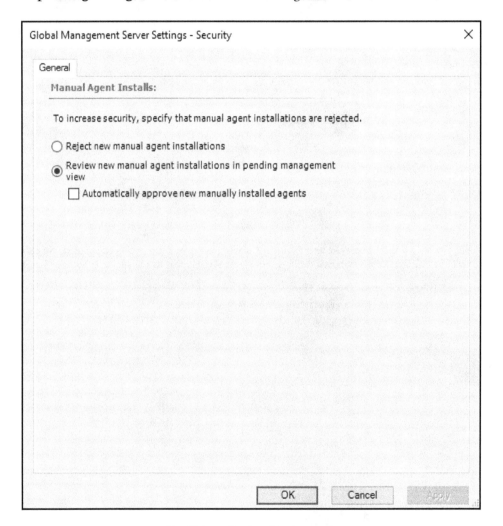

Global Management Server Settings - Security   ✕

General

Manual Agent Installs:

To increase security, specify that manual agent installations are rejected.

◯ Reject new manual agent installations

⦿ Review new manual agent installations in pending management
  view

    ☐ Automatically approve new manually installed agents

                                        OK   Cancel   Apply

Figure 20. Approve Nano Server: Manual agent install

5. Once you approve the manual agent installation, open the **Agent Managed** list in the **Device Management** section of the **Operations Manager Console Administration** pane, and verify the Health State as shown in *Figure 21*:

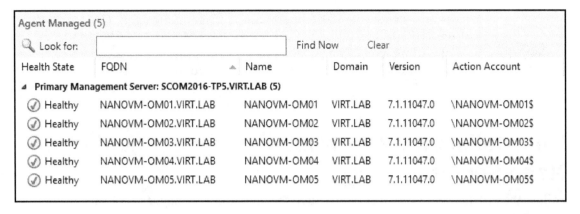

Figure 21. Health state: Agent managed

6. Once Nano Server is reported as **Healthy**, you can start monitoring it as you would monitor any Windows Server instance. *Figure 22*, shows an example of a critical error detected on Nano Server:

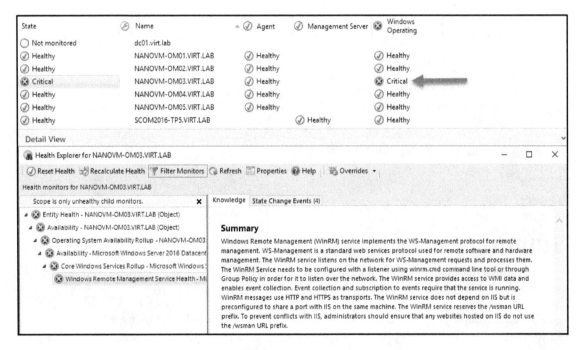

Figure 22. The health explorer: Critical error

Microsoft system center 2016 operations manager nano agent **Update Rollups (UR)** will be uploaded separately from SCOM 2016 UR. At the time of writing, you can download the system center 2016 operations manager nano agent CAB file for UR2 from the following link:

https://www.microsoft.com/en-us/download/details.aspx?id=54790.

Uninstalling the operations manager agent from Nano Server

Follow the instructions if you want to remove the operations manager agent from your Nano Server.

Open an elevated PowerShell console on the operations manager management server, and navigate to the following path:

```
cd "C:\Program Files\Microsoft System Center 2016\Operations
Manager\Server\AgentManagement\Nano\NanoServer"
```

Run the following command to remove the SCOM agent manually using PowerShell.

```
# Uninstall Nano Server SCOM
Agent.\UninstallNanoServerScomAgentOnline.ps1-
ManagementServerFQDNSCOM2016.VIRT.LAB-ManagementGroupNameSCOM2016-
NanoServerFQDNNANOVM-OM03.VIRT.LAB
```

The management server FQDN, management group, and Nano Server name to match your environment.

Summary

In this chapter, we discussed how to manage and monitor Nano Server using system center virtual machine manager and system center operations manager 2016.

We started by deploying Nano Server using VMM as a Hyper-V host using a bare-metal deployment, and then we deployed Nano Server as a virtual machine using VM templates.

We covered the available options on how to install the VMM agent; we also discussed how to manage and deploy network teaming on Nano Server using SET.

Deploying the SCOM agent is a bit different from VMM; with SCOM, we can push the agent to Nano Server in an automated fashion using the operations console or with PowerShell. However, in VMM we can add the SCVMM packages through the offline method (while creating the image) which is the recommended way. You can also add the packages online (while Nano Server is running), but, for either choice, it's a manual installation.

System center 2016 **Data Protection Manager** (**DPM**) is not supported on Nano Server. In other words, you cannot back up virtual machines running on top of Nano Server as a Hyper-V host.

Continue now to Chapter 6, *Managing Nano Server with Windows PowerShell and Windows PowerShell DSC*, to learn more about how to manage Nano Server using remote server GUI tools: Windows PowerShell and Windows PowerShell DSC.

6
Managing Nano Server with Windows PowerShell and Windows PowerShell DSC

In Chapter 5, *Deploying, Managing, and Monitoring Nano Server with System Center 2016*, we talked about how to deploy, manage, and monitor Nano Server using **System Center 2016 Virtual Machine Manager** (**SCVMM**) and **System Center 2016 Operations Manager** (**SCOM**).

One of the biggest fears of IT professionals that we heard a lot is, how will we manage a headless server without a local **User Interface** (**UI**); there is no remote desktop. Fortunately, it's not that difficult! You need to change your mindset from how you used to manage a traditional Windows Server in the past. In fact, Microsoft is laying the foundation of the future of Windows Server by introducing Nano Server. It is very important to keep in mind that Nano Server and Server Core is the future of Windows Server, so by embracing and investing the time in learning Nano Server will make your journey easier and take your organization to a complete new level.

There are a variety of ways you can manage Nano Server installation. PowerShell already become the foundation for many higher-level technologies, including PowerShell **Desired State Configuration** (**DSC**), and much more. PowerShell is everywhere now!

In this chapter, we will show you how to effectively manage Nano Server instance with:

- Remote server graphical tools
- Managing Nano Server with PowerShell
- Managing Nano Server with PowerShell DSC
- Managing Nano Server security settings with PowerShell DSC

Remote server graphical tools

Without the **Graphical User Interface** (**GUI**), it's not easy to carry out the daily management and maintenance of Windows Server. For this reason, Microsoft integrated Nano Server with all the existing graphical tools that you are familiar with such as Hyper-V Manager, failover cluster manager, Server Manager, registry editor, file explorer, disk and device manager, Server configuration, computer management, users and groups console, and so on. All these tools and consoles are compatible for managing Nano Server remotely. The GUI is always the easiest to use.

In this section, we will discuss how to access and set the most common configurations in Nano Server with remote graphical tools.

Server Manager

Before we start managing Nano Server, we need to obtain the IP address or the computer name of the Nano Server to connect to and remotely manage a Nano instance, either on a physical or virtual machine.

Login to your management machine and make sure you have installed the latest **Remote Server Administration Tools** (**RSAT**) for Windows Server 2016 or Windows 10.

You can download the latest RSAT tools from the following link:

```
https://www.microsoft.com/en-us/download/details.aspx?id=45520.
```

Launch Server Manager as shown in *Figure 1*, and add the Nano Server(s) that you would like to manage:

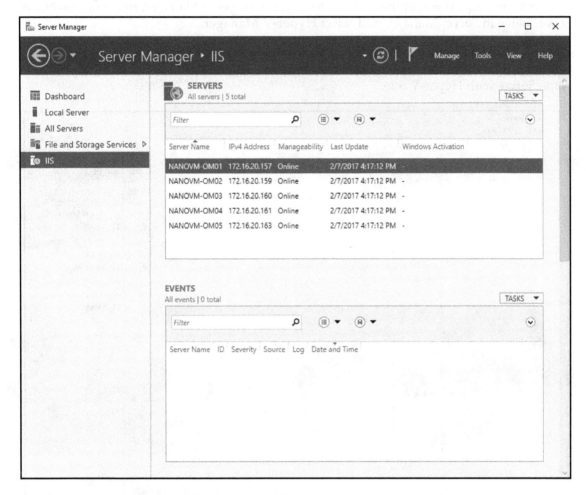

Figure 1: Managing Nano Server using Server Manager

You can refresh the view and browse all events and services you expect to see.

We want to point out that **Best Practices Analyzer (BPA)** is not supported in Nano Server. BPA is completely cmdlets-based and written in C# back during the days of PowerShell 2.0. It is also statically using some .NET XML library code that was not part of .NET framework at that time. So, do not expect to see best practices analyzer in Server Manager for Nano Server.

Hyper-V Manager

The next console that you probably want to access is Hyper-V Manager, right click on Nano Server name in Server Manager and select **Hyper-V Manager.**

Hyper-V Manager console will launch as shown in *Figure 2* with full support as you expect when managing Windows Server 2016 Hyper-V, free Hyper-V Server, Server Core and Nano Server with Hyper-V role:

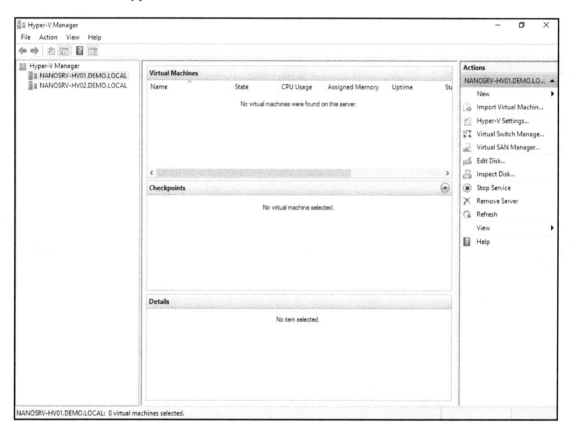

Figure 2: Managing Nano Server using Hyper-V Manager

Microsoft Management Console

You can use the **Microsoft Management Console** (**MMC**) to manage Nano Server as well:

- From the command-line type `mmc.exe`

- From the **File** menu, Click **Add/Remove Snap-in...** and then select **Computer Management** and click on **Add**

- Choose **Another** computer and add the IP address or the computer name of your Nano Server machine. Click on **Ok**

As shown in *Figure 3*, you can expand system tools and check the tools that you are familiar with like **Event Viewer**, **Local Users**, **Groups**, **Shares**, and **Services**. Please note that some of these MMC tools such as **Task Scheduler** and **Disk Management** cannot be used against Nano Server. Also, for certain tools, you need to open some ports in Windows Firewall:

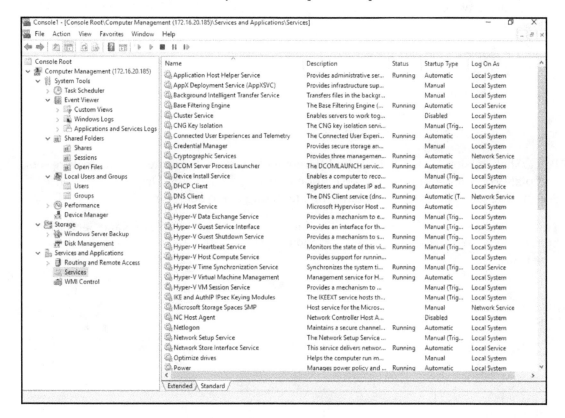

Figure 3: Managing Nano Server using Microsoft management console

Managing Nano Server with PowerShell

For most IT administrators, the graphical user interface is the easiest to use. But on the other hand, PowerShell allows for a fast and an automated process.

That's why in Windows Server 2016, the Nano Server deployment option of Windows Server comes with full PowerShell remoting support. The purpose of the core PowerShell engine is to manage Nano Server instances at scale. PowerShell remoting includes DSC, Windows Server cmdlets (network, storage, Hyper-V, and so on), remote file transfer, remote script authoring and debugging, and PowerShell Web access.

As discussed in `Chapter 1`, *Introduction to Nano Server*, Nano Server is deep refactoring initially focused on the cloud infrastructure roles (compute, storage, network) and born in the cloud applications. The model for Nano Server is to start small and then add only the features and components that you will use.

Some of the new features in Windows PowerShell version 5.1 on Nano Server support the following:

- Copying files via PowerShell sessions
- Remote file editing in PowerShell ISE
- Interactive script debugging over PowerShell session
- Remote script debugging within PowerShell ISE
- Remote host process connects and debug

PowerShell version 5.1 is available in different editions which denote varying feature sets and platform compatibility. Desktop edition targeting Server with Desktop Experience, Server Core and Windows 10, Core Edition targeting Nano Server and Windows IoT.

You can find a list of Windows PowerShell features not available yet in Nano Server here: `https://docs.microsoft.com/en-us/windows-server/get-started/powershell-on-nano-server`.

As Nano Server is still evolving, we will see what the next cadence update will bring for unavailable PowerShell features.

If you want to manage your Nano Server, you can use PowerShell remoting or, if your Nano Server instance is running in a virtual machine, you can also use PowerShell Direct; more on that at the end of this section.

In order to manage a Nano Server installation using PowerShell remoting, carry out the following steps:

1. You may need to start the WinRM service on your management machine to enable remote connections. From the PowerShell console type the following command:

   ```
   net start WinRM
   ```

2. If you want to manage Nano Server in a workgroup environment, open PowerShell console, and type the following command, substituting server name or IP with the correct value. Using your machine-name is the easiest to use, but if your device is not uniquely named on your network, you can use the IP address instead:

   ```
   Set-Item
   WSMan:\localhost\Client\TrustedHosts -
   Value "servername or IP"
   ```

3. If you want to connect multiple devices, you can use a comma and quotation marks to separate each device:

   ```
   Set-Item
   WSMan:\localhost\Client\TrustedHosts -
   Value "servername or IP, servername or IP"
   ```

4. You can also set it to allow connection to a specific network subnet using the following command:

   ```
   Set-Item
   WSMan:\localhost\Client\TrustedHosts -Value
   10.10.100.*
   ```

5. To test Windows PowerShell remoting against Nano Server and check if it's working, you can use the following command:

```
Test-WSMan -ComputerName " servername or IP" -
Credential servername\Administrator -
Authentication Negotiate
```

6. You can now start an interactive session with Nano Server. Open an elevated PowerShell console and type the following command:

```
Enter-PSSession -ComputerName "servername
or IP" -Credential servername\Administrator
```

In the following example, we will create two virtual machines on Nano Server Hyper-V host using PowerShell remoting. From your management machine, open an elevated PowerShell console or **PowerShell Scripting Environment** (**PSE**), and run the following script (make sure to update the variables to match your environment):

```
#region Variables$NanoSRV='NANOSRV-HV01'$Cred=Get-
Credential"Demo\SuperNano"$Session=New-PSSession-ComputerName$NanoSRV-
Credential$Cred$CimSesion=New-CimSession-ComputerName$NanoSRV-
Credential$Cred$VMTemplatePath='C:\Temp'$vSwitch='Ext_vSwitch'$VMName='
DemoVM-0'#endregion# Copying VM Template from the management machine to
Nano ServerGet-ChildItem-Path$VMTemplatePath-filter*.VHDX-recurse|Copy-
Item-ToSession$Session-DestinationD:\1..2|ForEach-Object{New-VM-
CimSession$CimSesion-Name$VMName$_-VHDPath"D:\$VMName$_.vhdx"-
MemoryStartupBytes1024GB`-SwitchName$vSwitch-Generation2Start-VM-
CimSession$CimSesion-VMName$VMName$_-Passthru
}
```

In this script, we are creating a PowerShell session and a CIM session to Nano Server. A CIM session is a client-side object representing a connection to a local computer or a remote computer.

Then we are copying VM templates from the management machine to Nano Server over PowerShell remoting. When the copy is completed, we are creating two virtual machines as generation 2 and finally starting them.

After a couple of seconds, you can launch Hyper-V Manager console and see the new VMs running on Nano Server host as shown in *Figure 4*:

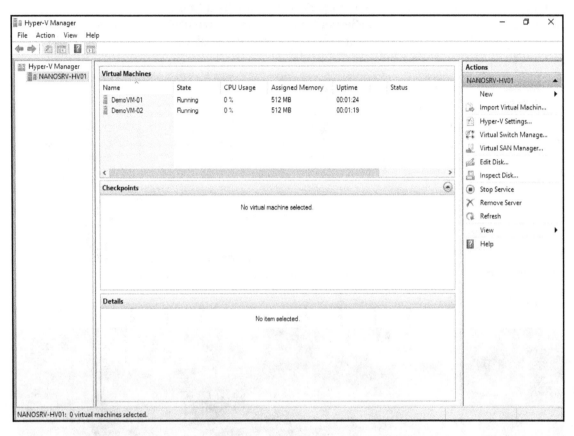

Figure 4: Creating virtual machines on Nano Server host using PowerShell remoting

If you have installed Nano Server in a virtual machine running on a Hyper-V host, you can use PowerShell Direct to connect directly from your Hyper-V host to your Nano Server VM without any network connection by using the following command:

```
Enter-PSSession -VMName <VMName> -
Credential.\Administrator
```

So, instead of specifying the computer name, we specified the VM Name. PowerShell Direct is so powerful; it's one of my favorite features, as you can configure a bunch of VMs from scratch in just a couple of seconds, without any network connection.

Moreover, if you have Nano Server running as a Hyper-V host, as shown in the example earlier, you could first use PowerShell remoting to connect to Nano Server from your management machine, and then leverage PowerShell Direct to manage your virtual machines running on top of Nano Server. In this example, we used two PowerShell technologies (PS remoting and PS Direct). This is so powerful and opens many possibilities to effectively manage Nano Server.

To do that, you can use the following command:

```
#region Variables$NanoSRV='NANOSRV-HV01'#Nano Server name or IP
address$DomainCred=Get-Credential"Demo\SuperNano"$VMLocalCred=Get-
Credential"~\Administrator"$Session=New-PSSession-ComputerName$NanoSRV-
Credential$DomainCred#endregionInvoke-Command-Session$Session-
ScriptBlock{
                Get-VM Invoke-Command-VMName(Get-VM).Name -
Credential$Using;VMLocalCred-ScriptBlock{
                                hostname Tzutil/g }
    }
```

In this script, we have created a PowerShell session in the Nano Server physical host, and then we used PowerShell Direct to list all VMs, including their hostnames and time zone.

The result is shown in *Figure 5*:

```
PS C:\> #regionVariables
$NanoSRV = 'NANOSRV-HV01' #Nano Server name or IP address
$DomainCred = Get-Credential "Demo\SuperBook"
$LocalCred = Get-Credential "~\Administrator"
$Session = New-PSSession -ComputerName $NanoSRV -Credential $DomainCred
#endregion

Invoke-Command -ComputerName $NanoSRV -Credential $DomainCred -ScriptBlock {
              param ($LocalCred)
              Get-VM
              Invoke-Command -VMName (Get-VM).Name -Credential $LocalCred -ScriptBlock {
                          hostname;Tzutil /g}
} -ArgumentList $LocalCred


Name        State    CPUUsage(%) MemoryAssigned(M) Uptime             Status              Version PSComputerName
----        -----    ----------- ----------------- ------             ------              ------- --------------
DemoVM-01 Running 0              512               14:26:48.2570000 Operating normally 7.0     NANOSRV-HV01
DemoVM-02 Running 0              512               14:26:43.3050000 Operating normally 7.0     NANOSRV-HV01
DemoVM-01
Pacific Standard Time
DemoVM-02
Pacific Standard Time
```

Figure 5: Nested PowerShell remoting

Managing Nano Server with PowerShell DSC

As discussed in the previous section, most of the Windows PowerShell cmdlets that you are familiar with can establish a remote connectivity and manage a Nano Server instance.

The usage for Nano is different, depending on if it's virtualized or not. Nano as a VM is meant to be just an engine; it might live for 10 seconds or 10 days, it is just a part of a huge application platform (the purpose is to execute apps on servers). But when running Nano on a physical machine, it is basically a cloud infrastructure (Hyper-V, storage, clustering) and nothing else. Nano is double-edged with dual purpose.

Nano Server was designed for high density deployment. Imagine trying to manage 1,000 Nano Servers using GUI-based tools. These tools might be fine for managing a relatively small number of servers, but are simply not practical for managing large-scale deployments. Nano Server is not really meant to be managed by a domain when running virtualized, it is designed to be a workhorse, managed by PowerShell DSC.

Microsoft clearly stated that its preferred management tool is Windows PowerShell.

DSC is a Windows PowerShell management platform that allows you to automate the deployment and configuration of software services and the environment in which these services run. DSC has many applications. These include, but are not limited to:

- Deploying and removing roles and features
- Deploying and managing configuration data
- Deploying software
- Managing registry settings, files, and directories
- Starting and stopping services
- Preventing configuration drift
- Discovering configuration states

In short, DSC is how you configure servers. This means that DSC provides definitions and descriptions of the desired end states configurations are declared. When DSC runs, it ensures that the end state matches the state defined by the DSC configuration so, if the configuration drifts on any server, DSC will make sure to bring it back to the desired state. Furthermore, the DSC engine, also known as the **Local Configuration Manager** (LCM), continues to ensure that the end states match the state declared by the DSC configuration: configurations are idempotent.

Best of all, because DSC is Windows PowerShell-based, it can scale to manage configurations for as many servers as is necessary. Remember, Nano Server was designed to be treated as cattle and not as a pet. The good news is, PowerShell DSC works on Nano Server as well. However, the following DSC features are not currently available on Nano:

- Decrypting MOF documents with encrypted password(s)
- Pull Server--you cannot currently set up a pull server on Nano Server

And the following DSC features are currently available on Nano Server:

- Both push and pull DSC modes are supported on Nano Server
- All DSC cmdlets that exist on a full version of Windows Server
- MOF encryption
- Event logging
- Azure automation DSC reporting

For the updated DSC features that are available on Nano Server, please check the following article:

`https://msdn.microsoft.com/en-us/powershell/dsc/nanodsc`.

The following section demonstrates how to use PowerShell DSC to remotely manage Nano Server. This example uses the xNetworking (`https://github.com/PowerShell/xNetworking`) PowerShell DSC module to set and manage built-in Windows firewall rules.

Creating a Nano Server image for PowerShell DSC

Before getting into how to use DSC to configure a Nano Server, you must create a Nano Server image that includes the `Microsoft-NanoServer-DSC-Package` package.

DSC on Nano Server is an optional package that is available in the `NanoServer\Packages` folder of the Windows Server 2016 media. The package can be added when you create a VHD(X) for a Nano Server by specifying `Microsoft-NanoServer-DSC-Package` as the value of the `packages` parameter of the `New-NanoServerImage` function, or by using `NanoServerPackage` provider online post deployment.

In the following example, we are creating five virtual machines; the script would look like the following:

```
#region variables# Staging path for new Nano image$StagingPath='C:\'#
Path to Windows Server 2016 ISO file $MediaPath='H:\'$Path=Join-Path-
Path$StagingPath-ChildPathNanoServer$Password=Read-Host-Prompt"Please
specify local Administrator password"-AsSecureString#endregion #region
Copy source filesif(-not(Test-Path$StagingPath)) {

  mkdir$StagingPath
}if(-not(Test-Path$Path)) {

  $NanoServerSourcePath=Join-Path-Path$MediaPath-ChildPathNanoServer-
Resolve Copy-Item-Path$NanoServerSourcePath-Destination$StagingPath-
Recurse} #endregion #region Generate Nano ImageImport-Module-Name(Join-
Path-Path$Path-ChildPathNanoServerImageGenerator) -Verbose
$ServicingPackagePath=@(
  'C:\NanoServer\Updates\Servicing stack update\Windows10.0-kb3211320-
x64.msu' 'C:\NanoServer\Updates\Cumulative Update\Windows10.0-
kb4010672-x64.msu')1..5|ForEach-Object{
    $ComputerName="NANOVM-OM0$_" $NanoServerImageParameters=@{

    ComputerName =$ComputerName MediaPath =$MediaPath BasePath =(Join-
Path-Path$Path-ChildPath$ComputerName)
    # .vhd for Gen1 VM and .vhdx for Gen2 VM TargetPath =Join-Path-
Path$Path-ChildPath($ComputerName+'.vhdx')
    AdministratorPassword =$Password Containers =$true Package
='Microsoft-NanoServer-DSC-Package' EnableRemoteManagementPort =$true
DeploymentType ='Guest' Edition ='Standard' ServicingPackagePath
=$ServicingPackagePath }

  New-NanoServerImage@NanoServerImageParameters}#endregion
```

Creating Nano virtual machines

Once the **Virtual Hard Disks** (**VHDX**) are created, you can simply copy them to your Hyper-V server and create a new virtual machine. It's worth noting that the VM must be a generation 2 VM, because you cannot attach a VHDX file to a generation 1 VM in the case of Nano Server.

To automate this process, you can run the following PowerShell script on your Hyper-V server:

```
#region create 5 NANO VIRTUAL MACHINES
#variables$vSwitchName01="vSwitch"$InstallRoot="D:\Hyper-
V"#endregion1..5|ForEach-Object{New-VHD-Path($InstallRoot+"\NANOVM-
OM0$_\NanoServer_D.vhdx") -SizeBytes50GB-DynamicNew-VM-
VHDPath($InstallRoot+"\NANOVM-OM0$_\NANOVM-OM0$_.vhdx") -Generation2-
MemoryStartupBytes4GB-NameNANOVM-OM0$_-Path$InstallRoot-
SwitchName$vSwitchName01Set-VMProcessor-VMNameNANOVM-OM0$_-Count4Set-
VM-VMNameNANOVM-OM0$_-AutomaticStopActionShutDown-
AutomaticStartActionStartIfRunningEnable-VMIntegrationServiceNANOVM-
OM0$_-Name"Guest Service Interface"Rename-VMNetworkAdapter-
VMNameNANOVM-OM0$_-NewName"MGMT"Set-VMNetworkAdapter-VMNameNANOVM-
OM0$_-Name"MGMT"-DeviceNamingOnAdd-VMScsiController-VMNameNANOVM-
OM0$_Add-VMHardDiskDrive-VMNameNANOVM-OM0$_-ControllerTypeSCSI-
ControllerNumber1-ControllerLocation0-Path($InstallRoot+"\NANOVM-
OM0$_\NanoServer_D.vhdx")Start-VM-NameNANOVM-OM0$_|Out-Null}
```

Importing the DSC xNetworking module

In this step, we will download and import the xNetworking module, which is a part of the DSC Resource Kit developed by the PowerShell Team. The xNetworking module contains the following DSC resources:

- xFirewall: Sets a node's firewall rules
- xIPAddress: Sets a node's IP address(es)
- xDnsServerAddress: Sets a node's DNS server address(s)
- xDnsConnectionSuffix: Sets a node's network interface connection-specific DNS suffix
- xDefaultGatewayAddress: Sets a node's default gateway address
- xNetConnectionProfile: Sets a node's connection profile
- xDhcpClient: Enables or disables DHCP on a network interface
- xRoute: Sets static routes on a node
- xNetBIOS: Enables or disables NetBIOS on a network interface
- xNetworkTeam: Sets up network teams on a node
- xNetworkTeamInterface: Adds network interfaces to a network team

- `xHostsFile`: Adds, edits or removes entries from the hosts file on a node
- `xNetAdapterBinding`: Binds or unbinds transport or filters to a network interface
- `xDnsClientGlobalSetting`: Configures DNS client global settings
- `xNetAdapterRDMA`: Enables or disables RDMA on a network adapter

You can choose any resource from the previous list to configure a node's IP Address, DNS Server Address, Firewall rules, Network Team and so on.

We need to download and install the `xNetworking` module on all Nano Servers, so open an elevated PowerShell console on your Hyper-V server and run the following script to automate this process:

```
#region variables$LocalPassword=ConvertTo-SecureString-
String'P@ssw0rd'-AsPlainText-Force$LocalCred=New-
ObjectSystem.Management.Automation.PSCredential('.\Administrator',$Loca
lPassword)#endregion# Download and Save xNetworking module locally from
PSGallerySet-PSRepository-Name'PSGallery'-
InstallationPolicyTrustedSave-Module-NamexNetworking-PathC:\NanoServer#
Copy and install xNetworking module on all Nano Servers1..5|ForEach-
Object{
        $S1=New-PSSession-VMNameNANOVM-OM0$_-Credential$LocalCred Copy-
Item-PathC:\NanoServer\xNetworking-ToSession$S1-Destination'C:\Program
Files\WindowsPowerShell\Modules'-Recurse-Force Invoke-Command-
Session$S1-ScriptBlock{ Import-Module-NamexNetworking-Verbose}
    }
```

In the first part of this script, we downloaded the `xNetworking` module from PowerShell gallery locally, and then we copied it through a PowerShell remote session and PowerShell Direct to all Nano Servers, instead of downloading the same module five times, and finally we imported it. PowerShell Direct is so powerful.

Push DSC configuration

Before we push the DSC configuration and set the firewall rules, the first step is to create a configuration file known as an MOF file. We generate the MOF file by using a Windows PowerShell script. The second step in the configuration process is to use the MOF file to configure the target Nano Server.

In an instance where you want to use DSC to enable built-in firewall rules onto the Nano Server, the first thing you will have to do is to write a PowerShell script that will create the required MOF file. Such a script might look as shown following:

```
# Variables$TargetNode='NANOVM-OM01','NANOVM-OM02','NANOVM-
OM03','NANOVM-OM04','NANOVM-OM05'ConfigurationxFirewallClient{
     # Importing the xNetworking DSC Module Import-DscResource-
ModuleNamexNetworking # List of Nano machine which needs to be
configured Node$TargetNode {
         # Enable Built-in ICMPv4-In xFirewallFirewallICMP4In {
             Name ='FPS-ICMP4-ERQ-In' Ensure ='Present' Enabled ='True'
Action ='Allow' Profile ='Any' }
         # Enable Built-in ICMPv6-In xFirewallFirewallICMP6In {
             Name ='FPS-ICMP6-ERQ-In' Ensure ='Present' Enabled ='True'
Action ='Allow' Profile ='Any' }
         # Enable Built-in File and Printer Sharing (SMB-In)
xFirewallFirewallSMBIn {
             Name ='FPS-SMB-In-TCP' Ensure ='Present' Enabled ='True'
Action ='Allow' Profile ='Any' }

         # Enable Built-in Hyper-V Replica HTTP Listener (TCP-In)
xFirewallFirewallHVRHTTPIn {
             Name ='VIRT-HVRHTTPL-In-TCP-NoScope' Ensure ='Present'
Enabled ='True' Action ='Allow' Profile =('Domain','Private')
         }

         # Enable Built-in Hyper-V Replica HTTPS Listener (TCP-In)
xFirewallFirewallHVRHTTPSIn {
             Name ='VIRT-HVRHTTPSL-In-TCP-NoScope' Ensure ='Present'
Enabled ='True' Action ='Allow' Profile =('Domain','Private')
         }
     }
}# Compile the MOF file xFirewallClient
```

In this block of code, we've created a configuration. The configuration is a built-in function, so you must give the configuration a name. In this case, we decided to name it xFirewallClient. The actual configuration details are enclosed in a series of braces.

In the first line of code, we specified the target Nano Servers that we need to configure. Please note that you can also use an IP address rather than a node name. The script works with both server names and IP addresses.

The second line of code within my configuration uses the Import-DscResource cmdlet followed by the xNetworking module name. This is necessary to import the various configuration items that DSC will use. The next line of code is Node followed by a variable named $TargetNode. In this case, we have added multiple Nano Server names into that variable. The main reason why we did this was to demonstrate the resulting MOF file will be server-specific. Hence, each Nano Server that you want to configure will usually need its own MOF file.

The next set of brackets defines the code that will be specific to the specified node. In this case, we are calling a built-in custom DSC resource called xFirewall. The xFirewall line includes FirewallICMP4In. FirewallICMP4In is just a name that we made up, and is useful in more complex scripts because of the way it allows you to call individual script sections. In this example, we are targeting five different built-in firewall rules. Please note that you can also add new firewall rules.

The next five lines of text are self-explanatory. First, we specified the built-in name for the firewall rule that we want to enable on the target server; the name is very important here. In this example, the name FPS-ICMP4-ERQ-In is corresponding to file and printer sharing (Echo Request-ICMPv4-In). Next is to ensure the specified rule is Present, and it's enabled True, the action is Allow, and the firewall profile is set to Any. For the Hyper-V Replica rule, we targeted the Domain and Private firewall profiles only.

The very last line of the script is xFirewallClient. Remember, the name xFirewallClient was assigned to the Configuration function at the beginning of the script. The xFirewallClient command at the end of the script calls this function, thereby generating all the MOF files.

The first thing you'll have to do is open a Windows PowerShell window and execute the configuration script. This causes Windows to create five MOF files based on this example (see *Figure 6*):

```
    Directory: C:\NanoServer\xFirewallClient


Mode                LastWriteTime         Length Name
----                -------------         ------ ----
-a----        18-Feb-17     9:29 PM         6790 NANOVM-OM01.mof
-a----        18-Feb-17     9:29 PM         6790 NANOVM-OM02.mof
-a----        18-Feb-17     9:29 PM         6790 NANOVM-OM03.mof
-a----        18-Feb-17     9:29 PM         6790 NANOVM-OM04.mof
-a----        18-Feb-17     9:29 PM         6790 NANOVM-OM05.mof


PS C:\NanoServer>
```

Figure 6: PowerShell DSC. Creating MOF files

Now you must use the MOF files to configure your Nano Servers. You can do this by using these four lines of code:

```
# Variables$LocalPassword=ConvertTo-SecureString-String'P@ssw0rd' –
AsPlainText-Force$LocalCred=New-
ObjectSystem.Management.Automation.PSCredential(".\Administrator",$Loca
lPassword)$TargetNode='NANOVM-OM01','NANOVM-OM02','NANOVM-
OM03','NANOVM-OM04','NANOVM-OM05'# Push DSC ConfigurationStart-
DscConfiguration-Path.\xFirewallClient –Verbose-Wait-
ComputerName$TargetNode-credential$LocalCred-Force
```

The first and second line of code simply retrieves a set of credentials and converts the password to secure string, storing it in a variable named $LocalCred. In the third line of code, we specified the target Nano Servers that we need to configure. In this example, we will push the configuration to five nano machines simultaneously, so we put the server names in a variable named $TargetNode.

The fourth line of code performs the actual configuration. For example, when we ran the script as shown in *Figure 6*, the script created five MOF files named NANOVM-OM01.mof, NANOVM-OM02.mof, NANOVM-OM03.mof, NANOVM-OM04.mof, and NANOVM-OM05.mof. These files are located in the same folder where we ran the script in the previous step. Therefore, we had to use the path for the configuration files when pushing the configuration (see *Figure 7*):

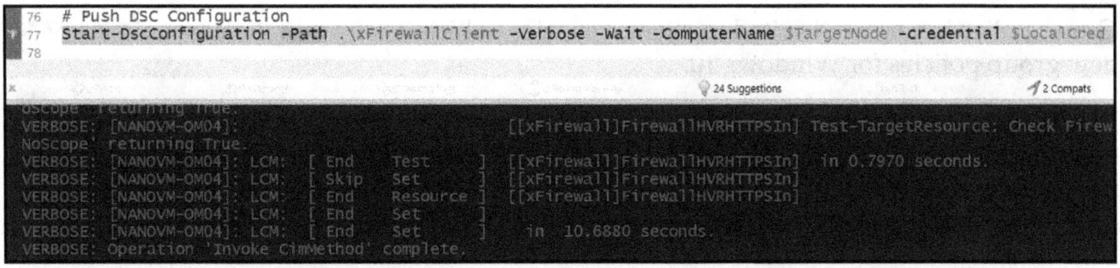

Figure 7: Push DSC Firewall rule configuration. Nano Servers

The DSC management platform makes it possible to apply a configuration to any Windows Server, including Nano Server. Even though this probably seems like a lot of work for such a simple configuration, the script can be modified to simultaneously configure large numbers of servers.

Managing Nano Server Security Settings with PowerShell DSC

As discussed in the previous sections, we can completely manage and configure Nano Server installation with Windows PowerShell and PowerShell DSC.

One of the things that makes Nano Server so interesting is that it takes up far less disk space, installs significantly faster, and needs far fewer updates and restarts compared to Server with Desktop Experience and Server Core. The image size for Server with Desktop Experience is around 11 GB, for Server Core it's 6 GB and for Nano Server it's 480 MB without any role or feature. To achieve this speed and small physical footprint, Nano Server has the smallest number of inbox components. Thus, group policy and the associated **Group Policy Management Console (GPMC)**, and **Local Policy Editor (LPEdit)** tools are not present on Nano Server. Even when domain joined, Nano Server will not consume and endorse group policy settings. This is to be expected because those tools are graphical components and Nano Server is headless and designed to be remotely managed.

This raises many questions around Nano Server group policy support. Many people including myself have invested a lot of resources for servers hardening with group policy, and many businesses have an investment in group policy, so not having Nano Servers accept it could cause slow adoption. What is the solution then?

DSC is the replacement for group policy, it provides better semantics for server scenarios, according to Mr. Jeffrey Snover (PowerShell inventor).

Group policy is very well suited to client scenarios, which is why you noticed a big set of new group policies for Windows 10.

In Windows Server 2016, Microsoft included four new PowerShell cmdlets to help manage security policy settings. While they are present on every installation option of Windows Server 2016, these are mostly useful on Nano Server because Nano Server does not support group policy. Please note that these cmdlets are used for managing local policy only.

You can access these cmdlets by running the following command (see *Figure 8*):

```
Get-Command -Module SecurityCmdlets
```

```
PS C:\> Get-Command -Module SecurityCmdlets | FT -AutoSize

CommandType Name                      Version Source
----------- ----                      ------- ------
Cmdlet      Backup-AuditPolicy        1.0.0.0 SecurityCmdlets
Cmdlet      Backup-SecurityPolicy     1.0.0.0 SecurityCmdlets
Cmdlet      Restore-AuditPolicy       1.0.0.0 SecurityCmdlets
Cmdlet      Restore-SecurityPolicy    1.0.0.0 SecurityCmdlets
```

Figure 8: Local Security Cmdlets in Nano Server

These security settings include two different kinds of files:

- .INF: This file contains security policy template settings. The .INF files can be generated with Backup-SecurityPolicy cmdlet on Server with Desktop Experience or Server Core installation.
- .CSV: This file contains advanced audit settings. The .CSV files can be generated with Backup-AuditPolicy cmdlet on Server with Desktop Experience or Server Core installation.

Once you have generated the `.INF` file and the `.CSV` file, then you can remotely invoke both the advanced audit and security template settings to your Nano Server installation by running the following command:

```
Import-ModuleSecurityCmdlets

# Replace the variables with the path to the .INF and .CSV files
$SecInf="C:\Nano\SecInf\GptTmpl.inf"
$AuditCsv="C:\Nano\Audit\audit.csv"

Restore-SecurityPolicy-Path$secInf
Restore-AuditPolicy-Path$auditCsv
```

Microsoft also released `GPRegistryPolicy` cmdlets, which will deal with `.POL` files containing registry policy settings (`https://msdn.microsoft.com/en-us/library/windows/desktop/aa374407(v=vs.85).aspx`).

The `.POL` files can be generated from your existing **Group Policy Objects** (**GPO**) backups, or they can be generated with `Export-GPRegistryPolicy` cmdlet.

`.POL` files will have either `Local Machine` or `Local User` registry key settings, which must be specified to the `Import-GPRegistryPolicy` and `Export-GPRegistryPolicy` cmdlets; more on that shortly. However, for Nano Server, all relevant security settings will be `Local Machine` only.

The `GPRegistryPolicy` can be installed from PowerShell gallery by running the following commands:

```
Install-Module -Name GPRegistryPolicy
```

Once you installed the module, you can start importing and exporting `.POL`, `.INF`, and `.CSV` files to Nano Server; you can also start applying security settings to Nano Server.

A sample configuration is shown following, you can download the current Security Baselines for Windows Server 2016 (`https://cdp.packtpub.com/b05331/wp-admin/post.php?post=38&action=edit`) and extract the `.inf`, `.csv`, and `.pol` containing the desired security settings from the exported GPO.

Once you extracted the `Windows-10-RS1-and-Server-2016-Security-Baseline.zip` file onto the Windows Server you wish to manage, there will be several GPOs in the `GPOs` folder, as shown in *Figure 9*:

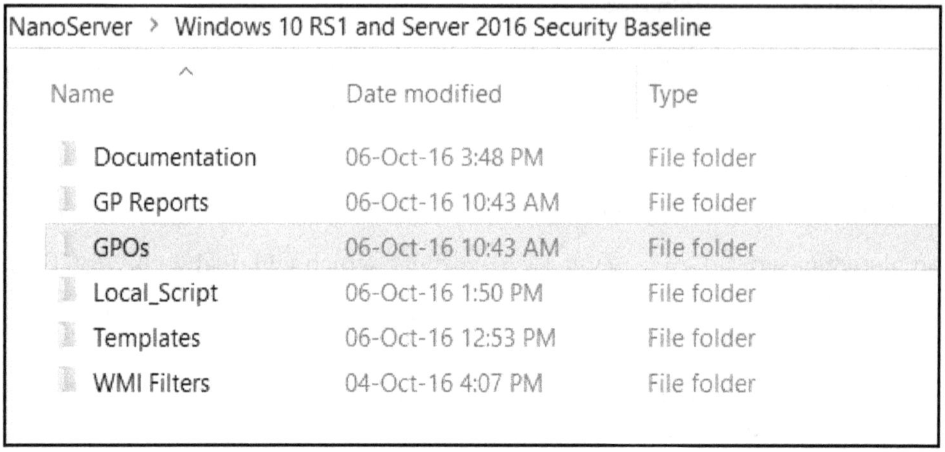

Figure 9: Security baselines for Windows Server 2016

Open the `GPOs` folder, and then from the GPO you wish to import, browse to:

```
DomainSysvol\GPO\Machine
```

If there is a `.POL` file in the root of this folder as shown in *Figure 10*, then you can remotely invoke the registry values in that `.POL` file into the registry of the targeted Nano Server:

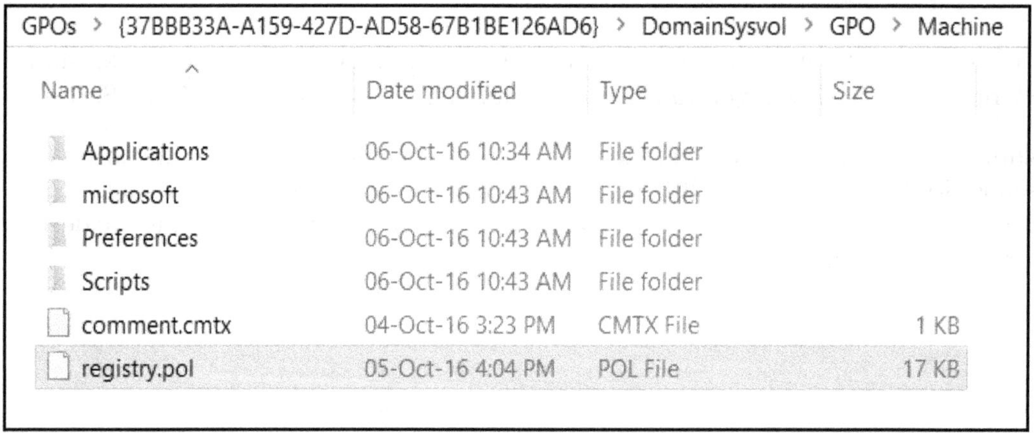

Figure 10: Registry POL file Windows Server 2016 security baselines

To import and apply the registry settings, open a remote PowerShell session onto Nano Server and run the following commands:

```
Import-ModuleGpRegistryPolicy

# Replace this string with the path to the .pol file
$GpoPol='C:\NanoServer\GPOs\{37BBB33A-A159-427D-
AD58-67B1BE126AD6}\DomainSysvol\GPO\Machine\registry.pol'

Import-GPRegistryPolicy-Path$GpoPol-LocalMachine
```

For some GPOs, there might also be advanced `Audit` or security template `SecEdit` files in the same folder under the following path (see *Figure 11*):

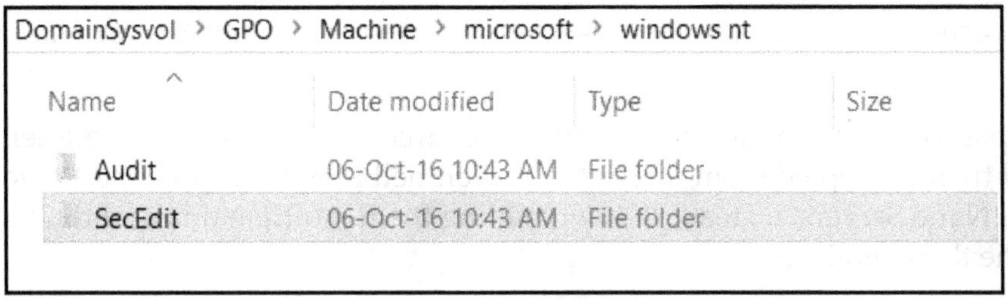

DomainSysvol > GPO > Machine > microsoft > windows nt			
Name ^	Date modified	Type	Size
Audit	06-Oct-16 10:43 AM	File folder	
SecEdit	06-Oct-16 10:43 AM	File folder	

Figure 11: Advanced Audit and security templates. Windows Server 2016 security baselines

You can also remotely invoke both the advanced audit and security template settings to Nano Server installation, as explained at the beginning of this section.

The security and registry cmdlets were designed to manage local policy. However, in the real world, no-one will deploy one or two Nano Servers. Nano Server was designed for high-density deployment; it's not practical for managing large-scale deployments.

For this reason, Microsoft released three new DSC resources building upon the previously released security and registry cmdlets for applying security settings on Nano Server by using PowerShell DSC.

First, we need to download and install these resources on all targeted Nano Servers, so open an elevated PowerShell console on your Hyper-V server and run the following script to automate this process:

```
#region variables
$LocalPassword=ConvertTo-SecureString-String'P@ssw0rd'-AsPlainText-
Force
$LocalCred=New-ObjectSystem.Management.Automation.PSCredential
('.\Administrator',$LocalPassword)
#endregion
```

```
# Download and Save Security Policy DSC resource locally from PSGallery
Set-PSRepository-Name'PSGallery'-InstallationPolicyTrusted
Save-Module-NameSecurityPolicyDsc,AuditPolicyDsc,GpRegistryPolicy-
PathC:\NanoServer

# Copy and install Security Policy DSC resource to all Nano Servers
1..5|ForEach-Object {
$S1=New-PSSession-VMNameNANOVM-OM0$_-Credential$LocalCred
Copy-Item-PathC:\NanoServer\SecurityPolicyDsc-ToSession$S1-
Destination'C:\Program Files\WindowsPowerShell\Modules'-Recurse-Force
Copy-Item-PathC:\NanoServer\AuditPolicyDsc-ToSession$S1-
Destination'C:\Program Files\WindowsPowerShell\Modules'-Recurse-Force
Copy-Item-PathC:\NanoServer\GpRegistryPolicy-ToSession$S1-
Destination'C:\Program Files\WindowsPowerShell\Modules'-Recurse-Force
Invoke-Command-Session$S1-ScriptBlock{ Import-Module-
NameSecurityPolicyDsc,AuditPolicyDsc,GpRegistryPolicy-Verbose }
}
```

In the first part of this script, we downloaded the three modules from PowerShell gallery locally, and then we copied them through a PowerShell remote session and PowerShell Direct to all Nano Servers, instead of downloading them multiple times, and finally we imported the three modules.

Second, you need to get the extracted `.inf`, `.csv`, and `.pol` files, as shown earlier, then simply pass the files into the new DSC resources and push the configuration onto your Nano Servers. A practical example could be updating Nano Servers using **Windows Server Update Service** (**WSUS**). What you could do is create a group policy on your active directory (Server with Desktop Experience or Server Core), then backup this policy and extract the `registry.pol` file as demonstrated earlier; then follow the following script to push the configuration: this will set the registry keys to all your Nano Servers to have it use your exiting WSUS Server.

 We strongly recommend a stage test deployment before you push any security settings in production!

Such a script might look like this:

```
# Variables
$LocalPassword=ConvertTo-SecureString-String'P@ssw0rd'-AsPlainText-
Force
$LocalCred=New-Object-
TypeNameSystem.Management.Automation.PSCredential-ArgumentList
('.\Administrator',$LocalPassword)
$TargetNode='NANOVM-OM01','NANOVM-OM02','NANOVM-OM03','NANOVM-
```

```
OM04','NANOVM-OM05'

ConfigurationSecurityBaseline
{
# Importing three DSC Modules
Import-DscResource-
ModuleNameAuditPolicyDsc,SecurityPolicyDSC,GpRegistryPolicy

# List of Nano machine which needs to be configured
Node$TargetNode
  {
SecurityTemplateSecurityBaselineInf
  {
 Path ="C:\NanoServer\GPO\GptTmpl.inf"
IsSingleInstance="Yes"
  }
AuditPolicyCsvSecurityBaselineCsv
  {
IsSingleInstance="Yes"
CsvPath="C:\NanoServer\GPO\audit.csv"
  }
RegistryPolicySecurityBaselineGpo
  {
 Path ="C:\NanoServer\GPO\registry.pol"
  }
  }
}

# Compile the MOF file
SecurityBaseline

# Push DSC Configuration
Start-DscConfiguration-Path.\SecurityBaseline-Verbose-Wait-
ComputerName$TargetNode-credential$LocalCred-Force
```

In this block of code, we've created a MOF configuration file. The configuration is a built-in function; you must give the configuration a name. In this case, we decided to name it SecurityBaseline. The actual configuration details are enclosed in a series of braces.

In the first line of code, we specified the target Nano Servers that we need to configure.

The second line of code within my configuration uses the `Import-DscResource` cmdlet followed by three modules: `AuditPolicyDsc`, `SecurityPolicyDSC`, and `GpRegistryPolicy`. This is necessary to import the various configuration items that DSC will use. The next line of code is: `Node` followed by a variable named `$TargetNode`. In this case, we have added multiple Nano Server names into that variable.

The next set of brackets defines the code that will be specific to the specified node. In this case, we are calling a built-in custom DSC resource called `SecurityTemplate`. The `SecurityTemplate` line includes `SecurityBaselineInf`. This is just a name that we chose.

The next line of text is self-explanatory. First, we specified the path for the `.inf` file. The next line of text we specified the `IsSingleInstance`. What `IsSingleInstance` means is it ensures that a configuration can set the security policy for a target node only once. The `IsSingleInstance` is limited to a single value `Yes`, by using a `ValueMap`.

We repeated the same process for the `AuditPolicyCsv` and `RegistryPolicy` custom DSC resources. However, we did not specify Single-Instance for the `RegistryPolicy`, because you can reapply the registry settings more than once.

Before the last line of the script is `SecurityBaseline`. The `SecurityBaseline` command calls the `Configuration SecurityBaseline` function, thereby generating all the MOF files.

The last line of the script is `Start-DscConfiguration`; this will push the configuration to all targeted Nano Servers and apply the desired security settings.

 All the codes provided in this chapter and other chapters are a companion to this book.

Summary

In this chapter, we discussed how to manage a Nano Server installation using remote server graphic tools, Windows PowerShell remoting, and PowerShell DSC.

As you have seen in this chapter, Microsoft invested heavily to bring PowerShell support onto Nano Server. PowerShell relies on the .NET Framework; as you noticed, Nano Server is a small OS and only has the Core of **Common Language Runtime (CLR).** The Core CLR is a tiny subset of the .NET Framework, but the PowerShell team went ahead and actually refactored all PowerShell to run on Core CLR, which was a huge effort. The good news is that PowerShell users will probably not miss any of the most important features. It has full language compatibility and supports PowerShell remoting, so you can use any of the most popular remote commands such as `Invoke-Command`, `New-PSSession`, `Enter-PSSession`, and so on.

Each Nano Server image contains by default Core CLR which is 45 MB of space; PowerShell itself takes up about 8 MB of space and there is 2 MB for the two built-in modules. PowerShell remoting is turned on by default, so a Nano Server installation will always be ready to be remoted into and be managed remotely.

If you are reading this chapter by Fall 2017, Microsoft is working on a new Management GUI tool focused on on-premises, disconnected server deployment. The upcoming solution is replacing the previous **Server Management Tools** (**SMT**) preview service in Azure, which is being retired on June 30, 2017. Stay tuned!

Continue now to `Chapter 7`, *Managing Nano Server with Third-Party Tools*, to learn more about how to manage Nano Server using 5nine Manager powered by 5nine software.

7
Managing Nano Server with Third-Party Tools

In Chapter 6, *Managing Nano Server with Windows PowerShell and Windows PowerShell DSC*, we talked about how to effectively manage Nano Server installations with remote server graphic tools, Windows PowerShell, and PowerShell **Desired State Configuration** (**DSC**).

The common question that we keep hearing is, How will admins be able to efficiently operate the next generation of datacenters built on top of Nano Servers? Windows PowerShell and DSC will be a popular choice; however they will require intermediate learning skills which challenge many users. As mentioned in the previous chapter, one of the biggest fears of IT professionals that we hear a lot is how to manage a headless server without a GUI. Fortunately, with 5nine Manager (http://www.5nine.com/5nine-manager-for-hyper-v-product.aspx) you can get a full user-friendly management UI to remotely deploy, configure, manage, and optimize a Nano Server installation.

In this chapter, we will show you how to manage Nano Server with 5nine Manager and cover the following topics:

- Nano Server administration using 5nine Manager
- Creating and managing Nano Server failover clusters with 5nine Manager

Nano Server administration using 5nine Manager

5nine Manager from 5nine software (`http://www.5nine.com/`) provides a centralized and easy-to-use graphical user interface. It allows administrators to create, manage, and monitor their Nano Server clusters, hosts, and VMs, in the same way as a traditional Hyper-V infrastructure.

At the time of writing, the current version of 5nine Manager is V9.4. The minimum supported version to manage Nano Server is V9.3 and later. You can download a trial version from the following link:

`https://www.5nine.com/5nine-manager-for-hyper-v-product.aspx`.

Assuming you have installed 5nine Manager in your environment, open the console and add the desired Nano Server that you want to administer.

As shown in *Figure 1*, we can specify the Name, IP Address, or use **Active Directory** to discover Nano Hyper-V hosts:

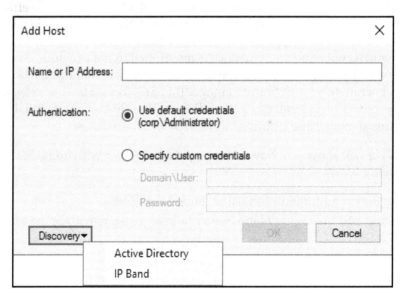

Figure 1. 5nine Manager adding nano hosts

When you click on **Active Directory**, you can select the desired Nano host that you want to manage (see *Figure 2*):

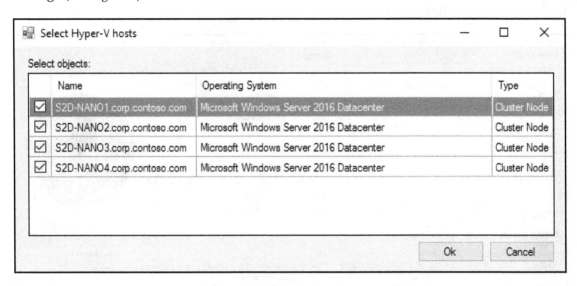

Figure 2. 5nine Manager add Nano hosts - Active Directory

The 5nine Manager console allows you to navigate and view summarized information at the datacenter, cluster, host, or virtual machine level. It integrates almost a dozen separate interfaces similar to what you would find in Windows Server or System Center to simplify management for new or experienced Hyper-V users.

The **Summary** tab, as shown in *Figure 3*, pulls together all the critical data you need about your Nano Server clusters, hosts, and VMs. You will see VM health, critical resources, disk utilization, and any recent alarms:

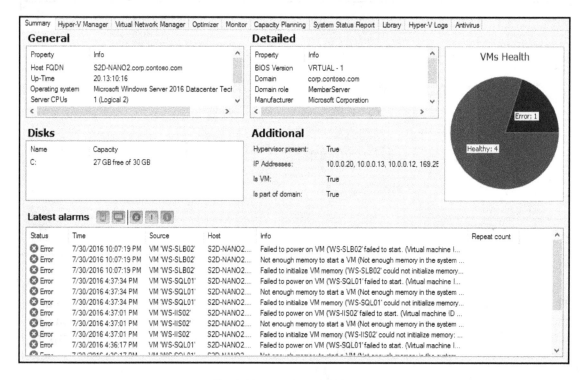

Figure 3. 5nine Manager Summary tab information

The **Hyper-V Manager** tab will allow you to manage all your virtual machines running Nano Server along with every other supported OS. In *Figure 4*, you can see a Nano Server VM being selected, allowing the user to perform traditional actions, such as starting or stopping a VM, along with some more advanced controls, such as checkpoints, exports, cloning, live migration, configuring, and monitoring VM replication. The display is customizable so you can filter the list to show Nano Server VMs with attributes that you are interested in, including the IP Address of the VM:

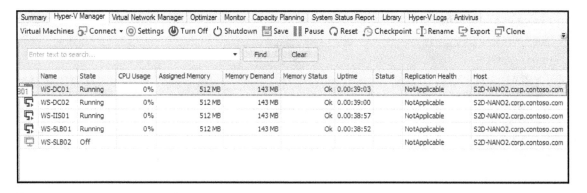

Figure 4. 5nine Manager Hyper-V Manager tab information

The **Virtual Network Manager** is used to manage external, internal, and private Nano Server virtual networks. *Figure 5* shows a user remotely managing several different types of network:

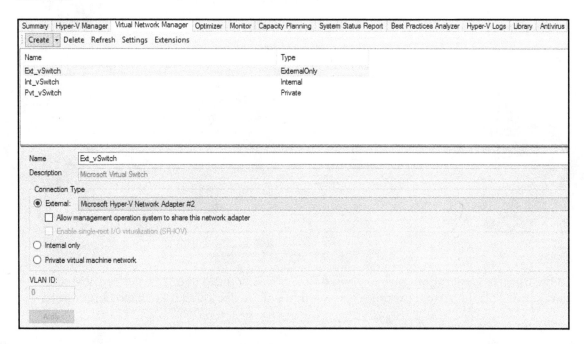

Figure 5. 5nine Manager Virtual Network Manager tab information

To help you maintain a healthy Nano Server environment, 5nine Manager will also let you monitor and optimize your configuration. There are numerous troubleshooting and logging tools built-in, and most management tasks can be simplified through wizards.

In *Figure 6*, a new virtual machine being created on a Nano Server Hyper-V host:

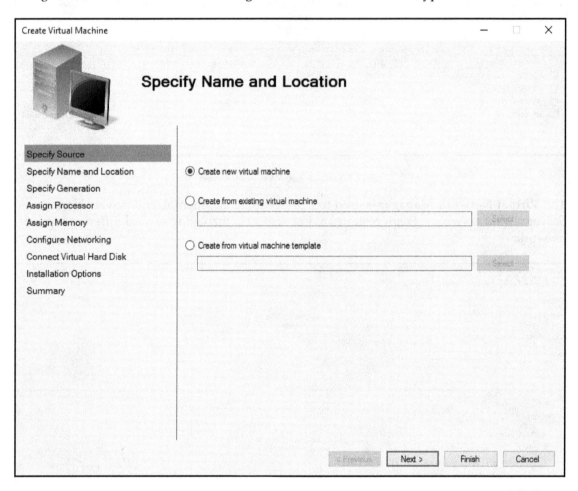

Figure 6. 5nine Manager create virtual machine wizard

In the **Specify Generation** page as shown in *Figure 7*, you can specify a desired VM generation and the virtual machine version that will be deployed on a Nano Server host:

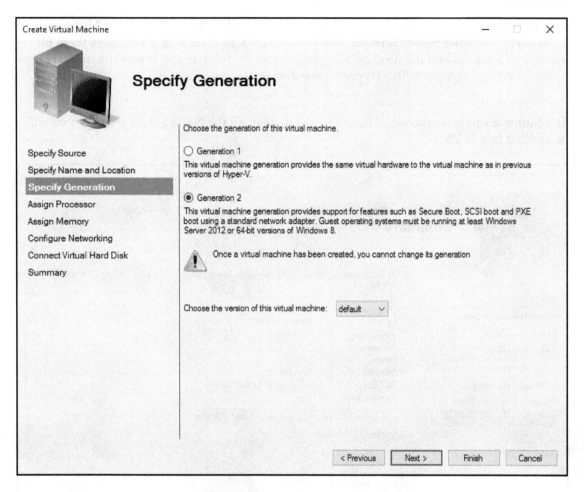

Figure 7. 5nine Manager Create Virtual Machine Wizard - Specifing VM generation

In earlier releases of Hyper-V, whenever you upgrade your host to a new release, the moment Hyper-V sees your virtual machines the configuration version will be upgraded automatically behind the scenes.

This behavior has been changed in Windows Server 2016 Hyper-V including Nano Server. When you import a virtual machine, Hyper-V will not automatically upgrade your virtual machine version. Upgrading a virtual machine configuration version is a manual operation that is separate from upgrading the host. This gives you the flexibility to move individual virtual machines back to Windows Server 2012 R2 Hyper-V if needed.

As a reference, version 5.0 is the configuration version of Windows Server 2012 R2. Version 2.1 was for Windows Server 2008 R2 SP1. The configuration version was always there for internal usage based on the functionality and not on the release, and it was not displayed to users. In Windows Server 2016 Hyper-V, the default VM version is 8.0.

The **Summary** page as shown in *Figure 8*, will display all the Nano Server settings that will be applied to this VM:

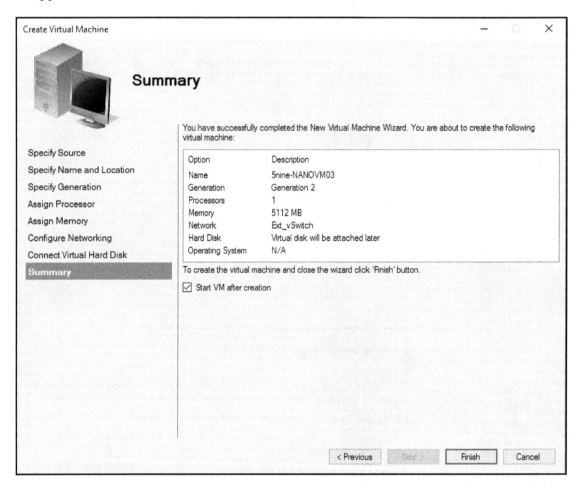

Figure 8. 5nine Manager Create Virtual Machine wizard, Summary

The 5nine Manager **Monitor** tab displays real-time and historical data about key performance metrics for Nano Server hosts and virtual machines. This includes CPU (%), memory (%), disk I/O (%), and network traffic (kbps), along with detailed data about cluster disk usage. In *Figure 9,* is an example of a Nano Server host, along with predictive utilization trend lines.

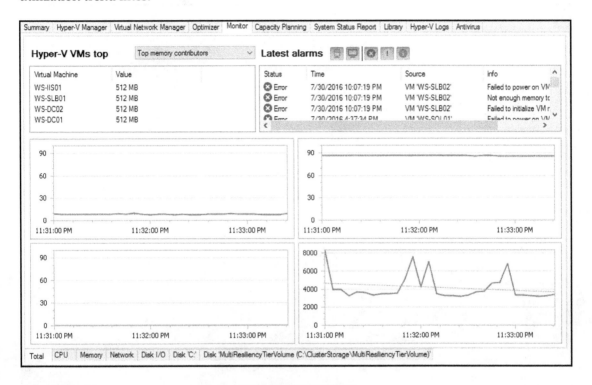

Figure 9. 5nine Manager Monitor tab

 Monitoring and history are available on a per-cluster-node level.

It is also possible to set custom alert thresholds from the **Options** on the **View** Menu. These thresholds allow you to set certain resource utilization limits for warnings and email alerts as shown in *Figure 10*. If one of these metrics is exceeded, you will be notified about the issue:

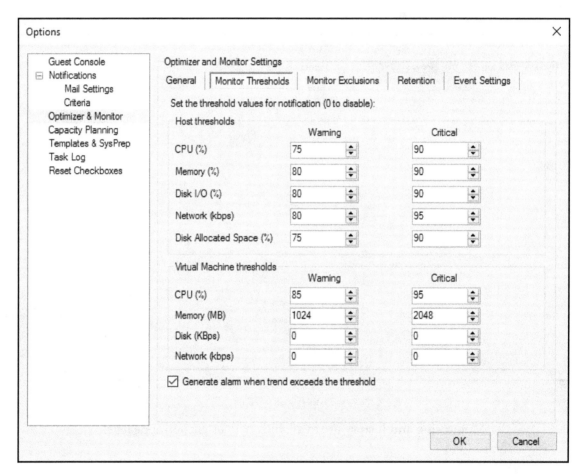

Figure 10. 5nine Manager setting custom alert thresholds

Any individual resource can be ignored if desired and there is also the ability to exclude any host or VM from being monitored at all. 5nine Manager also monitors the health of your disks, as shown in *Figure 11*, so you have enough storage capacity, notifying you if you are running low on space for your Nano Server virtual machines:

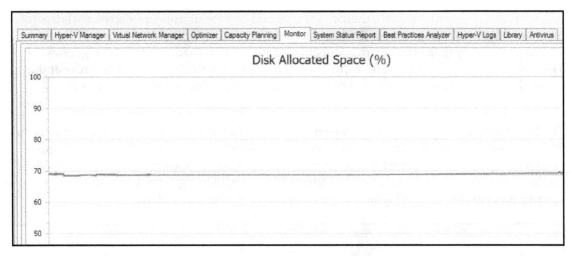

Figure 11. 5nine Manager monitor disk allocated space

5nine Manager's **Capacity Planning** tab, as shown in *Figure 12*, collects data from key performance indicators the Nano Server hosts and virtual machines, including CPU, memory, disk, and network utilization:

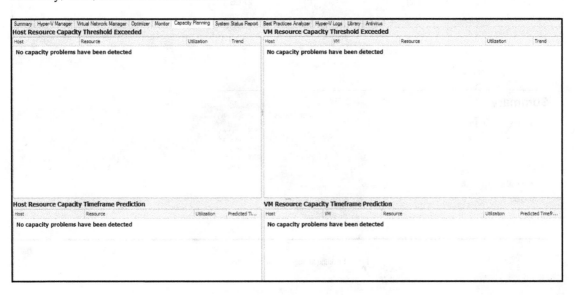

Figure 12. 5nine Manager Capacity Planning tab

After 5nine has monitored these metrics for a period of time, it uses predictive analytics to estimate the rate of utilization and when each resource will be fully consumed. This allows you to proactively make hardware acquisition requests, eliminating a lot of the guesswork. This solution lets you understand future needs to allow your infrastructure to grow at the optimal pace, and ensuring you do not get surprised when you are suddenly out of capacity.

The 5nine Manager **System Status Report** tab is used to dynamically create a report of each Nano Server host and the VMs running on it. After selecting key report information, the graphical report will inventory the configuration and settings of each component. This data can be saved and exported in several different file types, helping those with compliance reporting needs. In *Figure 13*, you can see an example of the useful data:

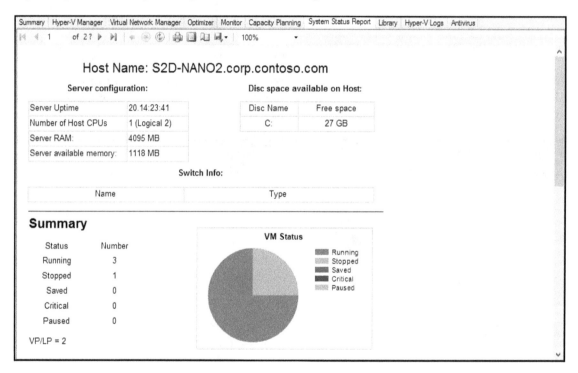

Figure 13. 5nine Manager System Status Report tab

5nine Manager also makes troubleshooting easy by integrating dozens of cluster, host, and virtual machine logs into the console. It is easy to filter and view different event information to help identify the source of your issues. See *Figure 14*:

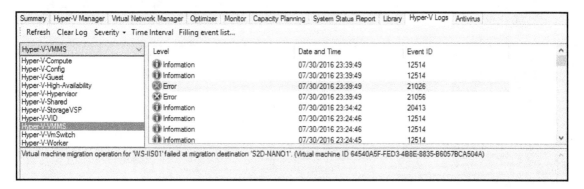

Figure 14. 5nine Manager Hyper-V Logs tab

Creating and managing Nano Server failover clusters with 5nine Manager

5nine Manager provides you with standard failover cluster operations, allowing you to create, validate, and configure a highly-available Nano Server infrastructure. The cluster best practice analyzer is even integrated into the process so you can ensure the highest uptime possible for your Nano Server virtual machines.

In this section, we will show you how to create and manage a Nano Server failover cluster with 5nine Manager.

Creating a cluster

5nine Manager lets you discover hosts and create a failover cluster. It will allow you to specify nodes, run cluster **Validation**, provide a client access point, and then create the cluster as shown in *Figure 15*:

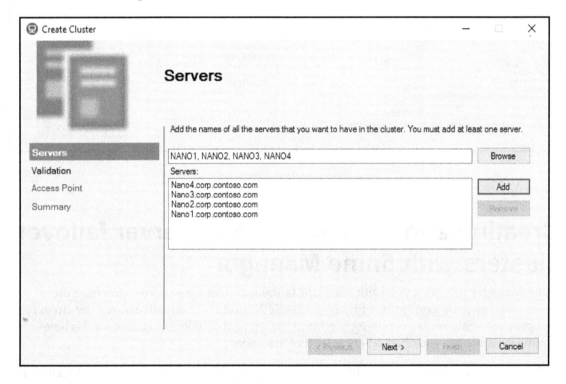

Figure 15. Create cluster wizard

Validating a cluster

Failover cluster validation is an essential task in all deployments as it is required for your cluster to be supported by Microsoft. With 5nine Manager, you can test the health of your cluster during configuration, or afterwards as a troubleshooting tool. You can granularly select the different tests to run as shown in *Figure 16*, and see the same graphical report you are familiar with:

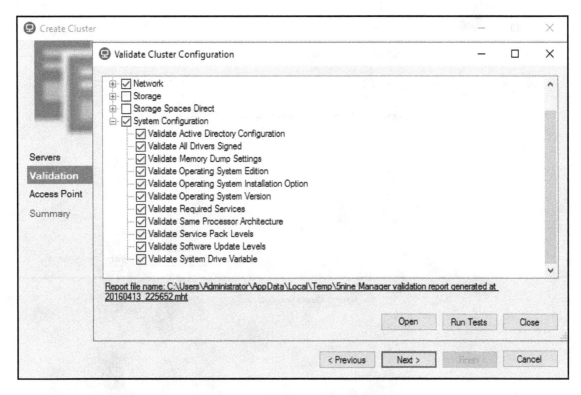

Figure 16. 5nine Manager Validate Cluster Configuration

Review the cluster validation report and click **Next**.

Specify the cluster **Access Point** name and add the static IP address as shown in *Figure 17*:

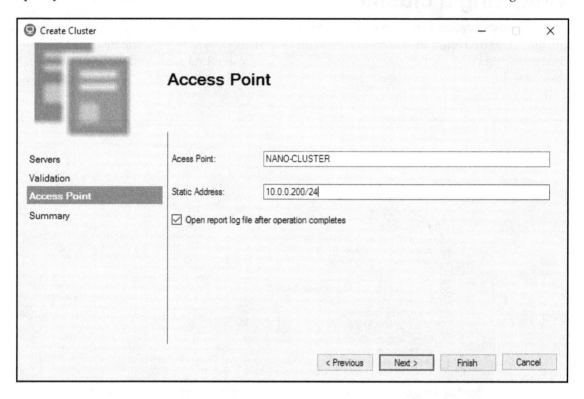

Figure 17. Creating Nano Cluster wizard

Click **Next**. Review the summary and click **Finish** (see *Figure 18*):

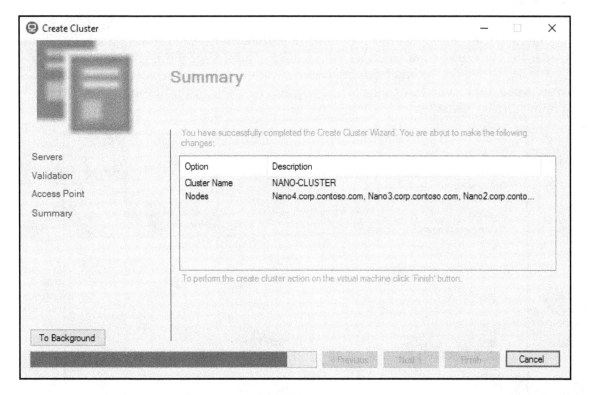

Figure 18. Creating Nano cluster summary

Configuring live migration settings

It is important to have a dedicated network for live migration to ensure that its traffic does not interfere with cluster heartbeats or other important traffic. With 5nine Manager you can specify the number of simultaneous live migrations and storage live migrations, and even copy those settings to the other cluster nodes. It is a best practice to configure all your clusters nodes the same way so that a VM operates the same, regardless of which host it is running on (see *Figure 19*):

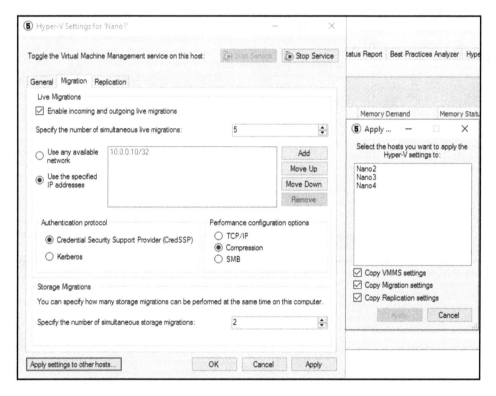

Figure 19. Configuring live migration settings

Viewing the cluster summary

5nine Manager has a summary dashboard that centrally reports the health of the cluster and its virtual machines. It quickly identifies nodes or VMs with problems, and lists any alerts from its resources. This Summary dashboard can also be refocused at the datacenter, cluster, host, and VM level for more refined results (see *Figure 20*):

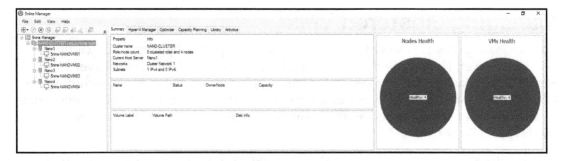

Figure 20. Cluster summary

Managing cluster nodes

With 5nine Manager, you can manage and configure your virtual disk and network settings. You can also perform standard maintenance tasks, such as to **Pause** and **Resume** a cluster node as shown in *Figure 21*, which will live-migrate VMs to other nodes as it evacuates a node to prepare for maintenance. A key point to mention is, when you let the cluster automatically choose nodes for placement (the best possible node), it will move the VMs to the node(s) with the most free memory. A list of active and failed cluster tasks is also displayed through the interface:

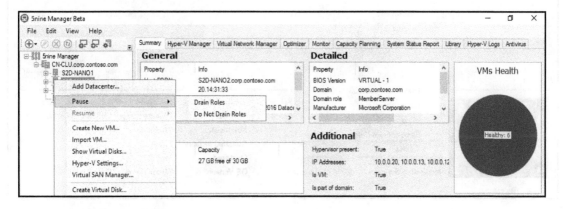

Figure 21. Pausing a cluster node

Managing clustered VMs

You can manage any type of virtual machine that is supported by Hyper-V, including Windows Server, Hyper-V Server, Windows, Linux, UNIX, and Windows Server 2016 Nano Server. 5nine Manager lets you centrally manage all your virtual machines, including the latest performance and security features for virtualization. The full GUI console even runs on all versions of Windows Server, including the otherwise GUI-less Windows Server Core and Hyper-V Server.

You can also **Set IP address** for Nano virtual machines, which makes remote network configuration much easier (see *Figure 22*):

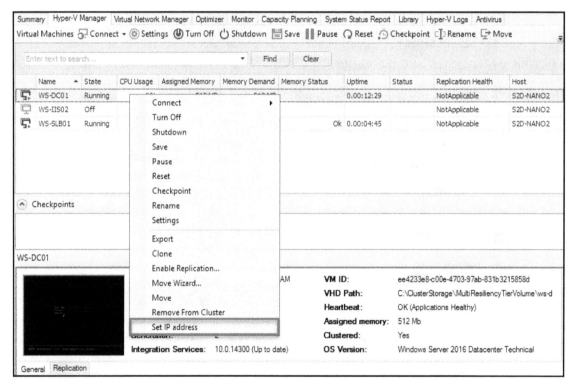

Figure 22. Set IP address on a Nano Server host

Host Load Balancing

5nine Manager allows you to group cluster nodes and hosts that will load-balance VMs. It live-migrates the VMs between hosts when customizable thresholds are exceeded. This type of dynamic optimization ensures that a single host does not get overloaded, providing higher-availability and greater performance for the virtual machines (see *Figure 23*):

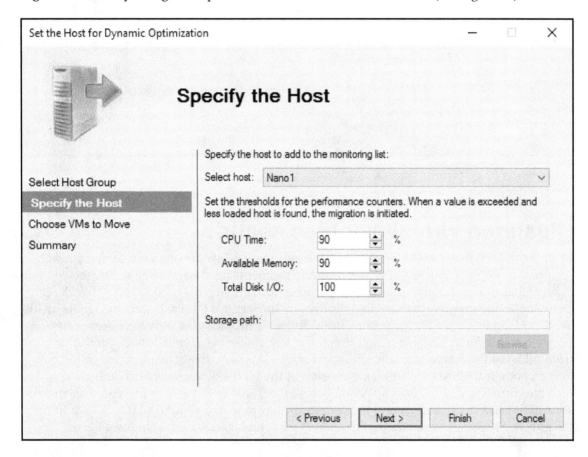

Figure 23. Host dynamic optimization

Failover clustering should be an integral part of your virtualized Nano Server infrastructure, and 5nine Manager provides a way to centrally manage all your clustered VMs.

Finally, you can also **Add Hyper-V Replica Broker** for the Nano cluster (see *Figure 24*):

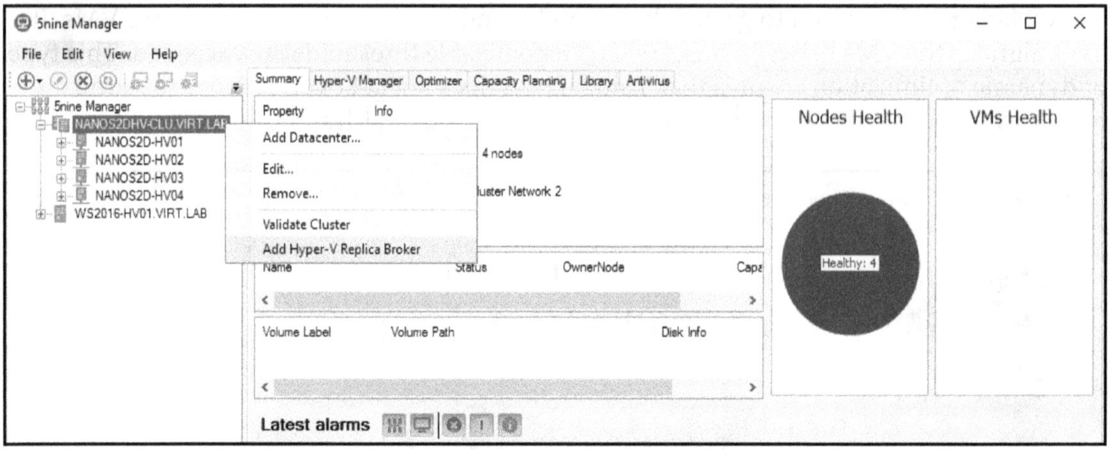

Figure 24. Adding Hyper-V replica broker

Clustered virtual machine security

In a physical environment, it is easy to install and manage agents on every server through endpoint protection. However, virtualized environments need to manage security differently from traditional data centers because virtual machines, disks, and networks can be dynamic and constantly changing. It's usually impractical to install security agents inside every VM. 5nine Cloud Security from 5nine Software provides the only agentless antivirus, firewall, and intrusion detection solution for Windows Server Hyper-V with protection from Bitdefender, Kaspersky labs, or ThreatTrack. This security software filters traffic going into and out of the VMs through an extension of the Hyper-V virtual switch, which provides protection at the host level and before the threat even reaches the VM. This means security is centrally managed and the user never has to worry about updating or scanning the guest OS, regardless of whether the VM is running Nano Server, Windows Server, Windows Client, or Linux.

> The antivirus functionality in 5nine Cloud Security is not supported for Nano Server-based Hyper-V hosts.

Get more information about 5nine Cloud security at:
`http://www.5nine.com/5nine-security-for-hyper-v-product.aspx`.

Summary

In this chapter, we discussed how to administer Nano Server using 5nine Manager from 5nine Software (`http://www.5nine.com`) and we showed you how to create and manage a Nano Server failover cluster.

Continue now to `Chapter 8`, *Running Windows Server Containers and Hyper-V Containers on Nano Server*, to learn more about Windows Server and Hyper-V Containers, and understand why Nano Server is a great platform for modern applications.

8
Running Windows Server Containers and Hyper-V Containers on Nano Server

When it comes to applications, historically IT administrators have deployed with a 1:1 application to server ratio. When the business needed a new application, it was deployed onto a newly provisioned physical system, to ensure no conflicts with existing applications and workloads. This resulted in a large number of physical servers, all with very low utilization.

Fast forward to a more modern datacenter today, where virtual machines are now prevalent, and you'll find significantly higher consolidation ratios, much greater utilization and significantly accelerated app deployment speeds as administrators deploy applications in minutes, compared to hours, days, or weeks in a purely physical datacenter.

There is however, a new and increasingly popular way to build, ship, deploy, and instantiate applications. Containers can further accelerate application deployment and streamline the way IT operations and development teams collaborate to deliver applications to the business.

In this chapter, we will talk about Windows containers, show you how to run containers on Nano Server, and we will cover the following topics:

- Container overview
- Windows Server containers and Hyper-V containers
- Running Windows containers on Nano Server

Container overview

Containers are an operating system-level isolation method for running multiple applications on a single control host. With developers building, and then packaging their applications into containers, and providing them to IT to run on a standardized platform, it reduces the overall effort to deploy applications, and can streamline the whole dev and test cycle, ultimately reducing costs. As containers can run on a host OS, which itself could be a physical or virtual machine, it provides IT with flexibility, and the opportunity to drive an increased level of server consolidation, all while keeping a level of isolation that allows many containers to share the same host operating system.

Container benefits

Applications are fueling the innovation in today's cloud-mobile world, and developers hold the keys to the power of those applications. The more streamlined and efficient the process for developers to build and deliver their applications, the faster more powerful applications can reach the business. This however, has to apply to both the developers and IT, who hold the keys when it comes to the infrastructure that the applications will run on.

For developers, containers unlock huge gains in productivity, and freedom; the ability to build an application, package it within a container, and deploy it, knowing that, wherever you deploy that container, it will run without modification, whether that is on-premise, in a service provider's datacenter, or in the public cloud using services such as Microsoft Azure. These containers don't have to be deployed independently - developers can model complex multi-tier applications, with each tier packaged within a container. This powerful abstraction of microservice architectures provides developers with incredible potential to deliver applications more rapidly than ever before. They can't however, do it without operations IT team support.

On the operations side, the Ops team benefit considerably from being able to gain ever higher levels of consolidation for applications and workloads than even virtualization could provide, and in addition they can put in place a platform that can rapidly scale up and down to meet the changing needs of the business. This standardized platform is easier to manage, yet provides developers with a consistent environment into which they can simply provide their app, and hit run.

This integration across development and operations is what's becoming known in the industry as DevOps. DevOps aims to integrate people, processes, and tools to streamline the application development and deployment life cycle. Ops can focus on providing a standardized infrastructure and a set of resources that can be consumed by the development teams, and developers can focus on designing, building, packaging, and testing their applications, using the platform that IT provides.

What is a container?

Now that we understand a little more about why containers are important to both operations and developers, it's important to understand just what a container is.

As shown in *Figure 1*, at the base we have a server. This could be physical, or a virtual machine, and at this stage it doesn't matter. On that server is a host operating system, which has container support within the kernel:

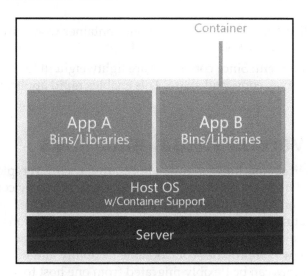

Figure 1. Container overview

If you think about an application, each app tends to have its own dependencies. This could include software, such as services, or libraries, or it could have hardware dependencies, such as CPU, memory, or storage. The container engine that exists within the host OS is essentially a lightweight virtualization mechanism that isolates these dependencies on an application basis, by packaging them into containers.

These containers run as isolated processes in the user space, on the host operating system, sharing the kernel with other containers. These containers can also be created instantly, which unlocks rapid scale-up and scale-down scenarios in response to changes in demand from the business.

There are a number of reasons why containers are attractive for developers and IT:

- **Fast iteration**: Containers allow for rapid iteration through the development process both because they are lightweight and because of the way the application is packaged with its dependencies.
- **Defined state separation**: Changes to the container don't affect other containers.
- **Resource controls**: You can constrain the resources used by a container. This ensures that a container gets resources such as CPU, RAM, and network bandwidth as specified and does not affect the performance of other containers running on the same host, because effectively a container can use what it needs if resources are not restrained. These resources are set at container runtime creation.
- **Immutability**: Changes made within one container won't affect containers running on the same host.
- **Rapid deployment**: Since containers are lightweight in terms of resources, they are easy to move, copy, and share. This enables rapid application deployment.

Containers versus virtual machines

If you think about a virtual machine as shown in *Figure 2*, each VM typically includes the app itself, the required binaries, libraries, and a guest OS, which may consist of multiple GBs of data. This runs on top of a hypervisor, and consumes a slice of resources from the underlying host operating system. One advantage of the virtualization approach is that the virtual machines can have different guest operating systems from one another, and from the host operating system, which provides considerable flexibility and high utilization. In addition, virtual machines can be flexibly migrated from one host to another, preserving state, and supplying administrators with considerable flexibility, especially in scenarios such as resource optimization and maintenance:

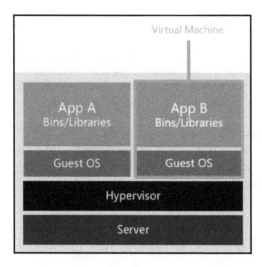

Figure 2. Virtual machine overview

Virtual machines also offer very high levels of isolation, both for resources and security, for key virtualized workloads.

However, you can achieve a best-of-both worlds approach, thus you can deploy containers inside virtual machines as shown in *Figure 3*:

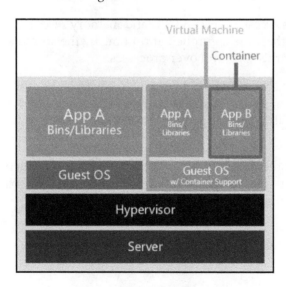

Figure 3. Container overview running in a virtual machine

Containers run on a host OS, but that host OS doesn't need to be a physical host. So, by running containers in virtual machines, you can deploy multiple, different VM operating systems, and inside, deploy multiple containers within those guest operating systems.

In this case, you would need fewer VMs to support a larger number of apps and fewer VMs would result in a reduction in resource consumption.

Each VM would support multiple isolated apps, albeit sharing the same guest operating system for the base image, but increasing overall density. This provides IT with considerable flexibility, as running containers inside VMs enables features such as live migration to increase service availability and host maintenance.

Windows Server containers and Hyper-V containers

Windows Server containers are isolated behind their own network compartment. This can be allocated a NAT DHCP or Static IP. Each container has an independent session namespace, which helps to provide isolation and security. The kernel object namespace is isolated per container, but it is shared with the same host operating system. The server that runs Windows Server container could be a physical or virtual machine.

Each container also has access to certain CPU and memory resources, along with storage and network capacity: these are controlled at runtime by the administrator, and this ensures a predictable and guaranteed control over processes.

As shown in *Figure 4*, there are two containers sharing a number of libraries. These packages also depend on a base OS image that describes the underlying operating system, such as Server Core, which has a large number of APIs that Windows supports, such as .NET, IIS, and so on.

Nano Server is also another base OS image; however, this has a much smaller surface, which will target apps that have been written from the ground up, with the cloud in mind; these are known as born-in-the-cloud applications:

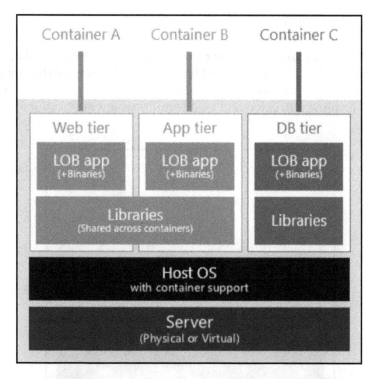

Figure 4. Windows Server containers

- The first challenge is, not enough isolation because the isolation is in user-mode, meaning a shared kernel. In a single environment where applications can be trusted this is not a problem, but in a multi-tenant or hosted environment, a malicious tenant may try to use the shared kernel to attack other containers.
- The second challenge is a dependency on the host OS version including the patch level, which may or may not cause problems; if a bad patch is deployed to the host, this could break the application running in the container.

Hyper-V containers have a slightly different approach to containerization. As shown in *Figure 5*, to create further isolation, each Hyper-V container has its own copy of the Windows kernel guest OS running in an optimized virtual machine, which is a key requirement for strong isolation.

Hyper-V is used for CPU, memory, and IO isolation (network and storage), which delivers the same level of isolation found in traditional VMs. Similar to VMs, the host only exposes a small, constrained interface to the container for the communication and sharing of host resources. This very limited sharing means Hyper-V containers have slightly less efficiency in terms of start-up times and density than Windows Server containers, but they have the isolation required to allow untrusted and hostile multi-tenant applications to run on the same host:

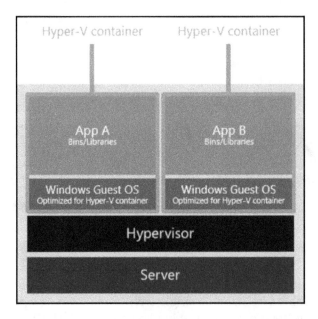

Figure 5. Hyper-V containers

Besides the optimizations to the OS that result from it being fully aware that it's in a container and not in a physical machine, Hyper-V containers will be deployed using Docker Engine (more on Docker in the following section) and can use the exact same packages that run in Windows Server containers. Thus, the trade-off between the level of isolation and efficiency and agility is a deploy-time decision, and not a development-time decision. The administrator of the host will decide whether to run the container in isolated mode or not.

Windows Server and Hyper-V containers will both take advantage of the smaller installation options, for Windows Server 2016: Server Core and the new deployment option Nano Server. Nano Server is a highly-optimized, headless deployment option for Windows Server that runs at a fraction of the Windows Server footprint and is ideal for cloud services.

What is Docker?

At a high level, Docker is an open source engine that automates the deployment of any application as a portable, self-sufficient container that can run almost anywhere. Docker is a management framework with a great set of management tools to manage the containers on whatever platform you are using.

In June 2014, Microsoft Azure added support for Docker containers on Linux VMs, enabling the broad ecosystem of **Dockerized** Linux applications to run within Azure's industry-leading cloud.

In October 2014, Microsoft and Docker Inc. jointly announced bringing the Windows Server ecosystem to the Docker community, through investments in Windows Server 2016, open-source development of the Docker Engine for Windows Server, Azure support for the Docker open orchestration APIs, and the federation of Docker Hub images into the Azure gallery and portal.

Windows containers can run in your private Datacenter, in a hosted service provider, or in any public cloud provider, and of course, Microsoft Azure.

Running Windows containers on Nano Server

Before we show you how to run Windows containers on Nano Server, we will discuss and explain the terminology that we will use in the subsequent sections:

- The host operating system that will run containers is called the container host. The containers could be either Windows Server containers or Hyper-V containers.
- Windows Server containers could be based on Server Core or Nano Server, which run without hypervisor dependency. Windows Server containers share the same kernel with the host, as well as each other.
- Hyper-V containers could also be based on Server Core or Nano Server, which run inside a special optimized virtual machine and require Hyper-V to be enabled on the container host operating system.

The following section will describe the deployment process for how to run Windows Server containers and Hyper-V containers on top of Nano Server, and then we will look at how to convert Windows Server containers to Hyper-V containers.

Creating a Nano Server image for Windows Server containers

The following section will detail the deployment of a very basic Nano Server configuration. For a more thorough explanation of deployment and configuration options for Nano Server, see `Chapter 2`, *Getting Started with Nano Server*.

Follow the steps mentioned to create a VHD(X) image for Nano Server to be used as a container host so we can run Windows Server containers:

1. Mount the Windows Server 2016 ISO medium on your machine. In this example, it's mounted on the `H` drive.

2. Start Windows PowerShell as an administrator, and run the following script to create a VHD(X) for virtual machine deployment that includes the `Container` package. You will be prompted for an administrator password:

```
#region variables$ComputerName="NANOVM-CRHOST"# Staging path for
new Nano image$StagingPath="C:\"# Path to Windows Server 2016 ISO
file$MediaPath="H:\"$Path=Join-Path-Path$StagingPath-
ChildPathNanoServer$Password=Read-Host-Prompt'Please specify local
Administrator password'-AsSecureString#endregion#region Copy source
filesif(-not(Test-Path-Path$StagingPath)) {mkdir-
Path$StagingPath}if(-not(Test-Path-Path$Path))
{$NanoServerSourcePath=Join-Path-Path$MediaPath-
ChildPathNanoServer-Resolve Copy-Item-Path$NanoServerSourcePath-
Destination$StagingPath-Recurse}#endregion#region Generate Nano
ImageImport-Module-Name(Join-Path-Path$Path-
ChildPathNanoServerImageGenerator) -Verbose$ServicingPackagePath=@(
   'C:\NanoServer\Updates\Servicing stack update\Windows10.0-
KB4013418-x64.msu' 'C:\NanoServer\Updates\Cumulative
Update\Windows10.0-KB4013429-
x64.msu')$NanoServerImageParameters=@{ComputerName =$ComputerName
MediaPath =$MediaPath BasePath =(Join-Path-Path$Path-
ChildPath$ComputerName)
   # .vhd for BIOS and .vhdx for UEFI system TargetPath =Join-Path-
Path$Path-ChildPath($ComputerName+'.vhdx')
   AdministratorPassword =$Password Containers =$true
EnableRemoteManagementPort =$true EnableEMS =$true DeploymentType
='Guest' Edition ='Datacenter' MaxSize =40GB ServicingPackagePath
=$ServicingPackagePath}New-
NanoServerImage@NanoServerImageParameters#endregion
```

The previous script will create a VHDX image file using Windows Server 2016 ISO mounted as the `H:\` drive. When creating the image, it uses a folder called `NanoServer` found on the root `C` drive. The file is placed under the same folder called `NANOVM-CRHOST`. In this example, the computer name is set to `NANOVM-CRHOST` and includes `Guest` drivers. We will deploy a generation 2 virtual machine, thus we created the image as VHDX.

We added the container package, which will ensure that the image has the container feature enabled so you can deploy Windows Server containers on top of Nano Server running as a container host.

We also enabled the remote management port, and finally we added the latest Windows Server updates to the image.

> The critical updates are required in order for the Windows Container feature to function properly.

Creating a Nano Server VM for Windows Server containers

Once the image is created, you need to create a virtual machine from this VHD(X).

The following is a quick PowerShell script that will create a Nano VM for you:

```
#variables$vSwitchName01="Ext_vSwitch01"$InstallRoot="D:\VMs\NANOVM-
CRHOST"$VMName="NANOVM-CRHOST"$adminPassword="P@ssw0rd"$localCred=new-
object-typenameSystem.Management.Automation.PSCredential`
            -argumentlist"Administrator", (ConvertTo-
SecureString$adminPassword-AsPlainText-
Force)$IP="172.16.20.185"$GWIP="172.16.20.1"$DNSIP="172.16.20.9"# Create
VMNew-VHD-Path($InstallRoot+"\NANOVM-CRHOST_D.vhdx") -SizeBytes50GB-
DynamicNew-VM-VHDPath($InstallRoot+"\NANOVM-CRHOST.vhdx") -Generation2-
MemoryStartupBytes4GB`
        -Name$VMName-Path$InstallRoot-SwitchName$vSwitchName01Set-VMMemory-
VMName$VMName-DynamicMemoryEnabled$falseSet-VMProcessor-VMName$VMName-
Count4Set-VM-VMName$VMName-AutomaticStopActionShutDown-
AutomaticStartActionStartIfRunningEnable-VMIntegrationService$VMName-
Name"Guest Service Interface"Rename-VMNetworkAdapter-VMName$VMName-
NewName"vmNIC-MGT"Set-VMNetworkAdapter-VMName$VMName-Name"vmNIC-MGT"-
DeviceNamingOnAdd-VMScsiController-VMName$VMNameAdd-VMHardDiskDrive-
VMName$VMName-ControllerTypeSCSI-ControllerNumber1-ControllerLocation0-
Path($InstallRoot+"\NANOVM-CRHOST_D.vhdx")Start-VM-Name$VMName|Out-Null#
```

```
Wait for VM to respondWait-VM-Name$VMName-ForHeartbeat# Set NANO VM IP
address statically using PowerShell DirectInvoke-Command-VMName$VMName-
Credential$localCred-ScriptBlock{
    New-NetIPAddress-InterfaceAlias"Ethernet"-IPAddress$Using:IP-
PrefixLength'24'-TypeUnicast-DefaultGateway$Using:GWIP Set-
DnsClientServerAddress-InterfaceAlias"Ethernet"-ServerAddress$Using:DNSIP
    # Initialize new data drive to store docker images Get-Disk|Where-
Object{$_.PartitionStyle -eq"RAW"} |Initialize-Disk-PassThru|`
    New-Partition-DriveLetterD-UseMaximumSize|Format-Volume-
AllocationUnitSize64KB-FileSystemNTFS-NewFileSystemLabel"Container Images"-
Confirm:$false}
```

The previous script will create a NanoServer as generation 2 VM, then will start the VM and wait for it to respond by using the `Wait-VM` cmdlet, and finally we set a static IP address and initialize a new data volume inside Nano VM using PowerShell Direct.

Creating a remote PowerShell session

Because Nano Server does not have an interactive log-on nor remote desktop capabilities, all management will be completed from a remote system using Windows PowerShell.

Since we did not add Nano Server to the domain, we need to add the Nano Server system to trusted hosts on our management machine so we can manage it remotely:

1. Replace the IP Address with the IP Address of your Nano Server:

    ```
    Set-Item WSMan:\localhost\Client\TrustedHosts "172.16.20.185" -
    Force
    ```

2. Create a remote PowerShell session by running the following command:

    ```
    $NanoIP = "172.16.20.185"$NanoCred = Get-Credential
    ~\Administrator $Session = New-PSSession -ComputerName $NanoIP
    -Credential $NanoCred
    ```

Installing Docker

Docker is needed to work with Windows containers. The Docker installer for Windows is now available in an online package repository. It can be found and installed using the Docker provider of the package management (a.k.a. OneGet) PowerShell module. The provider needs to be installed before we start using it.

The following PowerShell cmdlets can be used to install the provider.

1. Open a remote PowerShell session on Nano Server. This assumes that you have already completed the steps described earlier:

```
$Session | Enter-PSSession
```

2. Run the following command within the remote PowerShell session to install the Docker provider PowerShell module to the Nano machine:

```
Install-Module -Name DockerMsftProvider -Repository PSGallery -Force
```

3. Run the following command within the remote PowerShell session to install the latest version of Docker using the OneGet to Nano machine:

```
Install-Package -Name docker -ProviderName DockerMsftProvider
```

4. When the installation is completed, reboot the Nano Server machine.

```
Restart-Computer -Force
```

Installing base container images

The base OS images are used as the base for any Windows Server or Hyper-V container and their characteristics are described as follows:

- Container images are a read-only template used to start and create a container.
- These templates contain applications, dependencies, and instructions.
- These images can comprise multiple layers (that is you have a base OS image, and then you might have another layer on top of it for your web application).
- The layers are shared between containers. As an example: let's say you have deployed a base OS image named base01, the base OS image could be Server Core or Nano Server, then you installed Web Server onto it, and then you capture and create a new container image named web01 which contains, for example, an IIS server that you just installed. Then, you may redeploy web01 to new containers named App01 image and App02 image: these new container images have their own applications (that is HTML or PHP), but they share the same web server image, web01 and have a common base OS image, base01.
- The images might have process execution instructions known as bootstrapping (that is, every time you start a container based on a certain image, you can start a specific process).

- The images can be stored and retrieved from a container image repository (that is, a public repository such as Docker Hub).

If you are planning to use only Windows Server containers, the base OS image must match the container host operating system. In other words, if the container host OS is Nano Server as described in this chapter, then you can only run Nano containers. So, if you try to create a Server Core container on top of a Nano Server container host, you will encounter an error that states: The operating system of the container does not match the operating system of the host.

However, you can create containers based on a Server Core OS image, if you are planning to use only a Hyper-V container and have a Hyper-V hypervisor enabled on your Nano Server container host (more on that in the *Creating a Hyper-V Container* section).

The following steps will show you how to pull a Nano Server base OS image:

1. Open a remote PowerShell session on Nano Server. This assumes that you already completed the steps described earlier:

    ```
    $Session | Enter-PSSession
    ```

2. To download and install the latest Windows Nano Server base image on top of Nano Server container host, run the following command:

    ```
    Docker pull microsoft/nanoserver
    ```

3. To see the list of images that you have on that container host, run the following command:

    ```
    Docker images
    ```

    As shown in *Figure 6*, we have just one base OS image (Nano Server) that we downloaded in step 2:

```
[172.16.20.185]: PS C:\> docker images
REPOSITORY              TAG           IMAGE ID        CREATED         SIZE
microsoft/nanoserver    latest        d9bccb9d4cac    7 weeks ago     925 MB

[172.16.20.185]: PS C:\> |
```

Figure 6. Nano Server base OS image

4. The container images downloaded or created will be stored on the container host in the following default location:

```
C:\ProgramData\Microsoft\Docker\
```

5. It's also recommended you change the default image location path from drive C to another drive (more on that in the *Create Hyper-V Container* section).

Managing container networking

If you think about a Hyper-V host, we typically install several virtual machines on that host and each VM has its own IP address. The VM typically will have exposed the IP address as an endpoint like a physical system. If you want to access a resource that is being hosted on that VM, we used to access that VM directly. However, Windows containers support five different networking modes as follows:

- **Network Address Translation (NAT)**
- Transparent
- l2bridge
- l2tunnel
- Overlay

 For more information about the different container networking options, check the following article: https://docs.microsoft.com/en-us/virtua lization/windowscontainers/manage-containers/container-network ing.

For the remainder of this chapter, we will use the NAT networking option, as this is the commonly used scenario. With containers, we have a large density capability, we can literally deploy 1,000 containers on a single host. So rather than giving each container a publicly accessible IP address, we can put the container endpoint behind NAT. The container Nano host might have an IP address that is publicly available; however, the container itself has a non-routable IP address. When you want to access an application within the container, we will access the container host and then build port mapping between the external port on the host and the internal port on the container application. For example, the external and internal ports may be mapped (80:80, 81:80, and 82:80).

By default, when you install the Docker package on the container host, the Windows Docker Engine creates a default NAT network named `nat` with the IP prefix `172.16.0.0/12`. If you want to create a NAT network with a specific IP prefix, then you could do one of the following two things by changing the options in the Docker config `daemon.json` file located at `C:\ProgramData\Docker\config\daemon.json`. You need to create that file if it does not already exist (more on that in a bit):

- Use the `fixed-cidr": "< IP Prefix > / Mask` option, which will create the default NAT network with the IP prefix and match specified.
- Or else we can use the `"bridge": "none"` option, which will not create a default network; a user can create a user-defined network with any driver using the `docker network create -d`command.

Before changing either of the previous configuration options, the Docker service must first be stopped on the container host and any pre-existing NAT networks need to be deleted.

1. Open a remote PowerShell session on Nano Server:

    ```
    $Session | Enter-PSSession
    ```

2. You can check the current container NAT network subnet on the host by running the following command:

    ```
    Get-ContainerNetwork
    ```

    As shown in *Figure 7*, the current container network subnet is `172.26.64.0/20`:

```
[172.16.20.185]: PS C:\> Get-ContainerNetwork

Name Id                                    Subnets          Mode SourceMac DNSServers DNSSuffix
---- --                                    -------          ---- --------- ---------- ---------
nat  a5407c03-4215-40c4-b2a5-31dde98271e6  {172.26.64.0/20} NAT
```

Figure 7.Container Network Overview

3. We will change the container network subnet by running the following commands:

    ```
    Stop-Service dockerGet-ContainerNetwork | Remove-
    ContainerNetwork -Force
    ```

4. Next, we need to create a `daemon.json` file at
`C:\ProgramData\docker\config\daemon.json` on the Nano Server container host. Run the following command:

```
New-item -Type File C:\ProgramData\docker\config\daemon.json
```

5. Run the following command to edit the `daemon.json` file and add the desired network subnet:

```
Add-Content'C:\programdata\docker\config\daemon.json''{ "fixed-cidr":"172.21.16.0/20" }
```

6. Start the Docker service by running the following command:

```
Start-Service docker
```

7. Check the container NAT network again by running `Get-ContainerNetwork` and confirm that the new NAT subnet is created (see *Figure 8*):

```
[172.16.20.185]: PS C:\> Get-ContainerNetwork

Name Id                                      Subnets            Mode SourceMac DNSServers DNSSuffix
---- --                                      -------            ---- --------- ---------- ---------
nat  7f0ce07d-3250-45ef-b2a9-c9220e0b02a1    {172.21.16.0/20}   NAT
```

Figure 8. Create New container network

8. By default, the container endpoints will be connected to the default `nat` network.

To access applications running inside a container connected to a NAT network, we need to create port mappings between the container Nano host and the container endpoint.

Please note that port mappings must be specified at container creation time or while the container is in a `STOPPED` state.

In the following example, we will create a static mapping between port `8082` of the container host and port `80` of the container endpoint (more on that in the *Create Windows Server Container* section):

```
Docker run -it -p 8082:80 microsoft/nanoserver
```

Managing container storage

We discussed in the *Installing base container images* section how to install a container image. Container images are not designed for persistent data, because containers, by default, use a temporary scratch space on the container host's system drive media for storage during only the lifetime of the running container. So, if you put your database there and you stop or delete the container, the database is gone. It is possible to move the container scratch space location to a different drive (more on that in the *Create Hyper-V Container* section at the end of this chapter).

Container images are also not a good place to store secret data, because if you put any sensitive data on the container image and then you push that image to Docker Hub, then everybody can pull that image off and get access to the secrets.

A good option for container storage is volumes. Volumes are persistent storage for containers; you can map volumes into containers. You can enable read-only or read/write on a volume. And the most important aspect is that multiple containers running on the same container host can access the same location at the same time. Microsoft has just announced that you can also do network storage via SMB shares and access it through the container's network.

The following steps will show you how to use volumes by mapping a folder named `Container-Data` on the container host to a running container:

1. Create a folder on the container Nano host by running the following command:

   ```
   New-Item -Path D:\ -Name "Container-Data" -ItemType Directory
   ```

2. In this example, we will place a text file inside that folder for demo purposes. You can place anything you want:

   ```
   New-Item -Path D:\Container-Data\ -Name "database.txt" -
   ItemType File
   ```

3. When you create a container, you need to add the parameter (-v) for volume mapping to the command (`docker run`) followed by the location of the folder on the container host and the location path inside the container. The command will look like this:

   ```
   Docker run -it -v d:\Container-Data:c:\data
   microsoft/nanoserver powershell
   ```

In this example, we created a new Nano container and ran PowerShell in an interactive session. While in the container, you can see the `Data` folder is showing inside the container, and the text file that we created on the container host named `database.txt` is visible as well (see *Figure 9*):

```
Windows PowerShell
Copyright (C) 2016 Microsoft Corporation. All rights reserved.

PS C:\> ls


    Directory: C:\


Mode                 LastWriteTime         Length Name
----                 -------------         ------ ----
d----l        3/7/2017   7:51 AM                 data
d-----        3/7/2017   7:51 AM                 Program Files
d-----       7/16/2016   5:09 AM                 Program Files (x86)
d-r---        3/7/2017   7:51 AM                 Users
d-----        3/7/2017   7:51 AM                 Windows
-a----      11/20/2016   3:32 AM           1894 License.txt


PS C:\> Get-ChildItem -Path C:\data


    Directory: C:\data


Mode                 LastWriteTime         Length Name
----                 -------------         ------ ----
-a----        3/7/2017   7:16 AM              0 database.txt
```

Figure 9. Using volumes in a container

When the container starts-up, it sees an extra folder on the C drive called `data`. That folder is directly mapped to the container host, so anything you write to that folder shows on the container host (`D:\Container-Data`) in this example and vice versa. So, when that container is stopped and removed, all the data changes made in the container are still available on the container host's volume. This is the best approach for storing databases that support running SQL Server inside a container.

Managing Docker on Nano Server

Before we start creating Windows Server or Hyper-V containers, we need to manage Docker on Nano Server from a remote management system using the Docker command-line interface. This is because PowerShell Remoting, including PowerShell ISE, currently cannot redirect the **teletype** (**TTY**) terminal output of an interactive container shell to the initial client's prompt (see *Figure 10*).The interactive container command is docker run -it:

```
[172.16.20.185]: PS C:\> docker run -it microsoft/nanoserver cmd
docker : the input device is not a TTY.  If you are using mintty, try prefixing the command with 'winpty'
    + CategoryInfo          : NotSpecified: (the input devic...d with 'winpty':String) [], RemoteException
    + FullyQualifiedErrorId : NativeCommandError
```

Figure 10. Running the Docker command-line in a remote session

Please note that you can also manage containers with Docker PowerShell as an alternative to the Docker command-line interface (Docker), or alongside it. However, the PowerShell module is currently still in alpha status and is likely to change rapidly.

For more information about Docker-PowerShell module, please check the following repository: https://github.com/Microsoft/Docker-PowerShell.

For the remainder of this chapter, we will use the Docker command-line interface natively to manage Windows containers on top of Nano Server.

The following steps can be used to prepare a Nano container host for Docker remote management:

1. Open a remote PowerShell session on Nano Server:

   ```
   $Session | Enter-PSSession
   ```

2. Create a firewall rule on the Nano container host for the Docker remote connection. We will use port 2375 for an unsecure connection:

   ```
   New-NetFirewallRule -DisplayName 'Docker Inbound' -Name "Docker
   daemon" -Profile Any -Direction Inbound -Action Allow -Protocol
   TCP -LocalPort 2375 -Description "Inbound rule for Docker
   daemon to allow the Docker Engine to accept incoming
   connections over [TCP 2375]."
   ```

Please note that it is NOT recommended to use an unsecure connection in production. For more information on securing this connection over TCP port 2376 (Docker TLS), see `https://docs.microsoft.com/en-us/virtu alization/windowscontainers/management/manage_remotehost`.

3. Next, we need to configure the Docker Engine to accept an incoming connection over TCP port 2375. But first, we need to create a `daemon.json` file at `C:\ProgramData\docker\config\daemon.json` on the Nano Server container host. You can skip this step if you already created a `daemon.json` file in an earlier step:

```
New-item -Type File C:\ProgramData\docker\config\daemon.json
```

4. Next, run the following command to add connection configuration to the `daemon.json` file that we just created in the previous step. This configures the Docker Engine to accept incoming connections over TCP port 2375. (See *Figure 11*). You can add more than one configuration option to the `daemon.json` file, but you need to make sure to separate them with commas:

```
Add-Content 'C:\programdata\docker\config\daemon.json' '{ "hosts": ["tcp://0.0.0.0:2375", "npipe://"] }'
Cat -Path 'C:\programdata\docker\config\daemon.json'
```

```
[172.16.20.185]: PS C:\> Add-Content 'C:\programdata\docker\config\daemon.json' '{ "hosts": ["tcp://0.0.0.0:2375", "npipe://"] }'
[172.16.20.185]: PS C:\> Cat -Path 'C:\programdata\docker\config\daemon.json'
{ "hosts": ["tcp://0.0.0.0:2375", "npipe://"] }
[172.16.20.185]: PS C:\>
```

Figure 11. Adding a connection to daemon.json file

5. Finally, we will restart the Docker service on the Nano Server container host by running the following command:

```
Restart-Service docker
```

6. On the remote management system where you will be working, we need to download the Docker client by running the following command:

```
Invoke-
WebRequesthttps://download.docker.com/components/engine/windows
-server/cs-1.12/docker.zip-OutFile"$env:TEMP\docker.zip"-
UseBasicParsing
```

7. Next, we need to extract the compressed package that we downloaded in the previous step by running the following command:

```
Expand-Archive -Path "$env:TEMP\docker.zip" -DestinationPath
$env:ProgramFiles
```

8. Run the following command to add the Docker directory (client) to the system path. This will enforce the path setting even after the system is rebooted:

```
[Environment]::SetEnvironmentVariable("Path", $env:Path +
";C:\Program Files\Docker",
[EnvironmentVariableTarget]::Machine)
```

9. Once completed, the Nano container host can be accessed and managed remotely. We will create an environmental variable named DOCKER_HOST on the management system that will ease the interaction with the Nano container host so we can run Docker command-line remotely.

The following is the PowerShell command that can be used for this purpose:

1. Replace the IP address with the IP address of your Nano Server:

```
$env:DOCKER_HOST = "tcp://172.16.20.185:2375"
```

2. Once the variable is set as described in the previous step, you can start running the Docker command-line directly from your management system as shown in *Figure 12*:

```
PS C:\> docker images
REPOSITORY              TAG        IMAGE ID          CREATED         SIZE
microsoft/nanoserver    latest     d9bccb9d4cac      7 weeks ago     925 MB

PS C:\>
```

Figure 12. Running the Docker command-line locally against the Nano container host

Creating a Windows Server container

Before starting to create Windows containers (either a Server container or a Hyper-V container), we need a base OS image. As mentioned earlier, base OS images are available with either Server Core or Nano Server as the container operating system.

You can also create and build your own container images and upload them to Docker Hub; see the article at: `https://docs.docker.com/engine/getstarted/step_four/` for more information.

In this example, we will pull, from Docker Hub, a Nano Server-based OS image with the IIS role enabled.

The following steps are performed from the management system:

1. You can search the available images on Docker Hub by running the following command followed by a filter value (that is, IIS):

   ```
   Docker search IIS
   ```

2. Next, we will pull the image named `cobra300/nano-iis` it by running the following command:

   ```
   Docker pull cobra300/nano-iis
   ```

3. Once the base image is downloaded, you can confirm by running the following command (see *Figure 13*):

   ```
   Docker images
   ```

```
PS C:\> docker images
REPOSITORY           TAG       IMAGE ID         CREATED         SIZE
cobra300/nano-iis    latest    ed500c7136a7     7 weeks ago     1.01 GB
```

Figure 13. Docker images available on Nano a container host

4. To create a Windows Server container based on this image, run the following command (`docker run -dt` means that the detached containers can be started and will run in the background):

   ```
   Docker run -dt -p 8082:80 cobra300/nano-iis
   ```

5. To check if the container is created and running, you can run the following command (see *Figure 14*):

```
Docker ps
```

Figure 14. Windows Server container running on Nano container host

6. To see all containers available on the container host regardless of whether they are running or not, you can run:

```
Docker ps-a
```

7. To stop a container, you can run Docker stop followed by the container ID:

```
Docker stop 37cd2ca12e78
```

8. To start a container, you can run Docker start followed by the container ID:

```
Docker start 37cd2ca12e78
```

9. For all the available Docker command-lines, type `docker -help`.

10. For more information on a specific command, type `docker COMMAND --help` (see *Figure 15*):

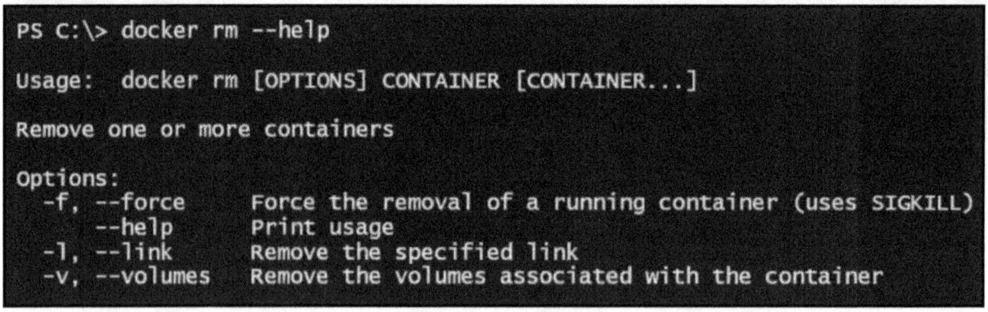

```
PS C:\> docker rm --help

Usage:  docker rm [OPTIONS] CONTAINER [CONTAINER...]

Remove one or more containers

Options:
  -f, --force      Force the removal of a running container (uses SIGKILL)
      --help       Print usage
  -l, --link       Remove the specified link
  -v, --volumes    Remove the volumes associated with the container
```

Figure 15. Docker COMMAND Help

11. On your management machine, open your favorite web browser and type the IP address of the container host followed by the TCP port (8082) that we specified in step 4. (See *Figure 16*):

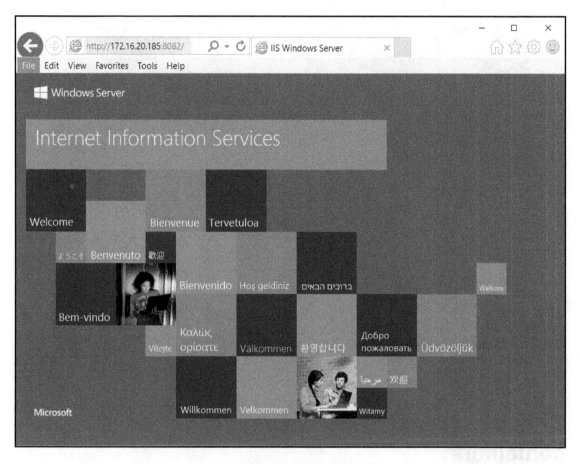

Figure 16.IIS running in a Nano container

As you can see, the container host will translate port 8082 from the external IP 172.16.20.185 to the container endpoint on port 80, the IIS welcome page is launched, and this confirms that IIS is running inside a Nano container.

12. To run a command in a running container, run the following command (see *Figure 17*):

```
Docker exec -it 37cd2ca12e78 ipconfig
```

We ran the command `exec` in an interactive mode using the `-it` parameter, followed by the container ID and the `ipconfig` command.

In this example, the IP address of the Nano container is `172.21.24.219`:

```
PS C:\> docker exec -it 37cd2ca12e78 ipconfig
[2J[H[37;40m


Windows IP Configuration


Ethernet adapter vEthernet (Container NIC 9297f000):


   Connection-specific DNS Suffix  . :

   Link-local IPv6 Address . . . . . : fe80::2581:6327:ea64:3add%14

   IPv4 Address. . . . . . . . . . . : 172.21.24.219

   Subnet Mask . . . . . . . . . . . : 255.255.240.0

   Default Gateway . . . . . . . . . : 172.21.16.1
```

Figure 17. Viewing the Nano container IP address

Creating a Nano Server image for Hyper-V containers

To run Hyper-V containers, the Hyper-V role is required to be enabled on a Nano Server container host. If the container Nano host is itself a Hyper-V virtual machine as described in the following example, then nested virtualization should be enabled before adding the Hyper-V role.

Follow the steps to create a VHD(X) image for Nano Server to be used as a container host, so we can run Hyper-V containers alongside Windows Server containers:

1. Mount the Windows Server 2016 ISO medium on your machine. In this example, it's mounted on the H drive.

2. Start Windows PowerShell as an administrator, and run the following script to create a VHD(X) for virtual machine deployment that includes the `Container` and `Compute` packages. You will be prompted for an administrator password:

```
#region variables$ComputerName="NANOVM-CRVHOST"# Staging path
for new Nano image$StagingPath="C:\"# Path to Windows Server
2016 ISO file $MediaPath="H:\"$Path=Join-Path-Path$StagingPath-
ChildPathNanoServer$Password=Read-Host-Prompt'Please specify
local Administrator password'-AsSecureString#endregion #region
Copy source filesif(-not(Test-Path-Path$StagingPath)) {

  mkdir-Path$StagingPath
}if(-not(Test-Path-Path$Path)) {

  $NanoServerSourcePath=Join-Path-Path$MediaPath-
ChildPathNanoServer-Resolve Copy-Item-
Path$NanoServerSourcePath-Destination$StagingPath-Recurse}
#endregion #region Generate Nano ImageImport-Module-Name(Join-
Path-Path$Path-ChildPathNanoServerImageGenerator) -Verbose
$ServicingPackagePath=@(
  'C:\NanoServer\Updates\Servicing stack update\Windows10.0-
kb3211320-x64.msu' 'C:\NanoServer\Updates\Cumulative
Update\Windows10.0-kb4010672-x64.msu')
  $NanoServerImageParameters=@{

  ComputerName =$ComputerName MediaPath =$MediaPath BasePath
=(Join-Path-Path$Path-ChildPath$ComputerName)
  # .vhd for BIOS and .vhdx for UEFI system TargetPath =Join-
Path-Path$Path-ChildPath($ComputerName+'.vhdx')
  AdministratorPassword =$Password Compute =$true Containers
=$true EnableRemoteManagementPort =$true EnableEMS =$true
DeploymentType ='Guest' Edition ='Datacenter' MaxSize =40GB
ServicingPackagePath =$ServicingPackagePath}
  New-NanoServerImage@NanoServerImageParameters#endregio
```

The previous script will create a VHDX image file using the Windows Server 2016 ISO mounted on the `H:\` drive. When creating the image, it uses a folder called `NanoServer` found on the `root C` drive. The file is placed in the same folder called `NANOVM-CRVHOST`. In this example, the computer name is set to `NANOVM-CRVHOST` and includes `Guest` drivers. We will deploy a generation 2 virtual machine, thus we created the image as VHDX.

We added both the container and compute packages; this will ensure that the image has the container feature enabled so you can deploy Windows Server and Hyper-V containers. We also enabled the remote management port, and finally we added the latest Windows Server updates to the image.

> The critical updates are required in order for the Windows Container feature to function properly.

Creating a Nano Server VM for Hyper-V containers

Once the image is created, you need to create a virtual machine from this VHD(X).

The following is a quick PowerShell script that will create a Nano VM and enable nested virtualization for you:

```
#Variables$vSwitchName01="Ext_vSwitch01"$InstallRoot="D:\VMs\NANOVM-
CRHOST"$VMName="NANOVM-CRVHOST"$adminPassword="P@ssw0rd"$localCred=new-
object-typenameSystem.Management.Automation.PSCredential`
            -argumentlist"Administrator",(ConvertTo-
SecureString$adminPassword-AsPlainText-
Force)$IP="172.16.20.185"$GWIP="172.16.20.1"$DNSIP="172.16.20.9"# Create
VMNew-VHD-Path($InstallRoot+"\NANOVM-CRVHOST_D.vhdx") -SizeBytes50GB-
DynamicNew-VM-VHDPath($InstallRoot+"\NANOVM-CRVHOST.vhdx") -Generation2-
MemoryStartupBytes4GB`
        -Name$VMName-Path$InstallRoot-SwitchName$vSwitchName01# Disable
dynamic memory for nested virtualizationSet-VMMemory-VMName$VMName-
DynamicMemoryEnabled$false# Configure virtual processor for nested
virtualizationSet-VMProcessor-VMName$VMName-Count4-
ExposeVirtualizationExtensions$true# Enable mac address spoofing and device
namingRename-VMNetworkAdapter-VMName$VMName-NewName"vmNIC-MGT"Set-
VMNetworkAdapter-VMName$VMName-Name"vmNIC-MGT"-DeviceNamingOn-
MacAddressSpoofingOnAdd-VMScsiController-VMName$VMNameAdd-VMHardDiskDrive-
VMName$VMName-ControllerTypeSCSI-ControllerNumber1-ControllerLocation0-
Path($InstallRoot+"\NANOVM-CRVHOST_D.vhdx")Set-VM-VMName$VMName-
AutomaticStopActionShutDown-AutomaticStartActionStartIfRunningEnable-
VMIntegrationService$VMName-Name"Guest Service Interface"Start-VM-
Name$VMName|Out-Null# Wait for VM to respondWait-VM-Name$VMName-
ForHeartbeat# Set NANO VM IP address statically using PowerShell
DirectInvoke-Command-VMName$VMName-Credential$localCred-ScriptBlock{New-
NetIPAddress-InterfaceAlias"Ethernet"-IPAddress$Using:IP-PrefixLength'24'-
TypeUnicast-DefaultGateway$Using:GWIP Set-DnsClientServerAddress-
InterfaceAlias"Ethernet"-ServerAddress$Using:DNSIP

   # Initialize new data drive to store docker images Get-Disk|Where-
Object{$_.PartitionStyle -eq"RAW"} |Initialize-Disk-PassThru|`
   New-Partition-DriveLetterD-UseMaximumSize|Format-Volume-
AllocationUnitSize64KB-FileSystemNTFS-NewFileSystemLabel"Container Images"-
Confirm:$false}
```

The previous script will create a Nano Server generation 2 VM. We disabled dynamic memory, and we enabled nested virtualization and MAC address spoofing. Then we start the VM and wait for it to respond by using the `Wait-VM` cmdlet; and finally we set a static IP address and initialize a new data volume inside Nano VM using PowerShell Direct.

Creating a Hyper-V container

Managing Hyper-V containers with Docker is almost identical to managing Windows Server containers. For more details, please refer to the sections entitled *Installing Docker, Managing container networking,* and *Managing Docker on Nano Server.*

In the following example, we will download a Windows Server Core base OS image with the IIS role enabled, and then we will run Hyper-V containers on top of the Nano Server container host.

Before you proceed, please make sure to complete the steps described earlier:

1. In this step, we will change the Docker images and the scratch space location on the container host. First, we need to create a `daemon.json` file at `C:\ProgramData\docker\config\daemon.json` on the Nano Server container host. You can skip this step if you already created this file in an earlier step. Run the following command:

   ```
   New-item -Type File C:\ProgramData\docker\config\daemon.json
   ```

2. Run the following command to edit the `daemon.json` file and add the desired container scratch space location. In this example, we have added the following three configuration options:

   ```
   Add-Content'C:\programdata\docker\config\daemon.json''{
   "hosts": ["tcp://0.0.0.0:2375", "npipe://"],"fixed-
   cidr":"172.21.16.0/20","graph": "D:\\ProgramData\\Docker" }'
   ```

3. Start the Docker service by running the following command:

   ```
   Start-Service docker
   ```

4. Download the Windows Server Core (IIS) image from Docker Hub by running the following command:

   ```
   Docker pull microsoft/iis
   ```

5. Once the base image is downloaded, you can confirm it by running the following command (see *Figure 18*):

```
Docker images
```

Figure 18. Windows Server Core base OS image with IIS

6. It's very important to note that the Nano Server base OS image is much smaller in size than the Server Core image (see *Figure 19*):

Figure 19. Server Core image versus Nano Server image

7. To create a Hyper-V container with the Docker command-line, the `--isolation=hyperv` parameter must be used as shown in the following example:

```
dockerrun-dt-p8082:80--isolation=hypervmicrosoft/iisdockerrun-
dt-p8083:80--isolation=hypervmicrosoft/iis
```

You might notice that creating a Hyper-V container for the first time can take a bit longer than a Windows Server container and this is expected because of the isolation around the hypervisor. You might also note that starting and stopping a Hyper-V container is also slower than a Windows Server container.

If you don't specify the `--isolation=hyperv` parameter, the container will be created as a Windows Server container by default.

In the previous example, we created two Hyper-V containers and mapped each one to a different TCP port:

1. On the container Nano host, the **virtual machine work process** (**vmwp**) is visible and the Hyper-V container is running in a specialized virtual machine that is encapsulating the running container and protecting the running processes from the container host operating system (see *Figure 20*):

```
[172.16.20.185]: PS C:\> Get-Process -Name vmwp -IncludeUserName | FT -AutoSize

Handles WS(K) CPU(s)    Id UserName                                                      ProcessName
------- ----- ------    -- --------                                                      -----------
      0 15516   3.88   312 NT VIRTUAL MACHINE\4FCB6FB4-884C-4A34-B978-8032F5C2F977 vmwp
      0 24028   1.75  2660 NT VIRTUAL MACHINE\CFA4A4CF-C4A2-4F73-858E-610A1B7D82ED vmwp
      0 22936   1.52  2956 NT VIRTUAL MACHINE\8855CB15-8624-4972-A028-F0C45E30027C vmwp
```

Figure 20. Virtual machine work process for a Hyper-V container

2. With Hyper-V containers, you can run multiple container instances concurrently on a container host; however, each container runs inside a special optimized virtual machine. This gives kernel level isolation between each Hyper-V container and the container host.

3. You can use the `Test-Connection` cmdlet from your management machine to check if the containers running on the container Nano host are responding through the external IP address with their specified TCP port (see *Figure 21*):

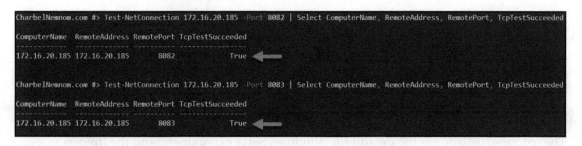

Figure 21. Tesing connection output for running containers

Converting a Windows Server container to a Hyper-V container

You can take any Windows Server container, develop it up, make sure it's working as expected, and then convert it to a Hyper-V container.

So, if you are developer and you are building an application, you can package it and deploy it as Windows Server container in a test environment probably, and then convert it to a Hyper-V container and run it in a more isolated environment. In this case, you don't have to change your application.

In the following example, we will demonstrate how to convert a Windows Server container to a Hyper-V container running on top of a Nano Server container host:

1. To find out what runtime or isolation technology you are using for those containers, you can add the parameter `--filter` to the `docker ps` command to list and filter by the isolation technology of the running containers. You can add the (`-a`) parameter to the same command to check whether all the existing containers are running or not.
2. In this example, we have three containers running; two of them are Hyper-V containers and the third one is a Windows Server container (see *Figure 22*):

```
Docker ps --filter "isolation=hyperv"Docker ps --filter
"isolation=process"
```

```
PS C:\> docker ps --filter "isolation=hyperv"
CONTAINER ID    IMAGE           COMMAND                 CREATED         STATUS            PORTS
cb6e6ccf21a5    microsoft/iis   "C:\\ServiceMonitor..." 13 hours ago    Up About an hour  0.0.0.0:8083->80/tcp
a59fff688fc7    microsoft/iis   "C:\\ServiceMonitor..." 13 hours ago    Up About an hour  0.0.0.0:8082->80/tcp

PS C:\> docker ps --filter "isolation=process"
CONTAINER ID    IMAGE             COMMAND                 CREATED         STATUS          PORTS
f654227ca0ac    cobra300/nano-iis "C:\\ServiceMonitor..." 20 minutes ago  Up 20 minutes   0.0.0.0:8085->80/tcp
```

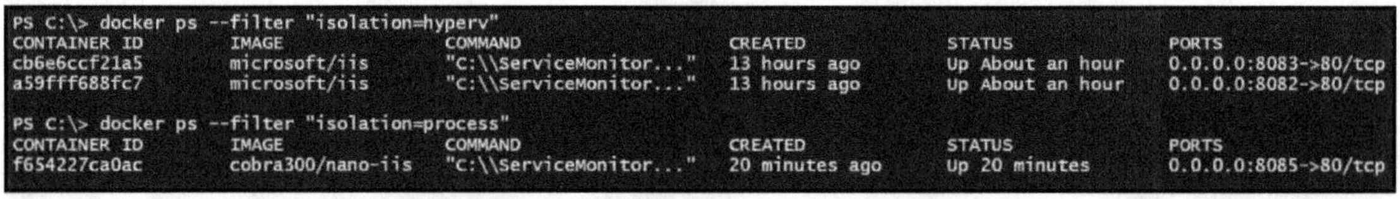

Figure 22. Filter running Hyper-V and Windows Server containers

The (process) isolation is the default for Windows Server containers, and the (hyperv) isolation is for Hyper-V containers.

The default isolation on Windows server operating systems is (process). Please note that the default and only supported isolation on a Windows 10 client operating system is (hyperv). An attempt to start a container on a client operating system with (`--isolation process`) will fail.

To convert a Windows Server container to a Hyper-V container, you need first to stop the container, then capture the current state that is creating a new image from the container's changes, and finally start the container with the isolation technology as hyperv (see *Figure 23*).

In this example, the container ID that we will convert is f654227ca0ac:

```
Docker stop f654227ca0acDocker commit --author "Charbel Nemnom"
f654227ca0ac nano-hvctn:CNDocker imagesDocker run -name
convert_wsctn_hvctn -dt -p 8085:80 --isolation=hyperv nano-hvctn:CN
```

```
PS C:\> docker ps --filter "isolation=process"
CONTAINER ID        IMAGE                COMMAND             CREATED          STATUS            PORTS
f654227ca0ac        cobra300/nano-iis    "C:\\ServiceMonitor..."  23 hours ago     Up 9 seconds      0.0.0.0:8085->80/tcp

PS C:\> docker stop f654227ca0ac
f654227ca0ac

PS C:\> Docker commit --author "Charbel Nemnom" f654227ca0ac nano-hvctn:CN
sha256:d379cea520b7ac98f019c1e538968777e1645afb121304cdcf8d65ff2044530f

PS C:\> docker images
REPOSITORY          TAG         IMAGE ID        CREATED          SIZE
nano-hvctn          CN          d379cea520b7    14 seconds ago   1.05 GB
microsoft/iis       latest      a3dd2dff392b    6 weeks ago      9.82 GB
cobra300/nano-iis   latest      ed500c7136a7    7 weeks ago      1.01 GB
microsoft/nanoserver latest     d9bccb9d4cac    8 weeks ago      925 MB

PS C:\> docker run --name convert_wsctn_hvctn -dt -p 8085:80 --isolation=hyperv nano-hvctn:CN
6af0a596f34cfa5d3eae8c9f6b7bfc5ab97e8ab0903fe6329ae34f4fb369593a

PS C:\> docker ps --filter "isolation=hyperv"
CONTAINER ID        IMAGE            COMMAND             CREATED          STATUS            PORTS
6af0a596f34c        nano-hvctn:CN    "C:\\ServiceMonitor..."  27 seconds ago   Up 22 seconds     0.0.0.0:8085->80/tcp
```

Figure 23. Converting a Windows Server container to a Hyper-V container

Summary

In this chapter, we discussed Windows containers and how they can change the way we deploy applications. We also talked about container benefits and how they can integrate across Dev and Ops teams to accelerate application delivery.

Finally, we showed you how to deploy and run a Windows Server container and a Hyper-V container on top of Nano Server using Nano base OS and Server Core images running IIS.

It's worth noting that not all web applications will run on Nano Server. IIS version 10 running on Nano Server targets applications developed and based on ASP.NET Core, so the full .NET Framework will not run. Applications written in Java and PHP will run with IIS on Nano.

Microsoft is working on reducing the size of the Nano base OS image footprint on disk by 50% and even more by the time you read this. This has two benefits: firstly, it will speed up the start-up time of containers, and secondly, it will minimize the bandwidth needed when you pull the image from Docker Hub. Please check Chapter 10, *Running Other Workloads on the Nano Server*, for more information about the future of Nano Server.

Microsoft is also working on bringing a new type of Linux container that can run on Windows Server 2016. The new type of Linux containers will use Hyper-V containers technology, because for now, Linux containers can run on Linux operating systems and Windows containers can only run on Windows host operating systems. Thus, by using Hyper-V containers isolation technology, we can run Linux containers alongside with Windows containers on the same container host.

Continue now to Chapter 9, *Troubleshooting Nano Server*, to learn more about how to troubleshoot a Nano Server installation running on a physical and virtual machine.

9
Troubleshooting Nano Server

In Chapter 8, *Running Windows Server Containers and Hyper-V Containers on Nano Server*, we talked about how to run Nano containers and Hyper-V containers on top of a Nano Server container host.

One of the most frequent questions that we hear a lot is, how do we troubleshoot a headless server without logging into it? There is no support for a remote desktop to administer and troubleshoot the system. Whether we like it or not, sometimes things go wrong and we need to troubleshoot. We already saw in Chapter 6, *Managing Nano Server with Windows PowerShell and Windows PowerShell DSC*, how to do things remotely. We also discussed that, as long as you can connect to the server through the various methods, you can do your troubleshooting with PowerShell or with the remote management consoles. However, sometimes even that isn't possible and you find yourself in a situation where the server does not boot correctly or is completely stuck. Here you need to troubleshoot and resolve the problem.

In this chapter, we will show you how to effectively troubleshoot a Nano Server installation with:

- Nano recovery console
- Emergency management services
- Kernel debugging
- Setup and boot event collection
- Enabling access to Nano Server event logs

Nano recovery console

You read in earlier chapters about all the benefits of Nano Server, such as performance, less disk footprint, less patches, security, and so on. But without the GUI, it's not easy to troubleshoot a Nano Server.

This is why in Windows Server 2016, the Nano Server deployment option of Windows Server comes with full Nano Server recovery console support. The purpose of the recovery console is to provide direct local access to a Nano Server operating system in order to re-establish remote network connectivity. The Nano recovery console does not provide you, command-line access nor PowerShell access locally. However, it does provide you with the ability to fix whatever might be causing remote management not to work. In this case, you can use the recovery console to fix your issues and get remote connectivity again. With the recovery console, you can configure networking, and Firewall rules, and reset the Windows remote management (WinRM) service, which is required for PowerShell remoting.

The recovery console is the default interactive console on every Nano Server installation. Just log in with local access using the administrator and password you supplied while creating the Nano Server image and the menu will be loaded.

When you log on to Nano Server interactively either in a virtual or physical machine, the recovery console looks as shown in *Figure 1*:

Figure 1. Nano Server recovery console logon Window

After you logon, you will see a screen that displays server information as shown in *Figure 2*:

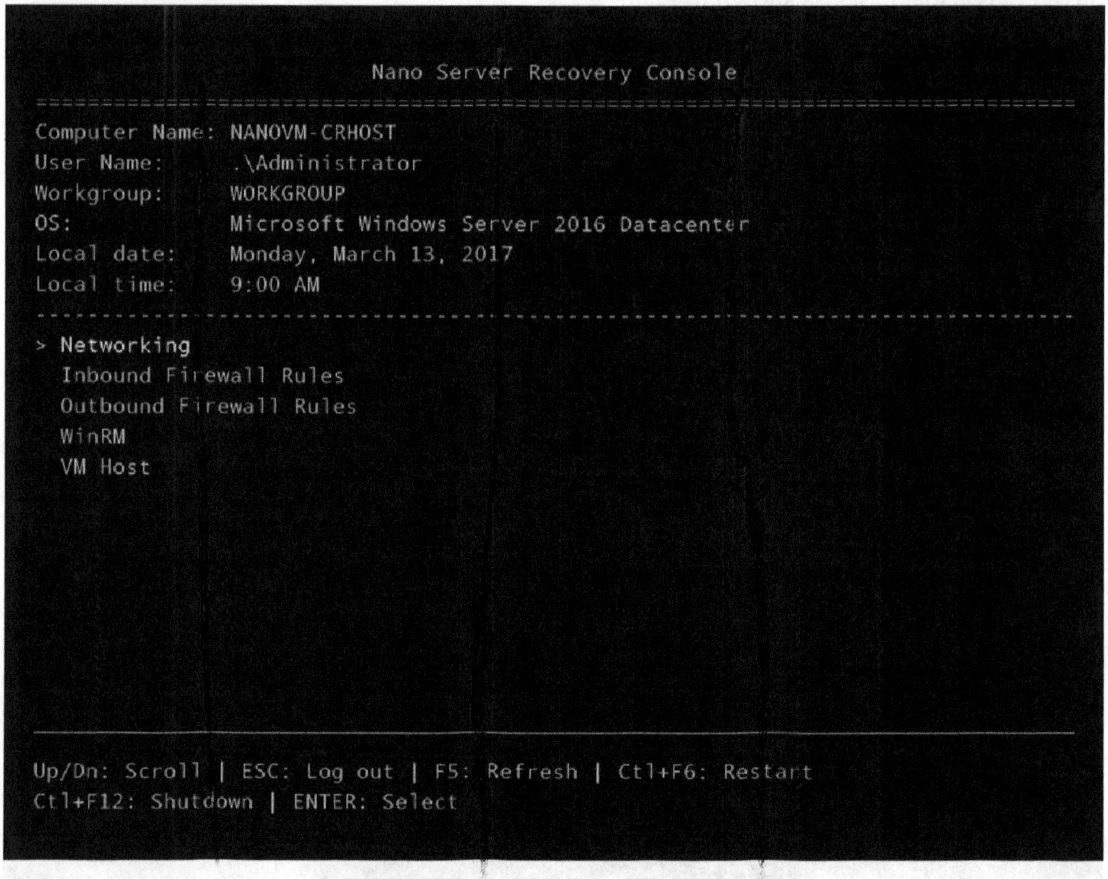

```
                    Nano Server Recovery Console
========================================================================
Computer Name: NANOVM-CRHOST
User Name:      .\Administrator
Workgroup:      WORKGROUP
OS:             Microsoft Windows Server 2016 Datacenter
Local date:     Monday, March 13, 2017
Local time:     9:00 AM
------------------------------------------------------------------------
> Networking
  Inbound Firewall Rules
  Outbound Firewall Rules
  WinRM
  VM Host




_____
Up/Dn: Scroll | ESC: Log out | F5: Refresh | Ctl+F6: Restart
Ctl+F12: Shutdown | ENTER: Select
```

Figure 2. Nano Server recovery console home page

You will be able to see the domain (or workgroup), version of the OS, the local date and time, Networking, inbound Firewall rules, outbound Firewall rules, WinRM, and the VM host (if Nano Server is running a Hyper-V host). More importantly you can use the following options:

- Select > Networking (by using the *Tab* key), scroll down with the arrow keys to select Inbound Firewall Rules, Outbound FirewallRules or WinRM and press *Enter*.

The Nano Server team has added the following capabilities that you can manage through the Nano Server recovery console:

- View computer name
- View domain/workgroup
- Logon/log out
- Shutdown/restart
- Enable/disable NIC
- View IPv4/IPv6 address
- Set IPv4/IPv6 address
- View gateway
- Set gateway IP address
- View routing table
- View primary/secondary DNS
- View MAC address
- View network driver name
- View network driver date
- View network driver version
- View network driver provider
- View network driver installation date
- Set Firewall rules (enable/disable)
- Reset WinRM service

Setting network configurations using the Nano Server recovery console

In this section, you will see how to set basic networking configurations in Nano Server without PowerShell or advanced command-lines.

To manage Nano Server installation using the recovery console, carry out the following steps:

1. Select **>Networking** by pressing the *Tab* key, and on the **Network** settings page, list all your network cards; you can select which NIC you want to view or configure (see *Figure 3*):

```
                        Network Adapter Settings
===================================================================================

Ethernet
Microsoft Hyper-V Network Adapter
- - - - - - - - - - - - - - - - - - - - - - - - - - - - - - - - - - - - - - - - - -

State            Started
MAC Address      00-15-5D-62-F4-3E

Interface
DHCP             Disabled
IPv4 Address     172.16.20.185
Subnet mask      255.255.255.0
Prefix Origin    Manual
Suffix Origin    Manual

Interface
DHCP             Enabled
IPv6 Address     fe80::4d15:60de:626a:7ab4
Prefix Length    64
Prefix Origin    Well Known
Suffix Origin    Link


Up/Dn: Scroll | ESC: Back | F4: Toggle | F10: Routing Table
F11: IPv4 Settings | F12: IPv6 Settings
```

Figure 3. Nano Server recovery console network adapter settings

Here you will see that:

- By pressing *F4*, you can toggle the state (disable/enable) for a specific NIC
- By pressing *F10*, you can see the routing table, and by pressing *F10* again, you can add a static route, or press *Delete* to delete the route
- By pressing *F11*, you can toggle the DHCP state for IPv4, and by pressing *Enter*, you can set/update the NIC IPv4 address for a particular NIC

- By pressing *F12*, you can toggle the DHCP State for IPv6, and by pressing *Enter*, you can set/update the NIC IPv6 address for a particular NIC

- You can go back to the main recovery console page by pressing the *Esc* key

2. Select **>Inbound Firewall Rules** on the main recovery console page, and on the **Firewall Rules** page, you can view all the inbound rules (see *Figure 4*):

```
                            Firewall Rules
========================================================================================
Select an inbound rule to view
- - - - - - - - - - - - - - - - - - - - - - - - - - - - - - - - - - - - - - - - - - - -
> File and Printer Sharing over SMBDirect (iWARP-In)
  Windows Remote Management (HTTP-In)
  Windows Remote Management (HTTP-In)
  Windows Remote Management - Compatibility Mode (HTTP-In)
  Remote Service Management (RPC)
  Remote Service Management (NP-In)
  Remote Service Management (RPC-EPMAP)
  File and Printer Sharing (NB-Session-In)
  File and Printer Sharing (SMB-In)
  File and Printer Sharing (NB-Name-In)
  File and Printer Sharing (NB-Datagram-In)
  File and Printer Sharing (Spooler Service - RPC)
  File and Printer Sharing (Spooler Service - RPC-EPMAP)
  File and Printer Sharing (Echo Request - ICMPv4-In)
  File and Printer Sharing (Echo Request - ICMPv6-In)
  File and Printer Sharing (LLMNR-UDP-In)
  Remote Event Log Management (RPC)
  Remote Event Log Management (NP-In)
  Remote Event Log Management (RPC-EPMAP)
_____

Up/Dn: Highlight | ENTER: Select | ESC: Back
```

Figure 4. Nano Server recovery console inbound Firewall rules

- By pressing *Enter* on any inbound rule, you can view all the details for a particular Firewall rule

- By pressing *F4*, you can toggle the state (disable/enable) for a particular Firewall rule

- You can go back to the **Inbound Firewall Rules** page by pressing *Esc* key

3. Select **>Outbound Firewall Rules** on the main recovery console page, and on the **Firewall Rules** page, you can view all the outbound rules (see *Figure 5*):

```
                          Firewall Rules
===================================================================
Select an outbound rule to view
- - - - - - - - - - - - - - - - - - - - - - - - - - - - - - - - - -
> File and Printer Sharing (NB-Session-Out)
  File and Printer Sharing (SMB-Out)
  File and Printer Sharing (NB-Name-Out)
  File and Printer Sharing (NB-Datagram-Out)
  File and Printer Sharing (Echo Request - ICMPv4-Out)
  File and Printer Sharing (Echo Request - ICMPv6-Out)
  File and Printer Sharing (LLMNR-UDP-Out)
  Windows Management Instrumentation (WMI-Out)
  Core Networking - Packet Too Big (ICMPv6-Out)
  Core Networking - Time Exceeded (ICMPv6-Out)
  Core Networking - Parameter Problem (ICMPv6-Out)
  Core Networking - Neighbor Discovery Solicitation (ICMPv6-Out)
  Core Networking - Neighbor Discovery Advertisement (ICMPv6-Out)
  Core Networking - Router Advertisement (ICMPv6-Out)
  Core Networking - Router Solicitation (ICMPv6-Out)
  Core Networking - Multicast Listener Query (ICMPv6-Out)
  Core Networking - Multicast Listener Report (ICMPv6-Out)
  Core Networking - Multicast Listener Report v2 (ICMPv6-Out)
  Core Networking - Multicast Listener Done (ICMPv6-Out)
-------------------------------------------------------------------
Up/Dn: Highlight | ENTER: Select | ESC: Back
```

Figure 5. Nano Server recovery console outbound Firewall rules

- By pressing *Enter* on any outbound rule, you can view all of its details for a particular Firewall rule.
- By pressing *F4*, you can toggle the state (disable/enable)
- You can go back to the outbound Firewall rules page by pressing the *Esc* key

 It is not possible to create a Firewall rule through the Nano Server recovery console. The entire idea of the console is to fix connectivity issues (inbound/outbound) if something went wrong. The moment you have restored connectivity; you should use remote management tools such as PowerShell remoting to create your desired firewall rules or do other tasks.

4. Select >WinRM on the main recovery console. The only option here is to press
    Enter to reset the WinRM service (see *Figure 6*). If the WinRM service is not
    running, it will start, and the service startup type will be set to automatic:

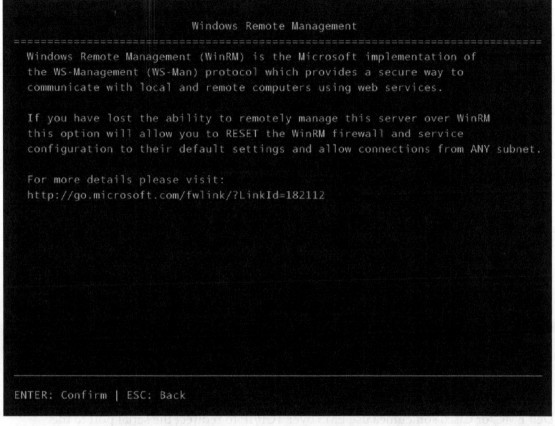

Figure 6. Nano Server recovery console reset WinRM

5. You can go back to the main recovery console page by pressing the *Esc* key, if you
    want to restart the Nano Server, you can press (*Ctrl+F6*) or shutdown (*Ctrl+F12*) if
    needed.

The Nano Server recovery console is completely different from Sconfig in Server Core;
there is no command-line shell nor server configuration running in the background.

The recovery console is divided into two parts: the frontend and backend:

- The frontend uses the usual Windows console API. The console used isn't really the full Windows console due to current renderer limitations in the Nano Server environment (no background colors, and so on).
- The backend almost exclusively uses WMI to manage the local Nano machine, with a few data points pulled from the registry where they weren't available from the WMI interface.

Emergency management services

Emergency Management Services (**EMS**) is a feature that provides remote management and system recovery options when other server administrative options are not available. It is also required for headless systems in which there is no GUI available, as in the case of Nano Server.

EMS works through the **Special Administration Console** (**SAC**) feature of Windows Server. The SAC channel provides a number of administrative features such as enabling the Windows command prompt (`cmd.exe`) channel for Windows CLI access, listing processes currently running on the system, obtaining IP address information, retrieving server hardware information, and rebooting the server, to name just a few. Another important feature of the SAC channel is the ability to monitor the boot and install progress of the server. For more information on EMS and SAC see the TechNet article at:

`https://technet.microsoft.com/en-us/library/cc784221(v=ws.10).aspx.`

PuTTY is an SSH and telnet client and it is one of the tools that can be used to access EMS using a serial port. The good news is, network software and server vendors such as HPE, Dell EMC, or Cisco sometimes use EMS over TCP/IP to redirect the serial port to the network card by virtualizing the serial port. Thus, if you have a baseboard management port in your server such as iLO or iDRAC, you can actually access a Nano Server machine over EMS in this way. Please refer to the section entitled *Windows EMS in a Physical Machine* in this chapter to learn more about the **Virtual Serial Port** (**VSP**) using HPE ProLiant Server.

Enabling EMS

In most installations, EMS is enabled by default, but in Nano Server this must be enabled when creating the image so you can use it when needed.

First you need to create a Nano Server image. See `Chapter 3`, *Deploying Nano Server in a Virtual Machine and on Physical Hardware*, for more details.

There are a couple of ways to enable EMS on Nano Server. We can use Windows PowerShell or DISM combined with Bcdedit.

Enabling EMS using PowerShell

To enable EMS using PowerShell, we need to use the `New-NanoServerImage` command when creating the image or after the image is created by using the `Edit-NanoServerImage` command included in the Nano Server PowerShell module.

The following is an example of both methods:

```
New-NanoServerImage
-MediaPath <media path>
-BasePath .\Basefolder
-TargetPath .\NanoServer-EMS.vhd
-EnableEMS
-EMSPort 3
-EMSBaudRate 9600
 Edit-NanoServerImage
-BasePath .\Basefolder
-TargetPath .\NanoServer-EMS.vhd
-EnableEMS
-EMSPort 3
-EMSBaudRate 9600
```

In the previous example, we enabled EMS over serial port COM 3 with a baud rate of `9600` bps. We choose the speed baud rate `9600`, because it's the default speed used by any terminal client such as PuTTY, or HyperTerminal. If you don't include those parameters, the default port for EMS is COM 1 and the speed is 115200 bps.

Enabling EMS using DISM

You can also use the DISM command-line tool to enable EMS in the image by running the following commands:

```
Dism /Mount-Image /ImageFile:.\NanoServer.wim /Index: 1
/MountDir:.\mountdir

Bcdedit /store \ mountdir \ boot \ bcd / ems {default} on

Bcdedit /store \ mountdir \ boot \ bcd / emssettings EMSPORT:3
EMSBAUDRATE:9600

Dism \ dism / Unmount-Image /MountDir:.\mountdir / Commit
```

In the previous example, we mounted a Nano Server image toward a directory called `mountdir` using index 1, because `NanoServer.wim` holds two Windows images:

- `Index: 1`: Windows Server 2016 `SERVERSTANDARDNANO`
- `Index: 2`: Windows Server 2016 `SERVERDATACENTERNANO`

Then you can use the `Bcdedit` tool, the boot configuration data editor, toward the mounted directory and then enable EMS. You can configure further EMS settings over serial `port 3` with a baud speed rate of `9600` bps. Finally, you should commit the changes by using DISM followed by the `/Commit` switch.

Windows EMS in a virtual machine

To use Windows EMS in a virtual machine, you need to use a generation 1 VM, because we need on use the emulated virtual COM Port. In generation 2 virtual machines, there are no COM ports by default. However, we can change this in PowerShell which needs further configuration; we will get into that in a bit.

Assuming you are using a generation 1 VM for Nano Server, the virtual COM port will communicate with the Nano Server VM through a named pipe.

A named pipe is an option that connects the virtual serial port to a Windows named pipe on the host operating system or another computer on the network.

A named pipes is a portion of memory that can be used by one process to pass information to another process, so that the output for one is the input for another. The second process can be local or remote.

Additional information about named pipe is available at: `https://msdn.microsoft.com/en -us/library/aa365590%28VS.85%29.aspx`.

First, we need to create a named pipe under the VM settings as shown in *Figure 7*:

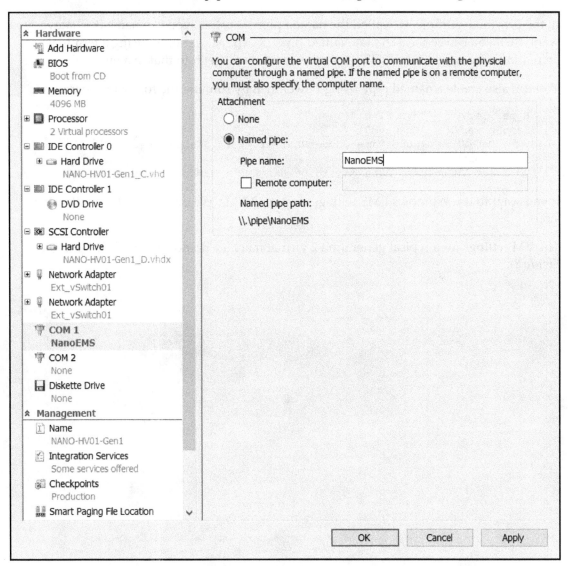

Figure 7. Enabling Virtual COM port, Nano Server Gen 1 VM settings

You do not need to have network connectivity to the VM to use EMS. You need to make sure to leave the EMSPort to the default port 1, because generation 1 or generation 2 virtual machines have only two virtual COM ports, COM 1 and COM 2.

In the previous example, we called the named pipe NanoEMS, you can name it whatever you want, then you can connect to that Named pipe \\.\pipe\NanoEMS using a terminal emulation program such as PuTTY for example; we will get into that in a bit.

You can also create a named pipe using PowerShell by running the following command:

```
$HyperVServer = "HVHOST-01"
$NanoServerVM = "NANO-VM01 "
$VM = Get-VM -ComputerName $HyperVServer -Name $NanoServerVM
$VM.ComPort1
$VM | Set-VMComPort -Path '\\.\pipe\NanoEMS' -Number 1 -Passthru
```

If you want to use Windows EMS with generation 2 VMs, please carry out the following steps:

The VM settings for a typical generation 2 virtual machine do not show a COM port (see *Figure 8*):

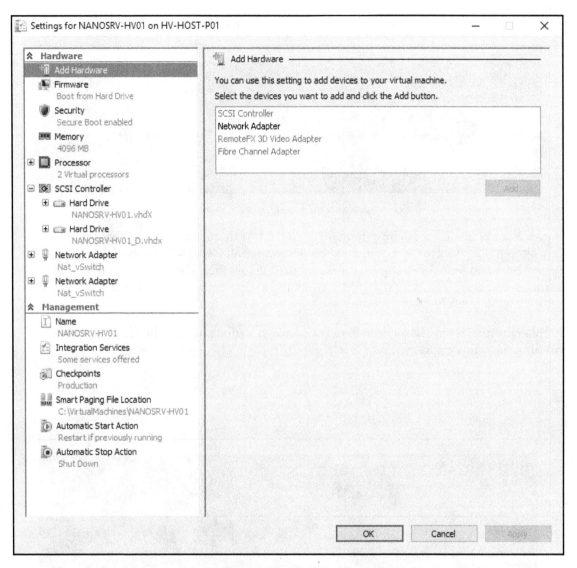

Figure 8. Nano Server Gen 2 VM settings

That is simply because the VM **Settings** in Hyper-V Manager will never show COM ports regardless of whether they are present or not in a generation 2 VM.

Let's run the following command in Windows PowerShell:

```
Get-VMComPort -VMName <VMName>
```

In PowerShell, we can see two COM ports for a generation 2 VM (see *Figure 9*):

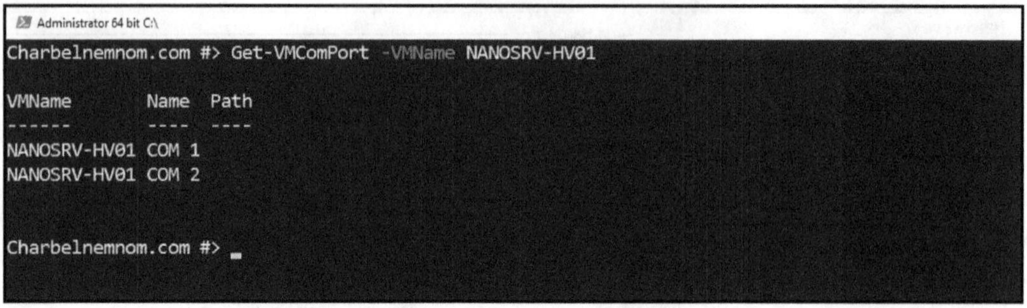

Figure 9. Virtual COM port, Nano Server Gen 2 VM settings

If you want to use kernel debugging with a Gen 2 VM there is a trade-off that you want to pay attention to. Secure boot is enabled by default for all Gen 2 virtual machines. However, secure boot and kernel debugging are incompatible together. Hence, if you need to use kernel debugging with Windows EMS, you need to disable secure boot in the firmware settings while the VM is off.

In this example, we will disable secure boot and set a pipe path for the COM 1 port by running the following commands (see *Figure 10*):

```
Stop-VM -VMName NANOSRV-HV01
Set-VMFirmware -VMName NANOSRV-HV01 -EnableSecureBoot Off
Set-VMComPort -VMName NANOSRV-HV01 -Path '\\.\pipe\NanoEMS' -Number 1
Get-VMComPort -VMName NANOSRV-HV01Start-VM -VMName NANOSRV-HV01 -Passthru
```

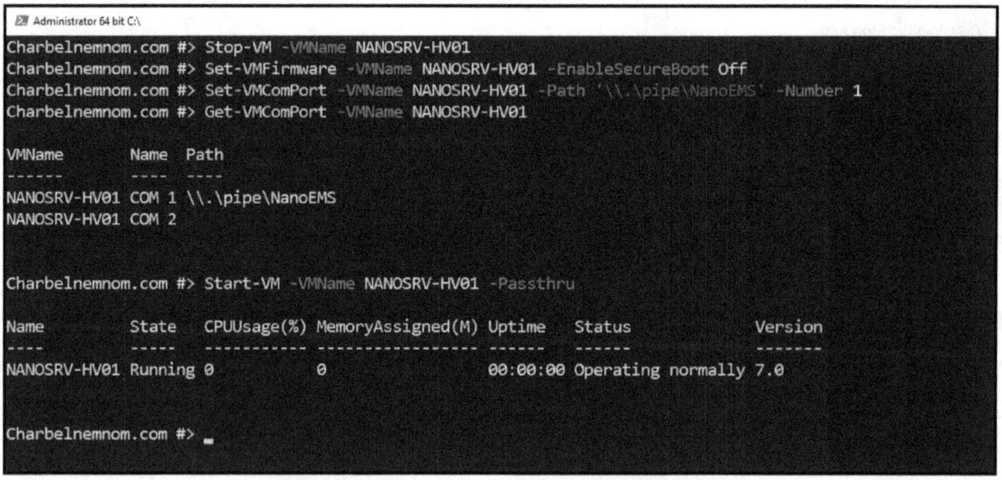

Figure 10. Enabling Virtual COM Port - Nano Server Gen 2 VM

Troubleshooting Nano Server VM using EMS

We assume you downloaded PuTTY (`https://www.chiark.greenend.org.uk/~sgtatham /putty/latest.html`). Launch it and access Nano VM using the named pipe that we created earlier, as shown in *Figure 11*:

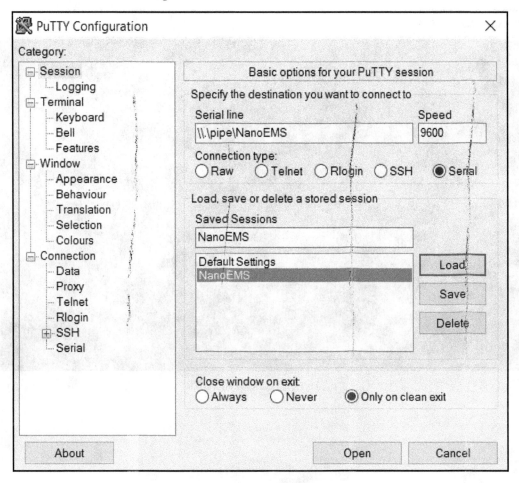

Figure 11. Accessing Nano Server VM using EMS

Type the named pipe in the **Serial line** field and set the speed accordingly, then click **Open** and press *Enter*. Recall that if you enabled EMS without setting the speed, the default is 115200.

As shown in *Figure 12*, we are in an emergency console session:

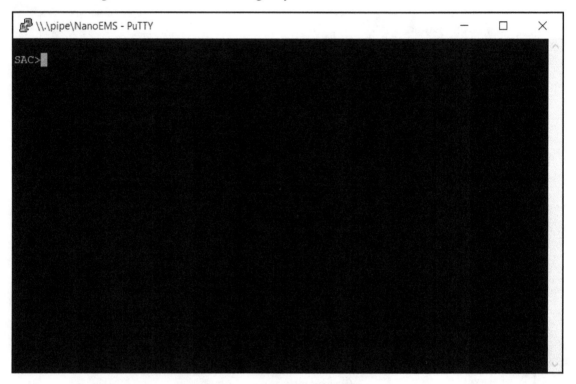

Figure 12. Log into Nano Server VM using EMS

You can type a question mark `?` or `help` to get all the commands available as shown in *Figure 13*:

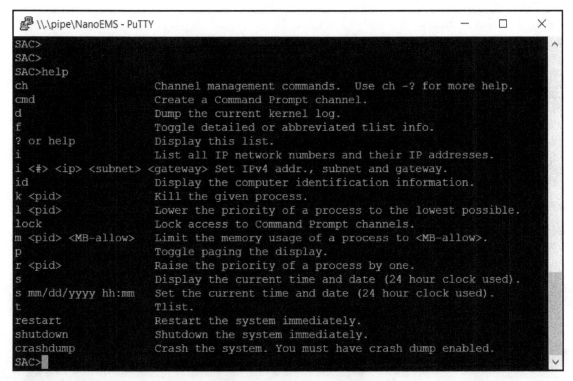

Figure 13. Emergency management service console help commands

To create a command channel, type `cmd`. A new channel will be created.

You can enter that channel as shown in *Figure 14* by typing: `ch -si 1` where `1` is the channel number associated with `Cmd0001`. In this example, the channel number is `1`:

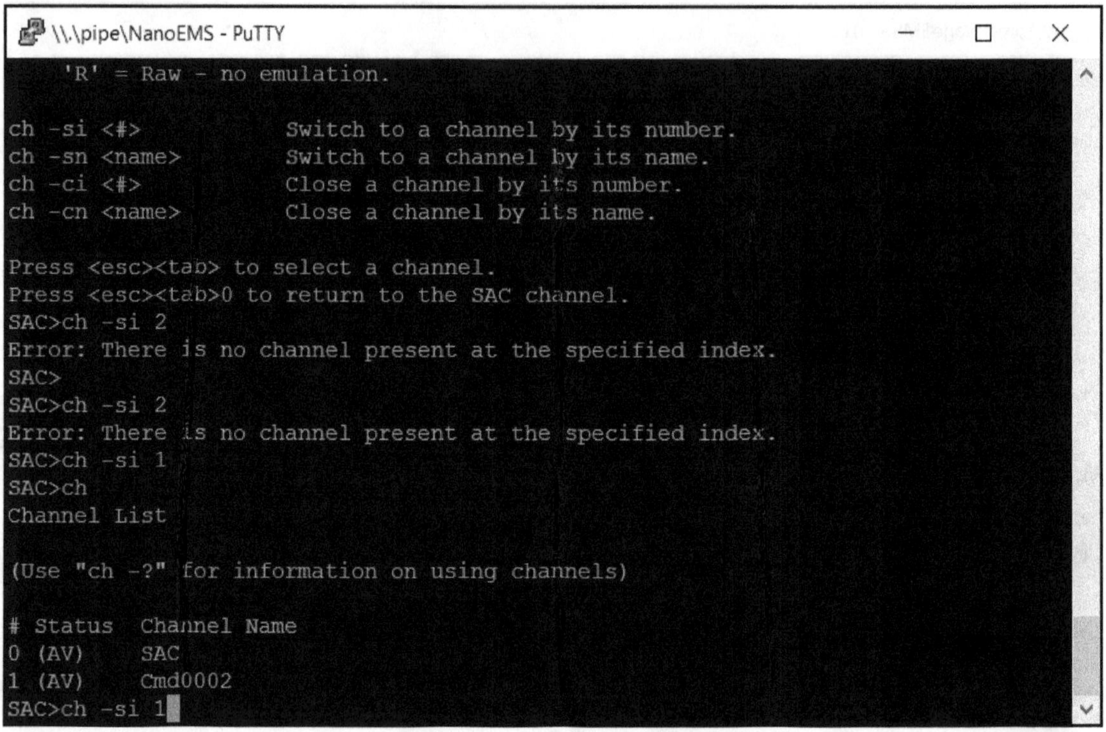

```
 \\.\pipe\NanoEMS - PuTTY                                       —   □   ×
    'R' = Raw - no emulation.

ch -si <#>            Switch to a channel by its number.
ch -sn <name>         Switch to a channel by its name.
ch -ci <#>            Close a channel by its number.
ch -cn <name>         Close a channel by its name.

Press <esc><tab> to select a channel.
Press <esc><tab>0 to return to the SAC channel.
SAC>ch -si 2
Error: There is no channel present at the specified index.
SAC>
SAC>ch -si 2
Error: There is no channel present at the specified index.
SAC>ch -si 1
SAC>ch
Channel List

(Use "ch -?" for information on using channels)

# Status   Channel Name
0 (AV)     SAC
1 (AV)     Cmd0002
SAC>ch -si 1
```

Figure 14. Emergency management Service channel creation

Press *Enter* twice to authenticate using the same credentials that you used when creating a Nano Server image (see *Figure 15*):

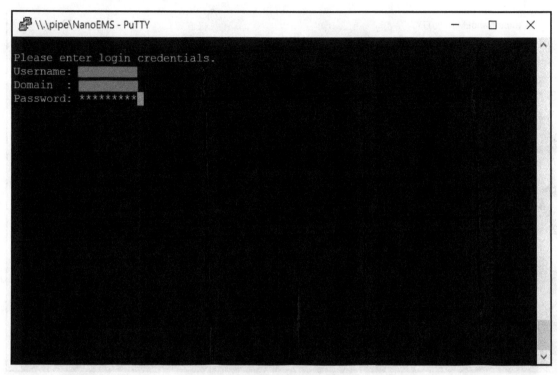

Figure 15. Emergency management service channel authentication

After authenticating, you are in the Windows command prompt (cmd) where you can start doing your normal troubleshooting as shown in *Figure 16*:

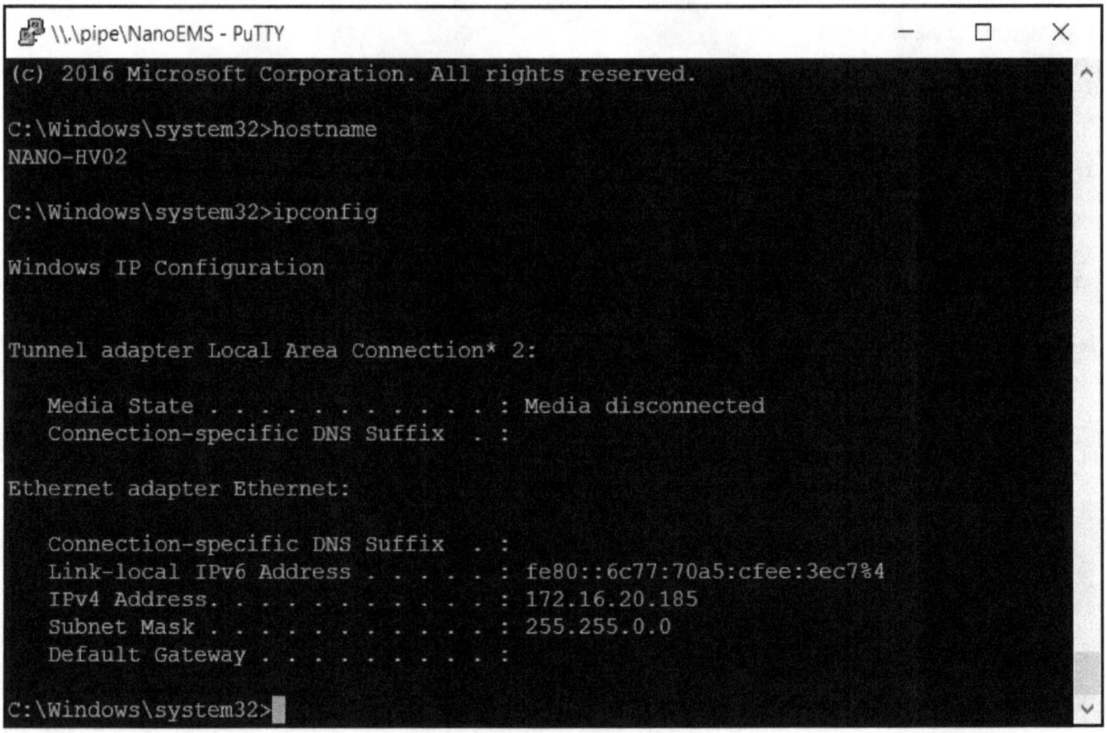

```
🖳 \\.\pipe\NanoEMS - PuTTY                                    —    □    ×

(c) 2016 Microsoft Corporation. All rights reserved.

C:\Windows\system32>hostname
NANO-HV02

C:\Windows\system32>ipconfig

Windows IP Configuration


Tunnel adapter Local Area Connection* 2:

   Media State . . . . . . . . . . . : Media disconnected
   Connection-specific DNS Suffix  . :

Ethernet adapter Ethernet:

   Connection-specific DNS Suffix  . :
   Link-local IPv6 Address . . . . . : fe80::6c77:70a5:cfee:3ec7%4
   IPv4 Address. . . . . . . . . . . : 172.16.20.185
   Subnet Mask . . . . . . . . . . . : 255.255.0.0
   Default Gateway . . . . . . . . . :

C:\Windows\system32>
```

Figure 16. Emergency management service cmd window

The greatest feature about SAC and cmd channel is PowerShell support; you can use Windows PowerShell (CoreCLR) through the EMS console as well.

In the command prompt window, type `PowerShell`; Windows PowerShell will launch as shown in *Figure 17*:

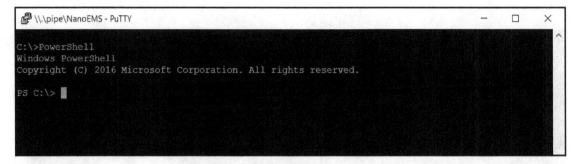

Figure 17. Using PowerShell over a Windows EMS Session with Nano Server

To get all the available PowerShell cmdlets, run the following command:

```
Get-Command | measure
```

We have `1152` PowerShell cmdlets available (see *Figure 18*):

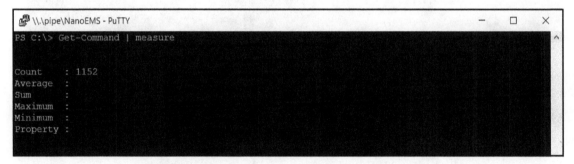

Figure 18. PowerShell cmdlets over a Windows EMS session with Nano Server

In the following example, we will change the IP address of Nano Server through a Windows EMS session.

While the EMS session is still open, type the following commands to update the IP address of Nano Server (see *Figure 19*):

- `Get-NetIPAddress-InterfaceAliasEthernet|SelectInterfaceAlias,IPAddress`
- `Remove-NetIPAddress-InterfaceAlias"Ethernet"-Confirm:$False`

- New-NetIPAddress-InterfaceAlias"Ethernet"-IPAddress172.16.20.140-PrefixLength'24'-TypeUnicast|Out-Null
- Get-NetIPAddress-InterfaceAliasEthernet|SelectInterfaceAlias,IPAddress

```
PS C:\> Get-NetIPAddress -InterfaceAlias Ethernet | Select InterfaceAlias, IPAdd
ress

InterfaceAlias IPAddress
-------------- ---------
Ethernet       172.16.20.185


PS C:\> Remove-NetIPAddress -InterfaceAlias "Ethernet" -Confirm:$False
PS C:\> New-NetIPAddress -InterfaceAlias "Ethernet" -IPAddress 172.16.20.140 -Pr
efixLength '24' -Type Unicast | Out-Null
PS C:\> Get-NetIPAddress -InterfaceAlias Ethernet | Select InterfaceAlias, IPAdd
ress

InterfaceAlias IPAddress
-------------- ---------
Ethernet       172.16.20.140


PS C:\>
```

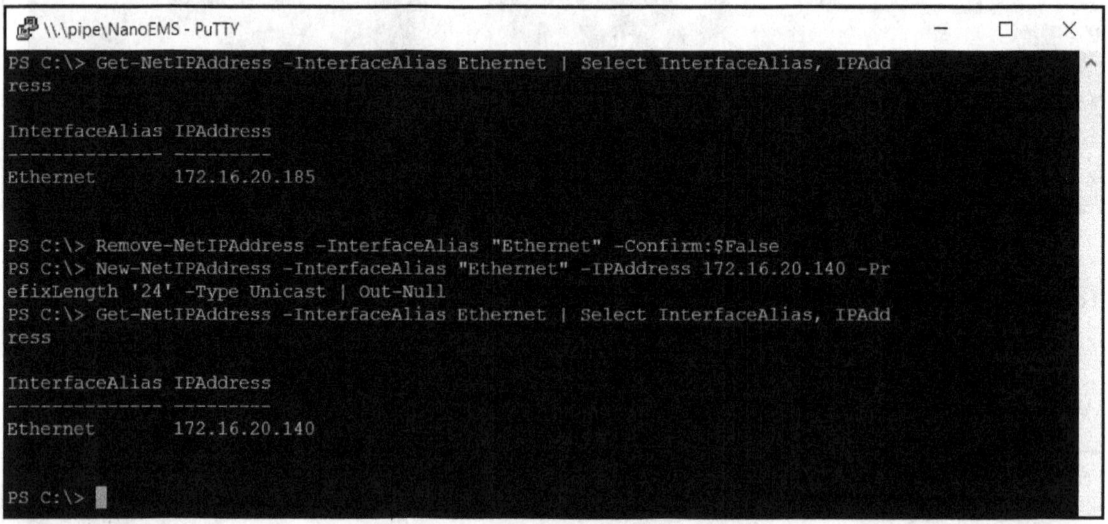

Figure 19. Changing IP Address over a Windows EMS session on Nano Server

Windows EMS on a physical machine

In this section, we will demonstrate the experience of using Windows EMS to troubleshoot Nano Server installed on an HPE ProLiant server. Please note that this operation is possible with other servers as well; please check with your OEM vendor.

Using Windows EMS to manage an HPE ProLiant server involves the following:

- Enabling virtual serial port
- Enabling the EMS port in ROM-based setup utility
- Enabling Windows EMS in the bootloader of Nano Server OS
- Using PuTTY or a similar terminal emulation program to establish an SSH connection to the ProLiant iLO IP address
- Using Windows EMS functionality to perform basic support administrative tasks

Enabling a virtual serial port

HPE **Integrated Lights-Out 3/4 (iLO 3 and 4)** allows administrators to manage their servers remotely using a variety of connection methods including a Web browser, telnet, SSH, and PowerShell. This section focuses on enabling a VSP for use with SSH.

To enable a VSP on the server:

1. Connect to the iLO IRC using a web browser (`http://<IP address of the iLO>`).
2. Logon to the iLO using the appropriate iLO credentials.
3. Power on the server.
4. Press the *F9* function key when displayed to enter system utilities.

For HPE ProLiant Gen8 (BIOS) systems:

1. Locate the `Virtual Serial Port` option using the following path, `System Options -> Serial Port Options -> Virtual Serial Port`.
2. Hit the *Enter* key to select from a list of options. For the purpose of this example, we'll select `COM 2` as shown in *Figure 20*:

Figure 20. Enabling virtual serial port on HPE Gen8 systems

3. A reboot is required for the change to take effect. Hit *Esc* three times to get back to Setup Utility and then *F10* to save and reboot the system.

If you have HPE Gen9 systems, please carry out the following steps, otherwise skip to the section titled *Enabling the EMS Port in ROM-Based Setup Utility (RBSU)*.

For HPE ProLiant Gen9 systems:

1. Locate the `Virtual Serial Port` option using the following path, `System Configuration` -> `BIOS/Platform Configuration (RBSU)` -> `System Default Options` -> `Serial Port Options` -> `Virtual Serial Port`.
2. Hit the *Enter* key to select from a list of options. For the purposes of this example, we'll select `COM 2`.
3. Hit *F10* to confirm and save the change.
4. A reboot is required for the change to take effect. Hit the *Esc* key until you are back to the System Utilities screen.
5. Scroll down and select `Reboot the System`.

The ProLiant VSP is now enabled. The next step is to enable the EMS console on the server.

Enabling the EMS Port in ROM-Based Setup Utility (RBSU)

The HPE ProLiant EMS Console option configures the ACPI serial port to redirect output to the Windows EMS console.

To enable the EMS console on the server:

1. Connect to the iLO IRC using a web browser (`http://<IP address of the iLO>`).
2. Logon to the iLO using the appropriate iLO credentials.
3. Power on the server.
4. Press the *F9* function key when displayed to enter System Utilities.

For HPE ProLiant Gen8 (BIOS) systems:

1. Locate the Virtual Serial Port option using the following path, `BIOS Serial Console and EMS` -> `EMS Console`.
2. Hit the *Enter* key to select from a list of options. Note: Be sure to select the COM port that matches the VSP COM port configured previously. For the purpose of this example, we'll select `COM 2` as shown in *Figure 21*:

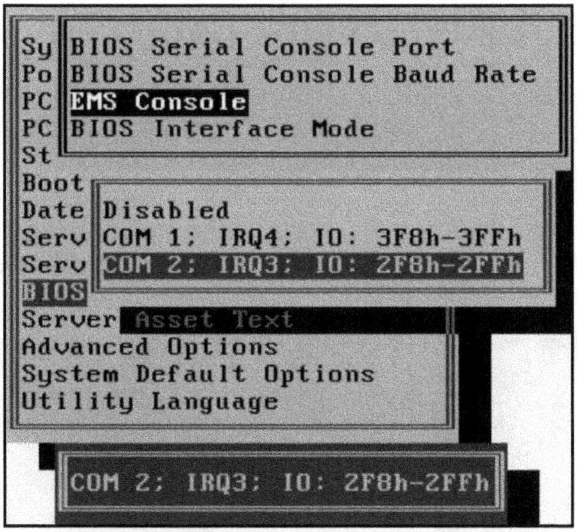

Figure 21. Enabling EMS Console on HPE Gen8 systems

3. A reboot is required for the change to take effect. Hit the *Esc* key twice and *F10* to save and reboot the system.

If you have Gen9 systems, please carry out the following steps, otherwise skip to the section entitled *Enabling Windows EMS in the bootloader of the Nano Server OS*.

For HPE ProLiant Gen9 systems:

1. Locate the **Virtual Serial Port** option using the following path, `System Configuration -> BIOS/Platform Configuration (RBSU) -> BIOS Serial Console and EMS -> EMS Console`.

2. Hit the *Enter* key to select from a list of options. It is important to be sure to select the COM port that matches the VSP COM port configured previously. For the purpose of this example, we'll select **COM 2**.

3. Hit *F10* to confirm and save the change.

4. A reboot is required for the change to take effect. Hit the ESC key until you are back to the System Utilities screen. Scroll down and select **Reboot the System**.

Enabling Windows EMS in the bootloader of the Nano Server OS

This section describes how to enable Windows EMS in the bootloader of the Nano Server operating system using the `Bcdedit` tool.

We need to enable and set the EMS port and baud rate in the boot database, but before doing that, let's look at the current boot database by running **bcdedit** at the command prompt as shown in *Figure 22*:

```
Windows Boot Loader
-------------------
identifier              {default}
device                  vhd=[C:]\Nano\NanoServer01.vhd
path                    \windows\system32\boot\winload.exe
description             Windows Server 2016 Technical Preview 4
locale                  en-us
inherit                 {bootloadersettings}
bootems                 Yes
custom:1600007e         Yes
allowedinmemorysettings 0x15000075
osdevice                vhd=[C:]\Nano\NanoServer01.vhd
systemroot              \windows
resumeobject            {5f5587db-dd6d-11e5-a382-806e6f6e6963}
nx                      OptIn
hypervisorlaunchtype    Auto
ems                     Yes
```

Figure 22. Bcdedit boot configuration data

As you can see, the VHD image that we have deployed on the physical server has EMS enabled but the port and the baud rate are not set.

Recall, from the previous section, that we enabled EMS and the Virtual Serial Port (VSP) in HPE RBSU and we selected COM 2.

We need to set the EMS to port 2 as well in the default bootloader and we will set the baud rate to 9600 bps.

Type the following commands at the command prompt:

```
bcdedit /ems {default} ON
bcdedit /emssettings EMSPORT:2 EMSBAUDRATE:9600
```

Using PuTTY to establish an SSH connection to the iLO IP address

This section describes how to establish an SSH connection to the Proliant iLO IP address, and logging in using Windows EMS and open a SAC channel. The following prerequisites must be met to continue:

- The OS boot loader entry associated with Nano Server is configured for EMS as described in the previous section
- The ProLiant server VSP is enabled as described in the previous section
- The ProLiant server EMS console is enabled as described in the previous section
- A terminal emulator program such as PuTTY is installed on your management station

Here are the steps for connecting using VSP:

1. Open a PuTTY session using putty.exe.
2. In the **Host Name** box in the **Session** category, enter the IP address or FQDN of the iLO.
3. Choose **SSH** as the connection type and ensure the Port is set to 22.

4. Optional: Add a friendly name in the **Saved Sessions** box and click the **Save** button to save it for future use (see *Figure 23*):

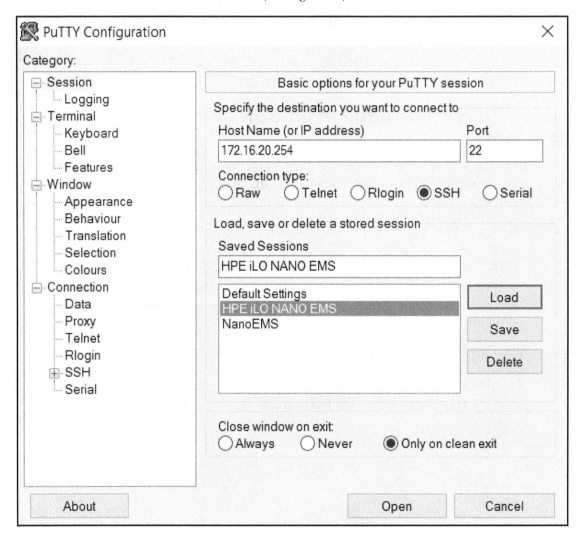

Figure 23. Using PuTTY to open SSH session to HPE iLO VSP

5. Click the **Open** button to establish a connection to the iLO.

6. If this is the first time a connection has been made to the ILO VSP from this computer, you may receive a PuTTY Security Alert pop-up. This is normal when using a SSH connection. Go ahead and click the Yes button to continue.

7. At the login prompt, enter an iLO user name and password.

8. After a successful login, you should see the following prompt, `</>hpiLO->`.

9. Type `VSP` and hit Return to open a VSP session.

10. If the connection is successful, you should now have an active VSP session (see *Figure 24*):

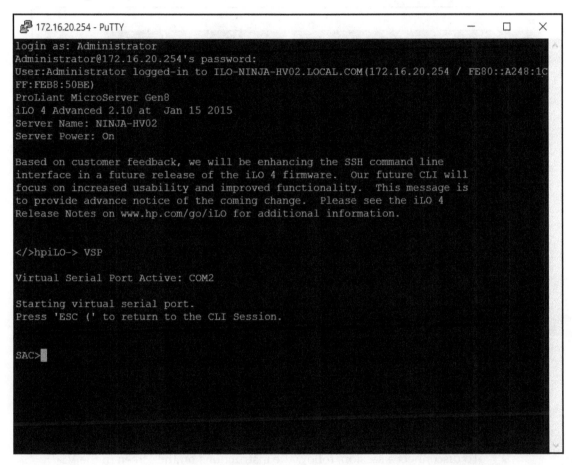

```
🖳 172.16.20.254 - PuTTY                                              —    □    ×
login as: Administrator
Administrator@172.16.20.254's password:
User:Administrator logged-in to ILO-NINJA-HV02.LOCAL.COM(172.16.20.254 / FE80::A248:1C
FF:FEB8:50BE)
ProLiant MicroServer Gen8
iLO 4 Advanced 2.10 at  Jan 15 2015
Server Name: NINJA-HV02
Server Power: On

Based on customer feedback, we will be enhancing the SSH command line
interface in a future release of the iLO 4 firmware.  Our future CLI will
focus on increased usability and improved functionality.  This message is
to provide advance notice of the coming change.  Please see the iLO 4
Release Notes on www.hp.com/go/iLO for additional information.


</>hpiLO-> VSP

Virtual Serial Port Active: COM2

Starting virtual serial port.
Press 'ESC (' to return to the CLI Session.


SAC>█
```

Figure 24. HPE iLO VSP logon screen

11. If the connection failed, double-check the VSP configuration following the steps provided earlier.

12. Once you have established a VSP session, your cursor may appear to be frozen and you are unable to interact with the server. This might be normal depending on the state of the server. With the connection still active, reboot the server.

13. Once the server is rebooted, you should start seeing output to the VSP interface, specifically system POST information. If you can see the system POST information displayed to the VSP session, as shown in *Figure 25*, the VSP is configured correctly:

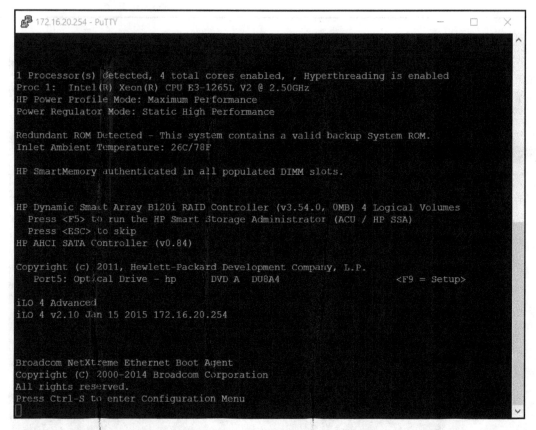

```
1 Processor(s) detected, 4 total cores enabled, , Hyperthreading is enabled
Proc 1:  Intel(R) Xeon(R) CPU E3-1265L V2 @ 2.50GHz
HP Power Profile Mode: Maximum Performance
Power Regulator Mode: Static High Performance

Redundant ROM Detected - This system contains a valid backup System ROM.
Inlet Ambient Temperature: 26C/78F

HP SmartMemory authenticated in all populated DIMM slots.

HP Dynamic Smart Array B120i RAID Controller (v3.54.0, 0MB) 4 Logical Volumes
   Press <F5> to run the HP Smart Storage Administrator (ACU / HP SSA)
   Press <ESC> to skip
HP AHCI SATA Controller (v0.84)

Copyright (c) 2011, Hewlett-Packard Development Company, L.P.
   Port5: Optical Drive - hp        DVD A  DU8A4                    <F9 = Setup>

iLO 4 Advanced
iLO 4 v2.10 Jan 15 2015 172.16.20.254



Broadcom NetXtreme Ethernet Boot Agent
Copyright (C) 2000-2014 Broadcom Corporation
All rights reserved.
Press Ctrl-S to enter Configuration Menu
```

Figure 25. POST information displayed to the VSP session of HPE ProLiant Server

To disconnect a session, follow the instructions on the screen in the VSP session as shown in *Figure 24*. Type the key combination, *Shift+Esc+9* (The number *9* on the main keyboard, not on the keypad or *F9*) to exit the session and go back to the </>hpiLO-> prompt. Type Exit to completely exit the SSH connection.

If the VSP was working up until Nano Server boots and then ceases, it means that EMS is not enabled in the BCD store of the operating system. If this is the case, then one or more configuration steps failed or were skipped. You will need to retrace the steps to figure out exactly where things went wrong.

Using Windows EMS functionality to perform basic support administrative tasks

This section describes how to use the Windows EMS and SAC channel to perform basic administration for Nano Server.

If VSP and Windows EMS are configured correctly, you should see output in the VSP session (see *Figure 26*):

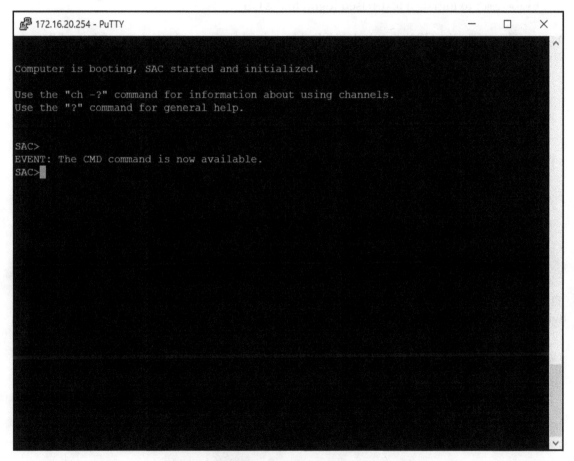

Figure 26. VSP session for HPE ProLiant Server connected to Windows EMS

Type `help` in the window to obtain a list of useful commands. Most noteworthy are:

- `I`: to obtain IP address information
- `id`: to list OS details
- `t`: to obtain a list of running processes
- `restart`: to reboot the OS
- `shutdown`: to initiate a shutdown of the OS
- `cmd`: to initiate a text-based logon to the OS

You can log on to the OS through the VSP channel using the credentials specified while creating a Nano Server image file. To do so, follow these steps:

1. Type `cmd` followed by the *Enter* key at the SAC prompt. You should see a message indicating a new channel has been created and the channel name. Most likely, the channel name is `Cmd0001`.
2. Type `ch` followed by *Enter* to see a list of available channels.
3. Find the channel number associated with the CMD channel created previously and type `ch -si 1` followed by the *Enter* key twice, where 1 is the channel number associated with `Cmd0001`.
4. You should be prompted with a login screen. Enter the username, password, and domain (if the server is domain-joined) of an administrative account on Nano Server.
5. You should now see a `C:\Windows\system32` prompt.

Through the local Windows VSP session, several commands are available for interacting with the OS. For example:

- `ipconfig.exe` : To display IP configuration
- `Powershell.exe` : To switch to a PowerShell session instead of the command-line

Type the following command while in a PowerShell session, to obtain OS information as shown in *Figure 27*:

```
Get-ComputerInfo w*x, oss*l
```

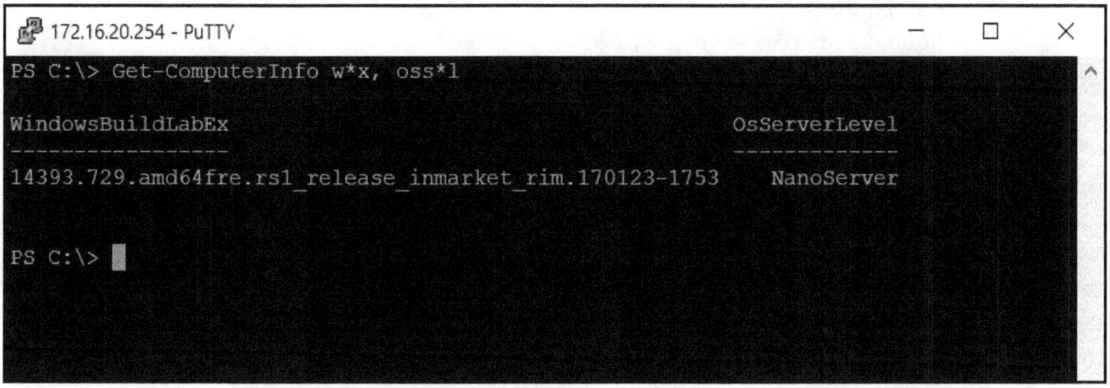

Figure 27. Obtain OS information using PowerShell over Windows EMS and VSP session

The VSP and EMS are great for monitoring the OS installation, obtaining the IP address, troubleshooting, and performing other support administrative tasks.

Kernel debugging

Kernel debugging is also a possibility with Nano Server. A Nano Server image supports kernel debugging through different methods. However, there is an extra step that you want to be aware of when using kernel debugging with Nano Server virtual machines. You need to include the `Compute` package and the corresponding PowerShell modules in the Nano image.

There are four methods to do kernel debugging with Nano Server. You can use either a serial port, a TCP/IP network, Firewire (IEEE1349), or USB.

To do so, we need to use the `New-NanoServerImage` command when creating the image or after the image is created by using the `Edit-NanoServerImage` command included in the Nano Server PowerShell module.

Please see `Chapter 3`, *Deploying Nano Server in a Virtual Machine and on Physical Hardware*, for more details.

The following is an example for each method:

- **Serial Port**

  ```
  New-NanoServerImage -MediaPath \\PathToMedia -BasePath .\BasePath -
  TargetPath .\PathToVHD -DebugMethod Serial -DebugCOMPort 1 -
  DebugBaudRate 9600

  Edit-NanoServerImage -BasePath .\ -TargetPath .\Nano-Server.vhdx -
  DebugMethod Serial -DebugCOMPort 1 -DebugBaudRate 9600
  ```

In the previous example, we configured kernel debugging over serial port 1 with a baud rate of 9600 bps. We choose the speed baud rate 9600, because it's the default speed used by any terminal client such as PuTTY or HyperTerminal. If you did not set the debug COM port and the baud rate, the defaults are port 2 and 115200 bps. However, if you plan on using EMS and kernel debugging, then you need to use a different port number, because they cannot coexist on the same port.

- **TCP/IP Network**

  ```
  New-NanoServerImage -MediaPath \\PathToMedia -BasePath .\BasePath -
  TargetPath .\PathToVHD -DebugMethod Net -DebugRemoteIP 172.21.22.13
  -DebugPort 64000

  Edit-NanoServerImage -BasePath .\ -TargetPath .\Nano-Server.vhdx -
  DebugMethod Net -DebugRemoteIP 172.21.22.13 -DebugPort 64000
  ```

In the previous example, we configured kernel debugging to be used by a specific computer IP address 172.21.22.13 over port 64000. Please note that the port you specify should be greater than 49152. This cmdlet will generate an encryption key in a file alongside the resulting VHD(X), which is needed for communication over the port. Alternatively, you can specify your own key with the -DebugKey <key> parameter.

- **Firewire (IEEE 1394)**

  ```
  New-NanoServerImage -MediaPath \\PathToMedia -BasePath .\BasePath -
  TargetPath .\ PathToVHD -DebugMethod 1394 -DebugChannel 3

  Edit-NanoServerImage -BasePath .\ -TargetPath .\Nano-Server.vhdx -
  DebugMethod 1394 -DebugChannel 3
  ```

If you plan to use this method, be aware that the parameter –DebugChannel is mandatory.

- **USB**

```
New-NanoServerImage -MediaPath \\PathToMedia -BasePath .\BasePath -
TargetPath .\PathToVHD -DebugMethod USB -DebugTargetName <nano>

Edit-NanoServerImage -BasePath .\ -TargetPath .\Nano-Server.vhd -
DebugMethod USB -DebugTargetName KernelDebuggingUSBNano
```

 The name behind the –DebugTargetName <name> parameter is the one you are going to use when connecting through a remote debugger.

Installing WinDbg from Windows SDK

If you just need debugging tools for Windows 10, you can download Windows SDK from the following link:

`https://go.microsoft.com/fwlink/?linkid=838916.`

You do not need the Windows 10 Assessment and Deployment Kit (ADK) or Visual Studio; you can install the debugging tools as a standalone component from Windows SDK.

In the installation wizard, select **Debugging Tools for Windows**, and deselect all other components as shown in *Figure 28*:

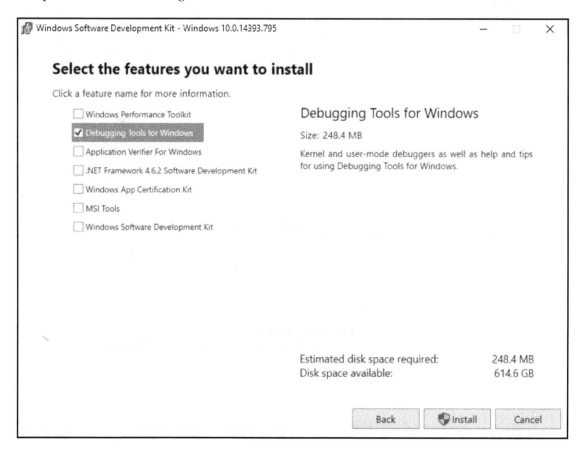

Figure 28. Installing Debugging Tools for Windows 10 from Windows SDK

Debugging Nano Server using WinDbg

After installing Windows SDK, open `WinDbg.exe` from the following location:

```
C:\Program Files (x86)\Windows Kits\10\Debuggers\x64\windbg.exe
```

Press *Ctrl+K* to open kernel debugging and connect to the name pipe of Nano Server as shown in *Figure 29*:

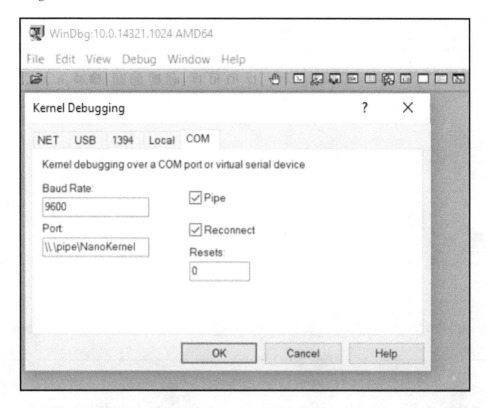

Figure 29. WinDbg kernel debugging over named pipe

At this point you can break in using *Ctrl+Break* as for normal kernel debugging processes (see *Figure 30*):

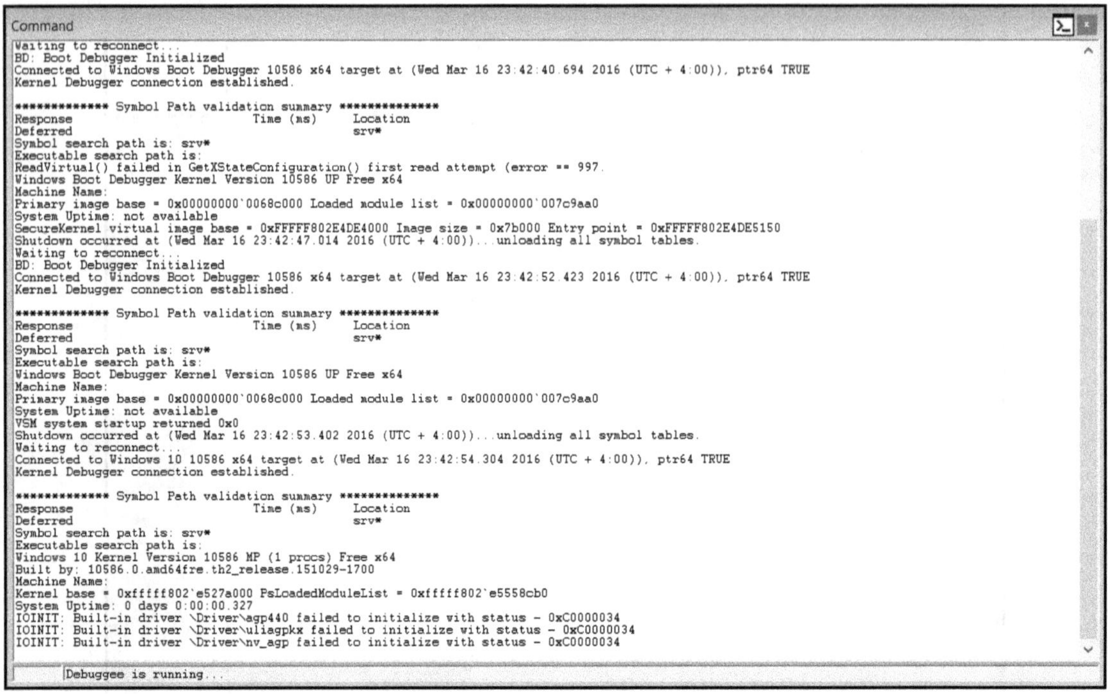

Figure 30. WinDbg kernel debugging connected to Nano Server

You can also use WinDbg with the command-line for live kernel-mode debugging as mentioned in the following article:

```
https://msdn.microsoft.com/en-us/library/windows/hardware/ff561306(v=vs.85).aspx.
```

To debug services in Nano Server, you need to first start kernel debugging on Nano Server.

Here is the link for kernel-mode debugging on Windows:

```
https://msdn.microsoft.com/en-us/library/windows/hardware/hh451166(v=vs.85).aspx.
```

There are two options to debugging a service in Nano Server:

- You can use the `sxe ld` debugger command to break when the service module is loaded: `https://msdn.microsoft.com/en-us/library/windows/hardware/ff539287(v=vs.85).aspx`

- You can configure the service to start with a console debugger, (that is `ntsd.exe`, attached in Nano Server). See this link: `https://support.microsoft.com/en-us/kb/824344#bookmark-8` using `ntsd.exe` instead of `windbg.exe`, and to control user-mode debugger from kernel debugger, check here: `https://msdn.microsoft.com/en-us/library/windows/hardware/ff539298(v=vs.85).aspx`

Setup and boot event collection (SBEC)

In this section, we will dive into **Setup and Boot Event Collection (SBEC)** which is a new feature introduced in Windows Server 2016. This feature is designed to help you to collect events and troubleshoot a headless machine-like Nano Server either locally or in a remote datacenter where you don't have access to it. SBEC allows you to remotely view the setup and boot event off-box; in other words, before the OS even boots. This feature will stream all events off during the boot and setup process to a collector machine in your environment and save them into an ETL file.

You can watch the events in real time, as it's going through the setup and boot process, and watch all the events that are coming in. Thus, you can see any failures that might occur. That's useful, especially when it comes to troubleshooting problems that occur during the boot process.

We want to emphasize that this service is not for Nano Server only. It's possible to use this feature with Server Core and Server with Desktop Experience as well.

To remotely collect ETW messages from physical or virtual machines, you should deploy a collector computer on your network as shown in *Figure 31*:

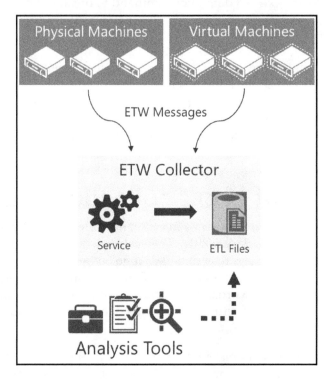

Figure 31. Setup and boot event collector diagram (image source - Microsoft)

Here are a few of the setup and boot events you can monitor with the Setup and boot event collection service:

- Loading kernel modules and drivers
- Enumeration of devices and initialization of their drivers (including devices such as CPU type)
- Verification and mounting of file systems
- Starting executable files
- Starting and completion of system updates
- The points when the system becomes available for logon, establishes connection with a domain controller, completion of service starts, and network shares are available

SBEC requirements

If the target computer (Nano Server) is running in a virtual machine, the VM must be hosted on Windows Server 2016 Hyper-V or Windows 10 as a virtualization host.

The collector computer must be running Windows Server 2016 (it can be either Server with Desktop Experience or Server Core), and the target computer must be running either Windows 10 or Windows Server 2016 including Nano Server.

The following combinations of a virtualized collector computer and target computer are known to work with SBEC:

Virtualization host	Collector virtual machine	Target virtual machine
Windows 8.1	YES	YES
Windows 10	YES	YES
Windows Server 2016	YES	YES
Windows Server 2012 R2	YES	NO

The SBEC service also works for physical machines.

Installing the collector computer

As mentioned earlier, the event collector service is available as an optional feature in Windows Server 2016. You can install the SBEC service using `DISM.exe` from the command-line or using Windows PowerShell.

Here is the command to install the service either way:

```
dism /online /enable-feature /featurename:SetupAndBootEventCollection
Install-WindowsFeature -Name Setup-and-Boot-Event-Collection -Verbose
```

You can also install the **Setup and Boot Event Collection** service with the **Add Roles and Features Wizard** in Server Manager as shown in *Figure 32*:

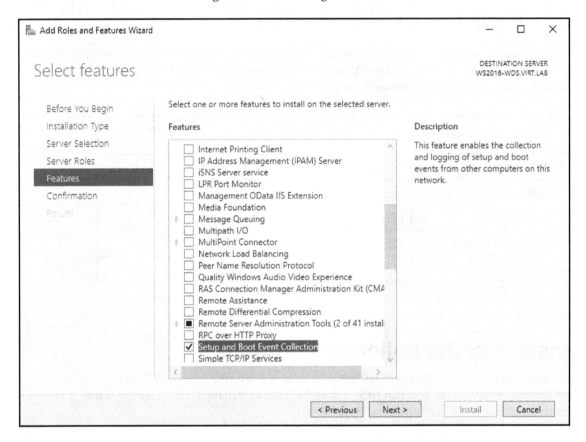

Figure 32. Installing Setup and Boot Event Collector Service using Server Manager

When the feature is installed, it creates a service called **BootEventCollector** (see *Figure 33*):

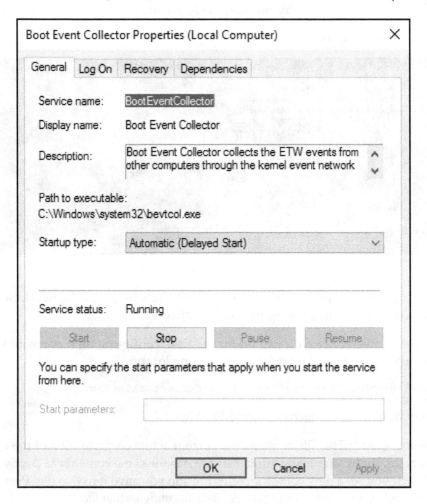

Figure 33. BootEventCollector service details

After installing the *Setup and Boot Event Collector* service, you can confirm if the installation succeeded and the service status by running the following command (see *Figure 34*):

```
Get-Service -DisplayName *boot*
```

```
CharbelNemnom.com #> Install-WindowsFeature -Name Setup-and-Boot-Event-Collection -Verbose
VERBOSE: Installation started...
VERBOSE: Continue with installation?
VERBOSE: Prerequisite processing started...
VERBOSE: Prerequisite processing succeeded.

Success Restart Needed Exit Code      Feature Result
------- -------------- ---------      --------------
True    No             Success        {Setup and Boot Event Collection}
VERBOSE: Installation succeeded.


CharbelNemnom.com #> Get-service -displayname *boot*

Status  Name               DisplayName
------  ----               -----------
Running BootEventCollector Boot Event Collector
```

Figure 34. Setup and Boot Event Collector Service Status

The boot event collector service should be running. It runs under the **Network Service Account** and creates an empty configuration file called `Active.xml`.

When you enable this service, you will find three XML configuration files created and stored on the collector computer under the following location:

```
C:\ProgramData\Microsoft\BootEventCollector\Config
```

Here is a brief description of each configuration file:

- `Active.xml`: This file contains the current active configuration of the collector service. Right after installation, this file has the same contents as `Empty.xml`. When you set a new collector configuration you save it to this file. Please refer to the section entitled *Creating the Active.xml configuration file*
- `Empty.xml`: This file contains the minimum configuration elements needed with their default values set. It does not enable any collection; it only allows the collector service to start in an idle mode
- `Example.xml`: This file provides examples and explanations of the possible configuration elements

There are several details to keep in mind when creating the `Active.xml` configuration file:

- The target computer, which is Nano Server. You can use its IPv4 address, a MAC address, or a SMBIOS GUID. Keep these factors in mind when choosing the address to use (more on that in the next section)
- The IPv4 address works best with static assignment of the IP addresses. **Kernel Debug Network Adapter** (**KDNET**) absolutely needs the DHCP, the target computer requires DHCP enabled. You can reserve the IP and MAC address through DHCP server for static assignment.
- A MAC address or SMBIOS GUID is convenient when they are known in advance but the IP addresses are assigned dynamically.
- IPv6 addresses are not supported by the EVENT-NET protocol.
- It is possible to specify multiple ways to identify the computer. For example, if the physical hardware is about to be replaced, you can enter both the old and the new MAC addresses, and either will be accepted.
- The encryption key used for the communication with the collector computer.
- The name of the target computer (Nano Server). You can use the IP address, host name, or any other name as the computer name.
- The name of the ETL file to use including its size.

Creating the Active.xml configuration file

1. On the collector computer, open an elevated Windows PowerShell console and change the directory to
   `C:\ProgramData\Microsoft\BootEventCollector\Config`
2. Type `notepad .\NewActiveConfig.xml` and then press *Enter*. An empty file will open in Notepad.
3. Copy the following example configuration into Notepad and save the file (see *Figure 35*):

The `NewActiveConfig.xml` file used in this example accompanies this book, you can download it.

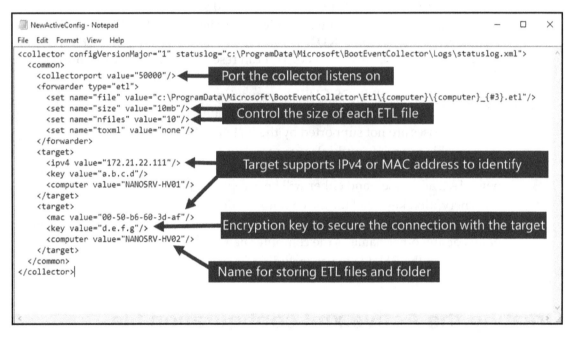

Figure 35. Creating the NewActiveConfig.xml using Notepad

4. As noted in the previous configuration file, you need to specify the collector port value, the recommended range is (50000-50039); next you need to specify the size of each ETL file (that is 10 MB) including the maximum number of ETL files to be created (that is 10 MB). Then you need to enter the details for each target computer separately under the `<target>` element. Please adjust the IPv4 addresses, MAC, and computer values based on your environment, and finally save the file and close Notepad.

5. Switch back to Windows PowerShell and apply the new configuration by running the following command:

```
$result = (Get-Content .\NewActiveConfig.xml | Set-SbecActiveConfig);
$result
```

The output should return the success value equal to `True` as shown in *Figure 36*:

```
Charbelnemnom.com #> pwd

Path
----
C:\ProgramData\Microsoft\BootEventCollector\Config


Charbelnemnom.com #> notepad .\NewActiveConfig.xml
Charbelnemnom.com #> $result = (Get-Content .\NewActiveConfig.xml | Set-SbecActiveConfig); $result

Name                          Value
----                          -----
InfoString                    Configuration:262204:0x4004003c: The configuration defined the following co...
ErrorString
NewTimestamp                  1310227623920666615
ErrorType                     0
Success                       True
WarningString
```

Figure 36. Applying the new configuration file

The previous command will apply the new configuration file automatically and update the collector service without needing a restart. You can always restart the service yourself with one of the following commands:

- Windows PowerShell:

      Restart-Service BootEventCollector

- Command-line:

      sc stop BootEventCollector; sc start BootEventCollector

- You can perform a validity check on the configuration file by running the following command (see *Figure 37*):

      bevtcol.exe -config .\NewActiveConfig.xml -checkOnly

```
CharbelNemnom.com #> bevtcol.exe -config .\NewActiveConfig.xml -checkOnly
I 2017-03-18 17:16:59.943Z Collector: Collector:720904:0x800b0008: The minimal log severity level has been set to "INFO
".
I 2017-03-18 17:16:59.959Z Collector: Collector:720898:0x400b0002: Collector configuration information:
  Configuration:262204:0x4004003c: The configuration defined the following computers:
  Configuration:262202:0x4004003a: The <target> with <ipv4> 172.16.20.185 produces the computer name "NANOCRHOST".
  Configuration:262203:0x4004003b: The <target> with <ipv4> 172.16.20.185 uses the forwarder with file "c:\ProgramData\M
icrosoft\BootEventCollector\Etl\{computer}\{computer}_{#3}.etl" of type "etl".
  Configuration:262205:0x4004003d: The <target> with <ipv4> 172.16.20.185 has 1 key(s) defined for it.
CharbelNemnom.com #>
```

Figure 37. Validating the new XML configuration file with BootEventCollector

You should not see any error or warning when validating the XML configuration file.

Configuring the target and collector computer

The target computer, which will be the Nano Server in this example, will push the messages to the collector machine.

You need to configure two items to collect setup and boot events:

1. On target computers that will send the events (that is, the Nano Server whose setup and boot you want to monitor), enable KDNET/EVENT-NET transport and enable the forwarding of events.
2. On the collector computer specify which computers to accept events from and where to save them.

Configuring Nano Server as a target computer

The following steps will describe how to set up Nano Server as a target computer:

1. First, you need to create a Nano Server image. See Chapter 3, *Deploying Nano Server in a Virtual Machine and on Physical Hardware*, for more details. If you already have Nano Server deployed in your environment, please skip to *step 3*.
2. Next, you need to add AutoLogger registry keys to enable sending diagnostic messages. To do this, you need to mount the Nano Server VHD image created in *step 1*, then load the registry hive, and update the registry. In this example, the Nano Server image is stored in the D:\ drive. Your path might be different; you need to adjust the following steps accordingly:
   1. On the collector computer, copy the C:\Windows\System32\WindowsPowerShell\v1.0\Modules\Boot EventCollector folder and paste it into the C:\Windows\System32\WindowsPowerShell\v1.0\Modules directory on the computer you are using to modify the Nano Server VHD image.
   2. On the computer that you are using to modify the Nano Server image, start a Windows PowerShell console as Administrator and run the following command:

```
Import-Module BootEventCollector -Verbose
```

3. Enable `AutoLogger` by updating the Nano Server VHD registry as shown in *Figure 38*. To do this, run the following command:

```
Enable-SbecAutoLogger -Path D:\NANOVM-CRHOST.vhd -
Verbose
```

```
CharbelNemnom.com #> Enable-SbecAutoLogger -Path D:\NANOVM-CRHOST.vhd -Verbose
VERBOSE: Executing: reg load HKLM\{ccbf2fba-9ae2-4685-94e9-e219c02f4a18}
C:\Users\Charo\AppData\Local\Temp\aioro4yd.njt\Windows\System32\config\SYSTEM
VERBOSE: The operation completed successfully.
VERBOSE: Executing: reg unload HKLM\{ccbf2fba-9ae2-4685-94e9-e219c02f4a18}
VERBOSE: The operation completed successfully.
VERBOSE: Completed the SBEC Autologger settings.
CharbelNemnom.com #>
```

Figure 38. Enabling AutoLogger in Nano Server using Windows PowerShell

3. If you already have Nano Server deployed either physically or virtually in your environment, you could use the following PowerShell command to enable SBEC `AutoLogger` instead of mounting the Nano Server VHD as described in *step 2:*

```
$NanoIP = "172.16.20.185"

$NanoCred = Get-Credential ~\Administrator

Enable-SbecAutoLogger -ComputerName $NanoIP -Credential
$NanoCred -Verbose
```

4. Finally, we need to update the BCD settings in the Nano Server image to enable the Events flag and set the collector computer to ensure diagnostic events are sent to the right collector machine. Note carefully the collector computer's IPv4 address, TCP port, and encryption key that you configured in the collector's `Active.XML` file as described in the section entitled *Creating the Active.xml configuration file.*

Again, if you already have Nano Server deployed in your environment, please skip to *step 5.*

On the computer that you are using to modify the Nano Server image, run the following command in a Windows PowerShell console as Administrator (see *Figure 39*):

```
Enable-SbecBcd -Path D:\NANOVM-CRHOST.vhd -CollectorIp 172.16.20.12 -
CollectorPort 50000 -Key a.b.c.d -Verbose
```

```
CharbelNemnom.com #> Enable-SbecBcd -Path D:\NANOVM-CRHOST.vhd -CollectorIp 172.16.20.12 -CollectorPort 50000 -Key a.b.c
.d -Verbose
VERBOSE: Executing: bcdedit /store "C:\Users\Charo\AppData\Local\Temp\3d4ci3yh.q4r\Boot\BCD" /set {default} debug no
VERBOSE: The operation completed successfully.
VERBOSE: Executing: bcdedit /store "C:\Users\Charo\AppData\Local\Temp\3d4ci3yh.q4r\Boot\BCD" /set {default} event yes
VERBOSE: The operation completed successfully.
VERBOSE: Executing: bcdedit /store "C:\Users\Charo\AppData\Local\Temp\3d4ci3yh.q4r\Boot\BCD" /eventsettings net
hostip:172.16.20.12 port:50000 key:a.b.c.d
VERBOSE: Key=a.b.c.d
VERBOSE: Completed the SBEC BCD settings.
CharbelNemnom.com #>
```

Figure 39. Updating BCD settings in Nano Server using Windows PowerShell

You need to run the previous command on each Nano Server image on which you want to enable the Events flag and set the collector computer.

5. You can also use the following PowerShell command to set the BCD settings in Nano Server without mounting the VHD image:

```
$NanoIP = "172.16.20.185"
$NanoCred = Get-Credential ~\Administrator
Enable-SbecBcd -ComputerName $NanoIP -CollectorIp 172.16.20.13
-CollectorPort 50039 -Key e.f.g.h -Credential $NanoCred -
Verbose
```

 You can only mount and update the BCD settings for the Nano Server VHD image as described earlier. Recall that VHD for Nano image means generation 1 VM (BIOS).

There is a known issue when you try to update the BCD settings for Nano Server with a VHDX image. Recall that VHDX for Nano image means generation 2 VM (UEFI). Alternatively, you can always use PowerShell remoting to set the BCD settings for Nano Server either deployed in a virtual machine (Gen 1/Gen 2) or in a physical machine. However, if you want to enable and update the BCD settings for a Nano Server Gen 2 VM, you need to disable secure boot under **Security** in the VM settings first, and then use PowerShell remoting to update the BCD settings. When the secure boot policy is enabled, an error will occur if you attempt to modify the debugger settings. The value is protected by the secure boot policy and cannot be modified or deleted.

Configuring the collector computer

The last step is to update the collector computer to receive events sent by the Nano Server computer by adding either the IPv4 address, or the MAC address of the Nano Server to the configuration file `NewActiveConfig.xml` on the collector computer. See the section titled *Creating the Active.xml configuration file* for more details.

Analyzing and reading diagnostic messages

Once the valid configuration file is saved on the collector computer and a target computer is configured, as soon as the target computer is restarted the connection to the collector is made and events will be collected and saved to the following path (see *Figure 40*):

`C:\ProgramData\Microsoft\BootEventCollector\Etl`

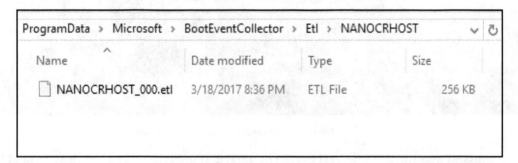

Figure 40. Collected ETL files

Then you can use any tool that can read an ETL file to read the diagnostic messages that are sent to the collector computer. Such tools are:

- Event viewer
- Message analyzer (`https://www.microsoft.com/en-us/download/details.asp x?id=44226`)
- Wevtutil (`https://technet.microsoft.com/en-us/library/cc732848.aspx`)
- Windows PowerShell `Get-WinEvent` (`https://msdn.microsoft.com/powershe ll/reference/5.1/microsoft.powershell.diagnostics/Get-WinEvent`)

The following is an example of reading the ETL log file using the `Get-WinEvent` cmdlet (see *Figure 41*):

```
Get-WinEvent -Path '.\NANOCRHOST_000.etl' -Oldest | Where-Object
{$_.LevelDisplayName -eq "Error"} | Sort-Object -Property TimeCreated -
Descending | Select-Object -First 3 | Format-list
```

```
CharbelNemnom.com #> Get-WinEvent -Path '.\NANOCRHOST_000.etl' -Oldest | Where-Object {$_.LevelDisplayName -eq "Error"}
 | Sort-Object -Property TimeCreated -Descending | Select-Object -First 3 | Format-List


TimeCreated  : 3/18/2017 10:04:29 PM
ProviderName : Microsoft-Windows-Kernel-Boot
Id           : 124
Message      : The Virtualization Based Security enablement policy check at phase 6 failed with status: {File Not
               Found}
               The file %hs does not exist.

TimeCreated  : 3/18/2017 10:04:29 PM
ProviderName : Microsoft-Windows-Kernel-Boot
Id           : 124
Message      : The Virtualization Based Security enablement policy check at phase 0 failed with status: {File Not
               Found}
               The file %hs does not exist.

TimeCreated  : 3/18/2017 9:00:46 PM
ProviderName : Microsoft-Windows-Kernel-Boot
Id           : 124
Message      : The Virtualization Based Security enablement policy check at phase 6 failed with status: {File Not
               Found}
               The file %hs does not exist.
```

Figure 41. Reading ETL file from an ETW event trace log using Get-WinEvent cmdlet

This command gets the three newest events in the log. It uses the `Get-WinEvent` cmdlet to get all the events from the ETL file. It pipes the event to the `Where-Object` cmdlet, which filters the event `Error` log results. Then, it pipes the events to the `Sort-Object` cmdlet, which sorts them in descending order by the value of the `TimeCreated` property. Then, it pipes the sorted events to the `Select-Object` cmdlet to select the three newest events. Finally, it uses the `Format-List` cmdlet to format the output of the command as a list of properties in which each property is displayed on a separate line.

Enabling access to Nano Server event logs

In the last section on troubleshooting a Nano Server installation, we will dive into how to enable and access Nano Server event logs.

To access the Event Logs on Nano Server that are located under the following path: C:\Windows\system32\winevt\Logs, you need to enable the following Windows firewall rules on Nano Server:

- Windows management instrumentation (DCOM-In)
- Windows management instrumentation (WMI-In)
- Windows management instrumentation (WMI-Out)

On your management machine, open an elevated PowerShell console, and create a new PowerShell remoting session to the Nano Server. If you still have your PowerShell prompt open from the previous section, you can use the existing $Session variable:

```
$NanoIP = "172.16.20.185"

$NanoCred = Get-Credential ~\Administrator

$Session = New-PSSession -ComputerName $NanoIP -Credential $NanoCred
```

Next, run the following command to enable the three firewall rules mentioned previously:

```
Invoke-Command -Session $Session -ScriptBlock {

Get-NetFirewallRule -Name WMI-RPCSS-In-TCP | Enable-NetFirewallRule -
PassThru | Format-List DisplayName, Enabled

Get-NetFirewallRule -Name WMI-WINMGMT-In-TCP | Enable-NetFirewallRule -
PassThru | Format-List DisplayName, Enabled

Get-NetFirewallRule -Name WMI-WINMGMT-Out-TCP | Enable-NetFirewallRule
-PassThru | Format-List DisplayName, Enabled

}
```

You should get the following output back showing that all three firewall rules are now
`Enabled`. (See *Figure 42*):

```
PS C:\> Invoke-Command -Session $Session -ScriptBlock {
     Get-NetFirewallRule -Name WMI-RPCSS-In-TCP    | Enable-NetFirewallRule -PassThru | Format-List DisplayName, Enabled
     Get-NetFirewallRule -Name WMI-WINMGMT-In-TCP  | Enable-NetFirewallRule -PassThru | Format-List DisplayName, Enabled
     Get-NetFirewallRule -Name WMI-WINMGMT-Out-TCP | Enable-NetFirewallRule -PassThru | Format-List DisplayName, Enabled
}


DisplayName : Windows Management Instrumentation (DCOM-In)
Enabled     : True




DisplayName : Windows Management Instrumentation (WMI-In)
Enabled     : True




DisplayName : Windows Management Instrumentation (WMI-Out)
Enabled     : True
```

Figure 42. Enabling Firewall rules in Nano Server using Windows PowerShell remoting

Once you have enabled the three firewall rules, you will be able to retrieve Nano Server
event log entries by running the following PowerShell script (see *Figure 43*):

```
CharbelNemnom.com #> .\B05331EN_08_1_Get-NanoServer-EventLogs.ps1 -Verbose

cmdlet B05331EN_08_1_Get-NanoServer-EventLogs.ps1 at command pipeline position 1
Supply values for the following parameters:
(Type !? for Help.)
NanoServer: 172.16.20.185
Username: Administrator
LogFile: System
Days: 1
VERBOSE: Enter the domain name
Enter domain name - Keep empty if Nano Server is not domain joined:
VERBOSE: Enter the Password for Administrator
Enter the Password for Administrator: *********
VERBOSE: Creating PSCredential Object
VERBOSE: Retrieving the Log Entries...
VERBOSE: Logs Retrieved... Completed!
VERBOSE: Opening the logs report...
CharbelNemnom.com #>
```

Figure 43. Retrieving Nano Server event logs using Windows PowerShell remoting

```
[CmdletBinding()]param(
    [Parameter(Mandatory,HelpMessage ='Nano Server Name or IP Address')]
[ValidateNotNullOrEmpty()] [String]$NanoServer,
```

```
[Parameter(Mandatory,HelpMessage ='Enter the username with
Administrator Privileges')] [ValidateNotNullOrEmpty()]
[String]$Username, [Parameter(Mandatory,HelpMessage ='LogFile =
Application, System, Security')] [ValidateNotNullOrEmpty()]
[ValidateSet('Application','System','Security')] [String]$LogFile,
    [Parameter(Mandatory,HelpMessage ='Last Number of Days')]
[ValidateNotNullOrEmpty()] [String]$Days) $head='<style>
  BODY{font-family:Verdana; background-color:lightblue;}
  TABLE{border-width: 1px;border-style: solid;border-color:
black;bordercollapse:
  collapse;}
  TH{font-size:1.3em; border-width: 1px;padding: 2px;border-style:
  solid;border-color: black;background-color:#FFCCCC}
  TD{border-width: 1px;padding: 2px;border-style: solid;border-color:
  black;background-color:yellow}
</style>'$header='<center><H1>Nano Server Event Logs
Results</H1></center>'# Prompting the Domain name.Write-Verbose"Enter
the domain name"[String]$DomainName=Read-Host-Prompt"Enter domain name
- Keep empty if Nano Server is not domain joined"# Formatting the
Credentials Username based on if the 'DomainName' Parameter was used or
not.If($DomainName)
{
    $CredsUsername="$DomainName\$Username"}If(!$DomainName)
{
    $CredsUsername="~\$Username"}# Prompting the username
password.Write-Verbose"Enter the Password for
$Username"$CredsPassword=Read-Host-Prompt"Enter the Password for
$Username"-AsSecureString# Creating a PSCredential Object to login to
the Nano Server.Write-Verbose"Creating PSCredential Object"$Creds=New-
Object-TypeNameSystem.Management.Automation.PSCredential-
ArgumentList($CredsUsername,$CredsPassword)# Retrieving and returning
back the Log Entries from the Log File passed in from the 'LogFile'
Parameter.Write-Verbose"Retrieving the Log Entries..."Get-WmiObject-
ComputerName$NanoServer-ClassWin32_NTLogEvent-
Filter("(logfile='$LogFile' "`
    +"AND (TimeWritten
>'$([System.Management.ManagementDateTimeConverter]::ToDMTFDateTime((ge
t-date).AddDays(-$Days)))'))") `
    -Credential$Creds|ConvertTo-HTML-head$head-body$header|Out-
FileNanoLogReport.htmWrite-Verbose"Logs Retrieved... Completed!"Write-
Verbose"Opening the logs report...".\NanoLogReport.htm
```

In the previous example, we retrieved the entries from the last, one day in the system log.

The following screenshot shows the output in the HTML file that is created after running the script, the report is saved in the current directory where the script is running (see *Figure 44*):

Nano Server Event Logs Results					
PSComputerName	**__GENUS**	**__CLASS**	**__SUPERCLASS**	**__DYNASTY**	**__RELPATH**
NANOVM-CRHOST	2	Win32_NTLogEvent		Win32_NTLogEvent	Win32_NTLogEvent.Logfile="System",Rec○
NANOVM-CRHOST	2	Win32_NTLogEvent		Win32_NTLogEvent	Win32_NTLogEvent.Logfile="System",Rec○
NANOVM-CRHOST	2	Win32_NTLogEvent		Win32_NTLogEvent	Win32_NTLogEvent.Logfile="System",Rec○
NANOVM-CRHOST	2	Win32_NTLogEvent		Win32_NTLogEvent	Win32_NTLogEvent.Logfile="System",Rec○

Figure 44. Nano Server event logs HTML report

Summary

In this chapter, we discussed how to troubleshoot a Nano Server installation using the Nano recovery console, **Emergency Management Services** (**EMS**), kernel debugging, and **Setup and Boot Event Collection** (**SBEC**), which is a new feature introduced in Windows Server 2016.

SBEC allows you to remotely view debug errors, events from your deployment process, the bootloader, OS, and services. It will help you to troubleshoot issues without interactive login or physical access and it works on both physical and virtual machines. It requires a little additional infrastructure and can be set up using PowerShell; you can access data in real time and it can be correlated with other diagnostic data to identify problems faster.

In the last section of this chapter, we covered how to retrieve and read Nano Server Windows event logs and display them in a nicely formatted HTML report.

Continue now to `Chapter 10`, *Running Other Workloads on the Nano Server,* to learn more about what other roles and features can run on Nano Server, and what Microsoft is planning for the next release of Nano Server.

10
Running Other Workloads on the Nano Server

In Chapter 9, *Troubleshooting Nano Server*, we talked about how to troubleshoot a Nano Server installation with Nano recovery console, emergency management services, kernel debugging, setup, and boot event collection including how to collect Nano Server event logs from a remote machine.

In this chapter, we will look at how to run other workloads on Nano Server and cover the following topics:

- Running DNS on Nano Server.
- Running IIS on Nano Server.
- Installing and managing Windows Defender on Nano Server.
- Managing a local administrator's passwords on Nano Server.
- Using MPIO on Nano Server.
- Using Windows Update on Nano Server.
- Update **Out of Box** (**OOB**) drivers for Nano Server.
- The future of Nano Server.

Running DNS on Nano Server

As discussed in earlier chapters of this book, Microsoft added DNS support for Nano Server. This support brings a convenient choice to run core infrastructure services on top of Nano Server which increase security and minimize disk footprint. So, instead of having a 12 GB image to run only **Domain Name System** (**DNS**) on Server with Desktop Experience and 7 GB for Server Core, you can use Nano Server with less than 1 GB of disk space and achieve the same thing.

The following section will detail the deployment of a very basic Nano Server configuration. For a more thorough explanation of deployment and configuration options, please check `Chapter 2`, *Getting Started with Nano Server*.

Follow the following steps to create a VHD(X) image for Nano Server to be used as a DNS server so we can run **Domain Name System** (**DNS**) on top of Nano Server:

1. Mount Windows Server 2016 ISO media on your machine. In this example, it's mounted on the `H` drive.

2. Start Windows PowerShell as administrator on your management machine which is a member of the same domain where you intend to deploy Nano Server, and then run the following script to create a VHD(X) for virtual machine deployment that includes the DNS package, `Microsoft-NanoServer-DNS-Package`. You will be prompted for an administrator password:

```
#region variables$ComputerName="NANOVM-DNS"# Staging path for new
Nano image$StagingPath="C:\"# Path to Windows Server 2016 ISO
file$MediaPath="H:\"$Domain="VIRT.LAB"$Path=Join-Path-
Path$StagingPath-ChildPathNanoServer$Password=Read-Host-
Prompt'Please specify local Administrator password'-
AsSecureString#endregion#region Copy source filesif(-not(Test-Path-
Path$StagingPath)) {mkdir-Path$StagingPath}if(-not(Test-Path-
Path$Path)) {$NanoServerSourcePath=Join-Path-Path$MediaPath-
ChildPathNanoServer-Resolve Copy-Item-Path$NanoServerSourcePath-
Destination$StagingPath-Recurse}#endregion#region Generate Nano
ImageImport-Module-Name(Join-Path-Path$Path-
ChildPathNanoServerImageGenerator) -Verbose$ServicingPackagePath=@(
   'C:\NanoServer\Updates\Servicing stack update\Windows10.0-
KB4013418-x64.msu' 'C:\NanoServer\Updates\Cumulative
Update\Windows10.0-KB4013429-
x64.msu')$NanoServerImageParameters=@{ComputerName =$ComputerName
MediaPath =$MediaPath BasePath =(Join-Path-Path$Path-
ChildPath$ComputerName)
   # .vhd for BIOS and .vhdx for UEFI system TargetPath =Join-Path-
Path$Path-ChildPath($ComputerName+'.vhdx')
   AdministratorPassword =$Password Package ='Microsoft-NanoServer-
```

```
DNS-Package' DomainName =$Domain ReuseDomainNode =$true
EnableRemoteManagementPort =$true EnableEMS =$true DeploymentType
='Guest' Edition ='Standard' MaxSize =10GB InterfaceNameOrIndex
='Ethernet' Ipv4Address ='172.16.20.185' Ipv4SubnetMask
='255.255.255.0' Ipv4Gateway ='172.16.20.1' Ipv4Dns ='172.16.20.9'
SetupCompleteCommand =('tzutil.exe /s "W. Europe Standard Time"')
   ServicingPackagePath =$ServicingPackagePath}New-
NanoServerImage@NanoServerImageParameters#endregion
```

This script will create a VHDX image file using Windows Server 2016 ISO mounted as `H:\` drive. When creating the image, it uses a folder called `NanoServer` found on the root `C` drive. The file is placed in the same folder, called `NANOVM-DNS`. In this example, the computer name is set to `NANOVM-DNS` and includes `Guest` drivers. We will deploy a generation 2 virtual machine, for this reason we created the image as VHDX.

We added the DNS package, this will ensure that the image has the DNS role installed so you can run Domain Name System on Nano Server. This script will also perform an offline domain join for the image, and if the same computer name does exist in the domain, it will reuse it.

We also enabled remote management port so we can manage Nano Server using PowerShell Remoting across different network subnets, we enabled **Emergency Management Services** (**EMS**), and added the IP address statically, DNS and Gateway.

Finally, we set the time zone to W. Europe Standard Time by using the `SetupCompleteCommand` parameter and added the latest Windows Server updates to the image.

Once the image is created, you need to create a virtual machine from this VHD(X), and connect to it using the **Hyper-V connect** option. There are several options to deploy Nano Server as a virtual machine, you can use **Hyper-V Manager**, **System Center Virtual Machine Manager**, or **Failover Cluster Manager**. In this example, we will use the following PowerShell script to automate this process:

```
#variables$vSwitchName01="Ext_vSwitch01"$InstallRoot="D:\VMs\NANOVM-
DNS"$VMPath="D:\VMs"$VMName="NANOVM-
DNS"$NanoServerImage="C:\NanoServer\NANOVM-DNS.vhdx"#region Create VM
directoryif(-not(Test-Path-Path$InstallRoot)) {
   mkdir-Path$VMPath-Name$VMName}#endregion#region copy Nano Imageif(-
not(Test-Path-Path($InstallRoot+"\NANOVM-DNS.vhdx"))) {Copy-Item-
Path$NanoServerImage-Destination$InstallRoot-Force}#endregion#region Create
VMNew-VHD-Path($InstallRoot+"\NANOVM-DNS_D.vhdx") -SizeBytes50GB-
DynamicNew-VM-VHDPath($InstallRoot+"\NANOVM-DNS.vhdx") -Generation2-
MemoryStartupBytes2GB`
      -Name$VMName-Path$InstallRoot-SwitchName$vSwitchName01Set-VMMemory-
```

```
VMName$VMName-DynamicMemoryEnabled$falseSet-VMProcessor-VMName$VMName-
Count2Set-VM-VMName$VMName-AutomaticStopActionShutDown-
AutomaticStartActionStartIfRunningEnable-VMIntegrationService$VMName-
Name"Guest Service Interface"Rename-VMNetworkAdapter-VMName$VMName-
NewName"vmNIC-MGT"Set-VMNetworkAdapter-VMName$VMName-Name"vmNIC-MGT"-
DeviceNamingOnAdd-VMScsiController-VMName$VMNameAdd-VMHardDiskDrive-
VMName$VMName-ControllerTypeSCSI-ControllerNumber1-ControllerLocation0-
Path($InstallRoot+"\NANOVM-DNS_D.vhdx")Start-VM-Name$VMName|Out-
Null#enregion
```

When deploying the DNS Server package to Nano Server, all PowerShell cmdlets are available locally. But before starting to manage DNS Server, you need to enable the DNS feature on Nano Server, because adding only the package to the image isn't enough.

To do so, you need to connect to Nano Server using PowerShell remoting and enable the DNS feature by using the following commands (see *Figure 1*):

```
$NanoIP="172.16.20.185"$NanoCred=Get-Credential~\Administrator$Session=New-
PSSession-ComputerName$NanoIP-Credential$NanoCred
$Session|Enter-PSSessionEnable-WindowsOptionalFeature-Online-
FeatureNameDNS-Server-Full-Role-VerboseGet-Service*dns(Get-Command-
ModuleDnsServer).CountExit-PSSession
```

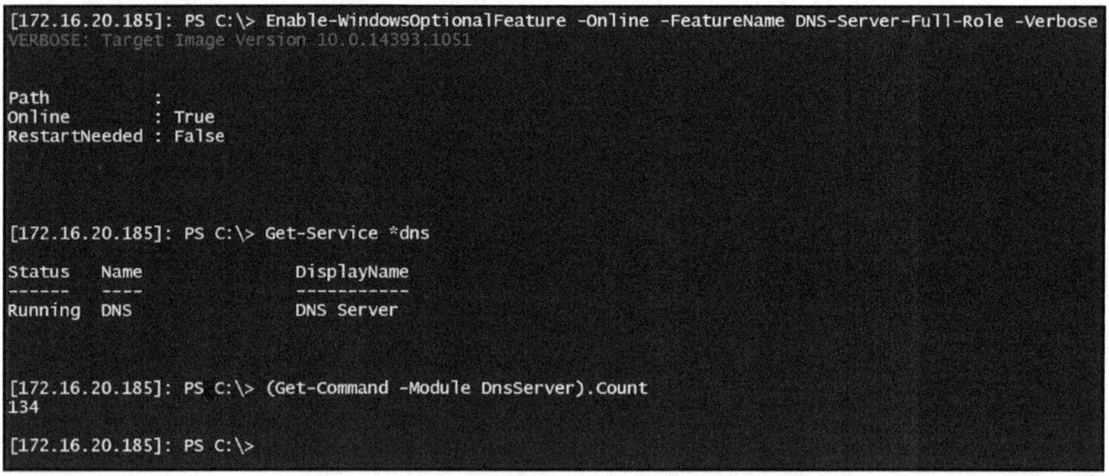

Figure 1. Running DNS Server on Nano Server

This server is now ready to run as DNS Server.

You can use PowerShell to remotely manage DNS using the `DnsServer` module which contains 134 cmdlets in Windows Server 2016, and you can, of course, use the DNS Server MMC console. You can do that by simply connecting remotely from your management machine with **Remote Server Administration Tools** (**RSAT**) enabled (see *Figure 2*):

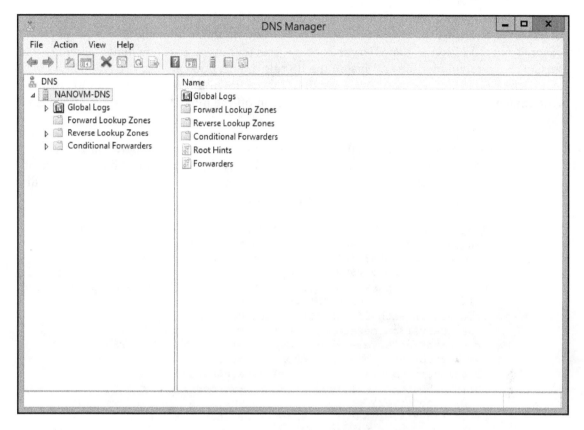

Figure 2. Connecting to Nano Server using DNS Console

Running IIS on Nano Server

With the release of Windows Server 2016, Microsoft announced that IIS 10 is also available as a role on Nano Server. With smaller memory and dramatically smaller disk footprint, web workloads are particularly suited to running on Nano Server, especially for high density web hosting.

Please note that not all Web Applications will run on Nano Server. IIS version 10 running on Nano Server targets applications developed based on ASP.NET Core, so full .NET Framework will not run. Applications written in Java and PHP will run with IIS 10 on Nano.

Mount Windows Server 2016 ISO media on your machine. In this example, it's mounted on the 'H' drive.There are many options, approaches, and methods to install IIS on Nano Server. You could use the Nano Server Package provider of the package management (a.k.a OneGet) PowerShell module and install the IIS role online, you can also use Nano Server **Image Builder** (**IB**). In this example, we will use the following PowerShell script to create a Nano image and add the IIS package to the image in offline mode (this is the recommended way according to Microsoft documentation).

1. Start Windows PowerShell as administrator on your management machine, and then run the following script to create a VHD(X) for virtual machine deployment that includes the IIS package `Microsoft-NanoServer-IIS-Package`. You will be prompted for an administrator password:

```
#region variables$ComputerName="NANOVM-IIS"# Staging path for new
Nano image$StagingPath="C:\"# Path to Windows Server 2016 ISO
file$MediaPath="H:\"$Path=Join-Path-Path$StagingPath-
ChildPathNanoServer$Password=Read-Host-Prompt'Please specify local
Administrator password'-AsSecureString#endregion#region Copy source
filesif(-not(Test-Path-Path$StagingPath)) {mkdir-
Path$StagingPath}if(-not(Test-Path-Path$Path))
{$NanoServerSourcePath=Join-Path-Path$MediaPath-
ChildPathNanoServer-Resolve Copy-Item-Path$NanoServerSourcePath-
Destination$StagingPath-Recurse}#endregion#region Generate Nano
ImageImport-Module-Name(Join-Path-Path$Path-
ChildPathNanoServerImageGenerator) -Verbose$ServicingPackagePath=@(
    'C:\NanoServer\Updates\Servicing stack update\Windows10.0-
KB4013418-x64.msu' 'C:\NanoServer\Updates\Cumulative
Update\Windows10.0-KB4013429-
x64.msu')$NanoServerImageParameters=@{ComputerName =$ComputerName
MediaPath =$MediaPath BasePath =(Join-Path-Path$Path-
ChildPath$ComputerName)
    # .vhd for BIOS and .vhdx for UEFI system TargetPath =Join-Path-
Path$Path-ChildPath($ComputerName+'.vhdx')
    AdministratorPassword =$Password Package ='Microsoft-NanoServer-
IIS-Package' EnableRemoteManagementPort =$true EnableEMS =$true
DeploymentType ='Guest' Edition ='Standard' MaxSize =10GB
SetupCompleteCommand =('tzutil.exe /s "W. Europe Standard Time"')
    ServicingPackagePath =$ServicingPackagePath}New-
NanoServerImage@NanoServerImageParameters#endregion
```

This script will create a VHDX image file using Windows Server 2016 ISO mounted as `H:\` drive. When creating the image, it uses a folder called `NanoServer` found on the root `C` drive. The file is placed in the same folder, called `NANOVM-IIS`. In this example, the computer name is set to `NANOVM-IIS` and includes `Guest` drivers. We will deploy a generation 2 virtual machine, for this reason we created the image as VHDX.

We added the IIS package, this will ensure that the image has the IIS role installed so we can host and run web services on Nano Server.

We also enabled Remote Management Port so we can manage Nano Server using PowerShell Remoting across different network subnets and we enabled Emergency Management Services. Finally, we set the time zone to W. Europe Standard Time by using the `SetupCompleteCommand` parameter and added the latest Windows Server updates to the image.

Once the image is created, you need to create a virtual machine from this VHD(X), please refer to the section titled *Running DNS on Nano Server* and see the example on how to automate the VM deployment using Windows PowerShell.

As soon as Nano Server with IIS is deployed, you can check if the default IIS page will launch by typing it's IP address in your favorite browser (see *Figure 3*):

Figure 3. Browsing IIS on Nano Server

As with any IIS installation on Windows Server (Server with Desktop Experience or Server Core), there are certain IIS sub-features enabled by default and some other features not enabled by default. As of this writing, the following set of IIS sub-features are enabled by default on Nano Server:

IIS Sub-Features enabled by default	Feature name
Default document	IIS-Default document
Directory browsing	IIS-Directory browsing
HTTP errors	IIS-Http errors
Static content	IIS-Static content
HTTP logging	IIS-Http logging
Static content compression	IIS-Http compression Static
Request filtering	IIS-Request filtering
IIS Administration module for Windows PowerShell	--

The following set of IIS sub-features are not enabled by default on Nano Server:

IIS Features available are not enabled by default	Feature name
HTTP redirection	IIS-Http redirect
Custom logging	IIS-Custom logging
Request monitor	IIS-Request monitor
Tracing	IIS-Http tracing
Dynamic content compression	IIS-Http compression dynamic
Basic authentication	IIS-Basic authentication
Client certificate mapping authentication	IIS-IIS certificate mapping authentication
Digest authentication	IIS-Digest authentication
IIS client certificate mapping authentication	IIS-Client certificate mapping authentication
IP and domain restrictions	IIS-IP security
URL authorization	IIS-URL authorization

Windows authentication	IIS-Windows authentication
Application initialization	IIS-ApplicationInit
CGI	IIS-CGI
ISAPI extensions	IIS-ISAPI extensions
ISAPI filters	IIS-ISAPI filter
Server-side includes	IIS-Server side includes
Web Socket protocol	IIS-Web sockets

To enable or disable any of the IIS sub-features, you can use either PowerShell or DISM to accomplish this. Please refer to the table above to get the corresponding feature name. For example, to install the application initialization feature on Nano Server, you need to use PowerShell remoting, and then run the following commands.

In this example, we will show you how to do the same using PowerShell and DISM:

```
#Connecting to Nano Server using PowerShell
remoting$NanoIP="172.16.20.158"$NanoCred=Get-
Credential~\Administrator$Session=New-PSSession-ComputerName$NanoIP-
Credential$NanoCred$Session|Enter-PSSession#Enable IIS-ApplicationInit
using PowerShellEnable-WindowsOptionalFeature-Online-FeatureNameIIS-
ApplicationInit-All #Disable IIS-ApplicationInit using PowerShellDisable-
WindowsOptionalFeature-Online-FeatureNameIIS-ApplicationInit#Enable IIS-
ApplicationInit using DISMdism/Enable-Feature/online/featurename:IIS-
ApplicationInit/all#Disable IIS-ApplicationInit using DISMdism/Disable-
Feature/online/featurename:IIS-ApplicationInitExit-PSSession
```

As for IIS management experience, PowerShell is front and center of the Nano Server management. This means you will be able to manage IIS on Nano using the new `IIS Administration` module for Windows PowerShell which includes 31 cmdlets (see *Figure 4*):

```
[172.16.20.158]: PS C:\> Get-Service W3SVC

Status    Name            DisplayName
------    ----            -----------
Running   W3SVC           World Wide Web Publishing Service


[172.16.20.158]: PS C:\> Get-Command -Module IISAdministration

CommandType    Name                                    Version     Source
-----------    ----                                    -------     ------
Cmdlet         Clear-IISCentralCertProvider            1.0.0.0     IISAdministration
Cmdlet         Clear-IISConfigCollection               1.0.0.0     IISAdministration
Cmdlet         Disable-IISCentralCertProvider          1.0.0.0     IISAdministration
Cmdlet         Disable-IISSharedConfig                 1.0.0.0     IISAdministration
Cmdlet         Enable-IISCentralCertProvider           1.0.0.0     IISAdministration
Cmdlet         Enable-IISSharedConfig                  1.0.0.0     IISAdministration
Cmdlet         Export-IISConfiguration                 1.0.0.0     IISAdministration
Cmdlet         Get-IISAppPool                          1.0.0.0     IISAdministration
Cmdlet         Get-IISCentralCertProvider              1.0.0.0     IISAdministration
Cmdlet         Get-IISConfigAttributeValue             1.0.0.0     IISAdministration
Cmdlet         Get-IISConfigCollection                 1.0.0.0     IISAdministration
Cmdlet         Get-IISConfigCollectionElement          1.0.0.0     IISAdministration
Cmdlet         Get-IISConfigElement                    1.0.0.0     IISAdministration
Cmdlet         Get-IISConfigSection                    1.0.0.0     IISAdministration
Cmdlet         Get-IISServerManager                    1.0.0.0     IISAdministration
Cmdlet         Get-IISSharedConfig                     1.0.0.0     IISAdministration
Cmdlet         Get-IISSite                             1.0.0.0     IISAdministration
Cmdlet         New-IISConfigCollectionElement          1.0.0.0     IISAdministration
Cmdlet         New-IISSite                             1.0.0.0     IISAdministration
Cmdlet         Remove-IISConfigAttribute               1.0.0.0     IISAdministration
Cmdlet         Remove-IISConfigCollectionElement       1.0.0.0     IISAdministration
Cmdlet         Remove-IISConfigElement                 1.0.0.0     IISAdministration
Cmdlet         Remove-IISSite                          1.0.0.0     IISAdministration
Cmdlet         Reset-IISServerManager                  1.0.0.0     IISAdministration
Cmdlet         Set-IISCentralCertProvider              1.0.0.0     IISAdministration
Cmdlet         Set-IISCentralCertProviderCredential    1.0.0.0     IISAdministration
Cmdlet         Set-IISConfigAttributeValue             1.0.0.0     IISAdministration
Cmdlet         Start-IISCommitDelay                    1.0.0.0     IISAdministration
Cmdlet         Start-IISSite                           1.0.0.0     IISAdministration
Cmdlet         Stop-IISCommitDelay                     1.0.0.0     IISAdministration
Cmdlet         Stop-IISSite                            1.0.0.0     IISAdministration
```

Figure 4. IIS Administration PowerShell cmdlets

In addition to PowerShell (IIS Administration) module, you can use the `appcmd.exe` to manage IIS remotely on Nano Server. `AppCmd.exe` is located in the `C:\Windows\System32\inetsrv\directory`. Because it is not a path of the Environment Variables default PATH, you need to use the full path to the executable when executing commands. Alternatively, you can manually add the `inetsrv` directory to the path on your management machine so that you can access `AppCmd.exe` directly from any location.

The IIS Manager console is not available as an option to manage Nano Server remotely, because of the missing API dependencies. However, Microsoft published an article on how to install and add all the required components to enable a web-based management UI for IIS administration on Nano Server.

https://blogs.iis.net/adminapi/microsoft-iis-administration-on-nano-server.

Creating a website on Nano Server is very easy, you can run the following PowerShell command to create a new site:

```
New-Item-PathC:\inetpub\wwwroot\-NameNanoWebSite-ItemTypeDirectoryNew-
IISSite-NameNanoWebSite-BindingInformation"*:80:NanoWebSite"-
PhysicalPathC:\inetpub\wwwroot\NanoWebSiteGet-IISSite-NameNanoWebSite
```

You can change the background image of the default IIS website by running the following command (see *Figure 5*):

```
$NanoIP="172.16.20.158"$NanoCred=Get-Credential~\Administrator$Session=New-
PSSession-ComputerName$NanoIP-Credential$NanoCred Copy-Item-
ToSession$Session-PathC:\NanoServer\iisstart.png-
DestinationC:\inetpub\wwwroot\-Force
```

Figure 5. Creating a website on Nano Server

Installing and managing Windows Defender on Nano Server

Nano Server 2016 does not come with an Antivirus client by default in contrast to Server with Desktop Experience and Server Core which both come with Windows Defender installed.

Nano Server also uses Windows Defender, however, it's a more lightweight version compared to other versions of Windows.

As we have seen in this book, all the roles and features for Nano Server come as additional packages that can be added on demand.

There are many different options that you can use to install Windows Defender on Nano Server. You could use the `New-NanoServerImage` cmdlet to create a Nano Server image and add the Defender package as part of the image in offline mode. You could also use Nano Server Image Builder. In this example, we will use Nano Server Package provider of the Package Management (a.k.a OneGet) and install the Defender feature in online mode.

Once the Nano image is created, you need to create a virtual machine from this VHD(X), please refer to the section titled *Running DNS on Nano Server* and see the example on how to automate the VM deployment using Windows PowerShell. This example also assumes that Nano Server is reachable over the network and has internet access.

First, you need to connect to Nano Server using PowerShell Remoting and install the Windows Defender package. The following is an example on how to use PowerShell to install the Windows Defender package using Nano Server Package provider:

```
$NanoIP="172.16.20.156"$NanoCred=Get-Credential~\Administrator$Session=New-
PSSession-ComputerName$NanoIP-Credential$NanoCred$Session|Enter-
PSSessionInstall-PackageProviderNanoServerPackageImport-
PackageProviderNanoServerPackageFind-NanoServerPackage-
Name*Defender*Install-NanoServerPackage-NameMicrosoft-NanoServer-Defender-
Package-Force
```

Once the Defender package is installed, you need to restart Nano Server using the `Restart-Computer` cmdlet, and then login again to update the virus definition file.

Please note that when deploying the Defender package, all the management tasks are performed from Windows PowerShell by using the Defender PowerShell Module.

The following is an example on how to use Windows PowerShell and command-line tool to manage and update the Antivirus signatures.

After connecting to Nano Server using PowerShell remoting, you can run the following commands (see *Figure 6*):

```
Import-ModuledefenderGet-Command-Moduledefender
```

```
[172.16.20.156]: PS C:\> Get-Command -Module defender


CommandType       Name                           Version   Source
-----------       ----                           -------   ------
Function          Add-MpPreference               1.0       defender
Function          Get-MpComputerStatus           1.0       defender
Function          Get-MpPreference               1.0       defender
Function          Get-MpThreat                   1.0       defender
Function          Get-MpThreatCatalog            1.0       defender
Function          Get-MpThreatDetection          1.0       defender
Function          Remove-MpPreference            1.0       defender
Function          Remove-MpThreat                1.0       defender
Function          Set-MpPreference               1.0       defender
Function          Start-MpScan                   1.0       defender
Function          Start-MpWDOScan                1.0       defender
Function          Update-MpSignature             1.0       defender
```

Figure 6. Windows Defender PowerShell Module

It's recommended to update the AV signature first by using the `Update-MpSignature` cmdlet, and then run a full system scan by using `Start-MpScan cmdlet.`

```
Update-MpSignature-UpdateSourceMicrosoftUpdateServer-Verbose Start-MpScan-
ScanTypeFullScan Get-MpComputerStatus
```

The `Update-MpSignature` cmdlet will use the Microsoft update server over the internet to update the AV signature.

If you are using Nano Server as a Hyper-V host, it's recommended to exclude certain processes, files, and folders from the Defender default scan.

These exclusions are made based on the Hyper-V file locations. The default location for

VM configuration files is, `C:\ProgramData\Microsoft\Windows\Hyper-V`, and for virtual hard disks is, `C:\Users\Public\Documents\Hyper-V\Virtual Hard Disks`. You might also need to exclude the cluster storage location `C:\ClusterStorage` if you are using failover clustering. Take a note of the current files and folder locations in your environment.

In this example, the following list of processes, files, and folder will be excluded from Windows Defender running on Nano Server:

- `D:\VMs`
- `*.vhdx` and `*.vhd`
- `Vmms.exe`, `Vmcompute.exe`, and `Vmwp.exe`

While you are still connecting to the Nano Server PowerShell session, run the following commands (see *Figure 7*):

```
Add-MpPreference-ExclusionExtension"*.vhdx","*.vhd"Add-MpPreference-
ExclusionPath"D:\VMs"Add-MpPreference-
ExclusionProcess"Vmms.exe","Vmwp.exe","Vmcompute.exe"Get-
MpPreference|FTExclusionExtension,ExclusionPath,ExclusionProcess-AutoSize
```

```
[172.16.20.156]: PS C:\> Add-MpPreference -ExclusionExtension "*.vhdx","*.vhd"
Add-MpPreference -ExclusionPath "D:\VMs"
Add-MpPreference -ExclusionProcess "Vmms.exe", "Vmwp.exe", "Vmcompute.exe"
Get-MpPreference | FT ExclusionExtension, ExclusionPath, ExclusionProcess -AutoSize


ExclusionExtension ExclusionPath ExclusionProcess
------------------ ------------- ----------------
{*.vhd, *.vhdx}    {D:\VMs}      {Vmcompute.exe, Vmms.exe, Vmwp.exe}


[172.16.20.156]: PS C:\>
```

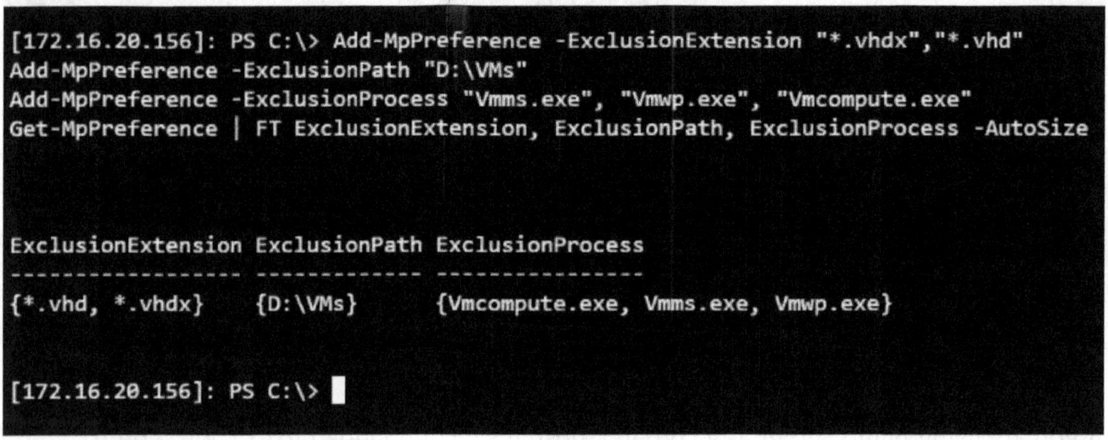

Figure 7. Windows Defender Exclusion

In some environments, Nano Server is deployed via a disconnected method without internet access, however, your company policy dictates that you still need to update the AV signature. In this case, you must download the AV signature files and then use a local or centralized UNC share to update and push the AV signature version on each Nano Server. This sounds like a manual approach; however, you can automate this option by using a daily single scheduled task that can pull the AV signature files from a central share location, and then update the signature version in an automated fashion.

The following example will show you how to download and update the AV signature in an offline or disconnected environment.

First, we need to download the AV signature files using the following PowerShell command (see *Figure 8*):

```
$destinationPath="D:\AVSignatures"#region create destination path if
doesnot existif(-not(Test-Path-Path$destinationPath)) {
mkdir-Path$destinationPath}#endregion#region Windows Defender Definitions
URL$x64S1="http://go.microsoft.com/fwlink/?LinkID=121721&clcid=0x409&arch=x
64"$x64D1=$destinationPath+"\mpam-
fe.exe"$x64S2="http://go.microsoft.com/fwlink/?LinkId=211054"$x64D2=$destin
ationPath+"\mpam-
d.exe"$x64S3="http://go.microsoft.com/fwlink/?LinkID=187316&arch=x64&nri=tr
ue"$x64D3=$destinationPath+"\nis_full.exe"#endregion#region Download
Windows Defender Definitions$WebClient=New-
ObjectSystem.Net.WebClient$WebClient.DownloadFile($x64S1,$x64D1)$WebClient.
DownloadFile($x64S2,$x64D2)$WebClient.DownloadFile($x64S3,$x64D3)#endregion
```

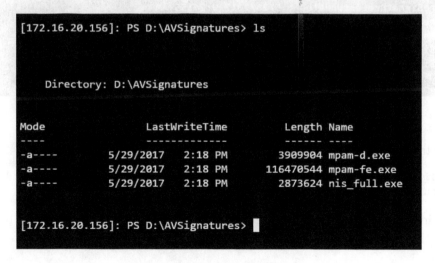

Figure 8. Download Windows Defender AV Signature Files

The second command is to update the AV signature version on Nano Server using the `MPCmdRun.exe` command-line instead of using `Update-MpSignature -UpdateSource FileShares`. This is the recommended approach suggested by Microsoft specifically for Windows Defender running on Nano Server.

Please note that every time you want to update the AV signature, you want to browse to `C:\Program File\Windows Defender` and then run the `MPCmdRun.exe` command-line tool from there. To work around this issue, you can create a new alias in PowerShell to speed up the process (more on that in a bit).

Before we update the Windows Defender definition, you can check the existing AV version installed by running the following command (see *Figure 9*):

```
Get-
MpComputerStatus|FLAMEngineVersion,AMProductVersion,`AntispywareEnabled,Ant
ispywareSignatureLastUpdated,`AntispywareSignatureVersion,AntivirusEnabled,
`AntivirusSignatureLastUpdated,AntivirusSignatureVersion
```

```
[172.16.20.156]: PS D:\> Get-MpComputerStatus | FL AMEngineVersion, AMProductVersion, `
AntispywareEnabled, AntispywareSignatureLastUpdated, `
AntispywareSignatureVersion, AntivirusEnabled, `
AntivirusSignatureLastUpdated, AntivirusSignatureVersion


AMEngineVersion                  : 1.1.13804.0
AMProductVersion                 : 4.10.14393.1198
AntispywareEnabled               : True
AntispywareSignatureLastUpdated  : 5/28/2017 9:24:55 AM
AntispywareSignatureVersion      : 1.245.154.0
AntivirusEnabled                 : True
AntivirusSignatureLastUpdated    : 5/28/2017 9:24:56 AM
AntivirusSignatureVersion        : 1.245.154.0
```

Figure 9. Windows Defender AV Signature Version

To update the AV signature version, run the following command:

```
New-AliasMpCmd"C:\program files\windows defender\MpCmdRun.exe"MpCmd-
SignatureUpdate-PathD:\AVSignatures
```

As shown in *Figure 10*, the AV signature version was updated from `1.245.154.0` to `1.245.198.0`:

```
[172.16.20.156]: PS C:\> MpCmd -SignatureUpdate -Path D:\AVSignatures

Signature update started . . .
Signature update finished.
[172.16.20.156]: PS C:\> Get-MpComputerStatus | FL AMEngineVersion, AMProductVersion, `
AntispywareEnabled, AntispywareSignatureLastUpdated, `
AntispywareSignatureVersion, AntivirusEnabled, `
AntivirusSignatureLastUpdated, AntivirusSignatureVersion


AMEngineVersion                : 1.1.13804.0
AMProductVersion               : 4.10.14393.1198
AntispywareEnabled             : True
AntispywareSignatureLastUpdated : 5/29/2017 11:10:58 AM
AntispywareSignatureVersion    : 1.245.198.0
AntivirusEnabled               : True
AntivirusSignatureLastUpdated  : 5/29/2017 11:10:59 AM
AntivirusSignatureVersion      : 1.245.198.0
```

Figure 10. Update Windows Defender AV Signature Version

Managing the Local Administrator's Passwords on Nano Server

As we covered in Chapter 6, *Managing Nano Server with Windows PowerShell and Windows PowerShell DSC*, the Group Policy and the associated **Group Policy Management Console** (**GPMC**) tools are not present on Nano Server, even when the domain is joined, because Nano Server will not consume and endorse Group Policy settings. This is expected because those tools are graphical components and Nano Server is headless and designed to be remotely managed. A question that you find yourself asking is, how am I going to manage a local administrator's password for high density Nano Server deployment?

The good news is that Microsoft brought the implementation of the **Local Administrator Password Solution** (**LAPS**) client for Nano Server, so that managing the local administrator's passwords will be possible as well. For more information about LAPS, please check the following article:

https://technet.microsoft.com/en-us/mt227395.aspx

In summary, LAPS is a free Microsoft product that enables client and server machines to automatically change the passwords on local accounts and store those passwords as attributes of the computer objects in Active Directory.

In this section, we will discuss and show you how to implement and manage Local Administrator's Passwords on Nano Server using the LAPS solution.

Prerequisites

The following prerequisites must be met to use LAPS on Nano Server:

- LAPS Client for Nano is only supported for Nano Server and it is not designed to run on any other version of Windows.
- LAPS Client for Nano depends on PowerShell DSC because LAPS is a client/server tool that runs as a Group Policy client-side extension on your computers. But since Group Policy is not supported on Nano Server, you need to make sure that Microsoft-NanoServer-DSC-Package is added to the image. For more information, please check Chapter 6, *Managing Nano Server with Windows PowerShell and Windows PowerShell DSC*, about how to manage Nano Server with Windows PowerShell DSC.
- LAPS Client for Nano also depends on Active Directory. You need to make sure that all Nano Servers that you want to manage using LAPS are joined to the domain. Please check Chapter 2, *Getting Started with Nano Server*.
- As for the classic LAPS Client for Windows Server, the LAPS Client for Nano also requires AD permissions delegation (more on that in a bit).

Installation

This example assumes that you already have a couple of Nano Servers deployed in your environment that include the DSC package.

First, we need to download LAPS.Nano.DSC module from PowerShell gallery, and then install it on all Nano Servers that you want to manage with LAPS.

Open an elevated PowerShell console on your management machine and then run the following script to automate this process:

```
#region variables update the password$LocalPassword=ConvertTo-SecureString-
String'P@ssw0rd'-AsPlainText-Force$LocalCred=New-
ObjectSystem.Management.Automation.PSCredential('.\Administrator',$LocalPas
sword)#endregion# Download and Install LAPS.Nano.DSC module locally from
PSGallerySet-PSRepository-Name'PSGallery'-InstallationPolicyTrustedInstall-
Module-NameLAPS.Nano.DSC-Force# Copy and install LAPS.Nano.DSC module on
all Nano Servers$Source='C:\Program
Files\WindowsPowerShell\Modules\LAPS.Nano.DSC'$Destination='C:\Program
```

```
Files\WindowsPowerShell\Modules'1..5|ForEach-Object{
     $S1=New-PSSession-VMNameNANOVM-OM0$_-Credential$LocalCred Copy-Item-
Path$Source-ToSession$S1-Destination$Destination-Recurse-ForceInvoke-
Command-Session$S1-ScriptBlock{ Import-Module-Name LAPS.Nano.DSC-Verbose}
  }
```

In the first part of this script, we downloaded and installed LAPS.Nano.DSC module from PowerShell gallery locally, and then we copied it through PowerShell remote session and PowerShell Direct to all Nano Servers instead of downloading the same module five times, and finally we imported it. PowerShell Direct is so powerful.

When the LAPS.Nano.DSC module is installed on all Nano Servers, we move onto creating configuration data in the registry. By default, Microsoft shipped a sample configuration and installation files within the DSC module that you can use or modify if necessary to match your environment (see *Figure 11*):

NanoServer > LAPS.Nano.DSC > 1.0.0.5 > Config			
Name	Date modified	Type	Size
LAPS.Nano.DSC.Config.ps1	23-Nov-16 11:19 AM	Windows PowerShell Script	4 KB
LAPS.Nano.DSC.Install.ps1	23-Nov-16 11:19 AM	Windows PowerShell Script	1 KB

Figure 11. LAPS Nano DSC Configuration and Installation Files

- You need to create the corresponding MOF file(s) before you push or pull the configuration and update the registry on each Nano Server.
- In this example, we've updated the LAPS.Nano.DSC.Config.ps1 file to match our environment where we want to configure the registry for LAPS on five different Nano Servers.

 The LAPS.Nano.DSC.Config.ps1 and LAPS.Nano.DSC.Install.ps1 files used in this example are companion accompanied with this chapter, you can download and use them for your convenience.

- Open Windows PowerShell on your management machine, browse to the folder where you saved the `LAPS.Nano.DSC.Config.ps1` script, and run the following commands (see *Figure 12*):

```
$ConfigNode='NANOVM-OM01','NANOVM-OM02','NANOVM-OM03','NANOVM-
OM04','NANOVM-OM05'.\LAPS.Nano.DSC.Config.ps1-
ConfigNode$ConfigNode
```

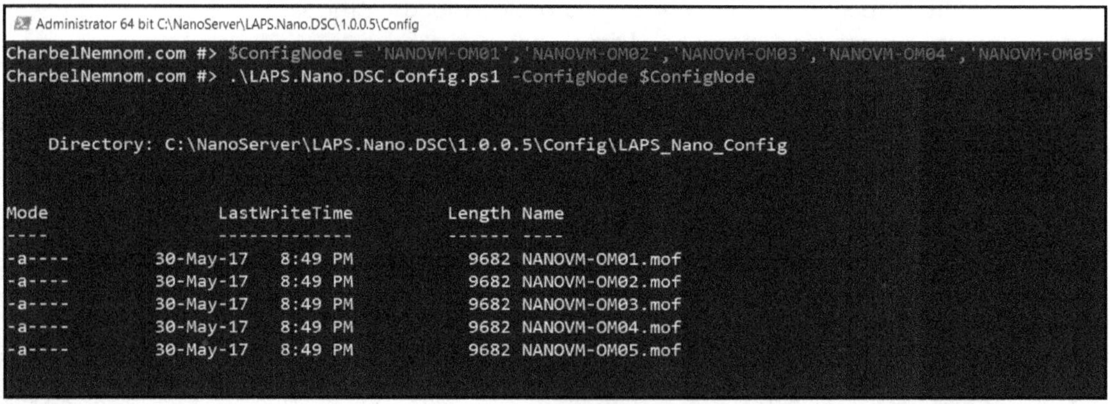

Figure 12. LAPS Nano DSC Registry Configuration- Creating MOF Files

Now you must use the MOF files created in the previous step to update the registry on your Nano Servers. You can do this by using the following four lines of code:

```
#region variables update the password$LocalPassword=ConvertTo-SecureString-
String'P@ssw0rd'-AsPlainText-Force$LocalCred=New-
ObjectSystem.Management.Automation.PSCredential(".\Administrator",$LocalPas
sword)#endregion#Push DSC ConfigurationStart-DscConfiguration-
Path.\LAPS_Nano_Config-Verbose-Wait-ComputerName$ConfigNode-
Credential$LocalCred-Force
```

After the configuration is applied, you should see the configuration created in registry on all Nano Servers as shown in *Figure 13*:

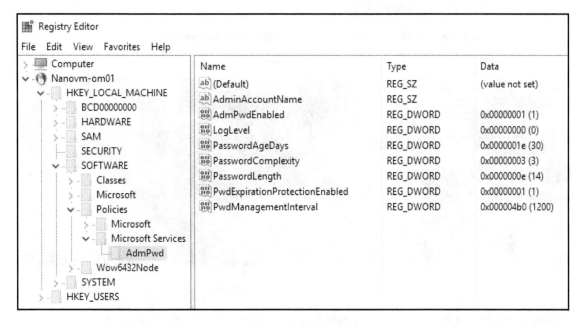

Figure 13. LAPS Nano Registry Configuration

Next, we move on to installing the LAPS client on all Nano Servers.

- In this example, we've updated the `LAPS.Nano.DSC.Install.ps1` file to match our environment where we want to install the LAPS client on five different Nano Servers.

- Open Windows PowerShell on your management machine, browse to the folder where you saved `LAPS.Nano.DSC.Install.ps1` script, and run the following commands (see *Figure 14*):

  `.\LAPS.Nano.DSC.Install.ps1-ConfigNode$ConfigNode`

```
Administrator 64 bit C:\NanoServer
CharbelNemnom.com #> $ConfigNode = 'NANOVM-OM01','NANOVM-OM02','NANOVM-OM03','NANOVM-OM04','NANOVM-OM05'
CharbelNemnom.com #> .\LAPS.Nano.DSC.Install.ps1 -ConfigNode $ConfigNode


    Directory: C:\NanoServer\LAPS_Nano_Install


Mode                LastWriteTime         Length Name
----                -------------         ------ ----
-a----        6/12/2017     4:35 PM         1960 NANOVM-OM01.mof
-a----        6/12/2017     4:35 PM         1960 NANOVM-OM02.mof
-a----        6/12/2017     4:35 PM         1960 NANOVM-OM03.mof
-a----        6/12/2017     4:35 PM         1960 NANOVM-OM04.mof
-a----        6/12/2017     4:35 PM         1960 NANOVM-OM05.mof
```

Figure 14. LAPS Nano DSC Client Installation- Creating MOF Files

Now you must use the MOF files created in the previous step to install the LAPS client service on all Nano Servers. You can do this by using the following four lines of code:

```
#region variables update the password$LocalPassword=ConvertTo-SecureString-
String'P@ssw0rd'-AsPlainText-Force$LocalCred=New-
ObjectSystem.Management.Automation.PSCredential(".\Administrator",$LocalPas
sword)#endregion#Push DSC ConfigurationStart-DscConfiguration-
Path.\LAPS_Nano_Config-Verbose-Wait-ComputerName$ConfigNode-
Credential$LocalCred-Force
```

After the installation is performed, you should see the `LAPS.Nano` service installed and running on all Nano Servers as shown in *Figure 15*:

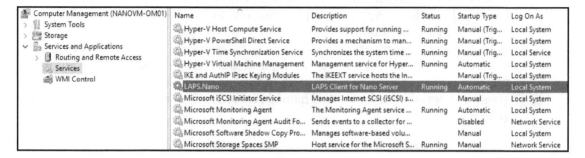

Figure 15. LAPS Nano Client Service

In the last step, you need to configure LAPS in your environment and extend the AD schema and delegate permissions:

1. You can download LAPS from the following link which is at version 6.2 as of this writing:

   `https://www.microsoft.com/en-us/download/details.aspx?id=46899.`

2. Install LAPS management tools on a member server in your domain environment. If you want to use LAPS for Nano Server only, then you don't need to install GPO Editor templates, because LAPS for Nano does not use GPO at all.

3. Run `Update-AdmPwdADSchema` from PowerShell to extend AD schema as shown in *Figure 16*:

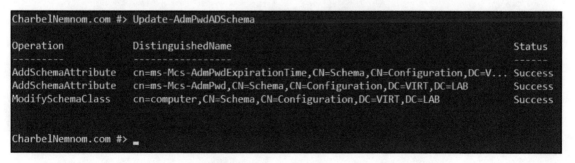

Figure 16. Modifying the AD schema for LAPS

4. To delegate computer permission to write a password on your Nano clients, you use the `Set-AdmPwdComputerSelfPermission` cmdlet to apply them to the Active Directory **organizational unit** (**OU**) objects which contain your LAPS client Nano Servers. Applying the permissions to the OUs causes them to be inherited by all the subordinate objects in those OUs, including other OUs. Please note that you must repeat this command with the name of every OU having the computer objects of LAPS Nano clients, unless the OU is subordinate to another OU that you have already configured. In this example, we will delegate the write password permission for the OU named Nano. The PowerShell will look like this (*Figure 17*):

`Set-AdmPwdComputerSelfPermission-Identity:NANO`

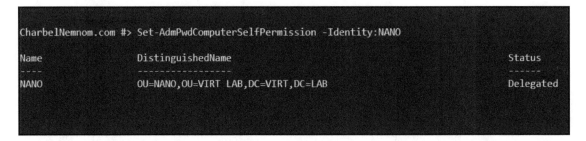

Figure 17. Delegate OU write permission

5. Wait some time and then check the password of a managed administrator account on Nano machines reported to AD using the LAPS UI tool as shown in *Figure 18*:

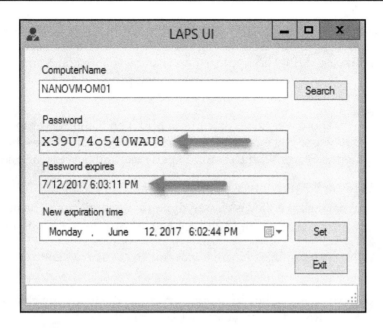

Figure 18. Delegate OU write permission

Using MPIO on Nano Server

Multipath I/O (MPIO) is a fault-tolerance and performance-enhancement technique that defines more than one physical path between the CPU in a computer system and its mass-storage devices through the buses, controllers, switches, and bridge devices connecting them. If one or more of these components fails, causing the path to fail, the multipath I/O logic uses an alternate path for I/O so that applications can still access their data.

In Chapter 4, *Deploying Hyper-V Cluster on Nano Server*, we covered how to deploy Nano Server in Hyper-Converged model using S2D. However, MPIO is not supported with S2D. In other words, there should be no MPIO on your S2D system because S2D is all single connection non-shared.

For more information about multipath I/O in Windows Server, please check the following article: https://technet.microsoft.com/library/cc725907.aspx.

In some scenarios, you need to connect Nano Server to iSCSI, Fiber Channel, and **Serial Attached Storage (SAS)** SAN by establishing multiple sessions or connections to the storage array. In this case, MPIO is supported and can be enabled on Nano Server to leverage fault-tolerance and performance-enhancement provided by the storage fabric component.

In this section, we will show you how you can use MPIO on Nano Server to support these type of scenarios. But before you enable MPIO, there are some differences that you want to be aware of compared to Server with Desktop Experience, and Server Core, such as:

- The Microsoft DSM is only supported on Nano Server
- The Load Balancing Policy is chosen dynamically and cannot be modified
- For more information about MPIO policies, please check the following article:

  ```
  https://technet.microsoft.com/en-us/library/dd851699(v=ws.11).asp
  x
  ```

- The Load Balancing policy for Nano Server has the following characteristics:
  - RoundRobin (active/active) Default
  - LeastBlocks - SAS HDD
  - RoundRobin with Subset - ALUA
- Path states (active/passive) for ALUA arrays are picked up from the target array
- Storage devices are claimed by bus type (that is Fibre Channel, iSCSI, or SAS). When MPIO is installed on Nano Server, disks are still exposed as duplicates (one available per path) until MPIO is configured to claim and manage the disks. Microsoft published a sample script on how to claim or unclaim disks for MPIO at the following link:

  ```
  https://technet.microsoft.com/en-us/windows-server-docs/get-star
  ted/mpio-on-nano-server.
  ```

- iSCSI boot is not supported

Enabling MPIO needs to be done after you have deployed Nano Server. As we have done multiple times through the course of this book, you are simply going to use PowerShell remoting or PowerShell Direct to connect to Nano Server and then run the following command:

```
Enable-WindowsOptionalFeature-Online-FeatureNameMultiPathIO
```

Or you can use Server Manager to connect to Nano Server and enable **Multipath I/O** in the **Add Roles and Features Wizard** as shown in *Figure 19*:

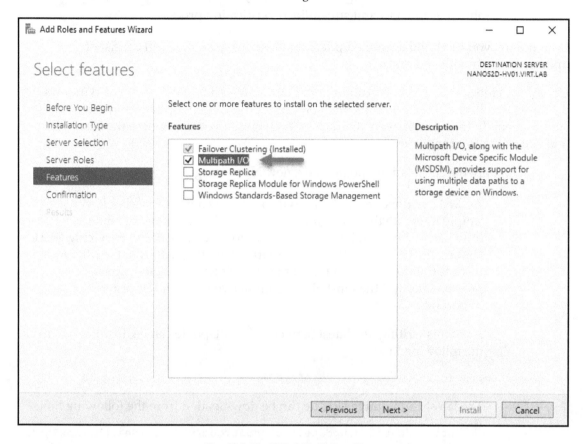

Figure 19. Enabling Multipath I/O using Server Manager

Using Windows Update on Nano Server

In Windows Server 2016 including Nano Server, Microsoft simplified and streamlined Windows updates and patching process which will help in reducing operating expenses costs by delivering:

- Predicable monthly update cadence you can plan for
- Fewer updates to manage

- Cumulative updates that have everything you need
- Proactive notification of updates before they cause downtime
- Simplified test matrix and streamlined verification process

In summary, you can build a simple update maintenance plan that will consist of: one update, once a month and that's it.

Updating Nano Server is slightly different than updating any other version of Windows. Basically, there are different options that you can choose from to update your Nano environment. In this section, we will touch on each one so you can choose the best option that suits your environment:

1. Apply the cumulative update into a new Nano image:

   As we have done multiple times through the course of this book, you can simply integrate the latest update directly when creating the image so that it's fully patched on first boot. You should download the latest **Servicing Stack Update** (**SSU**) and the latest **Cumulative Update** (**CU**) from the Microsoft Update Catalog and then install the Servicing Stack Update first as a prerequisite, and then install the Cumulative Update. The order is very important.

   As of this writing, the latest Servicing Stack Update can be downloaded from the following link:

   `http://catalog.update.microsoft.com/v7/site/Search.aspx?q=KB4013418`

   The latest Cumulative Update can be downloaded from the following link:

   `http://catalog.update.microsoft.com/v7/site/Search.aspx?q=KB4023680`

   After downloading the `.msu` files from the Microsoft Update Catalog, save them to a network share or local directory, and then use the `New-NanoServerImage` cmdlet followed by the `-ServicingPackagePath` parameter to integrate the latest update as part of the image. Remember, you need to specify the Servicing Stack Update `.msu` file first, and then the Cumulative Update `.msu` file.

The PowerShell command will look like the following, make sure to add the other parameters as needed, please check `Chapter 3`, *Deploying Nano Server in a Virtual Machine and on Physical Hardware,* for the complete list of the required and optional parameters:

```
New-NanoServerImage-
ServicingPackagePath'C:\NanoServer\Windows10.0-KB4013418-
x64.msu','C:\NanoServer\Windows10.0-KB4023680-x64.msu'
```

2. Apply the cumulative update into an existing Nano image:

   In this option, you can apply the latest update directly into your existing Nano Server image that you have built previously, so that Nano machines created using this image are fully patched on first boot.

   After downloading the `.msu` files from the Microsoft Update Catalog, save them to a network share or local directory, and then use the `Edit-NanoServerImage` cmdlet followed by the `-ServicingPackagePath` parameter to integrate the latest update as part of the existing image.

   The PowerShell command will look like the following, make sure to add the other parameters as needed:

   ```
   Edit-NanoServerImage-
   ServicingPackagePath'C:\NanoServer\Windows10.0-KB4013418-
   x64.msu','C:\NanoServer\Windows10.0-KB4023680-x64.msu'-
   TargetPathC:\NanoServer.wim
   ```

3. Apply the cumulative update to an existing offline VHD(X):

   In this option, you can apply the latest update directly into your existing virtual hard disk Nano image either in VHD or VHDX format. You need to make sure the virtual hard disk is not in use by either shutting down the VM or unmounting the virtual hard disk file. After downloading the `.msu` files from the Microsoft update catalog, save them to a network share or local directory, and then use the following PowerShell commands:

   ```
   Mount-WindowsImage-ImagePathC:\NanoServer.vhdx-
   PathC:\MountDir-Index1Add-WindowsPackage-PathC:\MountDir-
   PackagePathC:\NanoUpdatesDismount-WindowsImage-
   PathC:\MountDir-Save
   ```

The first command will mount the VHDX file and use a mounting directory called `MountDir`. The second command will add all Windows Updates that are located under `C:\NanoUpdates` to the mounting directory, and the final command will dismount and save the changes to the image.

4. Apply the cumulative update to a running Nano Server:

In this option, you can apply the latest update directly to a running Nano Server either in a virtual machine or physical host. After downloading the `.msu` files from the Microsoft Update Catalog, save them to a local directory on your management machine such as `C:\ServicingPackages`.

Then use `Expand.exe` utility to extract the `.cab` files from the `.msu` files into separate directories.

Open Windows PowerShell and run the following command to extract the `.cab` files (see *Figure 20*):

```
Expand.exe.\Windows10.0-KB4013418-x64.msu-
F:*.\Expand.exe.\Windows10.0-KB4023680-x64.msu-F:*.\
```

```
CharbelNemnom.com #> Expand.exe .\Windows10.0-KB4013418-x64.msu -F:* .\
Microsoft (R) File Expansion Utility
Copyright (c) Microsoft Corporation. All rights reserved.

Adding .\WSUSSCAN.cab to Extraction Queue
Adding .\Windows10.0-KB4013418-x64.cab to Extraction Queue
Adding .\Windows10.0-KB4013418-x64-pkgProperties.txt to Extraction Queue
Adding .\Windows10.0-KB4013418-x64.xml to Extraction Queue

Expanding Files ....

Expanding Files Complete ...
4 files total.
CharbelNemnom.com #> cd 'C:\NanoServer\Updates\Cumulative Update\'
CharbelNemnom.com #> Expand.exe .\Windows10.0-KB4023680-x64.msu -F:* .\
Microsoft (R) File Expansion Utility
Copyright (c) Microsoft Corporation. All rights reserved.

Adding .\WSUSSCAN.cab to Extraction Queue
Adding .\Windows10.0-KB4023680-x64.cab to Extraction Queue
Adding .\Windows10.0-KB4023680-x64-pkgProperties.txt to Extraction Queue
Adding .\Windows10.0-KB4023680-x64.xml to Extraction Queue

Expanding Files ....
Progress: 1 out of 4 files
Expanding Files Complete ...
4 files total.
```

Figure 20. Expand Windows Updates .cab Files

Finally, you need to copy the `.cab` files to Nano Server. If you're applying a servicing stack update, please make sure to restart the server after applying the servicing stack update before applying the latest cumulative update.

Open Windows PowerShell and run the following commands:

```
#Update the IP address according to your
environment.$NanoIP="172.16.20.185"$Session=New-PSSession-
ComputerName$NanoIP-CredentialAdministratorCopy-Item-ToSession$Session-
PathC:\ServicingPackages\-DestinationC:\-Recurse-Force$Session|Enter-
PSSessionSet-LocationC:\#Apply the Servicing Stack Update first and then
restartAdd-WindowsPackage-Online-
PackagePathC:\ServicingPackages\Windows10.0-KB4013418-x64.cabRestart-
Computer; exit#After restarting, apply the Cumulative Update and then
restart$Session=New-PSSession-ComputerName$NanoIP-Credential
Administrator$Session|Enter-PSSessionSet-LocationC:\Add-WindowsPackage-
Online-PackagePathC:\ServicingPackages\Windows10.0-KB4023680-
x64.cabRestart-Computer; exit
```

To confirm that all updates are installed successfully, you can connect to Nano Server and then run `Get-WindowsPackage` cmdlet as shown in *Figure 21*:

```
#Update the IP address accordingly$NanoIP="172.16.20.185"$Session=New-
PSSession-ComputerName$NanoIP-CredentialAdministrator$Session|Enter-
PSSessionSet-LocationC:\#Get a list of installed updatesGet-WindowsPackage-
Online|Where-Object{$_.ReleaseType -match"Update"}
```

```
CharbelNemnom.com #> #Update the IP address accordingly
CharbelNemnom.com #> $NanoIP = "172.16.20.185"
CharbelNemnom.com #> $Session = New-PSSession -ComputerName $NanoIP -Credential Administrator
CharbelNemnom.com #> $Session | Enter-PSSession
[172.16.20.185]: PS C:\Users\Administrator\Documents> Set-Location C:\
[172.16.20.185]: PS C:\>
[172.16.20.185]: PS C:\> #Get a list of installed updates
[172.16.20.185]: PS C:\> Get-WindowsPackage -Online | Where-Object {$_.ReleaseType -eq "Update"}


PackageName  : Package_for_KB4013418~31bf3856ad364e35~amd64~~10.0.1.0
PackageState : Installed  <----------
ReleaseType  : Update
InstallTime  : 6/11/2017 11:52:00 PM

PackageName  : Package_for_RollupFix~31bf3856ad364e35~amd64~~14393.1230.1.1
PackageState : Installed  <----------
ReleaseType  : Update
InstallTime  : 6/11/2017 12:05:00 PM
```

Figure 21. Verify installed Windows Updates

5. Download and install the cumulative update to a running Nano Server:

> In this option, you can apply the latest update directly to a running Nano Server either in a virtual machine or physical host without downloading the .msu files separately from the Microsoft Update Catalog. You can use the Windows Update WMI provider to download and install Windows updates while Nano Server is running.
>
> Connect to a running Nano Server machine using PowerShell remoting, and run the following commands:

```
#Update the IP address
accordingly$NanoIP="172.16.20.185"$Session=New-PSSession-
ComputerName$NanoIP-CredentialAdministrator$Session|Enter-
PSSessionSet-LocationC:\
```

- Scanning for available updates (see *Figure 22*):

```
$CimSess=New-CimInstance-
Namespaceroot/Microsoft/Windows/WindowsUpdate-
ClassNameMSFT_WUOperationsSession$ScanResults=$CimSess|Invoke-
CimMethod-MethodNameScanForUpdates-
Arguments@{SearchCriteria="IsInstalled=0";OnlineScan=$true}$Sca
nResults.Updates
```

```
[172.16.20.185]: PS C:\> $CimSess = New-CimInstance -Namespace root/Microsoft/Windows/WindowsUpdate
-ClassName MSFT_WUOperationsSession
[172.16.20.185]: PS C:\> $ScanResults = $CimSess | Invoke-CimMethod -MethodName ScanForUpdates -Argu
ments @{SearchCriteria="IsInstalled=0";OnlineScan=$true}
[172.16.20.185]: PS C:\> $ScanResults.Updates


Description       : Install this update to resolve issues in Windows. For a complete listing of the
                    issues that are included in this update, see the associated Microsoft Knowledge
                    Base article for more information. After you install this item, you may have to
                    restart your computer.
KBArticleID       :
MsrcSeverity      :
RevisionNumber    : 200
Title             : Update for Windows Server 2016 for x64-based Systems (KB4013418)
UpdateID          : 025c4f16-fea1-4ea9-91fd-32209b4d8998
PSComputerName    :

Description       : A security issue has been identified in a Microsoft software product that could
                    affect your system. You can help protect your system by installing this update
                    from Microsoft. For a complete listing of the issues that are included in this
                    update, see the associated Microsoft Knowledge Base article. After you install
                    this update, you may have to restart your system.
KBArticleID       :
MsrcSeverity      : Moderate
RevisionNumber    : 202
Title             : 2017-05 Cumulative Update for Windows Server 2016 for x64-based Systems
                    (KB4019472)
UpdateID          : 95ff788a-8fe4-4584-bfca-7051b92405b2
PSComputerName    :
```

Figure 22. Scanning for available updates - WMI provider

- Installing all available updates (see *Figure 23*):

```
$CimSess=New-CimInstance-
Namespaceroot/Microsoft/Windows/WindowsUpdate-
ClassNameMSFT_WUOperationsSessionInvoke-CimMethod-
InputObject$CimSess-MethodNameApplyApplicableUpdatesRestart-
Computer; exit
```

```
[172.16.20.185]: PS C:\> $CimSess = New-CimInstance -Namespace root/Microsoft/Windows/WindowsUpdate
-ClassName MSFT_WUOperationsSession
[172.16.20.185]: PS C:\> Invoke-CimMethod -InputObject $CimSess -MethodName ApplyApplicableUpdates

HResult ReturnValue PSComputerName
------- ----------- --------------
      0           0


[172.16.20.185]: PS C:\> Restart-Computer; exit
```

Figure 23. Installing all available updates - WMI provider

- After applying the updates, you might want to check whether they are installed (see *Figure 24*):

```
Get-WindowsPackage-Online|Where-Object{$_.ReleaseType -
match"Update"}
```

```
[172.16.20.185]: PS C:\> Get-WindowsPackage -Online | Where-Object {$_.ReleaseType -match "Update"}


PackageName   : Package_for_KB4013418~31bf3856ad364e35~amd64~~10.0.1.0
PackageState  : Installed
ReleaseType   : Update
InstallTime   : 6/11/2017 3:31:00 PM

PackageName   : Package_for_RollupFix~31bf3856ad364e35~amd64~~14393.1198.1.6
PackageState  : Installed
ReleaseType   : SecurityUpdate
InstallTime   : 6/11/2017 3:38:00 PM
```

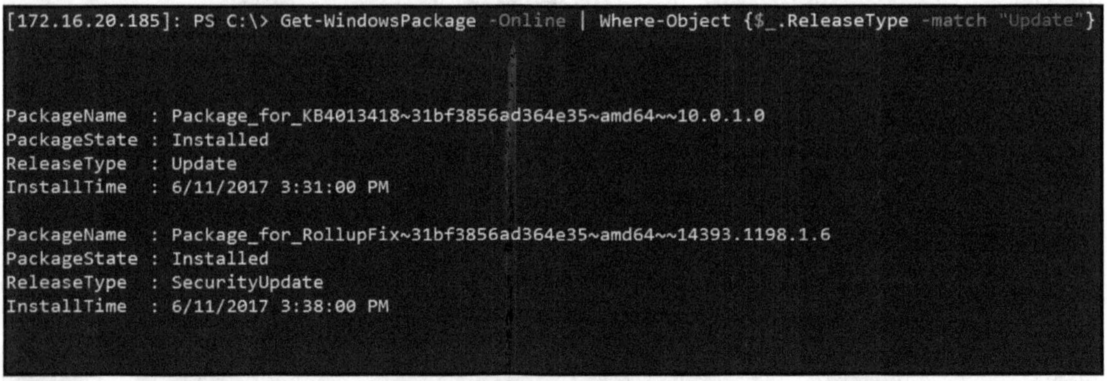

Figure 24. Checking installed updates

6. Using Windows Server Update Services to update Nano Server:

In this option, you can leverage your existing **Windows Server Update Services** (**WSUS**) in your environment to update Nano Server. As we discussed earlier, Nano Server does not support group policy, hence you cannot use the Group Policy Management console to apply WSUS policy on Nano Server. The alternate way is to manually modify WSUS registry entries for Windows Update. For more information about configuring Automatic Updates using Registry Editor, please check the following article:

```
https://msdn.microsoft.com/en-us/library/dd939844(v=ws.10).aspx
```

You can use the Registry Editor to connect to Nano Server by using the Connect Network Registry MMC and update the registry entries as shown in *Figure 25* and in *Figure 26*.

Nano Server is only concerned with the following four registry keys:

- `WUServer`:
  `HKEY_LOCAL_MACHINE\Software\Policies\Microsoft\Windows\WindowsUpdate`
- `WUStatusServer`:
  `HKEY_LOCAL_MACHINE\Software\Policies\Microsoft\Windows\WindowsUpdate`

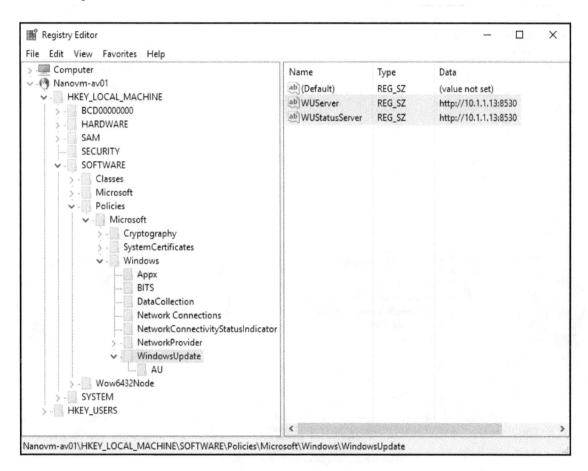

Figure 25.Registry keys for Windows Update

- UseWUServer:
  HKEY_LOCAL_MACHINE\Software\Policies\Microsoft\Windows\WindowsU
  pdate\AU

- AUOptions:
  HKEY_LOCAL_MACHINE\Software\Policies\Microsoft\Windows\WindowsU
  pdate\AU

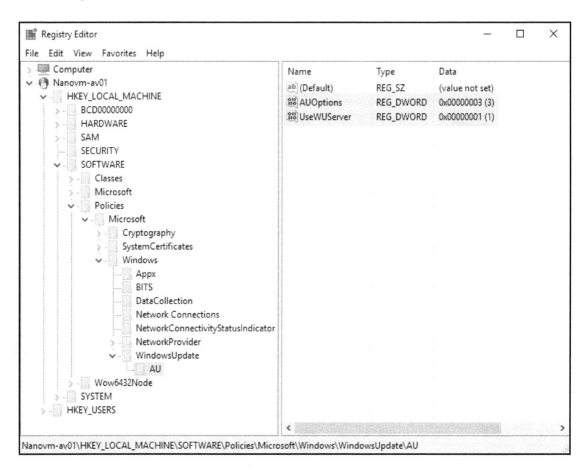

Figure 26. Registry keys for Automatic Update configuration options

You can also use Windows PowerShell and Windows PowerShell DSC to automate and create the same registry keys for a large number of Nano Servers.

The following commands will help you to create the necessary registry keys using PowerShell (if it does not already exist):

```
New-Item-Path"HKLM:
\Software\Policies\Microsoft\Windows"-NameWindowsUpdateNew-ItemProperty-
Path"HKLM:
\Software\Policies\Microsoft\Windows\WindowsUpdate"-NameWUServer-
PropertyTypeString-Value"http://10.1.1.13:8530"New-ItemProperty-Path"HKLM:
\Software\Policies\Microsoft\Windows\WindowsUpdate"-NameWUStatusServer-
PropertyTypeString-Value"http://10.1.1.13:8530"New-Item-Path"HKLM:
\Software\Policies\Microsoft\Windows\WindowsUpdate"-NameAUNew-ItemProperty-
Path"HKLM:
\Software\Policies\Microsoft\Windows\WindowsUpdate\AU"-NameUseWUServer-
PropertyTypeDWord-Value"1"New-ItemProperty-Path"HKLM:
\Software\Policies\Microsoft\Windows\WindowsUpdate\AU"-NameAUOptions-
PropertyTypeDWord-Value"3"
```

To confirm that all registry keys are created successfully, you can run the following command (see *Figure 27*):

```
Get-ChildItem-PathRegistry::HKLM\Software\Policies\Microsoft\Windows\-
Recurse|Where-Object{$_.Name -match"WindowsUpdate"}
```

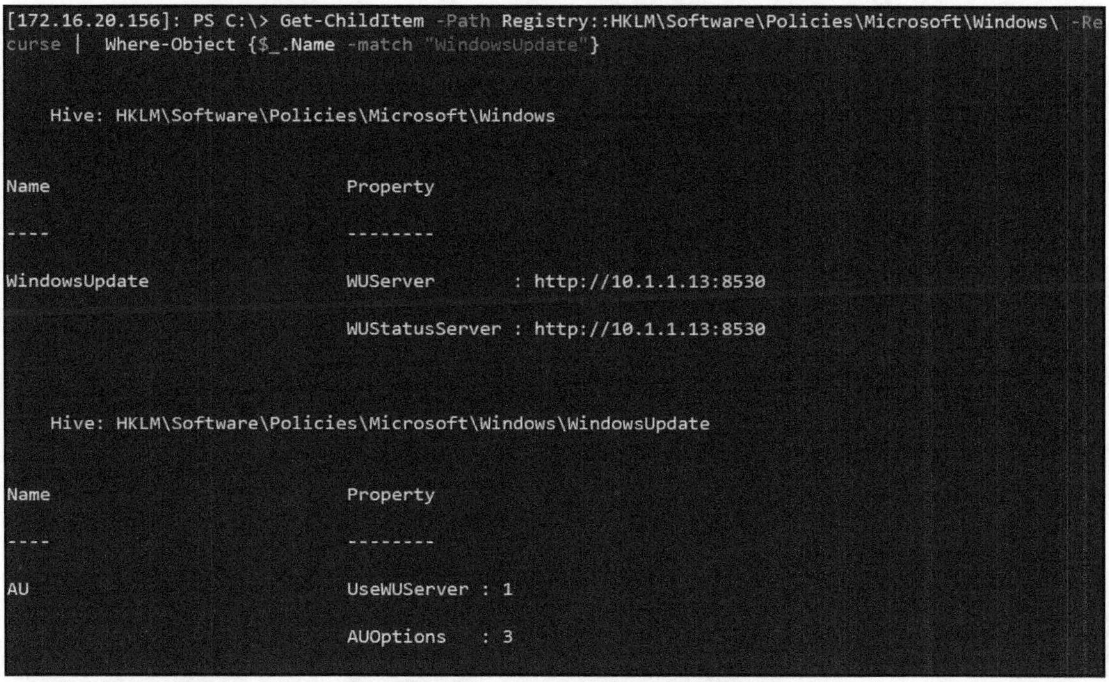

Figure 27. Browsing registry keys for Windows Updates

7. Using a Scheduled Task to Update Nano Server:

   Updating Nano Server using Task Scheduler is possible, if you want to automate this process, you need to create and register a scheduled task for each Nano Server to check for new Windows updates on a regular basis. The PowerShell command for a registered scheduled task will look like this:

   ```
   $Action=New-ScheduledTaskAction-Execute"PowerShell.exe"-
   Argument{-
   file"C:\NanoServer\NanoServerUpdate.ps1"}$trigger=New-
   ScheduledTaskTrigger-Weekly-At"1:00 AM"-
   DaysOfWeekFriday$User="Domain\AdminUser"Register-ScheduledTask-
   TaskName"NanoServerUpdate"-Trigger$trigger-User$User-
   Action$Action
   ```

The scheduled task above will trigger Nano Server to execute a specified PowerShell script to run every Friday at 1.00 AM.

To view the list of scheduled jobs, use the `Get-ScheduledTask` cmdlet. And to remove a scheduled job, use the `Unregister-ScheduledTask` cmdlet.

8. Using System Center Virtual Machine Manager to update Nano Server:

   If you have a System Center Virtual Machine Manager instance deployed in your environment, you can use SCVMM and WSUS server to update Nano Server deployment. Please refer to the following article to learn more about setting up update servers in the **System Center 2016 - Virtual Machine Manager (SCVMM)** fabric.

   ```
   https://docs.microsoft.com/en-us/system-center/vmm/update-se
   rver
   ```

9. Using Cluster-Aware Updating to update Nano Server:

    Cluster-Aware Updating (**CAU**) is also supported on Nano Server. However, the self-updating mode is not available for Nano. In other words, you can use a CAU server to update the cluster nodes, but you cannot schedule CAU to run on a specified date and time in self-updating mode. There are some points that you want to be aware of to make sure CAU runs successfully such as:

    - Make sure your system running CAU is Windows Server 2016 and you have the components to fully manage your Nano nodes from that server. This includes the Cluster management modules on your Nano Server, and the cluster management tools on your CAU server.
    - The orchestration of the updating must be from the external server. The CAU orchestrator runs .NET Framework and Nano doesn't support that version of .NET.

Update Out of Box (OOB) drivers for Nano Server

For certain system components, there may be a need to update the inbox version of the Nano Server driver to the most up-to-date. This will apply only for physical host deployment.

The following PowerShell command can be used to retrieve a list of all driver versions currently installed on the local system (see *Figure 28*):

```
Get-PnpDevice|Select-ObjectName,@{l='DriverVersion';e={(Get-
PnpDeviceProperty-InstanceId$_.InstanceId -
KeyName'DEVPKEY_Device_DriverVersion').Data}} -Unique
```

```
Name                                                                                              DriverVersion
----                                                                                              -------------
Intel(R) Xeon(R) E7 v3/Xeon(R) E5 v3/Core i7 DDRIO (VMSE) 0 & 1 - 2FBE                             10.1.2.77
Intel(R) Xeon(R) E7 v3/Xeon(R) E5 v3/Core i7 Power Control Unit - 2F98                             10.1.2.77
Intel(R) C610 series/X99 chipset SMBus Controller - 8D22                                           10.1.2.77
Intel(R) Xeon(R) E7 v3/Xeon(R) E5 v3/Core i7 PCIe Ring Interface - 2F34                            10.1.2.77
Intel(R) Xeon(R) E7 v3/Xeon(R) E5 v3/Core i7 DMI2 - 2F00                                           10.1.2.77
Intel(R) Xeon(R) E7 v3/Xeon(R) E5 v3/Core i7 Integrated Memory Controller 1 Channel Target Address Decoder - 2FGA   10.1.2.77
Intel(R) Xeon(R) E7 v3/Xeon(R) E5 v3/Core i7 Unicast Registers - 2FE4                              10.1.2.77
Intel(R) Xeon(R) E7 v3/Xeon(R) E5 v3/Core i7 DDRIO (VMSE) 2 & 3 - 2FB9                             10.1.2.77
ACPI Module Device                                                                                10.0.14393.0
Volume                                                                                            10.0.14393.0
Intel(R) Xeon(R) E7 v3/Xeon(R) E5 v3/Core i7 PCI Express Root Port 2 - 2F07                        10.1.2.77
Cluster Disk Driver                                                                               10.0.14393.0
Microsoft VHD Loopback Controller                                                                 10.0.14393.1198
Programmable interrupt controller                                                                 10.0.14393.0
Microsoft ACPI-Compliant Power Meter Device                                                       10.0.14393.0
HPE Ethernet 25Gb 2-port 640SFP28 Adapter                                                         1.45.15407.0
HPE Ethernet 25Gb 2-port 640SFP28 Adapter #2                                                      1.45.15407.0
iLO 4 (CHIF)                                                                                      3.30.0.0
Intel(R) C610 series/X99 chipset PCI Express Root Port #7 - 8D1C                                  10.1.2.77
Microsoft System Management BIOS Driver                                                           10.0.14393.0
Intel(R) C610 series/X99 chipset PCI Express Root Port #1 - 8D10                                  10.1.2.77
Microsoft ISATAP Adapter #11                                                                      10.0.14393.0
Plug and Play Software Device Enumerator                                                          10.0.14393.0
HPE Ethernet 25Gb 2-port 640FLR-SFP28 Adapter                                                     1.45.15407.0
HPE Ethernet 25Gb 2-port 640FLR-SFP28 Adapter #2                                                  1.45.15407.0
Intel(R) C610 series/X99 chipset PCI Express Root Port #5 - 8D18                                  10.1.2.77
Microsoft Virtual Disk                                                                            10.0.14393.0
Microsoft Failover Cluster Virtual Adapter                                                        10.0.14393.1066
```

Figure 28. Retrieve a list of all driver versions

To update the **Out of Box** (**OOB**) drivers for Nano Server, you need to obtain the right driver version from your favourite hardware vendor first, and then you need to login to Nano Server using PowerShell remote session and use the pnputil.exe command. You can install the drivers individually or all of them. For example, assuming the driver pack is located at C:\HPE-SPP-10.60 (in this example), you can install all of them with the following command:

```
pnputil.exe/add-driverc:
\HPE-SPP-10.60\*.inf/subdirs/install
```

This command will recursively install all the drivers automatically for you.

If you want to install just a single driver, use the following command instead:

```
pnputil.exe/add-driverc:
\HPE-SPP-10.60\<driver>\<filename.inf>/install
```

In this example, we will install all the drivers as shown in *Figure 29* and then reboot the system.

```
Adding driver package:   HPEStoreEverTapes\hpul.inf
Driver package added successfully.
Published Name:          oem39.inf
Driver package installed on matching devices.

Adding driver package:   HPEStoreEverTapes\HPUSBMSC.inf
Driver package added successfully.
Published Name:          oem40.inf
Driver package installed on matching devices.

Adding driver package:   HPH2xxSASSATAHBA\lsinodrv.inf
Driver package added successfully.
Published Name:          oem41.inf
Driver package installed on matching devices.

Adding driver package:   HPH2xxSASSATAHBA\lsi_sas2.inf
Driver package added successfully.
Published Name:          oem42.inf
Driver package installed on matching devices.

Adding driver package:   iLO34CI\hpqilo3chif.inf
Driver package added successfully.
Published Name:          oem43.inf
Driver package installed on matching devices.

Adding driver package:   iLO34MgmtCtrlPkg\hpqilo3core.inf
Driver package added successfully.
Published Name:          oem44.inf
Driver package installed on matching devices.

Total driver packages:  51
Added driver packages:  50
System reboot is needed to complete install operations!
[172.16.19.21]: PS C:\> Restart-Computer
```

Figure 29. Installing OEM drivers for Nano Server

The future of Nano Server

The future of Nano Server is all about containers. In the next release of Windows Server and beyond, Microsoft will optimize Nano Server image for containers. The uncompressed Nano container image in Windows Server 2016 is about 1 GB in size, this includes components not relevant for containers such as components needed for physical and virtual machines. Microsoft is significantly working on reducing the size of the image on disk by 50% and even more by the time you read this. This has two benefits. Firstly, it will speed up the start-up time of containers, and secondly, will minimize the bandwidth needed when you pull the image from Docker Hub (repository). All the components not relevant for containers and modern application development will be removed from the image. The optional components will be delivered as layers. Let's say, you need to pull a Nano optimized container image, and if you want .NET Core, you need to pull .NET as a layer on top of the image, and if you want PowerShell, you need to pull PowerShell as layer on top as well, so on and so forth.

For more information about Windows containers, please check Chapter 8, *Running Windows Server Containers and Hyper-V Containers on Nano Serve*.

In the future release of Windows Server, Microsoft is also bringing the Windows insiders program to Windows Server like in Windows 10. If you are familiar with the Windows 10 flights model (weekly update), Windows Server will follow the same method. This will help provide access to frequent and regular builds of Windows Server to anyone in the world. This will also mean that you can download Windows Server ISOs from the insider portal and pull the container images from the Docker Hub as well.

Windows Server will also move to Windows Server as a Service model, this new model works as semi-annual channel (pilot) and the semi-annual channel (broad). The **pilot** means that new features will be introduced followed by feedback from users and a stabilization period, however, the **broad** means that it's broadly declared after receiving feedback from the pilot phase, the broad release is stable for production deployment, so no new features will be added, and Microsoft will only release bug fixes. These changes attempt to realign Windows 10 and Windows Server with the new model of big features delivered twice a year in March and September. However, the **Long-Term Servicing Channel** (**LTSC**) for Windows 10 and Windows Server will remain identical to old versions of Windows where users receive security updates and bug fixes every month but no new features and enhancements will be installed. The next LTSC of Windows Server will be released on a typical release schedule (2-3 years). The minimum length of servicing lifetime for LTSC is 10 years (5 years mainstream support + 5 years extended support) or up to 16 years if you purchased premium assurance. As of this writing, if you require to receive all the new features of the next release of Windows Server, you should switch from LTSC to semi-annual channel by performing a fresh installation (No in-place upgrade), or if you are using failover clustering, you could move from LTSC to SAC by performing a cluster operating system rolling upgrade without any downtime.

Nano Server moving forward will be specifically used for container-optimized runtime. In the next release of Windows Server, Microsoft is intending to deprecate the host and guest VMs functionality in Nano Server, and focus exclusively on getting the container technology as small as possible by removing the host and virtual machine dependencies from the image. In other words, Nano Server will not be supported to run on physical and virtual machines. As an aside, the focus on containers was very well-received by many customers since the GA release of Windows Server 2016 in October 2016.

The infrastructure roles for Nano Server in Windows Server 2016 will remain fully supported as of today, because Nano Server was released under CBB servicing model (now is called Semi-annual Channel), that means the first Nano Server release (Version 1607) was released back in October 2016 it is still supported until spring 2018. You can still use Nano Server for physical host, virtual machine deployment as well as for containers. In fact, most of the topics and examples covered in this book will work the same whether you are using Server Core or Server with Desktop Experience.

Microsoft is also working on optimizing Windows Server Core for cloud host (physical machine) deployment which is the backbone for Azure (public cloud) and for Azure Stack (hybrid cloud). Windows Server Core will be also used as container hosts to run Nano container images as well as for **Software-defined Datacenter** (**SDDC**) hosts.

Summary

In the last chapter of this book, we discussed how to run DNS and IIS on Nano Server. We also covered additional updates and tools that will help you streamline your experience by using Nano Server.

Finally, we discussed the future of Nano Server including Windows Server moving forward.

We hope this book has been informative for you, and we would like to thank you for reading.

Index